SECOND EDITION

HUMAN

GEOGRAPHY

8

SECOND EDITION

HUMAN
GEOGRAPHY
8

Graham Draper • Lew French • Jennifer Farrell-Cordon

NELSON | EDUCATION

NELSON / EDUCATION

Human Geography 8

Authors
Graham Draper, Lew French, Jennifer Farrell-Cordon

General Manager, Social Studies
Carol Stokes

Publisher, Social Studies
Doug Panasis

Managing Editor, Development
Karin Fediw

Product Manager, Social Studies
Doug Morrow

Assistant Editor
Kimberly Murphy

Editorial Assistant
Jordana Camerman

Production Manager
Helen Jager-Locsin

Senior Production Coordinator
Sharon Latta Paterson

Design Director
Ken Phipps

Interior Design
Studio Montage

Cover Design
Eugene Lo

Printer
Transcontinental Printing Inc.

Focus Strategic Communications Inc.

Project Manager
Adrianna Edwards

Project Coordinator
Lisa Dimson

Developmental Editors
Linda Aspen-Baxter,
Adrianna Edwards

Copy Editor
Susan McNish

Proofreaders
Linda Szostak, Christi Davis-Martell,
Layla Moola

Index
Carol Roberts

Art Director
Adrianna Edwards, Lisa Dimson

Compositor
Valentino Sanna

Photo Research and Permissions
Natalie Barrington

Consultants and Reviewers

The authors and the publisher wish to thank the consultants and reviewers for their input—advice, ideas, directions, and suggestions—that helped to make this learning resource more student-friendly and teacher-useful. Their contribution in time, effort, and expertise was invaluable.

Consultants

Brenda Davis
Education Consultant
Six Nations of the Grand River

Patricia Healy
Curriculum Consultant (retired)
York Region District School Board

Karen Iversen
Educational Consultant
Edmonton, Alberta

Pina Sacco
Vice-Principal
Father Bressani Catholic High School
York Catholic District School Board

Reviewers

Heather Chalmers
Teacher
St. Augustine Catholic High School
York Catholic District School Board

Nancy Christoffer
Bias Reviewer

Karlene Elliott
Teacher
Toniata Public School
Upper Canada District School Board

Margaret Hoogeveen
Bias Reviewer

Mark Lowry
Geography Consultant
Toronto District School Board

John MacPhail
Teacher
St. Dominic Elementary School
Halton Catholic District School Board

Linda Memmo
Teacher
St. Fidelis Catholic School
Toronto Catholic District School Board

Patricia Perkin
Teacher
Kawartha Pine Ridge District School Board

Luci Soncin
Principal (retired)
St. Fidelis Catholic School
Toronto Catholic District School Board

Contents

· ·

Features to Help You Use This Book

KEY VOCABULARY

A Key Vocabulary list is found on the first page of each chapter to let you know the terms that are new or difficult in the chapter.

Before Reading questions and activities help you to think about what you already know about the topic. Your own experiences can give you some insights into the ideas presented. You are sometimes asked to share your thoughts with others. This helps you to improve your communication skills.

Fact File

Each Fact File is a small piece of information about the topic you are studying. Often, these facts are quite unusual in that they make you look at things from a different angle.

These questions help you understand key points. They can help you check that you understand what you are reading.

After Reading activities help you identify main ideas, make conclusions, and apply the ideas you have just learned to new situations.

LITERACY TIP

Helpful Hints

Literacy Tips are helpful hints that will make it easier for you to read, understand, and communicate ideas. These tips are linked to activities or information on or near the page where they are found.

These margin notes send you to the Nelson Social Studies website to learn more about the people, places, and events discussed in this textbook.

Go to Nelson Social Studies

GeoSkills

GeoSkills help you learn useful geographic and literacy skills. They show you steps that you can take to practise difficult skills that you will use in everyday life.

Go Geo-Green

Each Go Geo-Green feature lets you know about an interesting action that people have taken to help protect our environment. They show what people can accomplish when they set their minds to it.

BE A GLOBAL CITIZEN

These features are reports about actions that people have taken to help others around the world. They show how we are all connected to the world community.

CASE STUDY

A case study gives details about one example activity. It shows the bigger ideas that have been discussed in the chapter. Take the time to look for the connections.

Map Appendix

The Map Appendix, on pages 312 to 324, is a set of maps you will need to help you understand and do the work in this book.

Glossary

The Glossary, on pages 325 to 328, gives meanings for all the words that are printed in **bold** throughout the book. It is like a mini-dictionary.

Index

The Index, on pages 329 to 332, is a list of terms that you can find in the book and on what pages they are found. It is a quick way of finding out on what pages a topic is located.

End-of-Chapter Exercises

At the end of every chapter, there are four types of questions. These questions are designed to let you test yourself on how well you understand the chapter, to get you to stretch your geography skills, and to allow you to demonstrate your readiness to move on to new material.

Knowledge and Understanding

Inquiry/Research and Communication Skills

Map, Globe, and Graphic Skills

Application

Patterns in Human Geography

IN THIS UNIT

- identify the main patterns of human settlement and identify the factors that influence population distribution and land use
- use a variety of geographic representations, resources, tools, and technologies to gather, process, and communicate geographic information about patterns in human geography
- compare living and working conditions in countries with different patterns of settlement, and examine how demographic factors could affect your own life in the future

2 Imagine trying to get from place to place on this street in New Delhi, India. As cities become more and more crowded, new problems arise. What problems do you see resulting from this situation?

1 What message does this cartoon send about the problems we face on Earth?

CONGRATULATIONS! IT'S YOUR 6 BILLIONTH! WHAT DO YOU THINK HE'LL BE WHEN HE GROWS UP?

HUNGRY, CROWDED, AND POOR!

3 This family is fortunate. They can take care of their basic needs. What are human basic needs? Do people have a right to have them met?

Population Breakdown for China by Age

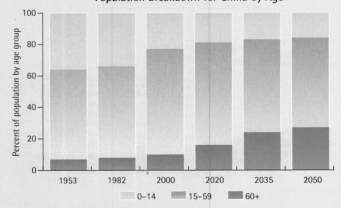

Percent of population by age group — 1953, 1982, 2000, 2020, 2035, 2050

0–14   15–59   60+

4 China is the world's most populous country, with 1.2 billion people. It is home to 20 percent of the world's population. China has made efforts to slow population growth in recent decades. How effective have these efforts been? How will the percentage of people under the age of 15 change in China from 2000 to 2035?

5 Humans change the environment. This is Tokyo, Japan, the world's largest city region. How do you think much of the land was used a century ago, when the city was much smaller?

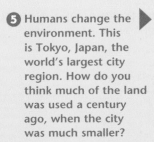

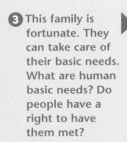

6 This graph illustrates how city land is usually used. Does land use in the community you live in or near match this pattern?

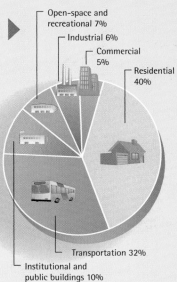

Open-space and recreational 7%

Industrial 6%

Commercial 5%

Residential 40%

Transportation 32%

Institutional and public buildings 10%

7 Computers have changed the way we work. What other jobs require good computer skills and knowledge?

Baby Boomer Retirement Statistics, 2005–2029

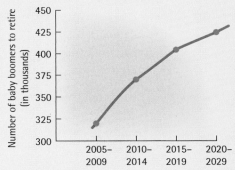

Number of baby boomers to retire (in thousands)

450
425
400
375
350
325
300

2005–2009 2010–2014 2015–2019 2020–2029

8 Canada's population is aging. The baby boomers are reaching retirement. How will this affect opportunities for new business?

9 Global warming and air pollution are two major threats today. Might the next big growth area for jobs be related to the environment? What kinds of jobs might they be?

10 Because of closer global connections and the industrialization of food production, we can get foods from all over the world. What are some advantages and disadvantages of this?

1 Population Distribution and Density

IN THIS CHAPTER

- identify three patterns of settlement: linear, scattered, and clustered
- identify and explain the factors that affect where people live
- compare the characteristics of places with high and low population densities
- make up questions to guide research about population characteristics and patterns

KEY VOCABULARY

Aborigine
arable
census
choropleth map
cluster
demography
dense
developed country
developing country
economic development
linear
population density
population distribution
scattered
sparse

Growing Pains

1. How many people have you met in your life? Predict how many people you are likely to meet between now and when you become a senior citizen.

2. a) What might be some reasons to look at the total number of people in the world?

   b) In what ways might the size of the world's population affect you personally?

For thousands of years, Earth was home to relatively few people. At the end of the last Ice Age—roughly 10 000 years ago—about 4 million people existed worldwide. The population started to grow quickly around 1950. Throughout the first years of the twenty-first century, the world population grew by around 76 million people a year. That is more than twice the population of Canada. The United Nations predicts that by the year 2050, the world's population will grow to more than 9 billion people. It will keep growing over the next two centuries.

Counting Heads

Demography is the study of human population. "Demographers" study data on populations. These scientists analyze information about where and how well people live. Their research helps us understand why people live where they do. It also tells us why some countries have population problems.

LITERACY TIP

Using Headings to Predict

It is a good idea to skim a textbook chapter before you start reading it. The headings and subheadings in each section will give you a general idea of the content you will be reading. As you read the headings, think of questions you want answered.

Figure 1.1

The world population was estimated to be 6.76 billion in March 2009. In 2013, the world's 7 billionth person may be born into your community. However, chances are much greater that he or she will be born in an economically developing part of Africa or Asia. What challenges might this person face because of where he or she is born?

Demographers also do the following:

- help countries, regions, and cities predict what the population will be in the future
- work for governments and businesses to recommend how to provide services and goods for people

Figure 1.2

What message does this cartoon send about world population growth?

LITERACY TIP
. . . .

Reading Cartoons

Cartoons are humorous drawings that cartoonists use to make comments about issues or events. Cartoonists want to get readers thinking about a topic. You will need to read the speech balloons and look carefully at the clues given in the drawing to understand the cartoonist's message. (Refer to GeoSkills on pages 192–193 in Chapter 9.)

Fact File

Ninety-seven percent of all population growth occurs in countries that are economically developing. These countries are still trying to provide their citizens with good quality of life. They are working to provide health care and school systems to meet the needs of their people. If these countries cannot provide enough health care and education for their growing population, should they give up?

The Census

How are all the people in a country counted? Every five years, many governments collect information about the number of people living within their borders. Every 10 years, they conduct a more detailed **census**. In Canada, the government hires people to conduct door-to-door surveys. They collect information about age, ethnic background, language, family size, and other topics. Statistics Canada conducts the Canadian census.

World Population Growth, 1750 to 2050

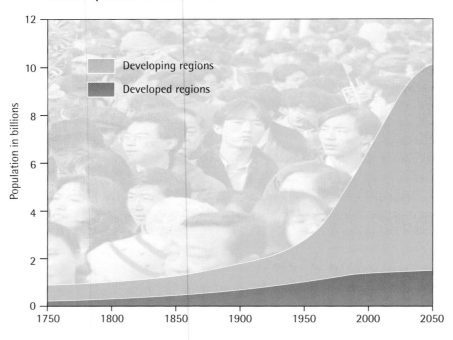

Developing regions

Developed regions

Figure 1.3

This graph shows world population growth in developing and developed regions, from 1750 to 2050 (estimated). What do demographers mean when they say there has been a population "explosion"?

A Timeline of the World's Population Growth in Billions

1804	1927	1960	1975	1987	1999	2012	2028	2042
1 billion	2 billion	3 billion	4 billion	5 billion	6 billion	7 billion	8 billion	9 billion

Figure 1.4

This timeline shows when the world's population reached billions of people. It took millions of years of human history to reach 1 billion people. The timeline also estimates when the world's population will reach the next billion people in the future. How old will you be when the population is expected to reach 9 billion?

LITERACY TIP
Reading a Graph

When reading a graph, remember TAPP: Title, Axes, Pattern, and Purpose. TAPP will help you understand and connect to the information in the graph. TAPP will also help you make meaningful observations. (Refer to GeoSkills on page 30 in Chapter 2.)

1. Look at the line graph in Figure 1.3. Write down three observations that you can make about the information in this graph. Observations could be about patterns that you see, high or low values, predictions about the future, and so on.

2. Use Figure 1.3 to predict the number of people that may live on Earth in 100 years.

3. Use the timeline in Figure 1.4 to determine the length of time it took to add each new billion people. What do you notice as you calculate the time period for each new billion people? What are two factors that could affect the length of time it takes for the world to add a billion new people to its population?

Population Distribution

Look at the World Population Density map on page 314 of the Map Appendix. People are not evenly distributed on Earth's surface. Many people live in the following four huge **clusters**, or groups, of population:

- eastern North America
- western Europe
- southern Asia
- southeast Asia

In other parts of the world, small numbers of people are **scattered** over large areas. Notice how the population is spread over the Arctic and central Australia. Settlement does not occur everywhere. However, very few places are free of human activities. Permanent, year-round research bases exist even in Antarctica. Where people live is called **population distribution**. **Population density** is how many people live within a given area. While these terms may seem similar, Figure 1.5 shows the difference. Regions A and B have the same population density. Note how the population distribution is different for each.

Population Distribution Patterns

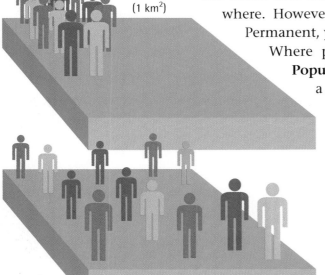

A
(1 km²)

B
(1 km²)

Figure 1.5

Regions A and B both have the same population density. There are 12 people per square kilometre. However, different patterns of population distribution exist. Region A shows an unequal distribution, or cluster, of people. In region B, the population is more evenly distributed, or scattered, throughout the area. Think about the region in which you live. Is the pattern of population distribution clustered or scattered?

Population Density

The population density of a place tells us how many people live in an area. It is usually measured by the average number of people for each square kilometre (km²). To calculate this, you divide the number of people living in a country or region by the land area in which they live. For example, Australia has a population of 20.6 million and an area of 7 687 000 km²:

$$\frac{20\ 600\ 000}{7\ 687\ 000} = 2.7 \text{ people per km}^2.$$

Bangladesh has a population of 153.5 million and an area of 144 000 km²:

$$\frac{153\ 500\ 000}{144\ 000} = 1066.0 \text{ people per km}^2.$$

As these two examples show, population density varies greatly from place to place. In fact, population densities around the world range from less than one person per square kilometre to thousands of people per square kilometre. Review what demographers do (see page 5). How might they use information about population density?

Fact File

Australia has over 50 times more land area than Bangladesh, but it has only one-seventh the population. Why do you think fewer people live in a country that has more land area?

Figure 1.7

The population density in Osaka, Japan, contrasts sharply with that of a rural area (see Figure 1.8). What is the most visible sign of high population density?

Population Density by Country

Country	Population Density (persons per km²)
Australia	3
Bangladesh	1 035
Belgium	348
Brazil	22
Canada	3
China	138
Dominican Republic	476
Hong Kong	6 308
Egypt	73
Iceland	3
Japan	338
Macau	20 346
Mongolia	2
Nigeria	156
Russia	8
Singapore	6 785
Sudan	15
United Kingdom	251
United States	31

Figure 1.6

What do you notice about the population densities of countries around the world? Which countries are the least densely populated? Which are the most densely populated?

Figure 1.8

This is a rural area in Africa. What is the most visible sign of low population density?

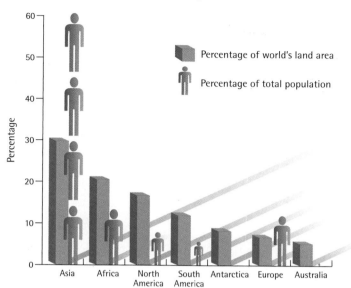

Comparing Land Area and Population

Figure 1.9

This graph compares the areas of the continents to their populations. Which continent has the greatest population density?

Canada and Australia are large in area but have small populations. These countries have a low or **sparse** population density. Some countries, like Bangladesh, have large populations living in a small area. The people live and work packed closely together. These countries have a high population density, or a **dense** population. Countries with a moderate population density are somewhere in the middle. They average from 15 to 150 people per square kilometre. France has a population density of 112 people per square kilometre. Therefore, it has a moderate population density.

Population density refers to how close or how far apart people live to one another. Understanding population density can help communities plan what services are needed. It is also needed to know where to build new schools, houses, businesses, and transportation routes. Looking at population densities also helps us compare different regions of the world.

To learn more about population topics around the world,

Go to Nelson
Social Studies

1. Describe the population distribution in your area or community.

2. Calculate the population density of your classroom by finding the number of people per square metre.

3. a) The average population density of Canada is 3 persons per square kilometre. Based on what you observe, how does your community or area compare to this average value?

b) Explain why an average population density may not tell us much about the conditions in a country or region.

4. a) The population density in Nunavut is 0.01 persons per square kilometre. Identify two challenges such a sparse population might face.

b) The population density of the city of Toronto is 881.5 persons per square kilometre. Identify two challenges such a dense population might face.

GeoSkills

Reading a Choropleth Map

A map is a drawing that shows physical and human features of Earth's surface. Reading a map is not the same as reading a piece of text. Maps combine visual information and text to show data.

The map in Figure 1.10 is a specific type of map known as a **choropleth map**. It comes from two Greek words: *choros* (place) and *pleth* (value). Choropleth maps are thematic maps of places that show one type of data (or values). Patterns of distribution are clear when only one type of data is shown. Look at the maps on pages 312–324 of the Map Appendix. What specific type of data does each map show?

A choropleth map is one of the simplest ways to show data.

- First, place the data into groups of numbers or percents from lowest to highest (for example, under 2, 2–20, 20–40, 40–100, and so on).
- Then, use a graded colour series to represent the data groups on the map. This means that you choose light to darker shades within the same colour family (for example, shades of green or brown). Choose the lightest shade within a colour family to show the group with the lowest numbers or percents. Then, use a slightly darker shade to represent the next highest data group, and so on. The darkest shade shows the group with the highest numbers or percents.

Population density maps are choropleth maps because they show one type of data (population density). Density information is expressed as people per square kilometre (ppl/km²). Use the steps of the TLC method to read and understand choropleth maps. (See the choropleth map and steps on page 11.)

For Step Four, answer the following questions:

1. a) Which region of Canada has the sparsest population density?

   b) Using what you already know about Canada's physical geography, explain why so few people live in this region.

2. a) Which region of Canada has the densest population?

   b) Using what you already know about Canada's physical geography, provide two reasons why so many people live in this region.

3. a) Use the World Population Density map on page 314 of the Map Appendix. Look for large areas around the world that have a population density of less than 10 people per square kilometre. Look at the legend to determine which colour represents that number set. List five of these regions.

   b) With a partner, provide a geographic reason why so few people live in each of these regions. Set up your answers in a table like the one below. The first column will name the region; the second column will show the geographic reason why so few people live in each of these regions; and the third column will show why the geographic reason prevents people from living in this region.

Region	Geographic Reason	Why This Geographic Reason Prevents People from Living in the Region
Northern Russia	very cold	difficult to grow crops and raise livestock for food

GeoSkills

Reading a Choropleth Map *(continued)*

Step One:

Read the *title*. The title will put the map into context for you.

Step Two:

Look for and read the *legend*. The legend will explain the symbols and colours used on the map. What do the colours represent in this legend?

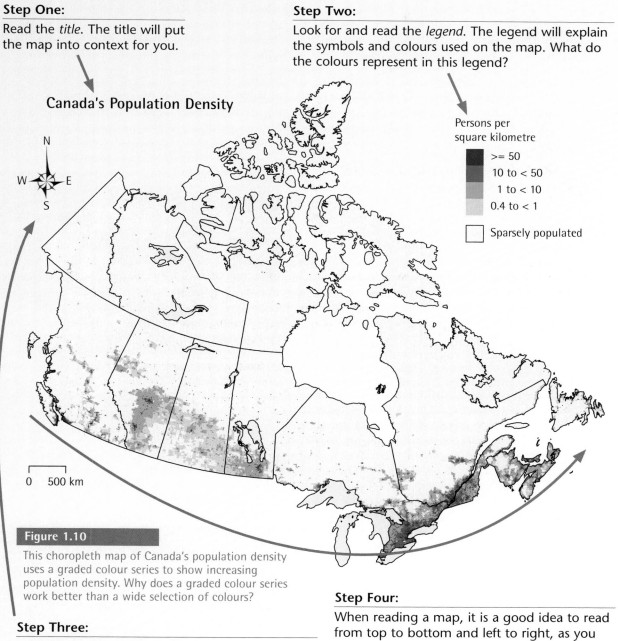

Canada's Population Density

Persons per
square kilometre

- >= 50
- 10 to < 50
- 1 to < 10
- 0.4 to < 1

☐ Sparsely populated

0   500 km

Figure 1.10

This choropleth map of Canada's population density uses a graded colour series to show increasing population density. Why does a graded colour series work better than a wide selection of colours?

Step Three:

Find the *compass*. Make sure you can identify the cardinal points of *north*, *south*, *east*, and *west*.

Step Four:

When reading a map, it is a good idea to read from top to bottom and left to right, as you would read a book. As you do this, look for any patterns of population density in Canada.

BE A GLOBAL CITIZEN

Overpopulation— Looking for Answers in a Crowded World

Imagine that you wake up one morning and find twice as many people living in your house. You have to share your bedroom, your clothes, your computer, and all of the items in your house. How would your life change?

The world faces a similar, but far larger situation. Our population is increasing at a rapid rate. We have only 14 percent of Earth on which to live. The rest of the planet is either water or too harsh for humans to settle. Humans use many resources from Earth, but how long will these resources last as use increases?

You live in a world that must face the problems of a growing population. Check out the work of organizations such as the Population Reference Bureau and the United Nations Population Fund. As a citizen of the world, you must help look for answers so that you can become part of the solution.

Figure 1.12

How would you feel if you had to share your home with twice as many people? What challenges would you face as twice as many people tried to live in the same amount of space?

Figure 1.13

This street in New Delhi, India, shows how serious the problem of overpopulation has become. How would you feel if you had to live in a city this crowded?

Problems Caused by a Rapid Population Increase in Your Home and the World

	Problems Caused if the Number of People in Your House Doubled	Problems Caused by Overpopulation
Fighting over resources	There may be fights over computer or bathroom use.	Many groups of people in the world are fighting over access to food and water resources.
Control over existing space	You may feel the need to protect your belongings.	Many wars are over land control and protection of resources.
Division of money	How will the money be divided? Will some get more money than others?	Some countries flourish while others sink into poverty.
Overuse of resources	Water and energy bills will increase. Your family will use more products.	People use more of Earth's resources.
Pollution	The garbage you produce will increase.	Imagine how much garbage over 6 billion people produce!

Figure 1.11

The problems caused by overpopulation are similar to the problems that would arise if the number of people in your house doubled. However, they are on a much larger scale.

NEL

Why Do People Live Where They Live?

LITERACY TIP

Brainstorming and Categorizing

Brainstorming means coming up with as many ideas about a topic as possible. Begin by writing down all your ideas. Then, add to, subtract from, join, or change ideas. Look for groups of ideas that go together. Categorize your ideas under headings. Finally, think about your ideas and choose the best ones.

1. Figure 1.5 on page 7 illustrates the difference between population distribution and population density. Design your own picture or other type of visual to show the difference between population distribution and population density.

2. a) With a partner, brainstorm a list of factors that might affect the population distribution and population density of a place.

   b) Organize your factors into two groups: natural factors and human factors.

We have seen that there are patterns to where people live in the world. The following factors work together to create these patterns:

* natural environment
* level of economic development
* history of a region

Natural Environment

Land for Human Settlement

The natural environment has a strong influence on where people live. About 71 percent of the world's surface area is water. Only 29 percent of the world is land surface. Of this area, less than half can support human settlement. The rest is too rocky, too steep, too dry, too cold, or too swampy to support many people. Much of the land that can be used for human settlement cannot support very large numbers of people, so population densities remain low. Approximately 90 percent of the people on Earth live on just 10 percent of its land area.

Figure 1.14

Most of Earth's surface cannot be used for human settlement. As Earth's population grows, what new types of settlements might people need to consider?

The World's Population on Earth's Surface

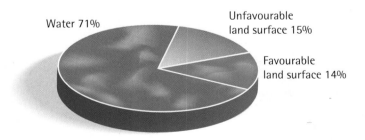

Water 71%

Unfavourable land surface 15%

Favourable land surface 14%

Which physical features would attract you to settle in a location? Places with **arable** land attract large numbers of people. Arable land has fertile soil. It also has a moderate climate and water for growing crops. The location of other natural resources also attracts settlement. Natural resources provide materials for food, shelter, and trade.

Would you settle where many other people have also decided to live? Many densely populated areas are found in the following locations:

- river valleys
- coastal regions
- on flat or gently rolling plains

The Great Lakes–St. Lawrence Lowlands region of Canada is densely populated. Its soils are fertile. The climate is moderate and the land is fairly flat. These conditions are ideal for agriculture. They are also perfect for building cities and transportation networks. People tend to settle where they find these favourable characteristics.

Would you rather settle where fewer people have decided to live? Areas with unfavourable environments usually have sparse population densities. Unfavourable environments include the following:

- rugged terrain
- extreme climate
- limited water supply
- few resources
- infertile soils

The Himalayan mountain range in India and the Gobi Desert of Mongolia have sparse population densities. These regions provide poor conditions for human settlement.

Fact File

The Great Lakes–St. Lawrence Lowlands is the smallest landform region of Canada, but it is the most densely populated area of Canada. What challenges might the people face in this region?

Figure 1.16

This vineyard is found in the Niagara Region of Ontario. Which characteristics of this land made it attractive to settlers during Canada's early history?

Figure 1.15

This area of the Arctic is found in Nunavut. Which conditions make this region too extreme for many humans to live there?

Water for Life

People tend to live where there is access to water, since it is needed for life. Areas with enough water for people, animals, crops, and industries can support large populations. Many of the world's largest cities are ports that developed in coastal areas. Think of New York, Cairo, Shanghai, Toronto, and Chicago.

The fertile land of the Great Lakes–St. Lawrence Lowlands attracted people. Another favourable factor for settlement is its excellent waterways. They are used for shipping, industry, and agriculture.

Figure 1.17

This busy port in Shanghai supports a large population.

Figure 1.18

The Welland Canal runs from Port Colborne on Lake Erie to Port Weller on Lake Ontario. It is a major link of the Saint Lawrence Seaway. The canal was built between 1912 and 1932, and it was deepened in 1972. It has eight locks to overcome the 100-metre difference in height between Lake Erie and Lake Ontario. In what ways might the building of the Welland Canal have affected the population densities of the Great Lakes area?

1. Think about the area where you live. In what ways have the natural environment and water bodies influenced where people live?

2. Use the World Population Density map in the Map Appendix (page 314) to identify five lakes, seas, or oceans that have likely been important in shaping the population distribution of the world. (You will need to use an atlas to name the lakes and seas.) For each water body, suggest a reason why it is important.

Economic Conditions

A region's level of **economic development** can impact its population patterns. Economic development refers to how wealthy and industrialized nations are. In **developing countries**, a large part of the population works at harvesting natural resources. They might be farmers. They might cut forests or mine minerals. These industries are often located in rural areas with low population densities. In **developed countries** such as Canada, a large part of the population is employed in jobs that provide services to other people. They work in retail stores, restaurants, hospitals, schools, banks, and so on. This means that most people in developed countries live in urban areas with high population densities. In recent years, countries such as Mexico and Malaysia have developed swiftly. The cities in these countries have also grown very quickly. Now, less than 50 percent of the people in these countries live in rural areas.

LITERACY TIP

Making Meaningful Connections

When reading information, it is important to find ways to personally connect to it. Doing so will make the information more meaningful and relevant to your own life.

China's Population Density

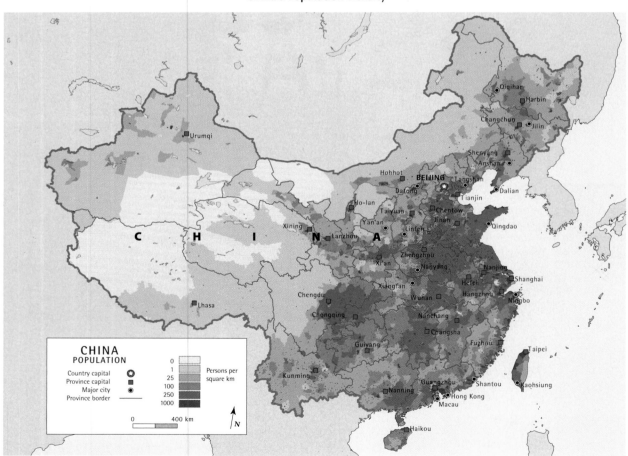

Figure 1.19

This map shows the population density of China. Describe the population distribution in this country. What do you suppose are important factors that shape the population density in China?

History

The history of a region influences the number of people that live there. Areas where people have lived together in one place tend to attract more inhabitants. Over time, the population grows in these settled communities. History helps to explain the high population densities in Europe and Asia. People have lived together on these continents for many thousands of years. Similarly, First Nations and Inuit have lived in North America for many thousands of years. However, they did not tend to live in large, settled communities. Therefore, North America did not experience population clusters until European newcomers came to North America and settled along the coasts. This explains the current population cluster on the East Coast.

Factors affecting population patterns work together. For example, plenty of water and fertile soil led to farming in North Africa thousands of years ago. The farmers cultivated the land close to the Nile River in Egypt. There, they could grow enough food to support many people. The people settled along the banks of the river. As they did, this population developed a **linear** pattern. Economic opportunities grew out of the settlement of this area. This encouraged more population growth. The Nile River Valley and Nile Delta supported a large population throughout history. (Use an atlas to find a map of North Africa and the Nile River.)

Figure 1.20

Tokyo is one of the largest cities in the world. Huge numbers of people use the subway system. Tremendous congestion occurs during rush hours. At some stations, white-gloved "pushers" are hired to push people into the trains. What might be one solution to this problem of overcrowding?

AFTER READING

1. Provide two reasons why it is useful to learn why people live where they live.

2. Examine the map showing population densities in North America on page 314 in the Map Appendix.

   a) Describe the pattern of population density that you see for Canada.

   b) Identify what are likely the two most important factors that shaped the density patterns of the Atlantic region and the Prairie region.

3. Predict what will be the population distribution and density patterns for Canada 100 years from now. Give reasons to explain your predictions.

CASE STUDY

Australia

The history of Australia provides an interesting example of population development. In the late 1700s, Britain sent thousands of its prisoners to work on prison farms in Australia. When they were released, they were offered a choice. They could return to Britain or stay in Australia. Many were offered supplies for 18 months and a grant of land if they stayed. Most of these people lived in poverty and had no opportunities for work in Britain. They chose Australia. In 1850, 400 000 people of British origin lived in Australia. There were many more sheep than people. In fact, there were 13 million sheep on the continent.

Gold was discovered in both New South Wales and Victoria in 1851. The population situation changed dramatically. The discovery of gold led to the economic development of Australia. During the 1850s, the population tripled.

The prisoners from Britain were not the first people to live in Australia. When the British arrived, as many as 700 000 **Aborigines** lived there, just as their ancestors had done for thousands of years. The British arrivals brought diseases with them, such as cholera and smallpox. Many Aborigines died from these diseases.

Today, Australia's population includes about 400 000 Aborigines. They make up about 2 percent of the population. Some live in the outback in the centre of Australia, or

Fact File

Disease brought by Europeans killed many First Nations peoples of North America. Smallpox wiped out most of the population in some villages. Other deadly diseases included typhus, measles, mumps, influenza, and pertussis (whooping cough). Why would these diseases be so deadly to First Nations populations?

Figure 1.21

Elder Mavis Foster, from the Waanyi tribe, is preparing for National Sorry Day held on May 26 each year. The purpose of this day is to remember the forced removal of almost 100 000 Aboriginal children from their families between 1910 and 1970. How does this compare with what Aboriginal peoples experienced in Canada?

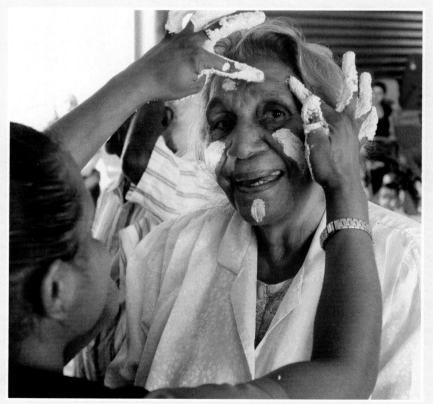

CASE STUDY

Australia (continued)

in the Northern Territories. Many work on ranches or farms. Others have moved to cities in the more densely populated southeast and southwest.

Most of Australia is sparsely populated with a very low population density. The south-eastern part of the continent has the most and best arable land. In this region, population densities are greater. Use an atlas to find a map of climate regions for Australia. What is the connection between population distribution and climate?

Dry climate and flat land throughout most of Australia are suited to livestock farming, especially sheep. Forests grow on the northern and southeastern coastal plains. These are the only parts of Australia with enough rain to support forests. Physical conditions affected population distribution in Australia. It has become the most urbanized continent. Eighty-five percent of the people live in cities. Australia is also the leading industrial country and the most economically developed country in the world.

Figure 1.22

This map shows the population density of Australia. Four out of every five Australians live in the densely populated coastal cities that make up only 3 percent of the country's land area. In what ways might this have affected the ways that industries developed in Australia?

LITERACY TIP
· · · · · · · · · · · · · · ·

Using Graphic Organizers

Question 2 asks you to compare the population distribution and densities of Australia and Canada. Using a graphic organizer, like a t-chart or a Venn diagram, allows you to see the relationship that exists between these two countries, and to arrive at your own conclusions. (Refer to pages 58 and 70 for examples of a t-chart and a Venn diagram.)

Population Density of Australia

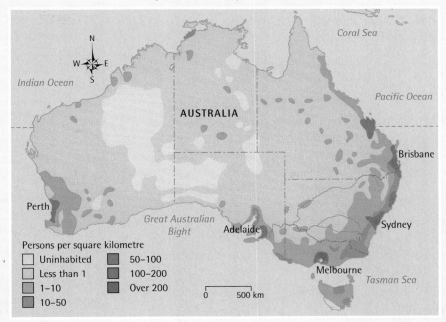

1. Identify the population density pattern of Australia.

2. What are some ways in which the population distributions and densities of Australia and Canada are the same and different? In order to compare similarities and differences, you could use a t-chart or a Venn diagram.

Knowledge and Understanding

1 In general, which factor that influences population patterns do you think is the most important? Give reasons for your opinion.

2 **a)** Make up three sketches or illustrations to show three patterns of settlement: linear (see page 17), scattered, and clustered (see page 7).

b) Use a road map or atlas to identify places in your province where you might find examples of these patterns.

3 Design a chart to compare living conditions in an area of high population density with living conditions in an area of sparse population density (refer to Figures 1.7 and 1.8 on page 8). You should be able to think of three ways for comparing the places.

4 Consider the population distribution and density patterns of Australia. What aspects of the patterns might be seen as opportunities? What aspects might be challenges? Give reasons to support your opinions.

Inquiry/Research and Communication Skills

5 **a)** Conduct a census of your class. To do this, develop a survey of five or six questions that will help you find information about the population characteristics and patterns of your classroom. Brainstorm with other class members to decide what information you wish to collect. Your questions must be related to what you have learned about population in this chapter. Consider the following topics as you construct survey questions:

- population distribution
- population density
- characteristics of your classroom population (Remember that people who are hired to conduct door-to-door surveys in their neighbourhoods collect information about age, ethnic background, language, family size, and so on.)
- factors that affect where people live from your classroom population (natural environment, economic developments, history)

b) Brainstorm with class members to decide how you can display your results. Consider the types of results you gathered and various ways that you can best record and display your results. For example, if you ask questions about where your class members live, you could plot their home locations on a community map to determine population distribution. If you ask questions about characteristics of your classroom population such as family size, you could graph your results.

6 Use the Internet, an almanac, and/or an atlas to list those countries in the world that have the top 10 total populations and those with the 10 highest population densities. Are there any countries that can be found on both lists? How do you explain your findings?

Map, Globe, and Graphic Skills

7 Look at the World Population Density map (page 314 of the Map Appendix). The darkest shades of colour show places with the highest population density. What patterns do you notice? Which parts of the world are uninhabited? Using an atlas, name the countries that appear to have the highest and lowest population densities.

8 The patterns of world population distribution show some strong correlations (similarities) to patterns of the natural environment.

a) Compare Figure 1.23 on page 21 with the World Population Density map (page 314 of the Map Appendix). What patterns do you observe?

b) Use an atlas to find thematic maps on world landforms, and climate and vegetation regions, and compare them with regions of dense, moderate, and sparse populations on the World Population Density map. Record your findings in a chart with the following headings:

Population Pattern	Landform Conditions	Climate Conditions	Vegetation Conditions
Dense populations			
Moderate populations			
Sparse populations			

c) Write a statement that draws a conclusion based on the evidence in your chart.

Water Deficiency and Surplus

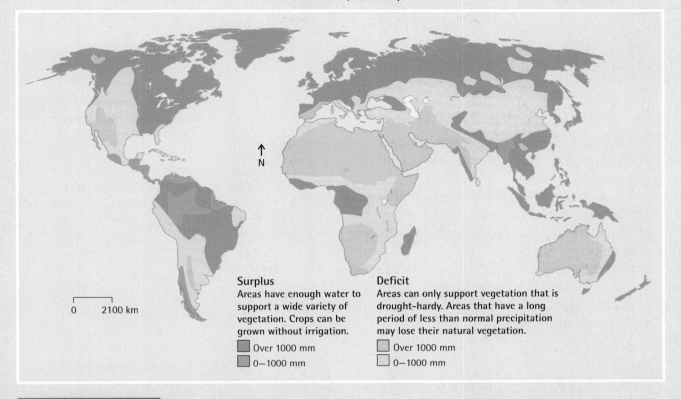

Surplus
Areas have enough water to support a wide variety of vegetation. Crops can be grown without irrigation.

◼ Over 1000 mm
◼ 0–1000 mm

Deficit
Areas can only support vegetation that is drought-hardy. Areas that have a long period of less than normal precipitation may lose their natural vegetation.

◼ Over 1000 mm
◻ 0–1000 mm

0   2100 km

Figure 1.23

This world map shows areas of water deficiency (drought) and surplus (flooding). What similarities can you observe between water supply and population distribution?

Application

9 **a)** What changes in world population distribution do you predict over the next 50 years? Give reasons for your prediction.

b) What changes in population density do you predict over the next 50 years? Give reasons for your opinions.

10 "The natural environment is the most significant factor that influences where people live." Do you agree or disagree with this statement? Give supporting reasons for your point of view.

11 Explain why it is impossible to get a truly accurate number for the present world population.

12 Consider your community as a place to live. What are the favourable and unfavourable factors about its location? Support your answers with evidence.

Figure 1.24

What is the natural environment in this photo of Sydney, Australia? Why do you think so many people live here?

2

Population Characteristics

KEY VOCABULARY

birth rate
death rate
fertility rate
gross domestic product (GDP)
Human Development Index (HDI)
infant mortality
life expectancy
literacy rate
natural increase
per capita income
population characteristic
population pyramid
replacement level
scatter graph

Which Is the Best Place to Live?

1. a) With a partner, brainstorm a list of places in the world where you think it would be best to live. What are the reasons for your choices?

b) With your partner, brainstorm a list of places in the world where you would not like to live. Give reasons for your choices.

From 1994 to 2000, Canada was ranked the best place in the world to live. In 1991, Canada lost its first-place position to Norway. In 2007, Canada ranked fourth behind Australia, Norway, and Iceland. Who decides which is the best country to live in? How is this decided? The United Nations looks at how well people live in 177 countries. It considers factors that measure how well each country is doing in three areas of human development:

- health—how long people can expect to live
- knowledge—how many people (15 years and up) can read and write, go to school, and what levels of schooling they reach
- standard of living—how much money people earn

These factors are expressed as statistics, information presented in number form. The United Nations combines these statistics into its **Human Development Index (HDI)**, which gives a general picture of living conditions in each country. (See Figure 2.2.)

Figure 2.1

Canada is a huge and diverse country. Do you think everyone in all parts of Canada would agree that our country is one of the best places to live? Why or why not?

Using Photographs for Information

Photographs provide additional information on what you are reading. Look at each photograph in Figure 2.1 and ask yourself the following:

- What is the main idea of the photograph?
- Where did I look first? Why?
- How does the photograph make me feel?
- What new information does it give about the topic?

Figure 2.2

These countries rate the highest and the lowest scores on the United Nations Human Development Index. On which continents are the countries with the highest scores? On which continent are the lowest-scoring countries?

Human Development Index Scores

10 Highest Scores	10 Lowest Scores
Iceland	Sierra Leone
Norway	Burkina Faso
Australia	Guinea-Bissau
Canada	Niger
Ireland	Mali
Sweden	Mozambique
Switzerland	Central African Republic
Japan	Chad
Netherlands	Ethiopia
France	Democratic Republic of Congo

Canada is near the top of the list of countries with the highest quality of life in the world. However, the United Nations Human Development Report is not all positive. This report shows concern about child poverty in Canada. Its treatment of Aboriginal peoples is also an issue. In Canada, child poverty has risen over the past two decades. Over 1 million children live in poverty. That means one in every six children. For the most part, they live in households with incomes under $20 000. Many of these are Aboriginal children.

A hopeful sign happened in June 2008. The government apologized to all Aboriginal peoples for the residential schools and the problems they created. The reason for these schools was to assimilate (absorb) Aboriginal children into mainstream society. School staff taught Aboriginal children to fit in with European ways of life. Parents had no say in the matter. All children had to attend these government- and church-run schools, which were often far from home. Before the 1940s, there were only a few residential schools across Canada. By 1955, there were 69, and by 1975, there were 207. Students often suffered from abuse at these schools The abuse and the separation from families led to many problems. They include loss of culture, poverty, increased despair, and emotional and social problems.

Figure 2.3

More than 16 percent of Canadian children live in poverty, such as these First Nations children living on a reserve in Alberta. If Canada is such a wealthy country, why do you think there is poverty?

Number Crunching

Statistics is the science of collecting different kinds of data and then interpreting and presenting the data in number form. Statistics involves counting people, events, or things. How many TVs do people purchase in a year? How many people are serving in the military in a country? How much energy does each person use? When these statistics are mapped, they show global patterns.

Demographers use statistics as a tool. They collect, study, and try to understand the numerical information in order to do the following:

- understand the past and present
- solve problems
- manage resources
- plan for the future

Population Characteristics

Population characteristics are factors that tell us how a population is changing. They also tell us how well people live in a country. Groups such as the following use population characteristics to plan for the future:

- large corporations
- hospitals
- retail stores
- school systems
- non-governmental organizations (NGOs) like UNICEF (the United Nations Children's Fund) or Amnesty International
- individuals

These groups plan for the products and services that will be needed by a changing population. For example, if more babies are being born, school systems must prepare for an increased number of students. If people are living longer, hospitals need to be ready to meet the medical needs of older patients. NGOs must prepare for the needs of increasing populations in developing countries.

Many different population characteristics are used, such as the following:

- birth rates
- literacy rates
- death rates
- life expectancy

These characteristics are like pieces of a giant puzzle. Demographers put all the pieces together to get a clearer picture of what a country is like and how well its people live.

Figure 2.4

Every family is different. Do you think there is a "best" size for a family? Why?

Figure 2.5

Since the fertility rate worldwide has decreased, do you think this child might be the man's only grandchild? Why?

Fact File

The fertility rate in developing regions of the world is 2.9. Some countries have very high fertility rates, with an average of more than 7 children born per woman. That means many women must have more than 10 children! Why do parents in developing regions have more children?

Counting the Babies

How many children are there in your family? The average number of children born in Canada is about 1.5 per family. This does not mean that there are one and a half children for each Canadian family! It means that this is the average number of babies born in the country in a woman's lifetime.

To find the **fertility rate**, you add up all the known births in a country (those reported in medical records) during one year, for women aged 15 to 44. Then, you divide the total births by the number of women in that age group. When a country looks at its future population growth, it must consider the following:

- current fertility rate
- **infant mortality**, or the number of infant deaths (one year of age and younger) per 1000 live births
- women who do not have children

To continue growing naturally, a country must have a fertility rate of 2.1. Demographers call this rate the **replacement level**. It means that enough babies are born in a given year to replace the number of people who die in that same year.

The average fertility rate for the whole world is 2.5 births per woman. During the 1950s, the average was more than 5 births per woman. Women everywhere in the world are now having fewer babies. The decline is greatest among African nations. Yet, because the world population is so high, there are far more mothers having babies today than there were in the 1950s. Even with lower fertility rates, our world will add nearly 3 billion more people by 2050.

Fertility Rates for Selected Countries, 1975, 1998, 2006

Country	1975	1998	2006
Albania	2.3	1.3	2.3
Australia	2.2	1.8	1.8
Brazil	5.8	2.6	2.4
Canada	1.8	1.5	1.5
China	5.8	1.9	1.7
Germany	1.5	1.0	1.4
Guatemala	6.4	5.1	4.6
India	5.7	3.4	3.1
Indonesia	5.2	2.9	2.4
Mexico	6.2	3.9	2.4
Rwanda	8.7	6.6	6.0
Tunisia	6.0	2.9	2.0
Yemen	8.5	7.6	6.0

Figure 2.6

This chart shows the change in fertility rates for selected countries from 1975 to 1998 to 2006. What is the general trend in fertility rates from 1975 to 2006?

1. a) The fertility rate of 2.1 is considered to be the replacement level fertility rate. This rate is high enough for a population to replace itself. How many countries in Figure 2.6 are below replacement level? What do you think this will mean for the populations of these countries in the future?

b) A number of countries listed in Figure 2.6 have a fertility rate above 2.1. What do you think this will mean for the populations of these countries in the future?

Going Up or Going Down?

One reason a country's population changes is that people are born and die each year. The **birth rate** tells us the number of babies that are born each year for every 1000 people in a country. The **death rate** tells us the number of people that die each year for every 1000 people in a country. If the number of births is greater than the number of deaths, the population goes up. Sometimes the death rate goes up sharply for one year due to events such as the following:

- a major catastrophe, such as a severe natural disaster
- a war
- an epidemic, which is a sudden outbreak of serious illness

The population goes up when the birth rate is higher than the natural death rate. A **natural increase** occurs. When the birth rate is lower than the death rate, a country's population goes down. Some countries in Europe have decreasing populations. In fact, Europe's overall population growth rate was −0.05 percent in 2005. In that year, more people died in Europe than the number of babies that were born. Birth rates are actually falling everywhere in the world. However, death rates are falling even faster. People are living longer due to better medical care and living conditions. Because death rates are decreasing faster than birth rates, the world population continues to grow.

Getting a Fix on the Numbers

In 2008, Canada's birth rate was 10.3 per 1000 or 10.3/1000. That same year, Canada's death rate was 7.6/1000. Because the death rate is lower than the birth rate, Canada has a natural increase every year. How do you calculate the natural increase of a country? Find the difference between the birth rate and the death rate. (Refer to Figure 2.7.)

Fact File

The world's most populous countries (2025 estimates) include the following:

Country	Population
China	1.45 billion
India	1.45 billion
United States	355 million
Indonesia	271 million
Brazil	228 million
Pakistan	225 million
Nigeria	210 million
Bangladesh	206 million
Russia	128 million
Ethiopia	125 million

Which countries are predicted to have the smallest populations in 2025?

Population Change Rates for Canada and Malawi, 1998, 2008

Canada

1998: $\dfrac{13}{1000} - \dfrac{7}{1000} = \dfrac{6}{1000} = 0.006 \times 100 = 0.6\%$

2008: $\dfrac{10.3}{1000} - \dfrac{7.6}{1000} = \dfrac{2.7}{1000} = 0.0027 \times 100 = 0.27\%$

Birth rate − Death rate = Natural increase for Canada
In 1998, for every 1000 people who lived in Canada, 6 more people were added to the population. In 2008, the natural increase dropped. For every 1000 people, 2.7 more people were added to the population.

Malawi

1998: $\dfrac{50}{1000} - \dfrac{20}{1000} = \dfrac{30}{1000} = 0.030 \times 100 = 3\%$

2008: $\dfrac{41.8}{1000} - \dfrac{17.9}{1000} = \dfrac{23.9}{1000} = 0.0239 \times 100 = 2.39\%$

Birth rate − Death rate = Natural increase for Malawi
There was a sizable drop in the birth rate from 1998 to 2008. Despite this drop, the death rate fell as well. The rate of natural increase for Malawi dropped in 2008. For every 1000 people, 24 more people were added to the population.

Figure 2.7

Canada's and Malawi's populations showed natural increases in 1998 and 2008. What are the differences in the way their populations changed?

Figure 2.8

Do you think it is important that Canada's population grows a great deal? Why?

Figure 2.9

On a typical day in Canada, about 950 babies are born and about 700 people die. Some 610 people come to Canada as immigrants, while 135 people emigrate, or leave Canada to live in other countries.

The global population growth was 1.8 percent in the early 1980s. Since then, it has gone down to 1.3 percent per year. The United Nations predicts that this may drop to 1 percent by the year 2025. Population growth tends to show the following patterns:

- Most industrialized countries have a low natural increase or a decreasing population.
- Most developing countries have higher rates of natural increase, usually between 2 and 3 percent.

Immigration also causes the population to change. Some people move out of a country. Others move in. The difference between the number of people leaving (emigrating) and those coming in (immigrating) is called the net migration. The population growth of a country depends upon both natural increase and net migration.

Fact File

The following table shows the net migration for Canada.

Years	Immigration	Emigration	Net
1976–1986	1 216 551	555 807	+660 744
1987–1997	2 339 155	440 144	+1 899 011
1998–2007	2 040 853	412 067 (est.)	+1 628 786

What trend do you see in the net migration for Canada? Why is this important for Canada's population growth?

Doubling Time

Imagine how your living conditions would change if the number of people in your family doubled over the next few years. Would there be enough room? Would there be enough money? What adjustments would you have to make in your life? When a country's population is growing quickly, people have to make adjustments in how they live. The government could have problems in providing the following:

- food
- housing
- education
- health care
- a healthy natural environment
- other basic requirements

Governments must know how fast a population is growing so they can plan for the future.

The faster the population grows, the less time it takes for a country's population to double. The average doubling time shows a huge gap between developed and developing countries:

- industrialized, more developed countries—500 years
- less industrialized, less developed countries—37 years

The population of several African countries will double in less than 25 years.

Fact File

If Canada's population continues to grow at current rates, it will be 66 million in 2085. How many years will it take for Canada's population to double? How old will you be when it doubles?

**Population Growth Rates and Doubling Time
for Selected World Regions, 2008**

Region	Growth Rate	Doubling Time
Europe	0.03%	2333 years
North America	1.00%	70 years
Latin America and Caribbean	1.30%	54 years
Africa	2.30%	30 years
East Asia	0.50%	140 years
Southeast Asia	1.40%	50 years
South Central Asia	1.70%	41 years
West Asia	1.90%	37 years
Canada	1.00%	70 years
Lowest growth rate	−0.60% (Ukraine)	Negative
Highest growth rate	3.40% (Liberia)	21 years

Figure 2.10

This table shows the population growth rates and doubling time for selected world regions. Which regions are expected to double their populations in less than 50 years? What challenges might these regions face as their population increases so quickly?

Figure 2.11

Rush hour in Dhaka, Bangladesh, depicts the pressure of a growing, densely populated region. From what you observe in this photograph, what challenges must the Bangladesh government face with such a high population density?

Figure 2.12

About one in every five people in the world lives in China. The Chinese government has tried to get people to limit their family size to only one child. They want to slow down China's population growth. China's natural increase is only 1.1 percent. However, China has a large population of 1.2 billion. The total number of people included in that 1.1 percent increase is huge. China's total population is expected to peak at 1.5 billion in 2035 and decline after that.

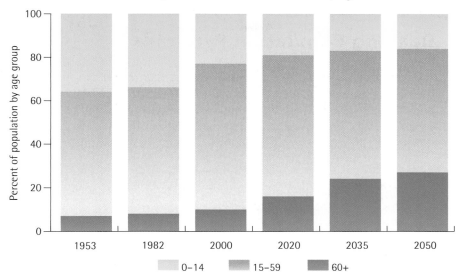

Population Breakdown for China by Age

Figure 2.13

Suppose you want to determine whether China's one-child policy is working to slow population growth. What information would you need to help you?

GEOSKILLS

Reading Population Pyramids

A **population pyramid** is a special type of horizontal bar graph. It shows the number of people in each age group and the balance between males and females in a country's population. When working with population pyramids, it is important to remember TAPP—Title, Axes, Pattern, and Purpose. Follow these steps to read the population pyramids below:

Step One:

Read each *title*. The titles tell you that you will look at two sets of population data: the population of Canada in the year 2007 and Canada's projected population for the year 2050. "Projected" means an educated guess.

Step Two:

Read the *axes*. The x-axis (horizontal) is labelled "Population (in millions)." With this type of graph, the x-axis is divided down the middle, starting with 0, to show males on the left and females on the right. The y-axis (vertical) is labelled with age groups from 0–4 to 90+. The age groups go up in fives, starting with the youngest population category at the bottom to the oldest at the top.

Step Three:

Look for *patterns* in the graphs. Some population pyramids look like true pyramids. In others, the numbers create different patterns. There is a bulge in the middle of the Canada 2007 pyramid. In 2050, the bulge has moved to the top of the pyramid.

Step Four:

Determine the *purpose* of the graphs. What do these graphs tell you about Canada's population? On the Canada 2007 graph, locate the bars that represent Canada's "baby boom" generation, 40–44, 45–49, and 50–54. The people in these age groups are part of a large group of children born after World War II, between 1946 and 1965. What impact does this group have on the shape of the population pyramid predicted for 2050? Suggest why the bar for females over 80 is longer than the bar for males over 80 in the 2050 graph. Look at the bars for 0–4 and 5–9. What is happening to our birth rate?

LITERACY TIP

Reading Graphs

The population pyramid is actually two horizontal bar graphs—one male and the other female—back to back.

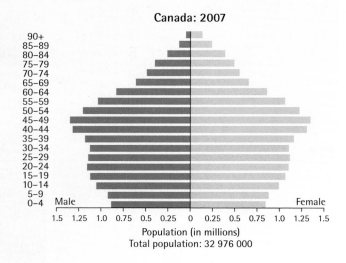

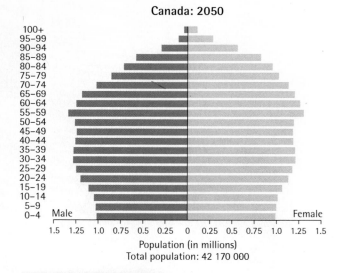

Figure 2.14

The top population pyramid shows the number of males and females in each age division in Canada for 2007. The bottom population pyramid shows the projected number of males and females in each age division in Canada for 2050.

Fact File

Italy is the world's "oldest" country. Half of its population is over the age of 40, and nearly 20 percent is over 65. Uganda is the world's "youngest" country. Half of its population is under the age of 15. How would the population pyramids differ for these countries? Which country would show the population pyramid of a developing country?

The Human Pyramid

Planners also need to study issues related to age and sex distribution of populations. Population pyramids are useful for this purpose. Canada's baby boomers create a bulge in the population pyramid. (Refer to GeoSkills, Step Four, and Figure 2.14 on page 30.) As this group ages, the bulge will move up to the top of the pyramid. Planners will know they must plan for the needs of senior citizens.

Countries with rapidly growing populations have very different age structures from those that grow slowly. The rapidly growing population of a developing country has a wide base at the bottom (a large number of young people) and a narrow top (few older people). The slowly growing population of a developed country has a narrow base and fairly equal numbers of people in all age groups.

Figure 2.15

What differences do you observe between the population patterns shown on the two graphs? Which of the graphs shows a greater increase in total population to 2050? Use the information from the graph to explain why.

1. Refer to Figure 2.15. Which regions will soon have a labour shortage? Where might these regions find workers?

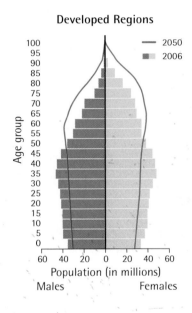
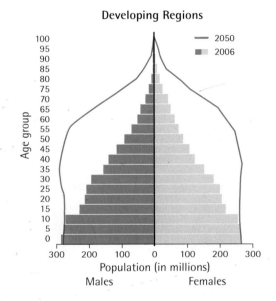

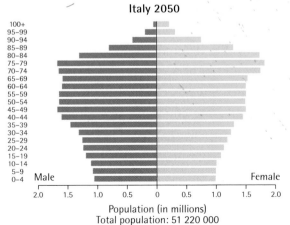

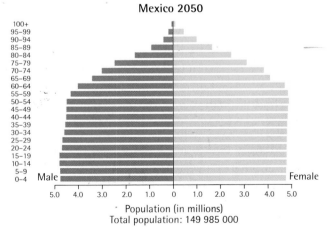

Figure 2.16

Compare these 2050 population pyramids with the bottom pyramid in Figure 2.14 on page 30. Identify whether each of the three countries (Canada, Mexico, and Italy) is expected to have a population that will increase quickly, increase slowly, decrease, or remain stable. How can you tell based on the age distributions?

Impacts of Population Characteristics

Population characteristics interconnect. A large percentage of the population in developing countries is under 15 years of age. Rapid growth in population will occur in these countries. Far more young people will soon be having children and adding to the population than there are old people who are dying. Even if the fertility rate goes down and these young people have fewer children than their parents did, the population will grow. Why? There are so many young people in the population who will have children in the next few years that this will keep the population growing for another 60 or 70 years.

Suppose medical treatment, sanitation, education, and food and water quality improved in the developing world. People could expect to live longer and death rates would continue to decrease. Would these two factors cause a further increase in population? These improvements in quality of life usually cause total population growth to slow. When people have a better quality of life, they tend to have fewer children.

To learn more about Earth's population growth through time,

Go to Nelson Social Studies

Figure 2.17

This family lives in Quetta, in northern Pakistan. With a fertility rate of 3.6, Pakistan, the world's sixth-largest country, has one of the highest population growth rates in the world.

AFTER READING

1. Name three population characteristics that tell us whether a country's population is changing (that is, whether it is growing, stable, or shrinking).

2. a) Identify two regions of the world experiencing a very high increase in population growth. Explain why the populations of these regions are increasing so much.

   b) Identify one region in which the population is declining. Explain why the population in this region is decreasing.

3. a) What is the difference between natural increase and fertility rate?

   b) How can lowering a country's fertility rate influence its rate of natural increase?

   c) How might lowering the fertility rate in a country be achieved?

4. Draw a sketch that shows the shape of a population pyramid for a typical developed country and a typical developing country.

1. In this section, you will read about different population characteristics that are used to measure quality of life. Based on what you know, what population characteristics would you use to measure quality of life in countries around the world?

LITERACY TIP

Making Jot Notes

Creating jot notes will help you remember the information in this section. First, think about the purpose of your reading: How is quality of life measured? Use the subheadings from the text as headings in your jot notes. Then record the information under each subheading in your own words.

Fact File

As a Grade 8 student in Canada today, you will probably do the following:

- complete high school and possibly go on to post-secondary education
- marry by the time you are 30 to 34 years old
- have one or two children
- have an annual income of $50 thousand to $60 thousand
- live at least 80 years
- enjoy good health most of your life

What quality of life can you expect? How might the expectations of a 14-year-old in a developing country differ?

Comparing Quality of Life

The United Nations rated Canada as the best place to live in the world from 1994 through 2000. Most Canadians have the following:

- clean drinking water
- lots of food
- comfortable housing
- full-time work

We often take these things for granted. Most Canadians know that standards of living differ greatly around the world. In some areas, such as the countries with the 10 lowest scores in Figure 2.2, many people cannot meet these basic needs. Other population characteristics help us to measure standard of living or quality of life.

Figure 2.18

Most Canadians are lucky to have all the basic requirements.

Life Expectancy

Life expectancy is the number of years that a baby can be expected to live under current conditions. Life expectancy at birth is a key sign of the health and quality of life of a society. Many people do not have access to the basic needs for a good quality of life (for example, health care, clean water, and abundant food). They can expect to live to around 50 or 60 years of age. Life expectancies are even lower in countries that are unstable or at war.

Population Characteristics for Selected Countries, 2005–2006

Country		Life Expectancy (years)	Per Capita Income (US$)	Doubling Time (years)	Literacy Rate for Ages 15–24 (% of pop.)	Birth Rate (per 1000)	Infant Mortality (per 1000)	Vehicles per 1000 People	CO$_2$ Emissions per Person (metric tonnes)
Bangladesh		64	450	35	50	28	52.5	1.1	0.3
Brazil		72	4 710	52	94	20	23.6	136	1.6
Canada		80	36 650	78	99	10	4.8	580	20.0
China		73	2 000	127	98	13	23.0	10.3	3.2
Ethiopia		53	170	25	31	41	86.9	1.6	0.1
Iceland		82	49 960	87	100	14	2.9	577	7.6
India		65	820	42	76	25	55.0	4.0	1.2
Japan		82	38 630	1 000	99	8	3.2	559	9.8
Mexico		76	7 830	55	96	21	16.7	147	4.2
Norway		79	68 440	118	100	12	3.3	498	19.0

Figure 2.19

Which countries listed here have the highest life expectancy? Suggest why this is so. Look for patterns as you examine the data in the columns. For example, do low scores in one column relate to low scores in another column? Do high scores in one column relate to low scores in another column?

Life Expectancy for Canadians

Life expectancy for Canadians reached a new high in 2007. It was 77 years for men and 83.8 years for women. Of the major nationalities of the world, only the Japanese, Icelanders, Swedes, French, and Swiss live longer. Men are more likely to die earlier than women will. Men show higher rates of heart disease, accidents, cancer, and suicide than women do.

Life expectancy tends to vary throughout Canada in the following ways:

- Southerners live longer than northerners.
- Those in high-density urban areas live the longest.

Life expectancies are lowest in the North, especially areas with large Aboriginal populations. Aboriginal peoples in the North are more likely to die earlier because of accidental injuries, cancer, respiratory diseases, and suicide.

1. Based on the statistics in Figure 2.19, to what year would a baby born in Canada today live? To what year would a person your age live?

LITERACY TIP

Reading a Table

Statistics are often presented in table form. Follow these steps to understand what the table is telling you.

1. Read the title to identify the purpose of the table.

2. Read the headings above each column to find out what the statistics are going to tell you.

3. Read the data under the headings.

4. Reread the data and look for any patterns or differences.

5. Use the information in the table and what you already know about the topic to make concluding statements.

Fact File

Many people have claimed that they lived to an exceptionally old age. However, they often lack birth certificates or other forms of proof. The record goes to Jeanne Calment. In 1997, she died in Arles, France, at the age of 122 years. This is the greatest confirmed age to which any human has lived! Who is the oldest person that you can claim to know?

Scatter Graphs

A **scatter graph** shows the relationship or interconnection between two population characteristics. Sometimes, this is called a correlation.

Figure 2.20 shows the relationship between life expectancy and birth rates, using 20 countries as a sample. Dots on the graph show the location of the two sets of data: birth rate on the *x*-axis and life expectancy on the *y*-axis. A line that comes closest to as many of the dots as possible is drawn on the graph so that it follows the overall trend of the dots. This line is called the "line of best fit." The positions of the dots in relation to the line of best fit tell demographers the following:

- If all the dots are close to this line, then these two characteristics have a *strong correlation*, or relationship.
- If the dots are scattered, with many of them farther away from the line, then there is a *weak correlation* between the two characteristics.

The direction of the line of best fit tells us the following:

- If the line extends from the upper left to the lower right, there is a *negative correlation*. When one of the numbers goes up, the other goes down.
- If the line extends from the lower left to the upper right, there is a *positive correlation*. When one number goes up, the other one goes up as well.

Birth Rate and Life Expectancy by Country

Country		Birth Rate	Life Expectancy
Australia		12	81
Brazil		20	72
Bulgaria		9	73
Canada		10	80
China		13	73
Colombia		21	73
Egypt		26	71
Ethiopia		41	53
France		12	81
India		25	65
Indonesia		20	71
Jamaica		21	73
Japan		8	82
Nepal		31	64
Poland		10	76
Rwanda		45	46
Syria		30	74
Thailand		20	71
Vietnam		21	74
Zambia		42	43

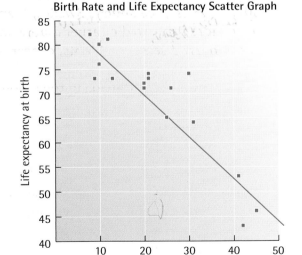

Birth Rate and Life Expectancy Scatter Graph

y-axis: Life expectancy at birth
x-axis: Birth rate per 1000 population

Figure 2.20

This scatter graph shows the relationship between birth rate and life expectancy for 20 countries. There is a strong negative correlation between birth rate and life expectancy. This means that the higher the life expectancy, the lower the birth rate. Countries with high life expectancies will have low birth rates. Do you think that this is a characteristic of a developed or a developing country?

GeoSkills

Creating a Scatter Graph

In order to create a graph, it is important to remember TAPP—Title, Axes, Pattern, and Purpose. Follow these steps to create and read a scatter graph using the data in Figure 2.21.

Infant Mortality Rates and Total Fertility Rates for Selected Countries, 2007

Country		Infant Mortality Rate (deaths/ 1000 live births)	Total Fertility Rate
Australia		5	1.8
Brazil		27	2.3
Bulgaria		9.7	1.4
Canada		5.3	1.5
China		27	1.6
Colombia		19	2.4
Egypt		33	3.1
Ethiopia		77	5.4
France		3.7	2.0
India		58	2.9
Indonesia		34	2.4
Jamaica		24	2.1
Japan		2.8	1.3
Nepal		51	3.1
Poland		6	1.3
Rwanda		86	6.1
Syria		19	3.5
Thailand		20	1.7
Vietnam		18	2.1
Zambia		100	5.5

Figure 2.21

This table shows the infant mortality rates and total fertility rates in 2007 for selected countries.

Step One

Read the title and the data in Figure 2.21 so you begin to understand the two sets of data you will be plotting on your scatter graph.

Step Two

Using graph paper and a ruler, create your two axes, and label them as follows:
- Title the *x*-axis (horizontal) "Infant mortality rate (deaths/1000 live births)." The highest infant mortality rate is 100, so make your *x*-axis go past 100 to 120. Your *x*-axis should start at 0. For every four squares on this axis, go up by 20. Therefore, your *x*-axis will be labelled 0, 20, 40, 60, and so on, with four squares between each labelled number. You will need to have 24 squares across to fit all of the numbers.
- Title the *y*-axis (vertical) "Total fertility rate." Start with 0 at the bottom of this axis. After every three squares, you will go up by 1. Therefore, your *y*-axis will be labelled 1, 2, 3, and so on. You will need 21 squares.

Step Three

Place a title at the top of your graph.

Step Four

Look at the data set, and begin to create your *pattern*. With a scatter graph, you will be placing a dot where the two numbers intersect. Starting with Australia, put a dot on the graph where 5 and 1.8 intersect. To find that point, start at 0 on your *x*-axis and go to where 5 is on the horizontal line. Now, go up your *y*-axis until you reach 1.8. Connect those two lines where they intersect and place a dot.

GeoSkills

Creating a Scatter Graph *(continued)*

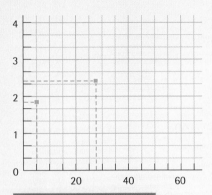

Figure 2.22

The first dot on this diagram shows where 5 and 1.8 intersect for Australia. The second dot shows where 27 and 2.3 intersect for Brazil.

Step Five

Continue by placing all 20 dots on your graph. Brazil will intersect at 27 and 2.3, Bulgaria at 9.7 and 1.4, and so on, until you have placed all 20 dots on your graph.

Step Six

Determine the line of best fit for this scatter graph. This is the straight line that comes closest to as many of the dots as possible. You need this line to determine the following:

- the overall trend
- the purpose for this graph

Step Seven

Look at the pattern you have created on the scatter graph. Are most of the dots close to the line? What type of correlation do the dots have? Remember what the direction of the line of best fit tells you:

- If the line extends from the upper left to the lower right, there is a *negative correlation*. When one of the numbers goes up, the other goes down.
- If the line extends from the lower left to the upper right, there is a *positive correlation*. When one number goes up, the other one goes up as well.

Step Eight

Determine *purpose*. What is the graph telling you about the relationship between these two different data sets? (Think about whether it is a positive or negative relationship.)

Figure 2.23

This scatter graph shows the intersection of the data for Australia, Brazil, and Bulgaria as shown in Figure 2.21. Plot this information on your own scatter graph and continue plotting the data for the remaining countries in Figure 2.21.

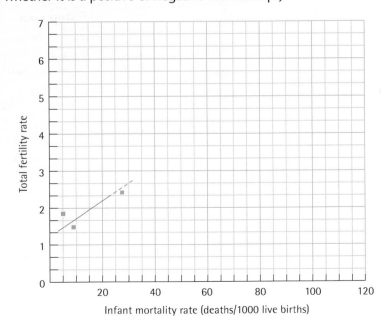

Literacy Rate

Literacy is the ability to read and write. It is important in helping people to learn and to improve their quality of life. The **literacy rate** is a measure of the population over 15 years of age who can read and write. More than 1 billion adults in the world cannot read and write because they do not have access to basic education. In many developing countries, children spend a great deal of their time producing food or working to earn money. This leaves little time or money for school. While world literacy rates are improving, less than 10 percent of children in most developing countries get as far as secondary school. In some countries, girls do not go to school at all. Statistics show that women who have received a basic education and are literate tend to have fewer children. This results in a lower fertility rate.

Fact File

In Brazil, illiterate women have an average of 6.5 children. Women with a secondary school education have an average of 2.5 children—almost 60 percent less! What do these statistics tell you about the connection between education and fertility rate?

Figure 2.24

Many girls and teachers in Afghanistan risk death by attending school. The Taliban threatens teachers frequently, telling them to leave their jobs or face the consequences.

Earning Power

One statistic that is often used to measure quality of life is **per capita income**. This is the average amount of money earned by each person in a country for one year. Per capita income is calculated by dividing all the money earned in a country in a year by the number of people in that country. Because this figure is an average, it can be misleading. For example, Kuwait has a high per capita income because it is rich in oil, which it sells to other countries. This brings in a lot of money for some Kuwaitis, but most earn low wages. There are a few very wealthy people in Kuwait, but many more people who are not wealthy.

A Different Kind of Gross—GDP

Gross domestic product (GDP) is the total value of all goods and services produced in a year in a country. To find GDP per capita, divide the country's total GDP by the number of people living in the country. GDP is sometimes used instead of per capita income. Per capita GDP can be used to show the difference between developed and developing countries. Yet, if everyone lived like people in North America, it would take at least another three Earths to support us.

GDP Comparisons between Kuwait and Canada

	Kuwait	Canada
World GDP rating	59th	15th
GDP per capita	$55 900	$38 600

Figure 2.25

Kuwait is ranked lower than Canada in terms of World GDP rating. Canada has more money-making potential in terms of producing goods and services. Yet Kuwait's GDP per capita is higher than Canada's GDP per capita. What could explain this? Does Kuwait's GDP per capita mean that the quality of life for everyone in Kuwait is higher than in Canada?

Fact File

	Haiti	Canada
Life expectancy (years)	57.6	81.2
Literacy rate (%)	53	99
GDP per capita (US$)	1 300	38 600

What do these statistics tell you about the connection between literacy rate and GDP per capita?

Learning More about Quality of Life and Population Patterns

Population characteristics include the following:

- birth rates
- death rates
- life expectancy
- literacy rates
- earning power

These types of statistics provide information about quality of life and how a population is changing. All communities and regions need this type of information to plan for the future. Demographers study these types of statistics. They look for patterns in order to provide information for future planning.

Figure 2.26

These photos show two views of Haiti. Haiti is one of the world's most impoverished countries. Population characteristics show a very low quality of life. Only 30 percent of the population has drinkable water. Overcrowded slums like the one shown in the photo directly above present serious problems for people who live in such poverty. The gap between the "haves" and "have nots" is widening. What are two things you think a developing country like Haiti can do to help reduce its poverty?

A demographer asks questions that connect different population characteristics. For example, what is the connection between literacy rates and birth rates? What is the connection between birth rates and life expectancy? Could answers to these questions provide information for future planning by governments and organizations? In this case, countries with low birth rates have higher literacy rates and longer life expectancies. Why is that the case? If countries want to lower their birth rates in order to bring about those positive effects, what steps might they take?

Think about other patterns these statistics reveal. How might they influence a country's growth and future? Look back at the tables in this chapter. What types of questions could you ask when researching population characteristics and the patterns they form? Use open-ended questions that will help you look for connections and patterns that could guide planning decisions. Your questions could take you even further. What plans can address connections between population characteristics? What can governments do? What can the people who make up the population do? What can people in other countries do?

LITERACY TIP

Asking Questions

Asking questions gives a focus to your reading and helps you understand what you read. There are two types of questions:

- Closed questions help you find facts in the text. For example: Which country has the highest literacy rate?

- Open-ended questions may require you to look beyond the text for an answer. For example: Why do developed countries have high literacy rates?

1. a) Use the statistics to the left of the scatter graph in Figure 2.20 to identify the countries that appear as the highest and lowest dots on the graph.

   b) In your own words, describe the correlation you see in the graph.

   c) Figure 2.20 shows statistics on birth rate and life expectancy. Construct one open-ended question that would help you research possible connections between these characteristics and other population characteristics described in this chapter. Meet with a group of students to share and compile your questions.

2. Re-examine the statistics for infant mortality rates (children dying before the age of one) and total fertility rates in Figure 2.21. Construct one open-ended question that would guide further research into possible connections between these characteristics. Meet with a group of students to share and compile your questions.

BE A GLOBAL CITIZEN

Students Improving Quality of Life

Have you ever wondered whether people in other countries see Canada as a great place to live? What makes our country so special? What do we have that other countries do not have? The United Nations ranks countries according to the Human Development Index. This index measures a country's achievement in three areas of human development: health, knowledge, and a decent standard of living. For the year 2007–2008, Iceland, Norway, Australia, Canada, and Ireland were the top five countries in the world. The lowest country on the index was Sierra Leone in Africa.

The issues that arise from the Human Development Index measurements affect many students. Students want to know how they can make a difference and improve the quality of life for people around the world. Many organizations offer opportunities for students to become involved—Water for People, UNICEF–Voices of Youth, and Save the Children are just a few.

Some students are so motivated that they find their own way to help the world. The Top 20 Under 20 award is presented to celebrate the leadership and achievement of Canadians under the age of 20. Eleven-year-old Bilaal Rajan received this award in 2008. Bilaal started helping people when he was four years old. He sold clementines, a type of mandarin orange, door to door to raise money for the people affected by the India earthquake. Since

Figure 2.27

Bilaal Rajan has used his experiences to write a book on methods to help every child reach his or her potential. How might you or your school create a fundraising campaign to help the less fortunate? Who would you need to ask for help?

Figure 2.28

Aleema Jamal is working to overcome barriers in education and to create a bridge between students and teachers from Kenya and Canada. How can you create bridges between people?

then he has raised millions of dollars to help less fortunate people around the world. Bilaal created an official fundraising website that shows his motto "Together we can help."

Seventeen-year-old Aleema Jamal also received a Top 20 Under 20 award. Her leadership resulted in Kenya's first public school Computer Resource Centre. She created a partnership with the Kenyan government and the Aga Khan Education Service to complete the project. Thirty-one primary students learned how to use a computer so they could train the remaining 1700 students in their school. Providing the computers and the training for these 31 students will empower a whole school and community.

. . . .

To learn about these amazing young people and other Top 20 Under 20 award recipients,

Go to Nelson Social Studies

We're All in It Together

1. When you hear about developing countries, what images come to mind? Share your thoughts with a partner.

2. As global citizens, should we be helping to improve the quality of life in other countries? Explain why or why not.

Most of us are aware of developing countries. We see images of these countries on television and in the movies. We read about them in books, magazines, and newspapers. Although this information may provide a snapshot view of parts of these countries, the focus is usually on hunger and poverty. This view can be narrow and misleading. What you rarely see in the media are the millions of people in developing countries who succeed in school, work hard at jobs, raise families, and pursue their hopes and dreams, just as many people in developed countries do.

Everyone in the world shares the same planet. We all use the precious resources available. However, there is a difference between developing and developed countries. We all do not use the same amount of resources or purchase the same amount of material goods.

At the beginning of the new millennium, the small number of developed countries had stable or declining populations. On the other hand, the populations of the many developing countries were growing quickly. The presence of more people means that Earth's natural resources are being used up more quickly. We produce more and more garbage and pollution. We must all help to make our world a better, healthier, and sustainable place for everyone.

Comparison of More Developed and Less Developed Regions

Measure	Less developed	More developed
Per capita GDP	$1 900	$33 800
Death rate (per 1000)	10.2	8.4
Birth rate (per 1000)	23.5	10.2
Total fertility rate (%)	3.3	1.5
Infant mortality rate (infant deaths per 1000)	59	7.5
Population under age 15 (%)	31	17
Doctors (per 1000)	0.4	3.7
Life expectancy (years)	64.1	75.6
Secondary school enrolment (male/female; %)	50/45	91/92

■ Less developed regions ■ More developed regions

Figure 2.29

This bar graph shows the gap between developed and developing regions. These figures are averages for more developed regions and less developed regions for 2000–2005. Why are averages sometimes misleading?

Figure 2.30

These students in schools in Chad, Africa, have brighter futures. The future looks more positive in many developing countries because more young people are attending school. What is the connection between education and a country's future?

Population Control

Most of the world's leaders seem to be concerned that Earth's population will continue to grow. In 1994, the leaders met in Cairo, Egypt, at a United Nations conference. They wanted to discuss population problems and issues and to find solutions. Many countries promised to work toward slowing population growth. They also agreed to promote sustainable population. That means that people would not use up Earth's resources at a fast rate and leave enough for future generations. The leaders agreed to spend money on voluntary family planning programs and other projects that would improve quality of life. However, not many of these promises have been kept.

The United Nations continues to work on this issue. They created Millennium Development Goals (MDGs) for the early twenty-first century.

Figure 2.31

Fifty years ago, former Prime Minister Lester B. Pearson said, "No other phenomenon casts a darker shadow over the prospects for international development than the staggering growth of population." Since he made this statement, the world's population has increased by 2 billion people!

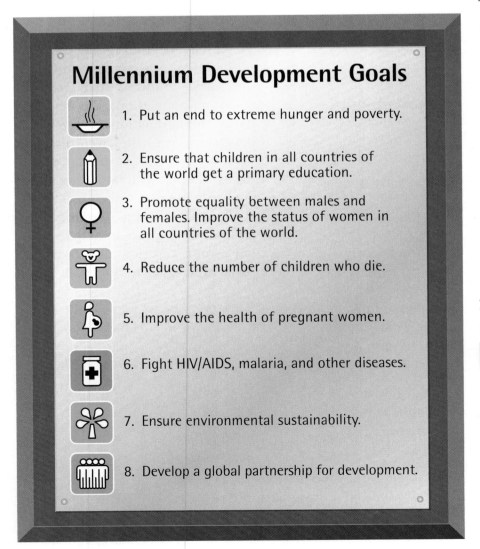

Millennium Development Goals

1. Put an end to extreme hunger and poverty.

2. Ensure that children in all countries of the world get a primary education.

3. Promote equality between males and females. Improve the status of women in all countries of the world.

4. Reduce the number of children who die.

5. Improve the health of pregnant women.

6. Fight HIV/AIDS, malaria, and other diseases.

7. Ensure environmental sustainability.

8. Develop a global partnership for development.

To learn more about meeting the MDGs,

Go to Nelson Social Studies

Figure 2.32

How do you think these goals will help improve the world? Do you think we will achieve these goals? Explain why you think the way you do.

Quality of Life—The Challenge

It is clear that everyone in the world cannot live like we do in the industrialized nations. There are too many people and not enough resources. We learned that the population characteristics of many countries, such as literacy rates and fertility rates, have key impacts on the people living in those countries. What can we do? How can we change our lifestyles to make the world a better place for all? How can we help improve conditions in other countries to make life more liveable and enjoyable for all? All global citizens need to think about and help find answers to these difficult questions.

Figure 2.33

As global citizens, we can all make a difference.

AFTER READING

1. Why is rapid population growth a concern for future generations? List three impacts or consequences that rapid population growth will have.

2. Why is the heading We're All in It Together on page 43 an important message for each of us to remember?

3. If you were given the opportunity to speak to world leaders, what is one idea you would suggest to them about improving the quality of life for millions of people?

CASE STUDY

Youthquake — Prospects for the Future

More than a billion teenagers in the world are just entering their reproductive years. That's about one-sixth of the people on the planet. Demographers sometimes refer to this group as a "youthquake." In the future, the population will grow enormously as this huge group begins to reproduce.

Over 95 percent of these teens live in developing countries. There, governments are already struggling to meet current needs for social services, education, jobs, family planning information, and health care. Millions of teens live on their own or on the streets. Many look after their siblings. These young people must have access to reproductive health information and services that will improve their quality of life. The decisions that young people everywhere make will help to decide the planet's future. Their families and their education will play an important role in helping today's youth make these decisions.

The story of Manoj shows how many teenagers live in developing countries. The challenges he faces contrast sharply with the lives of teenagers in developed countries.

▲▼▲▼▲▼▲▼ ▲

My name is Manoj, and I am 13 years old. I live in a village in Bihar province, India, with my mother, father, brother, and two sisters. My older sister, Riasa, died because of measles a few years ago. My country, India, grows enough food to feed us all, but the food is not evenly shared. Many of my friends—and sometimes my family and I—go to bed hungry at night.

My father works very hard. He works about 60 hours a week for part of the year, in the rice fields, scattering fertilizer by hand.

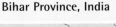

Bihar Province, India

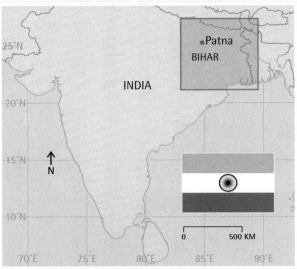

Figure 2.34

Manoj lives in Bihar province in northeastern India.

My mother works even longer—keeping the family clean, fed, and clothed; going to collect animal dung or wood for fuel; or walking to the market.

I am lucky because I am still at school, although this is my last year. The secondary school is too far away from my village, and my parents cannot afford to send me. There would be expenses for uniforms, supplies, and school fees. Dilip, my younger brother, goes to school, too. He and his classmates sit outside in the shade, as the school is too small for everyone. We cannot afford books or writing paper. We write on small pieces of slate. My parents have promised that Lakshmi and Gita, my two younger sisters, may attend school for two or three years. After that, Mother will need them to help at home. Father thinks he may have to send one of them to work in Patna, a large town, to earn money for the family.

CASE STUDY

Youthquake—Prospects for the Future (continued)

Last year, I visited a doctor to get medicine to cure my malaria. That was the first time I had ever been to see a doctor. The

Manoj helps his little brother Dilip with his schoolwork. How do their school supplies differ from yours?

Fifteen percent of the world's people live in India. India's population is growing at only 1 percent annually. Yet this adds 10 million people every year to the population. The large population is putting great pressure on the environment. This causes many problems such as deforestation, water pollution, and over-irrigation of the soil to grow rice (which causes soil to become salty and infertile).

medical clinic is a two-hour walk, and the doctor is not always there, although health care workers usually are.

Our house is made of mud with a tile roof. We have three wooden beds, four blankets, two wooden chairs, a bicycle, a solar-powered radio, metal and ceramic pots, a large basket, bags of rice, and jars of spices. Our statues of our Hindu gods protect our home. We are proud of owning our own well. It is in the courtyard of the house. We do not have electricity yet, but the government says we should get it soon in our village.

I am a good bike rider. When Father lets me, I ride the bike to the wrestling club in the village. Sometimes, when I have time, I make toys for my sisters from discarded items I pick up around the village.

My parents have picked out the girl I will marry when I am 16. I must decide whether to try to find work in the fields, which a landlord from the next town owns, or move to a large city and look for work there. I hope when I have children that they will have a better life than mine. My greatest wish is to be able to get a cow to provide milk for the family, and to go to school in the city to improve my chances of getting a good job.

AFTER READING

1. Identify 10 ways in which Manoj's life differs from yours.

2. Mohandas Ghandi, statesman and peacemaker, made the statement, "Live simply, so that others may simply live." How do Ghandi's words challenge you to alter how you live?

Knowledge and Understanding

1 Because you are reading this, you are literate. Suggest two reasons for the difference in literacy rates between Canada and developing countries, such as Bangladesh, Ethiopia, and India. (Refer to Figure 2.19.)

2 Create a population characteristics connections web.

a) Choose any five population characteristics and write them on a piece of paper. Draw a circle around each population characteristic.

b) Draw lines between the characteristics that are related to one another. Label each line "strong" or "weak," "negative" or "positive," to show the correlation between the population characteristics.

3 Create a quality of life ideas web. Write "Quality of Life" in a small circle at the centre of a half page of paper. What ideas come to mind when you think of quality of life? Record each of your ideas on the paper, scattered around the words "Quality of Life." Draw lines to show the connections between all the ideas.

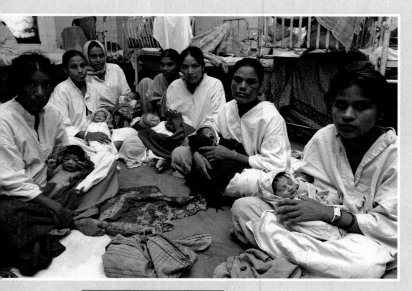

Figure 2.37

Babies are with their mothers in a maternity hospital in Mumbai, India. Why might a higher quality of life lead to a lower birth rate?

Inquiry/Research and Communication Skills

4 Work with a partner to make a sketch, collage, poster, or mobile to show how at least five population characteristics of Canadian life contrast with those in a developing country. Decide on a format with your partner, and identify the population characteristics you will depict. Decide who will portray your chosen population characteristics for Canadian life, and who will portray them for life in a developing country. Add labels and a title to your work.

Map, Globe, and Graphic Skills

5 Select two population characteristics from Figure 2.19. Draw a scatter graph, and plot the locations of the countries in Figure 2.19. Write an analysis of your graph to explain the correlation between the two characteristics and the differences between developed and developing countries.

6 Construct a population pyramid for your own community, or another community of your choice.

a) Research the population data for your community. Statistics Canada provides community profiles with statistics by age and sex for each community.

b) Collect the data for males and females for each age group in your community, and draw your pyramid.

c) Add labels and a title to your graph.

d) Imagine that you are a demographer. Remember the first "P" in TAPP. Describe two main characteristics of your community's population represented in your population pyramid. For example, one of your community's characteristics may be that it has a large group of seniors.

e) Consider how each of these characteristics might affect community planning for the future. Make two recommendations to the local government on how to provide better services to your community in the future.

7 Use the Literacy map on page 318 of the Map Appendix.

a) Look for the location of countries with high, moderate, and low literacy rates. Describe the global pattern of low literacy rates found on this map. In which regions of the world are they concentrated?

b) Choose another map that shows the pattern for another population characteristic such as life expectancy or family size. Describe the patterns you see for low life expectancy or high family size. Is the pattern similar to or different from the one in a)?

c) Suggest one reason that may explain the similarity or difference.

India's Estimated Population by Age and Sex for 2050

Age	Male	Female
0–4	60 000	57 000
5–9	60 500	57 500
10–14	61 000	58 000
15–19	61 700	58 500
20–24	62 500	58 500
25–29	63 000	58 000
30–34	62 500	57 000
35–39	61 600	57 000
40–44	61 500	56 800
45–49	60 000	56 200
50–54	59 000	54 900
55–59	52 500	52 000
60–64	46 000	47 500
65–69	40 000	42 500
70–74	32 500	38 500
75–79	26 000	33 200
80–84	17 000	24 500
85–89	9 000	16 000
90–94	4 800	10 000
95–99	1 100	5 000
100+	200	900

Population (in thousands)
Total population: 1 811 900 000

Figure 2.38

This table shows India's expected population by age and sex in 2050.

8 **a)** Use the statistical data in Figure 2.38 to construct a population pyramid for India. Follow the TAPP process:

- *Title* your graph—India.
- Create your *axes*: the vertical axis will show ages; the horizontal axis will show numbers of females and males. (Refer to GeoSkills on page 30.)
- Form your *pattern* using the data provided in Figure 2.38.
- Determine the *purpose* by answering questions 8b) and c).

b) Describe and explain the reasons for the patterns (shape) shown by the pyramid.

c) Compare your pyramid to the pyramids for Mexico and Italy in Figure 2.16. Which country's pyramid is most similar to India's population pyramid? Briefly describe the similarities.

Application

9 What is the connection between literacy rate and life expectancy?

a) Use the data for the countries listed in Figure 2.19 to draw a scatter graph. (Refer to GeoSkills on pages 36–37.)

b) Write an analysis of your graph to explain the correlation between the two characteristics.

c) What does this correlation tell you about the importance of education in your life?

10 What actions can you take to help ensure improved quality of life in developing countries?

a) Research ways that you can get involved through the work of organizations such as UNICEF—Voices of Youth, Water for People, Free the Children, and Save the Children.

b) Create a list of at least five actions that interest you.

c) From this list, choose one action that you will take. Create a plan to explain how you will take this action.

3

How People Use the Earth

KEY VOCABULARY

diversified
Greenbelt
imprint
land use conflict
megalopolis
official plan
settlement pattern
site
situation
urban sprawl
zoning bylaw

Pollution

Nature — It Is Indispensable!

BEFORE READING

1. Describe to a classmate how the natural environment affects your life. Make sure that you think about your needs for food, water, and shelter.

2. What are three ways that humans have changed the natural environment in order to make our lives more comfortable?

Nature takes care of us. When we need energy to heat our homes and transport us from place to place, our natural environment provides oil, gas, and other fossil fuels. We use trees from the forests for heating, and for lumber, paper, furniture, and other products. We harvest minerals to make metal products, such as steel and copper. Then, we shape these metals into consumer goods. By using the food chains in natural systems, we meet our needs for food and water. Unfortunately, our use of resources often harms the natural systems that support us.

Overfishing

Figure 3.1

Warning signs! Are we demanding too much of nature? Are we using the land wisely, or are we putting future generations at risk? There are many indications that the way people use Earth may be damaging natural systems that we need for life.

Species Extinction

Soil Erosion

Deforestation

1. Look at the photographs in Figure 3.1. For each problem shown, identify the following:

- an important cause of the problem
- one major effect or consequence of the problem
- one reason why people have difficulty solving the problem

LITERACY TIP

Using a Chart

To answer question 1, organize your ideas in a chart like the one shown. Make a separate row for each of the five problems illustrated in Figure 3.1.

Problem	Cause	Effect/Consequence	Reason Why It Is Difficult to Solve
Overfishing			

Use Our Planet Wisely!

Land is an important part of nature's interconnected systems. Of the 50 or so billion hectares of our planet's surface, only a little more than 8 billion hectares is land suitable for human use. There are almost 7 billion people (and counting) living on Earth. If the population were evenly distributed, each of us would have about 1.2 hectares of land to meet *all* our needs. That is not much land per person. We would be wise to look after the habitable land on Earth and use it in sustainable ways. We must also remember that we are not the only ones using this land. Many plant and animal species share this land with us.

A Bird's Eye View

Our use of nature leaves an **imprint** or mark on the physical environment. If you were riding high in the air in a hot air balloon and looking down at the land, you would see these imprints more clearly. This "big picture" view would give you evidence of how humans change the land. You would see many different patterns related to settlement and land use.

Settlement patterns show how people arrange themselves as they live on the land, either in urban or rural regions. Land use is the range of different ways in which people use Earth's surface.

1. Create a graphic organizer, such as a word web or Venn diagram, to show how you connect to, and depend on, nature.

2. Use a graphic organizer such as the one shown below to answer a) and b).

a) The human population will continue to grow, but there is no more land available to support the larger numbers. Suggest two consequences of having more people on the planet.

b) Suggest two actions people might take to reduce the overuse of natural resources.

c) Share the consequences and actions in your organizer with a partner.

| Consequences of having more people on the planet | ← | Human population keeps growing | → | Actions to reduce overuse of natural resources |

Fact File

A hectare is an area of 10 000 square metres. It is equal in area to one and a half Canadian football fields. How many football fields would be required to support 7 billion people?

Figure 3.2

Human imprints often form patterns on the land. Which activities can you see in these photos? Describe the patterns they form.

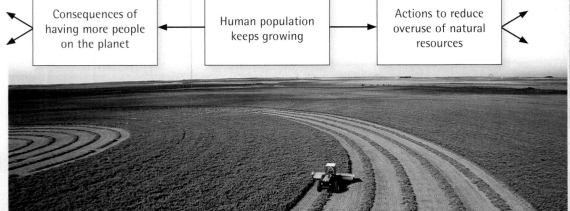

Settlement Patterns in Rural Areas

1. Have you ever looked down on the land from an airplane or tall building? What patterns did you see that people had created? What activities caused the patterns to form?

Most people live in settlements. The way settlements are arranged forms distinct patterns on Earth's surface. Settlements vary in the following ways:

- size
- density, or the number of people that live in an area
- function or purpose
- arrangement on the land

Settlement patterns can tell you something about the economic activities in a region. Patterns in a farming area are different from those in a fishing community or a mining town. In a fishing community, people settle in a wavy line along the coast, close to the water, which is their source of income. Farm families settle on their pieces of land, which is the way they make a living. Each family's buildings are separate from those belonging to their neighbours, who live on their own pieces of land. In mining towns, groups or clusters of buildings are linked by road to the mine, which is the main source of income for the community. Settlements with larger populations usually have many different economic activities. We say that these settlements are economically **diversified**.

Geographers study settlement patterns. They want to understand the following:

- how people are distributed in different parts of the world
- how settlements are connected to their natural settings
- the relationships that form as people, goods, and ideas move from one settlement to another

Using this information, geographers can help solve problems related to how people use the land.

Seeing Settlement Patterns

Geographers use the following tools to describe and analyze settlement patterns:

- maps
- aerial photographs
- satellite images

They look at how the land is divided among its owners. They also examine how buildings and different-sized settlements are arranged on the land.

Geographers often describe patterns according to their shape. There are three main types of settlement patterns in rural areas: linear, scattered, and clustered.

Rural Settlement Patterns

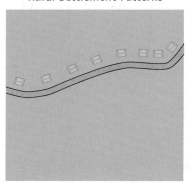

a) Linear
Linear patterns are sometimes called *strings*. This pattern consists of groups of houses or villages that form a line. The line can be straight (usually along a road or railway), or wavy (as found along the edge of a river or lake, or in a long, narrow valley).

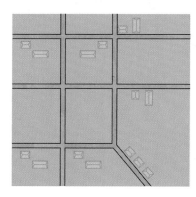

b) Scattered
Scattered patterns may be called *dispersed*. This is the main pattern found in agricultural regions of North America. Each house sits alone on a piece of land quite separate from its neighbours.

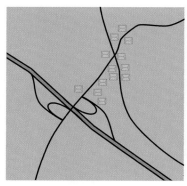

c) Clustered
Examples of this pattern could be a group of houses close together. These clusters are found in tiny hamlets or villages in agricultural areas, or a concentration of gas stations, motels, and restaurants at a highway intersection.

DURING READING

1. Which patterns of settlement have you observed in rural regions? How did the patterns suit the economic activities in those rural regions?

. . . .

To learn more about the
settlement of the Prairies,

**Go to Nelson
Social Studies**

Figure 3.4

Regina, Saskatchewan was
originally known as Pile of Bones,
the English translation of the First
Nation place name. First Nations
of the Plains people hunted bison
for food and clothing. The Cree
camped on the banks of a creek
where they laid bison bones in a
large pile. Is there any evidence
of the creek in the photo?

Change Is Constant

Looking at the past helps us to understand the geography of our
country today. The settlement patterns of European immigrants left
an imprint on the land. This imprint affected how the development
of human activities continued. As newcomers settled in the central
and western regions of Canada, each stage of settlement affected the
next stage. Figure 3.5 on page 56 shows three stages of development.
At one time, there were no towns and villages. Newcomers moved
west seeking new land and a new life. As the newcomers fenced
off the prairie, the First Nations who had occupied these lands for
thousands of years could no longer continue their traditional way
of life. The building of the railways linked Canadians from coast
to coast. New communities formed in a linear pattern along the
railways. Newcomers worked to make the land fit their needs. In the
process, natural ecosystems were changed or destroyed.

 1. a) Use Figure 3.5 on page 56
to identify three ways that the
settlement of immigrants on the
Canadian Prairies changed the
natural environment.

b) Consider the time period from the
beginning to the end of the 1900s. Note
three changes in each of the following human
patterns that occurred on the Prairies in the
twentieth century:

- transportation
- use of the land
- settlements

2. Draw a fourth part of the diagram in
Figure 3.5 to show how the Prairies might
look in the late 2000s. Keep in mind that
conditions in the past have an effect on
conditions in the future.

Figure 3.5

The settlement patterns and land uses on the Prairies changed
as newcomers moved in and built villages and towns.

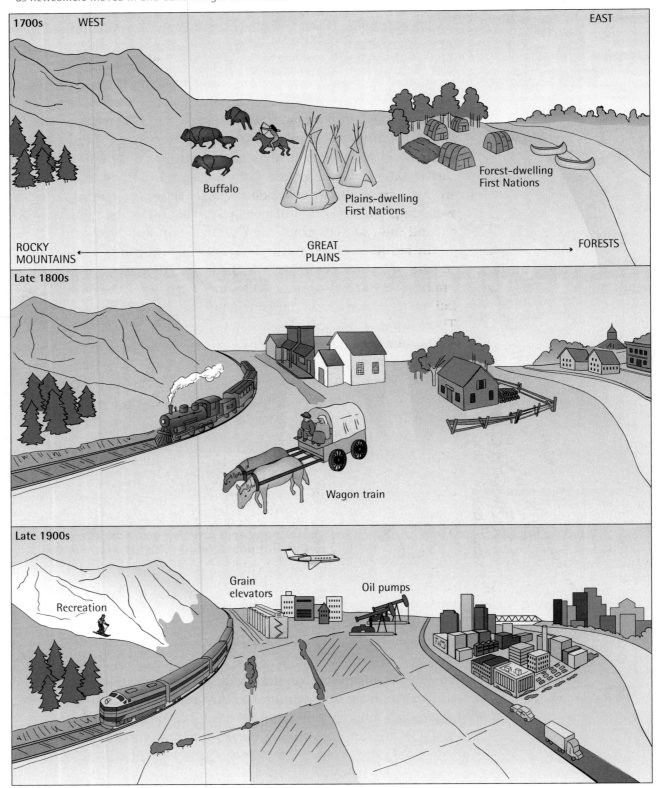

Changing Patterns

In the 1900s, the following changes transformed settlement patterns on the Prairies:

- population growth
- development of the rich lands and natural resources of the region
- advances in technology

Figure 3.6

Abandoned grain elevators, such as this one in Saskatchewan, are a sign of change on the Prairies. How does their destruction change the economy of the local area?

In the early 1900s, farmers still used ploughs to break the land. The population grew quickly, and newcomers settled on more land. Farmers began to use large machines to cultivate more land and produce more grain. The grain the farmers produced was stored in large wooden grain elevators beside the railway tracks. These structures were important centres of economic activity. Communities grew around the grain elevators.

In recent decades, grain elevators have been disappearing from the Prairie landscape. In 1981, there were 3117 grain elevators on the Prairies. By 2002, there were 412 left, and their numbers continue to fall. Farmers now haul their grain to larger, concrete storage facilities. These storage places are often located outside big urban centres. When a community's grain elevator closes down, basic services—such as the general store, the farm equipment dealer, the post office, and the bank—often close, too. The population of many towns has decreased, and many buildings stand vacant in those that still exist. Some towns have even disappeared altogether.

Because of changing technology in agriculture, farms are much larger than they were in the past. Farmers use bigger, more efficient machinery to farm more land. As a result, the number of farms has decreased, but the size of farms has increased overall. As more people move to urban centres and individual farmers farm more land, fewer people live in rural regions. The scattered settlement pattern of agricultural regions that you saw in Figure 3.3 is becoming even more scattered. Farm buildings with farm families living in them are farther apart. As a result of these human activities, the settlement patterns of rural regions are changing.

AFTER READING

1. Make a sketch to show the settlement pattern in your neighbourhood.

2. Look back at settlement patterns and land uses in Figure 3.5 on page 56. Based on what you know, how have human imprints on the land changed in your community or region

over the past 100 years? Consider changes in transportation methods, housing, and services such as stores.

3. In one sentence, identify how the number and variety of economic activities relate to the size of an area's population. Begin your sentence with, "The larger the population of an area…."

Urban Land Use

1. Create a t-chart with the headings Rural and Urban. Under each heading, write five words or phrases to describe what you think life is like in each setting. Then, write a one-sentence conclusion to sum up your chart.

Cities are the largest and most densely populated forms of settlement. In most parts of the world, cities are growing quickly. The people in growing cities use up increasing amounts of Earth's resources. They also deposit many different kinds of wastes. As cities grow into the surrounding countryside, they change the ecosystems there forever. Land is bulldozed and covered with buildings and pavement. The natural environment is buried under human-made materials. Cities close to one other can form one continuous urban area. In Japan, the three cities of Tokyo, Kawasaki, and Yokohama grew into one another. They formed one big **megalopolis**, or super city.

LITERACY TIP

Using T-Charts

Use a t-chart to compare two things. A t-chart has two columns, one for each topic you are comparing. Use point-form notes to complete a t-chart. Then, look for similarities and differences to sum up your comparison.

Rural	Urban
•	•
•	•
•	•

Figure 3.7

Tokyo Megalopolis is the largest urban area in the world.

Community Site and Situation Characteristics

Figure 3.8

Notice the site characteristics in the top diagram. This is a city built on a flat plain between the confluence of two tributaries, where the river empties into a larger body of water. A study of the situation reveals three bridges, industries built near a harbour, and good farmland on the outskirts of the city. What are the site and situation characteristics of the second community?

Site and Situation

People use technology to change the natural environment. For example, they build bridges and dams on rivers. The physical features of the environment affect people, places, and patterns. Geographers use the terms *site* and *situation* to describe the location of a town or city.

Site refers to the *physical features* in the area where the city is located. This could be a flat plain on the edge of a lake. It could be a narrow valley in the mountains. Settlements most often grow to become large cities when they are located in areas such as the following:

- wide river valleys
- places where two rivers join
- on a lake or ocean coast with a good harbour

Cities also grow in areas that have the following physical features:

- fertile soil
- moderate climate
- abundant natural resources

Situation refers to the general position of a city in relation to *human features*. Important aspects of a city's situation include the following:

- Transportation connections: Places that people can reach easily allow goods and people to move efficiently. This encourages growth.
- Intercommunity connections: Cities tend to grow when they interact with neighbouring cities.
- Resource connections: Urban communities that have access to natural resources also tend to grow. Cities can use resources such as good farmland, minerals, or forests to grow and prosper.

1. Describe the site and situation of your community, or an urban area in your part of the province.

Urban Places in Canada

Most Canadians now live in urban areas. The growth of towns and cities will probably continue over the next century. When urban areas spread out and grow into the surrounding rural areas, the result is **urban sprawl**. The invention of the automobile made urban sprawl possible. This technological change allowed people to travel faster and go longer distances.

People need extensive transportation networks to move from place to place. Many people commute to the city from the suburbs and surrounding towns. They spend as much as three hours each day driving back and forth to work. Commuters spend up to 15 hours a week, or two whole workdays, just going to and from work.

Fact File

Most people in Canada prefer cars to other forms of transportation. The average Canadian travels about 18 000 kilometres a year, over 88 percent of the time in a personal vehicle. (18 000 km is the same as driving from Toronto, Ontario to Buenos Aires, Argentina, and back again!) There are more than 18 million vehicles on Canadian roads today. As urban sprawl continues, how can the number of personal vehicles on the road be reduced? Figure 3.9 shows one way. Can you think of other ways?

Figure 3.9

High-occupancy vehicle lanes on highways encourage commuters to car pool.

GO GEO-GREEN

Ontario's Greenbelt

Joni Mitchell is a Canadian singer who wrote "Big Yellow Taxi." One of the lines of the song is "They paved paradise and put up a parking lot." These words relate to urban sprawl in southern Ontario. The cities and towns continue to grow and merge into one big megalopolis. The amount of open space, recreational land, and farmland gets ever smaller. Buildings are replacing the once-fertile soil. Animal and plant species are losing their habitats. Human use is straining the local watershed. People and politicians began to see this urban sprawl as a real threat to the environment. In 2005, a law was passed to create the **Greenbelt**.

Ontario's Greenbelt is more than 728 000 hectares of permanently protected green space. Farming, recreation, forests, wetlands, and watersheds are the only uses permitted for this land. Communities located in this protected area are not allowed to expand. The Greenbelt surrounds the area known as the Golden Horseshoe, which stretches around the western shore of Lake Ontario. It contains the Niagara Escarpment, the Oak Ridges Moraine, and

The Greenbelt in Ontario

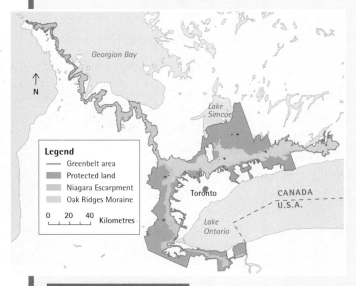

Figure 3.10

The Greenbelt surrounds many of the largest urban areas in southern Ontario. It stops urban growth from gobbling up the farmland of the region.

Figure 3.11

Ontario farms in the Greenbelt provide consumers with locally grown produce.

Rouge Park. These are all important environmentally sensitive lands. The purpose of the Greenbelt is to protect these lands from urban sprawl.

One of the goals of establishing the Greenbelt is to protect food resources. Many small towns in the region have farmers' markets. Consumers buy locally grown produce at these markets. The Greenbelt also offers places to go camping or hiking. There are many lakes and rivers for canoeing or kayaking. The Friends of the Greenbelt Foundation is a nonprofit organization that promotes the Greenbelt. They want everyone to know how important the Greenbelt is for the people of Ontario.

To help stop the "paving of paradise," your class could do one of the following:
- Plan a trip to one of the conservation areas, farms, or local farmers' markets in the Greenbelt. Find out more about their ecological, environmental, and economic importance.
- Host a fundraising lunch of locally made foods. Donate the money to a conservation organization.
- Encourage the cafeteria to support local farmers and buy produce from local farmers' markets.

By taking any of these small steps, you will be helping to protect green spaces today and for the future.

How People Use the Land

Many different activities go on in a city. Each one requires some use of land. Geographers refer to the different ways that people use land as "land use." Types of urban land use include the following:

- residential
- commercial
- industrial
- institutional
- transportation
- recreational
- open-space

City Land Uses

Open-space and recreational 7%

Industrial 6%

Commercial 5%

Residential 40%

Transportation 32%

Institutional and public buildings 10%

Figure 3.13

This circle graph shows land uses in a typical city.

Figure 3.12

These photographs show the types of land use found in most cities.

Residential land use is space occupied by homes. What types of homes do you see in this picture?

Places that sell goods and services to customers are examples of *commercial land use.* Name two examples of commercial land use in your community. Why are fast food restaurants considered commercial land use?

Industrial land use includes large factories and smaller industrial parks. What characteristics of large-scale industry can you see in this photo?

Schools, hospitals, places of worship, and government offices are included in *institutional land use*. What is one characteristic that distinguishes institutional land use from other land uses?

Recreational land use includes playing fields, playgrounds, golf courses, and arenas. What are some recreational land uses close to your home?

Transportation land use includes parking lots, train and bus stations, airports, and roadways. About what percentage of the land in your community is used for transportation land use?

Cemeteries and large parks are considered *open-space land use*. How is recreational land use different from open-space land use?

1. Explain how improved transportation technologies can lead to urban sprawl.

2. a) Identify an example of each of the types of urban land use described in Figure 3.13 in your local area.

   b) What do you think the most important land uses are in your local area? Why do you think your choices are the most important land uses in your local area?

Who makes decisions about how land will be used? Planners, developers, governments, and individuals do. Poor decisions can result in badly planned cities that can take up agricultural land, destroy natural habitats, and add to pollution. Expanding suburbs create transportation problems. Many people who live in the suburbs need to commute to work. Public transit often does not get them where they need to go. People choose to use their cars instead, adding to the greenhouse gases in the atmosphere.

GeoSkills

Viewing a Photograph: Looking for Land Uses

The pictures in this textbook help you read and understand the written text. Viewing photographs takes specific skills, just like reading maps or graphs. When you view a photograph, you make conclusions based on inferences, or educated guesses.

The chart in Figure 3.14 shows the I See, I Know, So method for viewing photographs. Examine land uses in the mountain valley shown in Figure 3.15. Use the I See, I Know, So method to develop your viewing skills.

I See... (what is in the picture)	I Know... (information based on what I already know or have experienced)	So... (I can make conclusions about where the photograph was taken and why it is included)
• ... the photo shows mountains in summer.	• ... they are tall because there is no vegetation on the summit of some of them. I know it is summer because there is no snow.	• ... the photograph was probably taken in the Rockies or in another tall mountain range. The photographer is on a mountain looking into a valley.
• ... in the middle ground, there is a curvy blue/white line of varying widths. In the left-middle ground, there is a fairly straight, thick, beige line.	• ... the curvy line is a river, in the middle of a valley. The straight line is human-made; it is a road in the distance.	• ... the valley has both natural and human-made transportation corridors.
• ... beside the river, there are some bright green, long curved shapes equally spaced apart, in the middle of dark green.	• ... that this is a golf course built into the forest.	• ... this is an area used for recreation.
• ... in the middle foreground is a very large building.	• ... that this is a hotel.	• ... this area caters to tourists.
• ... in the left-middle ground, there are a lot of buildings and straight lines. There are larger buildings on the small mountain, in the centre of the photograph.	• ... that this is a town site. You can see the grid patterns the roads make and the tops of a large number of buildings. You can also see that the town forms a cluster pattern.	• ... we can see that the town has many types of land uses. We can also see their distribution. The land uses shown include the following: – transportation (straight roads form a linear pattern) – recreational (the golf course and other park spaces form a linear pattern along the road) – institutional (larger buildings on small mountain in centre of photograph) – commercial (hotel in the middle foreground; large straight road in the left-middle ground and large buildings on either side) – open-space (parkland along the river)

Figure 3.14

Recording information about a photograph is a good way to determine what it shows.

GeoSkills

Viewing a Photograph: Looking for Land Uses *(continued)*

Figure 3.15

This is a scene of the Bow River Valley near Banff, Alberta.

Look at the photograph of Cairo in Figure 3.16. Draw an I See, I Know, So chart in your notebook. Focus on identifying land use when viewing this photo. Fill out the chart, and then share your ideas with a partner or a small group. Discuss any differences in the conclusions you drew. (Use this chart method for other visuals, as well.)

Figure 3.16

This is a view of Cairo, the capital city of Egypt.

Land Use Conflicts

Problems occur when people hold different views about land use decisions. Poor planning can result in **land use conflicts**. Examples include the following:

- a school built near a busy road
- a busy doughnut shop built where the extra traffic will cause congestion on local streets
- a new subdivision built close to a landfill site where the smell, noise, and constant garbage-truck traffic cause discomfort to residents

To try to avoid land use conflicts, town planners gather input from politicians and citizens. They use this information to create an **official plan** to reflect how the community wishes to grow. Town planners produce land use maps that illustrate the official plan. These maps show how property can be used (residential, commercial, industrial, and so on) and where different land uses will be allowed in the future. The municipal or regional government passes laws, called **zoning bylaws**, to make sure that everyone follows the official plan. A zoning bylaw controls what people can build. It also controls how big buildings can be on different properties. Different areas, or zones, are assigned different uses. Depending on the use, different types and sizes of buildings are allowed. There was a huge propane explosion and fire at a propane plant in northwest Toronto in August 2008. After that explosion, Toronto Mayor David Miller made an announcement that the city government would review zoning bylaws to check the safety of present land uses. They would decide if industrial areas should be farther from residential areas.

Figure 3.17

What are the location requirements for an elementary school?

Town planners are using some new ideas to make cities better places to live and less harmful to the environment. In the suburbs of big cities, large areas are used mainly for residential land use. People use their cars to go to work, to the library, or to the grocery store. This adds to air pollution. Now, town planners often design a mix of commercial and light industrial land in areas beside suburbs. These land uses provide jobs and services for people living nearby. They are also better for the environment.

Some architects are designing new suburban developments to include a mix of land uses.

Figure 3.18

Bicycle lanes make people feel safer riding on urban streets.

Fact File

Jane Jacobs was a writer and activist who campaigned for new approaches to urban planning. Jacobs compared cities to natural ecosystems — each element of a city works together like the parts of an ecosystem. What happens to one part of the system affects all of the other parts. Jacobs pushed for mixed-use urban development. Instead of areas designated for one type of land use, she said that cities need to integrate different building types and uses. Mixing city uses and users so that people of different ages are using areas at different times of the day is important to the city's development. "Intricate minglings of different uses in cities are not a form of chaos. On the contrary, they represent a complex and highly developed form of order."

AFTER READING

1. What land use changes might result if many people within a community chose to use bicycles instead of cars?

2. What are two choices that you and your family could make to lessen the impact of your activities on the land? How might these choices affect types of land use?

3. Look back to the examples of land use conflicts identified on page 66. Choose one of the examples and describe how three people might have very different views about the land use decision. For example, in the case of the school built near a busy street, you might describe the views of parents of schoolchildren, local residents trying to drive to work, and school officials.

CASE STUDY

Site and Situation of Montréal, Québec

This satellite image of Montréal shows some aspects of this city's site and situation.

Figure 3.19

Site can influence a city's land uses, and its problems. For example, the Lachine Rapids is a fast-flowing, dangerous section in the St. Lawrence River, just near where the river narrows in the image. You can see the white water created by the rapids. These rapids were a barrier to shipping. Look at the image and identify the St. Lawrence Seaway Canal, just to the south of the rapids and the Lachine Canal, which cuts across the island of Montréal.

Fact File

Samuel de Champlain set the tone for French relations with the Haudenosaunee Nation in the Montréal area in 1607, when he shot at a peace delegation. Conflict between the two peoples lasted 92 years.

CASE STUDY

Site and Situation of Montréal, Québec *(continued)*

Figure 3.20

This chart highlights the situation factors that influenced the settlement of Montréal. Which factor do you think influenced the location of the city most?

Physical Advantages
- The site had good agricultural land to feed the population.
- The water supply was plentiful.
- The rivers provided easy transportation routes.

History
- The first farms were long and narrow, built in a linear pattern along the river.
- Later farms had no river access.

Government Policy
- In the 1700s, France gave land to farmers based on long, narrow lots.
- The governments later added roads, power lines, and other features.

Technology
- Railroads and cars changed settlement patterns.
- The city is now more spread out.
- Houses built along roads and rail lines form a linear pattern.

The Great Lakes–St. Lawrence Lowlands provide flat land and fertile soils. Farmers cleared much of the land for agriculture. This land can also support a dense population. Montréal is on an island. Parts of this island are the most densely populated areas in Canada.

Montréal's situation on the St. Lawrence River illustrates how the city relates to its surroundings. Its location is 1600 kilometres from the Atlantic Ocean. It is far enough inland so no tides rise and fall. It also provides a gateway to the middle of North America. Before Montréal could take full advantage of this feature, canals and the St. Lawrence Seaway had to be built. Then, large ocean-going ships could enter the Great Lakes and continue on to other port cities such as Toronto, Thunder Bay, and Chicago.

Figure 3.21

These site factors influenced the settlement of Montréal.

Features of the Site of Montréal
- islands in the St. Lawrence River, which helped to shape the city
- river for fresh water and transportation
- rapids that were a barrier to water transportation
- flat, fertile agricultural land once the forests were cut down
- a series of rock terraces or step-like features on the main island (Île de Montréal), which provided a good vantage point for defence
- a large hill (Mount Royal), which is the remnant of an ancient volcano and now provides some green open space, as well as a scenic location for expensive housing developments
- sedimentary (limestone) rock layers, which provided building stones for many of the early buildings

Figure 3.22

The port of Montréal is a busy transportation hub where seaways, railways, and roadways connect.

1. Which feature of Montréal's site do you think has been the most important for determining the shape of the city?

2. Identify where the following types of settlement patterns occur on the satellite image in Figure 3.19: linear, dispersed, clustered.

3. Which type of land use would most likely be located around the port of Montréal? Explain your reasoning.

Knowledge and Understanding

1 How would you explain linear, scattered, and clustered patterns of human settlement to a young child? Record the words you would use to explain each pattern of human settlement and how you would demonstrate each pattern.

2 Complete a Venn diagram to compare a rural village and a neighbourhood in a city. Compare types of housing, population density, land uses, economic activities, and services, such as banks. Note common characteristics where the circles overlap in the centre area of your Venn diagram. Identify characteristics that are distinct in the outer areas of the circles.

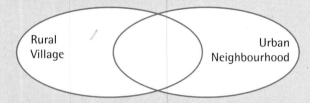

Rural Village | Urban Neighbourhood

3 **a)** Classify each of the land uses listed in Figure 3.23 under the appropriate urban land use category: residential, commercial, industrial, institutional, transportation, recreational, and open-space.

b) Add one more example to each of the categories. Then, explain why your example belongs in the selected category.

Skateboard park	Sports complex
Movie theatre complex	Airport
Scrap metal yard	Woodlot
Nuclear generating station	Shopping mall
Sewage treatment plant	Industrial park
Greenhouse	Apartment building
Senior citizens' home	University
Museum	Amusement park
Conservation area	Cement block plant
Golf course	Prison
Cemetery	Railway yard
Hospital	Convenience store

Figure 3.23

People use land in many different ways in urban centres.

4 Which of the land uses in Figure 3.23 would you want close to your home? Which ones would you not want to live near? Explain your reasons for at least two of your choices to a classmate.

Inquiry/Research and Communication Skills

5 Use ideas from this chapter to write an opinion paragraph about one of the following issues: "In order to look after the habitable land we have on Earth, we need to limit the extent to which urban regions can expand." OR "In order to look after the habitable land we have on Earth, we need to pass laws to protect more green space around urban regions." When you write an opinion paragraph, remember the 4 Cs: Catch, Commit, Convince, and Close.

- *Catch* the reader's attention in the first sentence by using an interesting fact, quotation, or question.

- *Commit* to a position on the topic in the second sentence by stating your opinion clearly.

- *Convince* the reader by proving your opinion with clear, concise evidence. You may need several sentences to do this. It is a good idea to "see" the points you will be making to prove the opinion you stated in the Commit step. Each point or reason you give should have an explanation supported with proof. Connect your points with transition words.

- *Close* your paragraph by writing a one- or two-sentence conclusion where you summarize the key point in your paragraph.

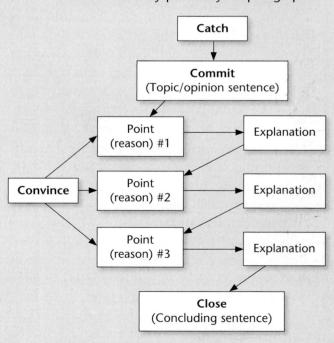

6 a) Ask your teacher for information from the planning department of your municipal or regional government. Use this primary source of information to find answers to the following questions:

- What steps does the planning department take to manage land uses in the local area?
- What actions is the planning department taking to reduce urban sprawl and its impacts?
- What process is in place to deal with land use conflicts that arise in your community?

b) Choose one of the following methods to share what you have learned:

- Create a chart or informative poster showing the answers to the research questions.
- Write a news report about planning in your community. Then, create an audio or video recording of your news report.
- Take digital images of locations in your community. Use them to develop a PowerPoint slide show or web page.

7 Has Ontario's Greenbelt helped to protect the rural areas and farmlands of southern Ontario?

a) Use the Internet and other resources to find two articles or reports on this plan. Use a three-column chart such as the following to record the points of view for each article.

Article Title, Author, Source (e.g.,website address, name of periodical), Publication Date	Point of View	Words That Express the Point of View

b) To learn about further points of view about the Greenbelt, share your findings with two other students.

c) Based on your research, what can you conclude about whether Ontario's Greenbelt has helped to protect the rural areas and farmlands of southern Ontario? Write your response using one of the following formats:

- an opinion paragraph (refer to question 5)
- a blog
- a letter to the editor

Map, Globe, and Graphic Skills

8 a) Sketch a map to show the main features of the site and situation of your local area. Use Figure 3.8 on page 59 as a guide to drawing sketch maps. Include information about physical features (shape of the land, drainage, soil and vegetation characteristics), and human features (transportation facilities, available natural resources, locations of other communities). Label the important features. Do not forget to follow the TLC method—Title, Legend, and Compass.

b) What are the three most important factors that have influenced the shape of your community?

9 a) Use the Internet or classroom resources to find one photograph showing an urban environment that you consider pleasant (one in which you would want to spend time), and another photograph showing conditions you consider unpleasant.

b) Use the I See, I Know, So method of viewing photographs described in GeoSkills on pages 64 and 65 to analyze the images.

c) Use a t-chart to record characteristics of pleasant and unpleasant urban areas. Examine the points in each column and write a paragraph describing each type of environment.

Application

10 How has technological change influenced settlement patterns over the past century? Choose one aspect of technological change, such as moving goods, disposing of wastes, or supplying energy. Make up three questions you could use to explore the topic. Begin each of your questions with one of the following: How …? How did …? What happened when …? What might …? Why …? Where …? (Refer to Geoskills on page 246 in Chapter 11.)

11 Ask your teacher for a land use map of your community from your municipal government. Does your community fit the types and percentages of land use in a typical Canadian city, as shown in Figure 3.13 on page 62? Explain.

4

People at Work

IN THIS CHAPTER

- identify and give examples of the three major types of industries—primary, secondary, and tertiary—and describe how these industries have developed in Canada
- use maps to identify economic patterns
- construct and study population pyramids in order to predict future trends in population characteristics
- research job trends and predict the skills that will be needed to meet the challenges of Canada's changing demographics

KEY VOCABULARY

cohort
demographic trend
downsize
globalization
hydroponics
knowledge worker
outsource
primary industry
secondary industry
tertiary industry

What about the Future?

BEFORE READING

1. What kind of work do you think you will do in the future?

2. Read the following quotation by futurist Frank Feather: "There are those that wait for the future to happen; those that go out and make the future happen for them; and those who are simply left to wonder what happened!" Think about how you will deal with what happens in the future. Will you be a "waiter," a "maker," or a "wonderer"?

Imagine riding on a train speeding through time. You race from year to year into the future, not sure where the train will take you. You see amazing new sights outside the windows. It is hard to predict what the future holds, but we do know that much will change, even more quickly than now. These changes will affect you, and you will need to adapt to them.

Sometime in the next five to ten years, you will probably enter the work market. Whether you do this directly from high school or after a post-secondary education, you will enter a very different workplace from the one your parents experienced. It is difficult to predict what types of jobs people will be doing in the rest of this century. Constant change means that many future jobs have not even been invented yet.

Figure 4.1

Banking has changed a lot all over the world in the past decade. People use bank machines and debit cards. If they have a computer, they can do their banking online. Banking jobs are also changing. People who work in banks need new skills to provide different kinds of personal banking services. One new service is providing telephone support for Internet banking customers with questions or problems. Ask your grandparents or other older people in your community how banking was different many years ago.

1. How might the work of the future differ from the kinds of work you see people doing today? What evidence can you use to support your predictions? Record your ideas and discuss them with a partner.

2. How do you think the nature of work has changed since you were born? Record your ideas and discuss them with a partner.

3. Now, examine Figures 4.2 and 4.3 to see how your ideas correspond with the information shown there.

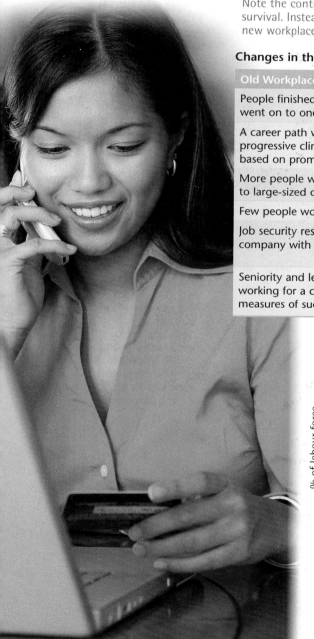

Figure 4.2

The work market has changed as the Industrial Age has changed to the Information Age. Note the contrasts in this table. In the Information Age, people focus less on material survival. Instead, they focus on the quality of life. Look at the characteristics of the new workplace. How can they improve quality of life?

Changes in the Workplace from the Industrial Age to the Information Age

Old Workplace (Industrial Age)	New Workplace (Information Age)
People finished their education and went on to one main career.	People will have several careers in their lifetime and will retrain every few years.
A career path was a steady, progressive climb in a company, based on promotions.	A career path will move in and out of different jobs, with more opportunities to work with a variety of people.
More people worked for medium- to large-sized companies.	More people work for small- to medium-sized companies or are self-employed.
Few people worked at home.	More people are working from home offices.
Job security rested in one career or company with one main job skill.	Performance contracts (workers hired on a project-by-project basis) require a broad range of skills.
Seniority and length of time working for a company were measures of success.	Performance and ability to adapt quickly are measures of success.

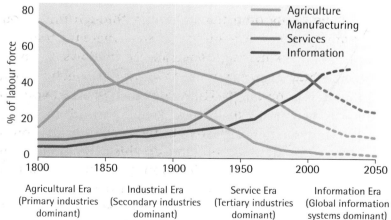

Percentage of Labour Force in Major Industries, 1800–2050

Legend: Agriculture, Manufacturing, Services, Information

y-axis: % of labour force (0, 20, 40, 60, 80)
x-axis: 1800, 1850, 1900, 1950, 2000, 2050

Agricultural Era (Primary industries dominant) — Industrial Era (Secondary industries dominant) — Service Era (Tertiary industries dominant) — Information Era (Global information systems dominant)

Figure 4.3

The changing nature of work is shown by the trend lines for work in agriculture, manufacturing, services, and information. Can you suggest a reason for the predicted decline in service jobs?

Trends

A trend is when things change in a general direction. Trends that cause industries to grow or decline include the following:

- technology trends, such as how well industries adapt to the use of technology in the Information Age
- social trends, such as the demand by customers for different products and services
- economic trends, such as a decrease in manufacturing jobs
- **demographic trends**, such as an aging population

Figure 4.4 shows that changes in the work market mean a trend toward more and more people working in part-time jobs. Geographers study how these trends affect employment and the workplace. They use such trends to help them predict what the future will be like.

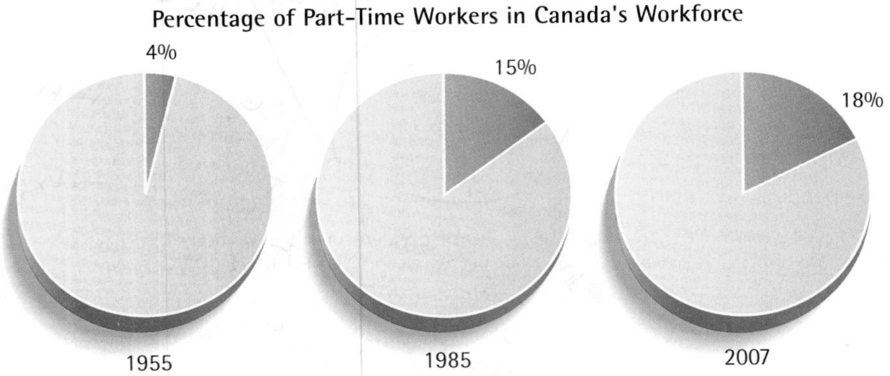

Percentage of Part-Time Workers in Canada's Workforce

4%   15%   18%

1955   1985   2007

Figure 4.4

These pie graphs show part-time workers as a percentage of Canada's workforce. The average income for part-time workers in 2005 was just over $15 000 a year. Twice as many women as men are employed part-time. What might account for this fact? Use the trend shown in these pie graphs to predict how Canada's workforce might change in the next 10 years. What impact could this trend have on Canadian workers?

Technology Trends

Computers and related technologies such as BlackBerries are changing the way people live and work. People can use the computer to do many things at home that they could once only do outside the home, such as work, shop, or send letters. People do more work away from offices or other places of business. They use laptops, cellphones, text messaging, and other methods of technology.

Social Trends

Social trends can affect the work market. A growing percentage of Canadians are changing their activities. These changes have created a need for new products and services.

LITERACY TIP

Finding Important Ideas

Pages 74 to 77 give a lot of information about trends in the workplace.

- Note how this section is divided into smaller sections.
- Each subsection has a heading that captures the main idea.
- Make a list of the subheadings and record one key point from each one to help you understand and remember the important information. Remember to look at important information in the figures and their captions as well.

Fact File

Self-employment has also increased at a rapid rate. About 43 percent, or 800 000, more Canadians were self-employed in 2007 than in 1990. Self-employed workers included 1.7 million men and 876 000 women. Why do you suppose almost twice as many men are self-employed?

The following social trends are creating many new jobs in Canada:

- Canadians spend more time at home on their computers than watching television.
- People want to spend more time enjoying outdoor activities such as hiking, kayaking, or snowboarding.

Economic Trends

The economic trend is toward a more global economy. For example, many Canadian automobile companies use car parts made in different countries, which are sent here for final assembly. Most running shoes are made in Asia. This trend toward global trading causes a great deal of change. It creates new jobs and makes other jobs disappear.

Figure 4.5

Individual or group kayaking adventures reflect the social trend of people spending more time taking part in outdoor activities. What jobs does this trend create?

Figure 4.6

The following trends are occurring in all parts of the industrialized world:

- More jobs are part-time.
- More people are self-employed.
- More people work at home.
- More women work outside the home while still doing unpaid work in the home.
- More workplaces are **downsizing**, or getting by with fewer employees, in order to compete by reducing costs.
- More people hold more than one job.
- More jobs are created in small or medium-sized companies than in large corporations.
- More jobs are **outsourced**; that is, employers are using temporary workers, or people who work for other companies, to perform tasks on a project-by-project basis.
- More people work in teams that are responsible to one another and that produce on their own initiative.

When you enter the workforce for the first time, which two of these trends will likely affect you?

Demographic Trends

Demographics affect the market in the following ways:

- The jobs that are needed in the economy and that are available to workers change.
- The workforce changes in some way, such as its age structure or how people are distributed in different ethnic groups.

The major demographic trend in Canada is the aging of its population. The baby boom **cohort** is nearing retirement. The retirement of this large group of people born in the time span from 1947–1960 will have a major impact on the job market. Examine the population pyramid for Canada's population in 2007 in Figure 4.7 to see how demographics have affected several generations of Canada's workforce.

To learn more about the Canadian population through population pyramids,

Go to Nelson
Social Studies

Figure 4.7

Each colour-coded section on the population pyramid below is a cohort, or a group of people born in a particular time span. Six cohorts are shown. Into which cohorts do the older members of your family fit?

Canada's Population in 2007

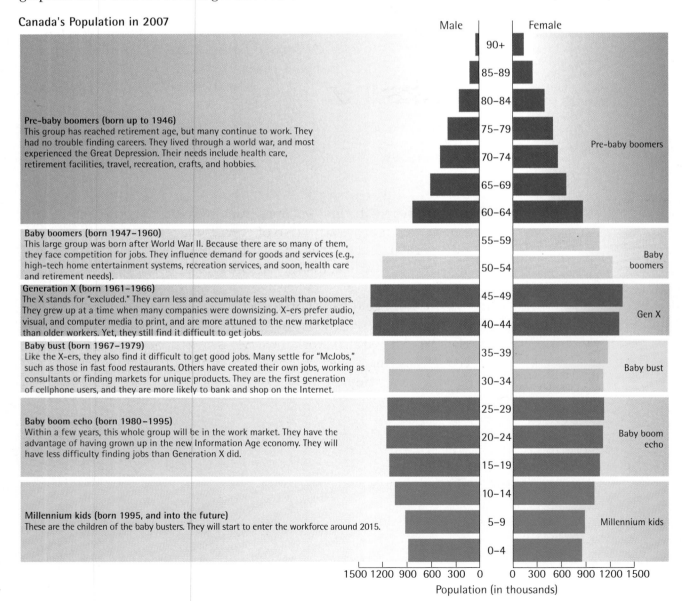

Pre-baby boomers (born up to 1946)
This group has reached retirement age, but many continue to work. They had no trouble finding careers. They lived through a world war, and most experienced the Great Depression. Their needs include health care, retirement facilities, travel, recreation, crafts, and hobbies.

Baby boomers (born 1947–1960)
This large group was born after World War II. Because there are so many of them, they face competition for jobs. They influence demand for goods and services (e.g., high-tech home entertainment systems, recreation services, and soon, health care and retirement needs).

Generation X (born 1961–1966)
The X stands for "excluded." They earn less and accumulate less wealth than boomers. They grew up at a time when many companies were downsizing. X-ers prefer audio, visual, and computer media to print, and are more attuned to the new marketplace than older workers. Yet, they still find it difficult to get jobs.

Baby bust (born 1967–1979)
Like the X-ers, they also find it difficult to get good jobs. Many settle for "McJobs," such as those in fast food restaurants. Others have created their own jobs, working as consultants or finding markets for unique products. They are the first generation of cellphone users, and they are more likely to bank and shop on the Internet.

Baby boom echo (born 1980–1995)
Within a few years, this whole group will be in the work market. They have the advantage of having grown up in the new Information Age economy. They will have less difficulty finding jobs than Generation X did.

Millennium kids (born 1995, and into the future)
These are the children of the baby busters. They will start to enter the workforce around 2015.

Fact File

In the last 15 years, the 500 largest manufacturing companies in the United States eliminated over 5 million jobs—over 25 percent of their total workforce. In Canada, 231 000 manufacturing jobs were lost between 2003 and 2007. In 2003, there were 2 275 000 manufacturing jobs in Canada; in 2007, there were 2 044 000. What might account for this loss in manufacturing jobs?

The Great Job Shift

Canada's economy is changing. It used to be based on industries that produce goods (for example, manufacturing, mining, construction, and agriculture). Today it is based more on providing services in areas such as the following:

- trade
- transportation
- health care
- education
- finance

This shift also reflects Canada's settlement pattern. Four out of five Canadians now live in urban environments.

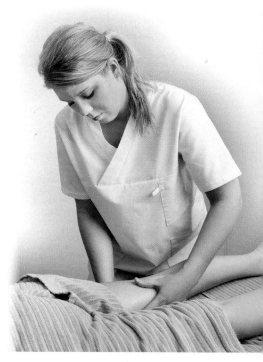

Figure 4.8

More Canadians than ever are working in personal services such as massage therapy and fitness training, retail sales, tourism (for example, hotels and restaurants), and entertainment (for example, theatres and video stores). Think of five adults that you know. How many of them work in personal services?

1. Figure 4.3 on page 73 predicts a future decline in the service sector. If we are in the Information Age, what trend will contribute to this decline? Watch for clues as you read the next section: Changes in Canada's Traditional Industry Sectors.

Shifting, But Not So Fast

In countries with rural societies, such as India, the job shift is happening, but more slowly. Two of every three people in India are considered rural. Much of the population lives in thousands of small rural villages. They work at traditional jobs such as farming and working in small village factories. Indian life is changing rapidly. The change is evident in large urban centres such as Mumbai and Calcutta. Urban Indians generally achieve higher education levels. A large middle class has formed that works in services and in jobs that require more education. This higher income group creates a need for the goods and services that many Canadians enjoy.

1. Figure 4.2 (page 73) and Figure 4.6 (page 75) provide information on how the workplace is changing. Which characteristics of the changing workplace have affected people in your family? How have they been affected?

2. Refer to Figure 4.3 (page 73), and describe the trends in both agriculture and information.

3. Into which cohorts on the population pyramid in Figure 4.7 (page 76) do you and your parents fit?

4. a) How might your career path differ from your parents' because of the trends and changes in the workplace?

   b) Which trends and workplace changes will affect this difference in your career path?

Changes in Canada's Traditional Industry Sectors

1. a) What are some traditional industries in Canada?

b) What jobs would you consider to be "traditional industry" jobs?

Primary industries take natural resources and make them into semi-finished products. An example is a wheat farm. The farmer that produces the wheat works in a primary industry. The company that buys the wheat and makes it into flour is a **secondary industry**. **Tertiary industries** include individuals or companies that provide services. The baker that uses the flour to bake the bread that customers order provides a service. The truck drivers that deliver flour and baked goods to supermarkets and grocery stores also work in tertiary, or service, industries. Who else provides services in supermarkets and grocery stores?

Deciding which sector of the economy a job fits into can be confusing. Workers in service industries are not always employed in the service (tertiary) sector. For example, a cook (a service job) may work in a logging camp (forestry is a primary industry). Or, a salesperson (also a service job) may work for a manufacturing company (secondary industry). Some people, such as clerical staff (administrative assistants, payroll clerks), work in all sectors of the economy.

Fact File

Canada's biggest companies in primary industries by total revenue in 2008 are as follows:

- oil and gas— Imperial Oil ($24B)
- mining—Rio Tinto Alcan ($20B)
- gold and diamonds— Barrick Gold ($6.5B)
- food products— McCain Foods ($6B)
- forest products— Abitibi Consolidated ($4B)

Which of these companies have you heard of?

Figure 4.9

Trends for the future indicate that major changes will continue in the primary industries. What do you notice about the future jobs in these sectors?

Figure 4.10

Scientists have taken a gene from a flounder (a type of fish) and combined it with tomato genes to make a new species of tomato. This tomato is more tolerant of cold weather. Many people are against this kind of bioengineered food (that is, cross species). Why do you think that is?

Farming
- fewer and fewer farmers
- larger farms owned by big companies
- computers used in all aspects of farming
- factory-like raising of animals in large, crowded areas
- robots replacing farm machines
- new crops invented through biotechnology
- increased greenhouse production using **hydroponics**, a system of producing plants in fertile water
- increased organic food production
- concerns about soil depletion, pesticide use, and safety of bioengineered foods
- typical jobs of the future: geneticist, computer programmer, plant biologist

Mining
- fewer ore drillers, blasters, mining engineers
- robots and computers will take over from human workers
- new materials such as plastics will replace metals in many products
- growth in mining the ocean floor
- typical jobs of the future: new-material engineer, polymerization scientist (make new natural or synthetic products such as cellulose or nylon)

Forestry
- fewer and fewer loggers and mill workers
- pulp and paper mills and sawmills increasingly automated
- laser-guided saws and robots moving wood to machines
- concerns about overuse of forest resources and the impact of clear-cutting
- typical jobs of the future: wildlife biologist, forest conservation officer

Changes to Primary Industries

Employment is declining in Canada's primary industries, such as mining, farming, and forestry. Before the Industrial Revolution, most people were farmers and were self-employed. People grew most of their own food and made their own clothing.

Many future jobs in the primary sector will require special training and skills. People may need skills in research, design, and engineering. Farmers are now using technologies, such as infrared satellite images and Global Positioning Systems (GPS), to see where to install drainage tiles or where to add more fertilizer on their fields. They need the know-how to use this technology in their work.

Figure 4.11

Mining in the future will rely more and more on robots rather than humans. Can you think of one advantage and one disadvantage of this trend?

Figure 4.12

Farmers breed fish in hatcheries, such as this one, and use them to replenish dwindling stocks. Can you think of two reasons why fish stocks decline?

Figure 4.13

Plants like this one generate power from coal and oil. These traditional sources of energy will be used less and less in the future. What is one advantage of this trend? What is one disadvantage? What are the alternatives?

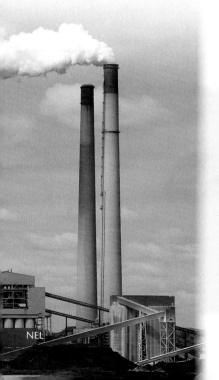

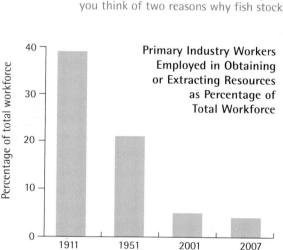

Primary Industry Workers Employed in Obtaining or Extracting Resources as Percentage of Total Workforce

(Percentage of total workforce vs. Year: 1911, 1951, 2001, 2007)

Figure 4.14

Over the last century, the percentage of workers needed to extract resources in Canada has declined greatly. How low do you think the percentage can go?

Energy

- energy demand will continue to increase
- switch away from oil and coal
- continued development of Canada's reserves of natural gas and tar sands
- jobs will shift to alternative fuel sources such as solar, electric, hydrogen fuel cell, wind, biomass, and nuclear fusion
- concerns about greenhouse gas emissions from burning fossil fuels and hazardous (nuclear) waste disposal
- typical jobs of the future: air quality analyst, solar cell technician, hazardous waste engineer, energy auditor

Fishing

- fewer fishers, small shipbuilders, machinists, navigators
- large factory trawlers will continue to "scoop up" fish
- increase in aquaculture (raising fish or seafood along seacoasts)
- intensive fish farming
- concerns about depletion of fish stocks, impacts of aquaculture (use of antibiotics, production of wastes, escape of fish that breed with wild stocks)
- typical jobs of the future: marine biologist, oceanographer, aquaculture farmer/consultant

Changes to Secondary Industries

Jobs in this sector of the economy are mainly in manufacturing. Better machines for making things have reduced the number of jobs in this sector. This includes the use of robots for routine work. Growth in manufacturing has also slowed down somewhat because of the baby boomers. They form the largest cohort, or age group, in society. This group already has much of what it needs and is not buying large quantities of manufactured goods. Some manufacturing industries have relocated to other countries. They move to developing countries, such as Mexico or Taiwan, to take advantage of low labour costs. However, some have just disappeared altogether.

Figure 4.15

Many people with disabilities work in manufacturing. This employee, who is blind, is working on a computer assembly line. Many manufacturing industries have slowed in recent years, but the demand for computers has increased steadily. Can you think of another growing manufacturing industry?

Changes to Tertiary Industries

Canadian society relies more and more on services. These include jobs related to information and communication technologies. Our economy is now called an information economy. People need to locate, read, understand, and process information, both at work and in everyday life. So much of modern communication depends on reading and writing. Literacy skills continue to be very important.

Fact File

The increased participation of women in the paid workforce has resulted in the need for services to replace some of the unpaid work that women did in the home, such as cleaning and child care. Do you think the increased participation of women in the paid workforce is connected to the increase in the number of knowledge workers? Why or why not?

Employment Trends in the Information Economy

The invention of computer technology created the need for new jobs. Workers are needed to make computer hardware (the computers themselves, monitors, printers, hard drives, and scanners) and to develop computer software (the programs used on computers). Many other computer-related jobs exist. Two examples are Internet webmaster and network maintenance specialist.

Today, one in every seven workers in Canada is a **knowledge worker**. This is the fastest-growing group of workers to appear in the past 25 years. Knowledge workers deal with information, and they have become essential in most industries. Knowledge workers will continue to replace factory workers. Experts estimate that by 2015, half of the workforce will be knowledge workers. They will design, plan, and develop ideas. They include social scientists (including geographers and psychologists), applied scientists, educators, system designers, and engineers. Some people think that fewer knowledge workers will be needed in the future. They expect that with new technologies, people will use computers to access the knowledge they need.

Careers in the tertiary sector related to the Information Age include the following:

- investigation
- publishing
- advertising
- data bank services
- software consulting
- law
- laboratory research
- engineering
- photography
- education

In the secondary sector, people work at jobs manufacturing items such as the following:

- computer equipment
- iPods
- telephone equipment
- photocopiers

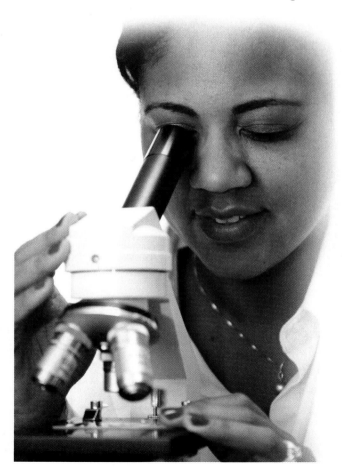

Figure 4.16

In 2005, more than 60 percent of technicians, engineers, and technical sales support staff in North America were women. What might attract more women than men to these careers?

The Power of Technology

We have moved away from the Industrial Revolution to the Information Revolution. We are also living with a Technology Revolution. The development of technology in the 1900s was awesome. Think about the progress from the automobile to spaceflight and the Internet. In the first decade of the twenty-first century, we already have the BlackBerry and new large-scale energy systems such as wind farms. It is difficult to predict what people will create next.

Personal computers, e-mail and the Internet, fax machines, and scanners make it easier to work at home. The trend toward home-based businesses will continue. Computers are doing much of the work people used to do, for example, in banking and assembling products in factories.

Computers have changed the job of the auto mechanic. Today's mechanics use computers to help them identify problems and keep cars in good repair.

Technology changes rapidly. Workers need knowledge about many different areas, including the latest in technology. In order to gain the knowledge they need, workers need to be literate, or able to read and write. Workers also need to be computer literate. They need to be able to use and operate computers, and to understand the language used in working with computer systems. Workers will need to retrain every few years to keep up to date and satisfy their customers. This will create a demand for more education and training.

Figure 4.17

Trades courses in secondary schools and colleges can lead to high-tech careers. What other trades would require good computer skills and knowledge?

1. Economist and Nobel Prize winner Wassily Leontief said, "Sophisticated computers will likely displace humans in the same way that work horses were eliminated by the introduction of tractors." When you consider technology trends, is it possible that computers will ever completely displace humans? Discuss this question in a small group. What evidence can you find within the text to support your opinion?

Robots Are Here to Stay!

In 2005, more than 12 000 robots did all kinds of jobs in Canada. Robots build cars and many other assembly-line products. They handle hazardous chemicals and defuse bombs. Robots will perform routine tasks in many Canadian households in the future.

Many companies use technology to save money. Robots are expensive, but they cost less than workers do. In the future, robotics may replace millions of jobs worldwide.

Figure 4.18

R2-D2 and C-3PO are well-known movie robots. In real life, robots are also doing amazing work. Researchers have developed small submarine robots with sensors and monitoring equipment to explore the oceans. Autonomous underwater vehicles (AUVs) can monitor wastes, explore for oil and gas, and research the role of oceans in climate change. They also helped pinpoint the position of the sunken *Titanic*. The ROVIO, with its webcam and ability to move around, can be used to check on things in the home—like whether the dog has food in its dish—while family members are at work or school.

 AFTER READING

1. What does it mean to be literate? What does it mean to be computer literate? Why is it important to be both literate and computer literate in today's workplace?

2. a) Using an organizer like the one shown, identify three primary industries and three secondary industries. For each industry, name the major product produced. For example, Kellogg's is an example of a secondary industry, and cereals is the product.

	Name of Industry	Product Made by This Industry
Primary industries	1.	
	2.	
	3.	
Secondary industries	1.	
	2.	
	3.	

b) What is the most important change that primary industries must face?

c) What is the most important change that secondary industries must face?

3. List three personal services you consider to be new types of services (that is, available for less than 15 years). Share your list with a classmate and add any new ones to your list.

Issues Affecting the Workplace

1. Impacts can be positive or negative.

a) What could happen in the workplace that a worker would identify as having a good impact?

b) What could happen in the workplace that a worker would identify as having a bad impact?

2. An *issue* is a large and complicated problem that creates discussion among people with different views. What issues might have an impact on Canadians in the workplace over the next few years? Brainstorm with a partner, and then share your ideas with another pair.

Many workplace issues will affect Canadians over the next few years. The workplace is changing, and many factors are responsible. Trends that have become issues include the following:

- increasing concern for protection of the environment
- the impact on the job market of the aging baby boomers, who are about to retire
- the impact of **globalization**, or global trade, and immigration on Canada

Up with the Environment!

More and more Canadians are working in environmental protection. This is a fast-growing industry. People today are concerned about the environment. We want more environmentally friendly products and services. Environmental protection services help companies and governments make their operations more efficient and less polluting.

LITERACY TIP . . . .

Checking Comprehension as You Read

While you are reading, stop and think about what you have read by doing the following:

- Ask a question.
- Clarify something.
- Make a comment.
- Make a connection.
- Make a prediction.

You have been reading a lot of information about the changing workplace in Canada. Interrupt your reading to think aloud. It will help you check your understanding of the text.

Figure 4.19

As the baby boomers get older, the number of people over 65 will increase to 25 percent of the total population by 2040. What opportunities for new business will this situation create?

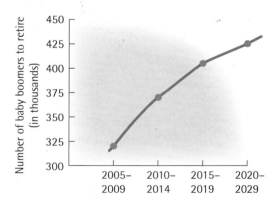

Baby Boomer Retirement Statistics, 2005–2029

Figure 4.20

Solar panels and wind farms are renewable, non-polluting energy sources. Might the next new age for jobs be the Environmental Age? What kinds of jobs could become available?

GO GEO-GREEN

Environmental Career Choices

Do you ever think about what you might be doing in 10 or 20 years? What career might suit your skills and learning style? People are becoming more aware of the environment. As they do, new environment-related opportunities are opening up.

You can learn about environmental careers on the Internet. Here are a couple of good places to start your search:

• GoodWork Canada: This is one of the most popular "green" job websites. It has connected people with environment-related job opportunities across Canada since 2001. GoodWork Canada provides the following:

  – listings of "green" jobs, internships, and volunteer positions

  – information about environmental events and workshops across Canada, where you experience some "green" jobs first-hand, or take part in forest cleanups and local fundraisers

• ECO (Environmental Careers Organization) Canada: This website provides details about many different environmental careers. What does an agricultural engineer do? How about an environmental geologist or an avalanche forecaster? The site offers profiles for these careers and many more. Each profile includes the following:

– an overview of the occupation's duties
– education needed to get into this occupation
– employment opportunities
– description of the work environment

For example, the profile for an avalanche forecaster explains it as a seasonal job that involves working outdoors, snowmobiling around, and gathering information on the weather and avalanche conditions. They use the information they find to assess the risk of an avalanche. Local ski resorts and news agencies then use this information to keep people safe in the mountains. This might be a good career choice for someone who enjoys outdoor activities such as skiing and snowmobiling.

What might be your ideal environmental job? Take the time to do a little research. You will begin a lifetime journey to have a career that you love and that will help the planet as well.

. . . .

To learn more about environmental careers,

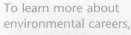

**Go to Nelson
Social Studies**

Figure 4.21

Working as an environmental geologist or avalanche forecaster often involves travelling and working outdoors in extreme conditions.

Not Enough Workers

Help wanted! In the 2000s, there will not be enough young people to fill all the jobs Canada has to offer. The following major trends will work together to produce a labour shortage in the next few years:

- Natural increase will remain low.
- The baby boom generation will retire and leave the workforce.
- There will not be enough new immigrants to fill all the jobs, unless the government increases the total number of immigrants that arrive each year.
- More workers will be needed because of the predicted growth in international trade.

The unemployment rate in Canada fell from more than 7 percent in the 1990s to 5.7 percent in 2007 and was predicted to fall to 4 percent by 2010. However, the global economic crisis that occurred in 2008 caused a jump in unemployment to 7.7 percent in 2009. When economic conditions improve, it is likely the unemployment rate will resume its decline due to Canada's population trends.

DURING READING

1. Discuss the following questions in a small group. Be ready to share the main points of your discussion with the rest of the class.

a) Many people are losing their jobs in primary industries and in manufacturing due to downsizing, changes in technology, globalization, and changes in the market.

Given this fact, how is it possible that a labour shortage is predicted in the future? (Hint: Look back at what you learned about trends in the workplace.)

b) What trends provide clues about which sectors will provide these jobs?

2. What will these trends mean for you as you enter the workforce?

Figure 4.22

Employers often search for new employees at job fairs held at colleges and universities.

CAREERS	
Landscape Research Analyst needed to assess properties for environmental protection and controlled development.	**Geographer/ Planner** needed to manage projects related to future development and city planning. Geographic information skills are a must.
Environmental, Geotechnical, Water, and Waste Water Engineers required to assist and direct upcoming rural and urban projects.	

Figure 4.23

Not long ago, jobs like these did not exist. They require knowledge and skills that are part of geographic training. Which words in the ads are related to geography?

Globalization, or Global Trade

Our planet is shrinking … or it seems to be because of the Technology Revolution! People can hop on an airplane and be anywhere in the world within a few hours. Satellites can beam images instantly to television sets anywhere on Earth. We import many products that we use every day from other countries. Workers in these countries make products such as appliances, running shoes, and jeans for less money than workers will in Canada.

Canada is known around the world for its satellite technology, fibre optics (light-based communication), and transportation equipment, from snowmobiles to subway cars. We live in a multicultural country with connections to every part of the world. Because of these factors, Canada can look forward to increased world trade. Many new jobs will be created in the following areas:

- marketing
- advertising
- transportation of Canadian products to export markets
- special career fields such as international law and communication

Increased global trade, or globalization, means more competition. This will put pressure on industries and businesses to cut their costs even more. Labour in North America is expensive. Therefore, many companies will try to reduce their workforces to as few as possible.

Fact File

The top five Information and Communications Technologies (ICT) companies in Canada by total revenue in 2008 were as follows:

- Bombardier ($17B)
- Nortel Networks ($11.4B)
- Celestica ($8B)
- IBM Canada ($6.8B)
- Research in Motion (RIM) ($6B)

How many of these companies are you familiar with? Why is ICT such a growing field of employment?

Figure 4.24

Since 1990, a growing field of employment has been Information and Communications Technologies (ICT). This includes workers such as computer programmers and systems analysts. In 1992, there were only 200 000 ICT workers in Canada. By 2006, there were more than 560 000. Cable and satellite communications have shown huge growth recently. People in these jobs earned 20 to 30 percent more than workers overall. Pick one business, such as a cable TV company. List as many different jobs as you can think of that are available within it.

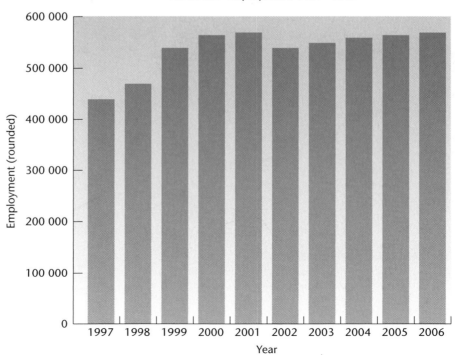

ICT Sector Employment, 1997–2006

GeoSkills

Reading a Flow Map— Major Exporting and Importing Regions, 2007

A flow map shows direction and distance of movement of people or goods. Lines or arrows show these movements. The arrows (or lines) begin at the source of the movement and end at the destination.

You have been reading about industry sectors and how Canada earns money through global trade. Canada is a country rich with resources. Many countries rely on Canada's products. Canada exports products, such as pulp and paper products, vehicles, electrical equipment, precious metals, and ores, to these countries. In return, Canada imports

products we do not have in our own country, such as plastics, aircraft, optical equipment, and machinery. Canada has four main trading partners—the United States, Japan, the United Kingdom, and other European Economic Community countries (for example, Germany, Belgium, the Netherlands). The flow map below shows you the following:
- where most of Canada's exports go
- how much Canada exports to these countries
- the amount of imports Canada gets from these four locations

Exports and Imports for Canada, 2007

Export	Import	Amount of trade (Can$, millions)
		250 000+
		24 000 to 33 000
		10 000 to 23 999
		Up to 9999

Figure 4.25

This flow map shows how much Canada exports to and imports from four regions in the world. Canada has a trade relationship with these four regions. How might you use this map to help explain this trade relationship?

GeoSkills

Reading a Flow Map—
Major Exporting and Importing Regions, 2007 *(continued)*

How do you read a flow map?

Step One

Look at the title first. For this flow map, the title is Exports and Imports for Canada, 2007. The information in the title provides a context for the map, and you can begin to use your prior knowledge of exports and imports to read this map.

Step Two

The legend is where you will learn information about the arrows. Which colour represents exports? Which colour represents imports? It is important to understand that the colours represent the movement of products to and from different locations. The arrows have beginning and ending points, showing that some products are being exported from Canada, while others are being imported into Canada.

Step Three

Use the legend to determine the meaning of the widths of the arrows. The greater the width, the more products are being traded.

1. a) With which country does Canada do the largest amount of trade? Why might this be the case?

   b) With which country do we import more than we export?

Exports and Imports for Canada, 2007

Country		Exports ($ millions)	Imports ($ millions)
United States		356 094.2	269 752.5
Japan		9 989.2	11 972.3
United Kingdom		14 154.8	9 894.3
Other European Economic Community countries		24 187.0	32 402.9

Figure 4.26

Why might a flow map be better suited to show you trade patterns than just a data table like this one?

Global Skills

What skills and traits do people need to work in global trade?

- the ability to understand trends and respond to them quickly
- language skills
- awareness of different customs and ways of doing business in other countries
- stamina to be "on the job" all the time—successful global companies "never sleep." Business activity is going on somewhere in the world all the time.

Immigration keeps adding to Canada's population. Immigrants help Canada in establishing successful global trade. They contribute skills in other languages that businesses need to communicate with global trading partners. They bring awareness of different customs and ways of doing business in other countries. This awareness is important to developing strong, respectful trading relationships.

Figure 4.27

Seventy percent of Canada's immigrants now come from Asia, Africa, and Latin America. How does this trend make sense when you consider increased globalization in trade?

Challenges of the Future

Most careers of the future will require workers to be skilled at the following:

- communicating
- problem solving
- decision making
- creative thinking
- teamwork
- adapting to meet the challenges of rapid change

Change is happening quickly. Jobs forecast for today may not be those needed a decade from now. This is why forecasters suggest people will have more and different jobs in the future. For the future workplace, you need the following:

- a rounded education
- an awareness of trends in society
- strong literacy and computer skills

Figure 4.28

Blueprint for the Future is a series of career fairs for First Nations, Inuit, and Métis students. These career fairs introduce Aboriginal youth to the wide range of possible careers. Organizers want to help students make solid career choices. Such services are important as Aboriginal youth are the fastest growing part of our population.

AFTER READING

1. Suggest a reason that shows why it may be very important for you to learn a second language.

2. At the beginning of this section, an issue was defined as a large and complicated problem that creates discussion among people with different views. Choose one issue affecting the workplace. Explain how it is a problem that creates discussion among people with different points of view.

3. Which of the issues affecting the workplace do you think will have the most impact on you as you prepare to enter the job market? Why?

CASE STUDY

GIS — An Expanding Career Area in the Information Economy

GIS is an acronym (a word made from the initials of other words) for Geographic Information Systems. It is predicted that this powerful computer-based technology will be used as widely in the future as word processing is today. A GIS combines a computer, specialized software, and geographic data (information) about places. Operators apply many different layers of data to maps of a particular location. Then, they use GIS to analyze patterns among the layers of data.

GIS is in great demand in the marketplace in the following areas:

- business and industry
- government
- institutions
- planning
- environmental management
- municipal services

GIS is used to plan where your school bus routes go, where the next McDonald's is built, or which farm fields or forest zones need protective action against disease or pests. Tens of thousands of jobs over the next few years will be created in the GIS field.

Why are people with GIS skills in such demand? Think of all the types of questions people in everyday jobs might ask. Then, think about how GIS might help them answer these questions.

Figure 4.29

The questions and problems that can be analyzed and solved using GIS are seemingly endless! Why are GIS answers better than what we did before?

Using GIS to Answer Questions

Job	Question	GIS Answer
Urban planner	Where should we build a bicycle trail in our community?	GIS can show where there are sites with fewer steep slopes and more scenic views.
Mayor of a city	Where should a new landfill site go?	GIS can show available land areas that are far away from populated areas, yet near to transportation links.
Police officer	Why do certain parts of my city experience more crime than others?	GIS can map out crime sites and compare these to areas of high population density and urban decay.
Environmentalist	What damage will occur if that river floods its banks?	GIS can create a map showing which buildings are too close to a river. It can also predict the total flooded area.
Sales manager	How do I divide up my sales territories so that my salespeople have an equal number of customers?	GIS can look at where customers live and draw boundaries so that each salesperson has the same number of customers.

Figure 4.30

GIS can help select appropriate sites for landfill garbage disposal. Can you think of other problems that GIS might help to solve?

CASE STUDY

GIS—An Expanding Career Area (continued)

GIS Career Profiles

Michelle Laronde is from the Mohawk Nation near Montréal. She has a university degree in geography and environmental studies. She also has a GIS diploma from Sir Sandford Fleming College. Michelle analyzes problems in natural resource management such as the impact of water pollution on local ecosystems and drinking water. Her work includes using different layers of information on maps of a watershed area to locate sources of pollution.

Greg Stamp is a recent graduate of the University of Lethbridge, where he specialized in mapping and GIS. He works for Stamp Seeds near Lethbridge, Alberta. Greg maps the yields of various crops over their land using a monitor on the combine. He uses the information along with a GPS (Global Positioning System) to see where different applications of fertilizers are required. The equipment for applying fertilizers can follow the schedule he creates from the map patterns. This saves energy and valuable fertilizer. He also maps their fields for soil quality and drainage.

GIS Application Profile

The Crime Analysis and Mapping Unit of the Peel Regional Police Force serves the needs of 1650 officers and 600 other employees. They produce maps of crime densities for different crimes. Then, they analyze the patterns and identify areas of higher crime. They also use mapping technologies in the following ways:

- to warn homeowners of a neighbourhood crime alert
- to respond to school incidents
- to predict likely target areas

Figure 4.31

Greg Stamp uses GIS to find ways to improve farming yields and save energy. All Ontario schools can use ESRI's ArcView GIS program. Ask your teacher or librarian to show you how to get started.

 AFTER READING

1. Why are people who work in the GIS field called knowledge workers?

2. What aspects of the profiles in this case study fit the pattern of current employment trends? Use a chart like the one below to answer this question. Scan the headings and subheadings in this chapter and choose those trends that apply to these profiles.

Employment Trend	Michelle Laronde	Greg Stamp	Peel Regional Police
Importance of the environment	She is using GIS to find major sources of river pollution. She is studying the impact of water pollution on the ecosystem.		
Use of technology			

Knowledge and Understanding

1 List two advantages and two disadvantages of working at home.

2 Identify one trend that is occurring in each of the industrial sectors: primary, secondary, and tertiary industries.

3 How do the following two quotations apply to trends about employment?

a) "People work any time and all the time, with no one keeping track of their hours, but with everyone watching their output." (William Bridges, former Microsoft employee)

b) "Don't count on the economy to produce new jobs; you've got to produce them yourselves."(Angus Reid, pollster, author of *Shakedown*)

Inquiry/Research and Communication Skills

4 **a)** Ask a parent or other older adult what skills were most important at the time they entered the workforce. Use a chart like the one below to make three lists of skills:

Skills Needed When a Parent or Other Older Adult Entered the Workforce	Skills Needed Today	Skills Needed in the Future
• • •	• • •	• • •

b) Compare the skills that were important when your interviewee entered the workforce to those needed today and those that will be needed in the future. Which are different? Which, if any, are the same?

c) Which skills will you need in order to be ready for the workplace of the future?

d) Which trends are most important for you to consider as you prepare to enter the job market?

Map, Globe, and Graphic Skills

5 Look at the labels on your clothing. Select one item of clothing and one school item, such as a notebook or ruler.

a) Write down where each product was made.

b) Use a tally sheet to collect the information from all students in the class.

Made in...	Total Number of Items Found in Class
Canada	
China	

c) Using an atlas and a blank map of the world, locate and label all of the countries listed on your class tally sheet.

d) Create a legend that shows the number of items made in each country that were tallied in your class (for example, 1 to 3 items = countries shaded in red; 4 to 6 items = countries shaded in green).

e) Connect all of the shaded countries to Canada by using arrows.

f) Is your map is complete?

• Does your map have a title?

• Does your legend identify the number of items made in each country?

• Does your map have a compass rose?

• Are the countries labelled and shaded neatly and correctly?

g) Using your map and information from this chapter, describe what is meant by the globalization of business.

6 Statistics Canada provides community profiles with statistics for communities in Canada. If your community is not listed, use the name of a larger community near you.

a) Is the population of your community increasing or decreasing?

b) Create two circle graphs to show the proportion of the community that is employed in primary, secondary, and tertiary industries: one graph for males and one for females. (Refer to GeoSkills on page 145 in Chapter 7.)

Primary includes agriculture and other resource-based industries. Secondary includes manufacturing and construction. The remaining categories are tertiary.

c) Create two additional circle graphs to show the same data for Ontario.

d) Write an analysis of your graphs:

- Which type of industry (primary, secondary, or tertiary) provides the most jobs in your community? Which type provides the least?

- What do you notice about the difference in patterns of female and male employment in your community? What reasons can you give for these differences?

- Do a few large companies employ most people, or do small- to medium-sized companies dominate?

- Suggest reasons for any similarities or differences between your community and Ontario.

Application

7 **a)** Investigate a career that interests you and that fits at least one of the major trends affecting the workplace. Research to find out the following:

- skills needed
- educational requirements
- a description of the day-to-day work done by someone in that field

b) Explain how this career fits at least one of the major trends affecting the workplace.

8 Examine the population pyramid in Figure 4.32.

a) Calculate the percent of the population that will be supported by the workforce in 2031. To do this, estimate the populations over 64 and under 15 from the population pyramid. Then, add these populations together and calculate this total as a percent of the 2031 population.

b) Compare this population pyramid to Figure 4.7 on page 76. Determine three major changes in Canada's age structure that will occur in the next quarter century.

c) How will these changes affect the Canadian workplace and trends in jobs?

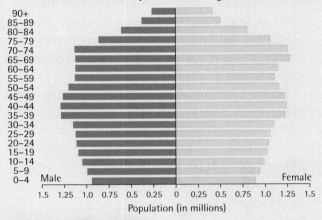

Canada's Predicted Population and Age Structure in 2031

Figure 4.32

Canada's total population is predicted to be 38 745 800 in 2031.

Figure 4.33

What economic, social, and demographic trends do these goods suggest to you?

5 Population Connections and Consequences

IN THIS CHAPTER

- summarize the factors that cause patterns in the ways that cities, industries, and transportation develop
- make up questions to guide research about population characteristics and patterns
- compare key characteristics of a number of developing and developed countries

KEY VOCABULARY

biofuel
food conglomerate
industrialization
infrastructure
monoculture
transnational corporation
urbanization

Riding the Wave

BEFORE READING

1. Think about a time when you experienced change in your life. How did you respond to that change? How was your response positive or negative? How could you have responded in a different way?

2. Think about your life. Give two examples of how one change (for example, the birth of a younger sibling, moving to a new home) caused other changes.

In earlier chapters, you have read that waves of change are sweeping over the world. These changes will affect everyone's future.

This chapter investigates some factors that are causing change in the following areas:

- **industrialization**—the rapid development of manufacturing in a society
- **urbanization**—the growth of cities as people move from rural areas to cities
- transportation—the movement of goods and people

It is hard to separate these three areas of society. The factors that affect one area affect the other areas, too. For example, a new highway might encourage the growth of manufacturing in a city and encourage more people to move to that city in search of jobs.

To complicate matters, urbanization, industrialization, and transportation vary greatly from one part of the world to another. For example, each country's industrial development is different. It depends on economic conditions and available resources. Each country faces a different set of problems as it copes with changes in urbanization, industrialization, and transportation.

Figure 5.1

Most bicycles sold in Canada are made in China. China is considered a country in transition, undergoing rapid industrialization. In what ways might transportation in China have to change in order to support the country's new industries?

Linking the Issues

Transportation, urbanization, and industrialization affect each other in complicated ways. Figure 5.2 shows how changes in one area affect the other areas. It also identifies issues that arise in developing countries because of these changes. Developed countries have different economic structures. Therefore, they deal with different conditions. In many developed countries, industries have moved to places where wages are lower. As a result, the populations of major cities have decreased.

How Transportation, Urbanization, and Industrialization Affect Each Other

Figure 5.2

When urbanization, industrialization, and transportation interact, changes occur. These changes raise many concerns and issues. In what ways might urban growth in Canada differ from urban growth in developing countries?

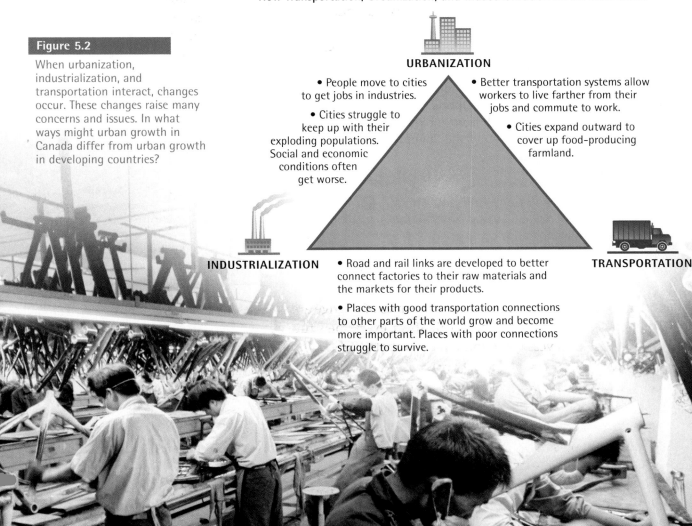

URBANIZATION

• People move to cities to get jobs in industries.

• Cities struggle to keep up with their exploding populations. Social and economic conditions often get worse.

• Better transportation systems allow workers to live farther from their jobs and commute to work.

• Cities expand outward to cover up food-producing farmland.

INDUSTRIALIZATION

TRANSPORTATION

• Road and rail links are developed to better connect factories to their raw materials and the markets for their products.

• Places with good transportation connections to other parts of the world grow and become more important. Places with poor connections struggle to survive.

Factors Causing Change

Many factors can cause change. We often group these factors under the following headings: social, political, cultural, economic, and environmental.

- Social factors have to do with how people get along with each other (for example, people take action to reduce poverty rates).

- Political factors are concerned with making decisions in groups (for example, governments pass laws to help people with low incomes).

- Cultural factors have to do with how groups of people get along with other groups of people (for example, local groups carry out plans to reduce poverty among young people in the community).

- Economic factors are concerned with how people earn a living and build wealth (for example, business leaders support programs to improve job skills among homeless people).

- Environmental factors have to do with nature and natural processes (for example, people work on environmental projects).

These factors do not work alone. They are very closely connected— that is, they are interconnected. They are also interdependent. That means that each factor depends on what is happening with the other factors. Look at an example of how factors are interconnected and interdependent:

In 1999, Nunavut was created because of agreements between the Inuit of Canada's North and the federal government. People were hopeful that the new territory would stimulate more jobs for the Inuit. They were also hopeful that social problems such as high school dropout rates could be improved. The agreements also included ways to protect the tundra of the region from damage.

Reading Complex Charts

Figure 5.3 is an example of a complex chart. It shows how daily decisions can affect our lives in many ways. To read the chart, begin in the middle, with the title, and work your way outward. Note that the five factors that affect change (listed in the middle circle), are also the titles to the five pie-shaped wedges. The information in each pie piece deals with one factor. The outer blue ring is not divided because all of the factors influence these topics.

Two important factors that work together and cause change are demographics and changing technology:

- *Demographics*—This has to do with population trends and patterns. Recent demographic trends include the movement of people from rural areas to cities, and rapidly growing populations in developing countries. Demographic trends can work to make problems like poverty even harder to solve.
- *Changing Technology*—New technologies may allow some problems to be solved more easily, such as finding ways to reduce pollution. But, advancing technologies may also mean that people who cannot afford them fall further and further into poverty.

How Change Factors Affect Daily Decisions and Everyday Life

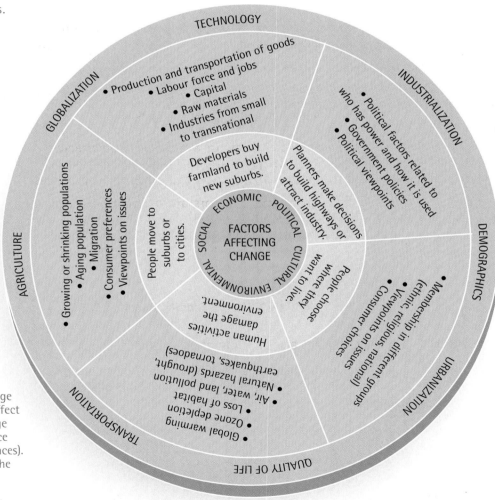

Figure 5.3

This chart shows that the change factors (centre of the circle) affect decisions made by people (beige spaces) which, in turn, influence many aspects of life (green spaces). All of these influences affect the broad topics around the edge of the chart. What decisions might you and your family make that could affect the topics around the edge of the chart?

1. Notice the decision "Developers buy farmland to build new suburbs" in Figure 5.3. How might this decision connect with each of the topics listed in the circle around the outside of the complex chart? Organize your ideas in a chart that looks like the one shown below. One connection has already been done for you.

Broad Topic	Connection to the Decision: Developers Buy Farmland to Build New Suburbs
Agriculture	Food-producing land near cities is lost to other uses, such as houses or businesses.
Demographics	
Globalization	
Industrialization	
Quality of life	
Technology	
Transportation	
Urbanization	

Bringing Change to Toronto's Port Area

The history of Toronto shows how changes in one area resulted in changes throughout a whole system. Toronto is a port city, welcoming shipping from around the Great Lakes and the world. In the past, the port activity encouraged the building of factories and warehouses along the shore. Railways and roadways connected the busy port to the rest of the province. By the 1950s, rail and road transportation improved due to changes in technology. Shipping companies began to lose business to rail and road transportation. Gradually, many of the factories along the shore closed down or moved to the growing suburbs. People began to see this rundown part of Toronto as an eyesore.

Figure 5.4

This photograph was taken around 1950. It shows the economic development around the port of Toronto. What transportation facilities can you identify in this picture?

New ways of thinking about Toronto's port have injected new life into this area. Tearing up most of the old rail lines made it easier for city dwellers to cross into this area. Other changes have included the following:

- the removal or conversion of old buildings to other uses such as condominium apartments
- the building of parks and walkways
- the opening of art galleries and trendy shops in the port area

In fact, one old distillery was transformed into an area of high-end shops and exclusive art galleries. All of these new uses take advantage of the unique characteristics of the original port area.

1. Identify three connections between urbanization, industrialization, and transportation in the renewal of Toronto's port area. You might use Figure 5.2 on page 97 as a model for organizing your ideas.

Figure 5.5

Many of the recent developments in the port area of Toronto have emphasized living and playing. This is a real shift from the industrial focus of the past. What factors do you think brought about these changes?

Figure 5.6

This is a streetscape in the renewed port area of Toronto. Why do you suppose developers converted old buildings instead of building new ones? Do you think you would want to live here?

The Industrialization of Food Supplies

BEFORE READING

1. With a classmate, brainstorm some ways that food items are changed from the time they are in their original state until they are served at your table.

The next time you are in a supermarket, spend a few minutes looking around at the products for sale. You will find an amazing variety of colours, shapes, and sizes. Thanks to technological advances in high-speed transportation and refrigeration, we can buy foods from every region of the world. Many of these foods are processed in factories by adding substances that preserve freshness, colour, and consistency. The large-scale processing of food is a direct result of the industrialization of food supplies.

Figure 5.7

The industrialization of food supplies means that we can choose from a wide variety of international products at the supermarket. What are the pros and cons of this fact?

Figure 5.8

Food supplies have been industrialized. Today, we can buy thousands of processed food products. How might this change in food supplies bring about changes in where people live and work?

Processing Potatoes into Potato Chips

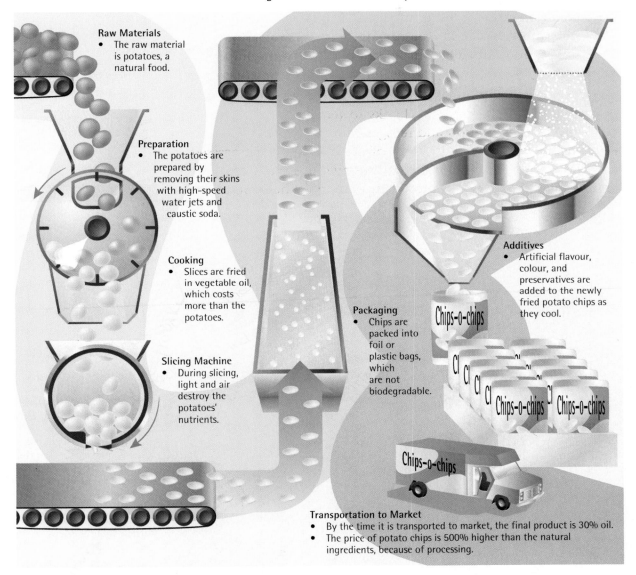

Raw Materials
- The raw material is potatoes, a natural food.

Preparation
- The potatoes are prepared by removing their skins with high-speed water jets and caustic soda.

Cooking
- Slices are fried in vegetable oil, which costs more than the potatoes.

Slicing Machine
- During slicing, light and air destroy the potatoes' nutrients.

Additives
- Artificial flavour, colour, and preservatives are added to the newly fried potato chips as they cool.

Packaging
- Chips are packed into foil or plastic bags, which are not biodegradable.

Transportation to Market
- By the time it is transported to market, the final product is 30% oil.
- The price of potato chips is 500% higher than the natural ingredients, because of processing.

More Mouths to Feed!

Many people see that industrialization of food supplies is the best way to meet growing food needs. As the global population rises, so does the demand for food. Most of the world's arable land is already being used to grow food. Therefore, we have to try to grow more and more food from the same amount of land. Many farmers believe that food production will have to become more intensive. That means using more seeds, fertilizers, chemical pesticides, tools, and machinery.

Not everyone agrees with this approach. Many people are concerned about the harmful effects of modern agriculture. These effects include the following:

- loss of biodiversity as farmers grow large quantities of one type of crop. This practice is called **monoculture**.
- pollution caused by intensive use of fossil fuels, chemical fertilizers, and pesticides
- soil erosion caused by use of farm machinery

Fact File

- Food production must rise by 50 percent by 2030 in order to meet growing food needs.
- In April 2008, the world had the highest food prices in 10 years.
- About 1 billion people in the world live on less than US$1 a day.

As the world population continues to grow, what challenges do these facts present?

Figure 5.9

In Canada, the use of pesticides threatens the survival of the burrowing owl. What animals in your area are endangered species? What is threatening these animals' survival?

Fact File

Agriculture uses over 50 percent of the world's available fresh water. Some parts of the world face severe water shortages. People use the available water far faster than nature can replenish it. Should those parts of the world with lots of water have to share their supply with those who face shortages?

Fact File

Transnational corporations control 80 percent of the world's trade and 80 percent of the world's croplands.

The top 200 transnational companies employ less than 1 percent of the world's total workforce. Should transnational corporations be allowed to get so big and have so much power?

The Big Players

Transnational corporations control much of the world's industrial food production. These large companies operate in many different countries. The prefix *trans* means "across." Transnational companies operate across national boundaries. Sometimes they are beyond the control of any government. That is, they do not belong to any one country. Some are so big that they earn more in a year than some developing countries earn. Kraft Foods Inc. is a transnational corporation and **food conglomerate**. It produces many common brand name food products such as Kraft, Post, Maxwell House, Danone, and Jell-O. Kraft sells its products in 155 countries.

Transnational corporations provide many jobs to the countries in which they operate. Sometimes the governments in these countries will give in to the corporations' demands in order to protect the jobs. Transnational corporations may demand that they pay little or no taxes. They may take action to weaken the strength of trade unions so that they can keep the cost of labour down. This is especially true in developing countries.

1. Identify two effects of the industrialization of food supplies. Label each effect that you identify as a political, social, cultural, economic, or environmental effect, and explain why it fits that category.

Figure 5.10

Transnational corporations operate in all parts of the world and in all areas of the economy. They include large oil companies and car manufacturers, electronic and entertainment companies, and food conglomerates. Some examples of transnational corporations are Coca-Cola, PepsiCo, Nike, Ford, Sony, Mitsubishi, and Microsoft Corporation. What are the pros and cons of transnational corporations operating in developing countries?

Globalization

The industrialization of food supplies has gone hand-in-hand with the globalization of the world food production system. Transnational corporations are producing more and more processed foods and other products. This growth is a sign of increasing globalization. Transnational corporations argue that they need to operate on a worldwide scale if they are to be successful. They buy raw materials in some countries, manufacture products in other countries, and sell their goods around the world. For example, a European-based company may buy chocolate produced in Africa, have it made into chocolate bars in Asia, and sell it to people in North America. Quick and efficient transportation of raw materials and finished products is key to globalization.

Increased globalization also contributes to urbanization. As industrialization increases in cities and countries that want a role in the global economy, workers migrate to these places in search of work. Cities like Beijing, China, and Mumbai, India, are expanding, at least in part, because of globalization.

1. Identify three connections between urbanization, industrialization, and transportation in the industrialization of food supplies. You might use Figure 5.2 on page 97 as a model for organizing your ideas.

2. Explain how globalization is linked to the industrialization of a product or good. To answer this question, consider the availability of raw materials and skilled workers, and the locations of markets.

Fact File

Ships carry 96 percent of world trade products by weight. Forty percent of trade products are moved in containers. These large metal shipping boxes are easy to transfer from ships to rail cars to trucks. How do you suppose container ships are loaded and unloaded?

Figure 5.11

Containers have made transporting all kinds of products faster and cheaper than ever before. How does this improvement in transportation relate to industrialization and globalization?

GO GEO-GREEN

Food Crisis: Food or Biofuels

If you eventually buy a car, what fuel will you use? Maybe you will just plug it in to recharge the batteries. Researchers are working on new forms of fuel as we try to use less oil. **Biofuels** are one of those new fuels. Biofuels are made from plants such as corn and grain, wood waste, and wheat straw. Many people see biofuels as a greener, more sustainable option than fuels such as gasoline and diesel. However, there is a problem with some biofuels. When crops are grown for fuel, they are not available for humans to eat. Croplands are limited. If we grow plants for fuel, where will we grow plants for food? Evidence suggests that the use of corn for biofuels has contributed to world hunger.

A growing food crisis around the world has pushed nearly 100 million people into poverty. That is because people have to spend more of their money on food. In 2008, the price of rice rose from $400 a tonne to $1000 a tonne—a rise of 250 percent. In Afghanistan, the price of wheat soared 300 percent. In countries where many people live in poverty, this means that some families have to spend all their money on food. The price of rice and other crops continues to rise as the demand for these grains for biofuels grows.

Fact File

In July 2008, the World Bank reported that biofuels have forced global food prices to rise by 75 percent since 2002. The report pointed out that 75 percent of global corn production between 2005 and 2008 has been used to produce the biofuel ethanol.

The following factors have made the problem even greater:

- As China and India grow more wealthy, their populations are buying more meat and grains than they did in the past.
- The price of oil fluctuates, but the overall trend has been up. This has pushed food prices up. Why? Oil is used to make chemical fertilizers. The fertilizers are now more costly, so it costs more for farmers to produce their crops. It also costs more to transport food to consumers.

It is hard to think that trying to do something good for the planet can cause so many new problems. As we try to improve technologies and burn less oil and other fossil fuels, we need to make sure that our choices do not cause harm in other areas. The following companies are making progress:

- Iogen Corporation has developed a biofuel made from non-food-based sources such as wheat straw. In 2008, Iogen received approval from the federal government to build an ethanol plant in Saskatchewan.
- Car companies are working on electric and hydrogen cars. In Japan in 2008, Honda introduced a zero-emission, hydrogen-fuel-cell car that emits only water.

Who knows? Maybe future cars will be fuelled up with tap water!

How can you get involved? You and your classmates could research the best ways to make use of biofuels or examine alternative energy options. You could also write to your Member of Parliament about the need to switch to renewable energy sources that do not reduce global food supplies.

Figure 5.12

What opinion does this cartoon present about biofuels? (Refer to GeoSkills on pages 192–193 in Chapter 9 and the Literacy Tip on page 5 in Chapter 1 for help in reading and understanding editorial cartoons.)

Swelling Cities

1. In this section, you will learn how urban growth and factors like technological change, economic development, and transportation are linked. Make up three questions about how these topics interconnect. Look for the answers as you read. Remember the 5 Ws and 1 H questions as you make your own questions. (Refer to the Literacy Tip on page 41 in Chapter 2 and GeoSkills on page 246 in Chapter 11.)

Advances in technology have influenced the shape and ways that cities work. New transportation and building technologies have been especially important. In turn, more people than ever live in cities. This process is called urbanization. The developing world is now experiencing the type of rapid urbanization that developed countries did in the early 1900s.

The world's urban population is growing quickly. Around 1950, the world's population was 2.5 billion. At that time, the percentage of the population that lived in urban areas was as follows:

- developing countries—17 percent
- developed countries—53 percent

Globally, fewer than 30 percent of the world's people lived in cities. This changed as people moved out of rural places in search of new opportunities in cities. Now, about half of the almost seven billion people on Earth live in towns and cities.

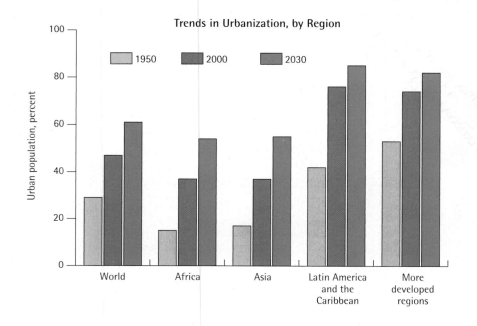

Trends in Urbanization, by Region

Figure 5.13

This graph shows the percentage of the urban population for different regions of the world. Which countries would be included in the category of More developed regions?

1. Look at Figure 5.13. Describe the trend you see. Why do you think that urbanization rates for Africa and Asia are below the world average?

2. Why do you suppose the change in urban population for more developed regions between 2000 and 2030 will be small? What factors might lead to such a small increase in their urban population?

To learn more about rapid urban growth in Gambia, a country in Africa,

Go to Nelson Social Studies

Figure 5.14

Providing services such as housing and transportation can be a challenge when a city experiences rapid population growth. In what ways might poor transportation facilities affect a city's economic development?

Rural Inhabitants "Vote with Their Feet"

Changes in food production, transportation, and industrialization are pushing people out of rural areas and pulling people toward cities. Just as people make choices when they vote, people who choose to move to the cities are voting to leave their rural homes. People leave rural areas for different reasons in developed and developing countries.

Fact File

The urban population of developing countries jumped from 304 million people in 1950 to 2.2 billion people in 2006. What factors push people from rural areas and pull them to cities in developing countries?

Figure 5.15

People choose to leave their homes in rural areas for different reasons in developed and developing countries. Suppose you live in a rural area. What factors might pull you to a city? What might encourage you to stay in the rural area?

Comparing Why People Leave Rural Areas in Developing and Developed Countries

Factors Pushing People to Cities in Developing Countries	Factors Pushing People to Cities in Developed Countries
High birth rates—Too many children are born for small farms to support.	*Low birth rates*—Populations in rural areas are dropping as birth rates reach record low values.
Small farms—Farms are divided into smaller and smaller plots as new generations inherit family farms. The divided farms are too small to support the families that own them.	*Large farms*—Farmers are using bigger, better machinery to farm more and more land. Advances in technology mean that fewer workers are needed in rural areas. This results in fewer jobs.
Few economic opportunities—Unemployment rates in rural areas are high. Unemployment in rural areas is often caused by large corporations buying up small subsistence farms for large-scale cash crops.	*Few economic opportunities*—Unemployment rates in rural areas are high. Unemployment in rural areas is often caused by the closing of services and businesses due to low demand from a shrinking population.
Natural disasters—Earthquakes or volcanic eruptions cause serious damage in rural areas. People have to leave their homes and villages.	*Few services*—The scattered, shrinking population means that services like health care and education are often limited. People have to travel long distances to get them.
Violent conflicts—War and other political upheavals affect land use.	*Little excitement*—Urban places seem more exciting than rural areas. Cities seem to offer more cultural, recreational, and entertainment services than rural areas.

Megacities

Another aspect of urbanization is the growth of very large urban areas. "Megacities" have spread out over the countryside, swallowing up farmland, towns, and cities. Megacities are found in both developed and developing countries. However, urban growth is happening more rapidly in developing countries. That makes urbanization a more urgent problem there. Massive urban areas such as São Paulo, Shanghai, and Mexico City have to cope with serious human and environmental problems. These issues include the following:

- poverty
- loss of farmland for food production
- air and water pollution
- traffic congestion
- lack of services such as electricity, water, sewage, and garbage disposal

- overworked **infrastructure** (structures and systems that a society needs to work well, such as roads and bridges, hospitals, schools, electricity)
- access to food, water, and housing

Developed countries struggle with similar challenges. However, the wealth that is found in their megacities means that they have more financial and people resources to help solve their problems. For example, taxes paid by citizens help to run hospitals and schools, and keep water systems operating.

Fortunately, in most developing countries (except China), the rapid growth of megacities is starting to slow down. In developed countries, there will be little growth, if any, in megacities.

Figure 5.16

This highway in Los Angeles shows some of the challenges of expanding the infrastructure of cities to meet the growing demand. Notice how the expressway overlaps the older grid pattern of city streets.

1. Imagine that you are a young person growing up in a rural area in Africa or Asia. Using information in this section, write a journal entry about making the following decision: Should you go to a large city, or stay in your home area?

The "Greening" of Cities

Around the world, people have started working to reduce the harmful impacts of cities. They want to make cities more resource-efficient and less polluting. Urban geographers and planners have offered the following ideas:

- Create mixed land uses so that people can live, shop, work, and enjoy their leisure time all in the same area. This will reduce the need to drive.

Figure 5.17

In a well-planned city, homes, schools, workplaces, and recreational centres are all within easy walking distance. Do you think this is a good way to live? Why?

- Make it easier for people to walk, bike, and take public transit so that they will not need to use their cars so often.

Figure 5.18

To encourage people to leave their cars at home, some Toronto buses have been equipped with bike racks. Passengers ride their bikes to and from their bus stops, then take their bikes the rest of the way by bus. Why would a city want to encourage people to use bicycles instead of cars?

- Encourage builders to construct high-density, affordable housing for people in all economic groups.

Figure 5.19

Houses that are close to the street and to one another create a sense of shared space and community. How might this type of housing help to prevent cities from spreading onto nearby farmlands?

• Restore and protect natural environments, such as woodlots, rivers, and wetlands, in cities.

Figure 5.20

People have made efforts to protect local environments so that natural systems in cities can work better. How could students in your school take action to protect the natural environment in your community?

• Support local agriculture and community gardens within cities.

Figure 5.21

By buying foods produced locally, city dwellers can buy less imported food. Why is this desirable?

• Promote recycling. Take steps to conserve energy and water, and to reduce waste and pollution.

Figure 5.22

Recycling and reducing waste can help to ease the impacts of cities on the environment. How can we use technology to help make cities "greener"?

AFTER READING

1. Look back at the questions you wrote for Before Reading question 1 on page 108. Write answers for the three questions you made up. If this section did not answer your questions, identify sources where you might find more information.

2. List four things that citizens can do to help make cities more sustainable.

3. Some people argue that, environmentally, large cities are disasters. Do you agree or disagree? Use the strategy outlined in GeoSkills on page 115 to give your opinion on this statement.

GeoSkills

Making an Informed Decision

Plan for Rouge Park pits green against greens

by Nicole Baute

It will be trees—and not subdivisions—that ultimately put some of the Toronto area's final farmers out of business. Two very important ideas of our time are going to be fighting against each other: land conservation and the local food movement.

The Rouge Park Alliance, which includes the Toronto and Region Conservation Authority, all levels of government, and a few other organizations, approved a seven-year rehabilitation plan for the park. This parkland includes the Toronto Zoo and protects a large portion of the Greater Toronto Area's rare green space. This plan allows for about 700 hectares of land to be converted from farmland and struggling natural area to lush forest and meadow. The program is to start in 2009.

The Rouge Park Alliance sees this program as a way to have a significant green corridor from the Oak Ridges Moraine to Lake Ontario. It will allow for a wider range of native wildlife species and improve the water quality of the lake and river. They see this program as a final opportunity, as the rest of the city has already been urbanized. It will also open up the land for a variety of recreational and educational opportunities.

This land is not unused space; in fact, it has been used for farming since the early 1800s. The land was expropriated (taken over by the government) in the 1970s, to make way for a new airport that was never built. But, many farmers have been renting the land to continue to grow local food. With global food shortages, high gas prices, and a growing awareness of the benefits of buying local foods, this idea seems to be short-sighted. As Fred Pike, a local farmer, says, "I think they think it's wasteland, that it's not being used, so that's why there's not much of an uproar, because trees are good—but I don't think they're good if you're taking agricultural land out of production."

Dale Reesor's family has been farming in this area since 1804. He currently farms about 360 hectares of soybeans and sweet corn, which he sells locally. He can't say for sure if he would be able to continue farming if he loses more land to the Rouge Park Alliance project.

The Toronto and Region Conservation Authority stresses that maintaining an agricultural presence in the park is a priority, especially with the growing awareness of the environmental benefits of local food. The general manager of Rouge Park says they do not see agriculture competing with naturalization. They are both needed in a large urban area. The farmers are concerned that not enough land will be set aside for agriculture, thus making it very hard for them to make a living off of their farms.

The plan will cost $5 million and the Rouge Park Alliance is looking for funding in order to begin this project as quickly as possible. The first phase will occur between 2009 and 2011.

Figure 5.23

How many different points of view can you identify in this newspaper article?

GeoSkills

Making an Informed Decision *(continued)*

LITERACY TIP

Newspaper Articles

A newspaper article should present facts without bias. It should answer the 5 Ws and 1 H questions. It has the following parts:

- headline—tells what the article is about and attracts the reader's attention
- lead—one or two sentences that tell the reader what happened, and "hook" the reader into wanting to know more
- background information— gives more details
- quotations—present specific points of view or opinions about the issue or event
- conclusion—one or two sentences about what might happen because of the event

Using the information in this article, suggest a solution that will protect the Rouge Park region.

To choose the best solution, you must identify the criteria you will use to make your final decision. Criteria are the standards you will use to judge the situation and the options. In this case, you must find a way to protect the Rouge Park region in a sustainable way that considers both the environment and the economic needs of the people.

Step One

To make an informed decision, look at all sides of the problem. In this case, several groups of people have an interest in the Rouge Park region. You can use an organizer to help you see the different perspectives.

Complete a chart like this one in your notebook.

Who	Wants/Needs	Effects on Rouge Park
The Rouge Park Alliance		
Local farmers		
GTA residents		

Step Two

Think about the points you put in your chart. Then, suggest a way to improve the Rouge Park region. Remember that you cannot please everyone. However, your plan should have some benefits for all the groups involved. Most important, your solution should protect the environment.

Step Three

Write a paragraph explaining your plan for protecting the Rouge Park region. Describe how you arrived at your decision. Be prepared to discuss your ideas in a group.

CASE STUDY

Mexico's Maquiladora Zone

Industrialization has come to Mexico in a big way! "Maquiladora" is a Spanish word for foreign-owned factories that make goods to be exported to the United States. The maquiladora zone is a strip of land along Mexico's border with the United States. More than 3000 factories have been built there to provide American consumers with the products that they want. Most of these factories are owned by large American transnational corporations, such as Ford, General Motors, Fisher Price, and Mattel (see Figure 5.24).

The manufacturers have come to the maquiladora zone because they can pay Mexican workers lower wages. Workers in the factories often make as little as US$1 an hour. About 60 percent of the workers are young women. Employers can pay females less money in Mexico, and they will still work in poor conditions. Most jobs are assembly-line positions that require few skills.

Reasons to Locate in the Maquiladora Zone

Wages—Hourly wages paid to Mexican workers are much lower than the wages paid to American or Canadian workers.

Work hours—In Mexico, the standard work week is 48 hours. In Canada and the United States, the average work week is 40 hours or less.

Transportation costs—Goods can be moved by road or rail transport to markets all over North America. This keeps production costs low.

Costs of production—The Mexican government has programs to keep start-up and operating costs low.

Figure 5.25

Foreign companies gain important advantages by locating in the maquiladora zone. What are some advantages of the zone for Mexico?

Mexico welcomes foreign manufacturers in this zone because they create jobs—over 1 million, or about 17 percent of all jobs in Mexico. The maquiladora factories produce 45 percent of the country's exports.

Figure 5.24

This map shows the location of the maquiladora zone in Mexico. The foreign-owned factories were built in the 105 kilometre-wide zone inside the Mexican border to keep transportation costs as low as possible. The zone impacts economic activities on both sides of the border. How do you suppose this changed life in border towns?

The Maquiladora Zone in Mexico

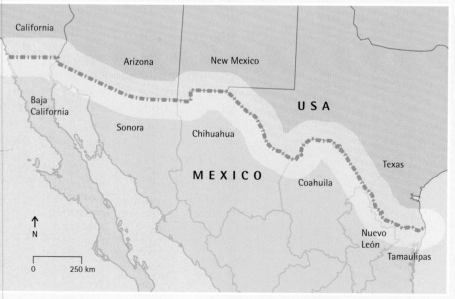

CASE STUDY

Mexico's Maquiladora Zone *(continued)*

Fact File

The maquiladora zone was set up in 1965. Foreign companies were offered large tax breaks as long as their products were immediately exported to the United States. Why do you suppose companies had to export their products right away to get tax breaks from Mexico?

Figure 5.26

In the maquiladora zone, jobs are usually on assembly lines. Why do you suppose workers stay at these jobs when wages are so low?

The maquiladora zone has drawn hundreds of thousands of Mexican workers to the region. The workers find homes in the fast-growing *colonias* (neighbourhoods) in the maquiladora zone. However, living conditions are poor. Workers often live in crowded huts, without water or proper toilet facilities. The manufacturers pay no local taxes, so no schools or social services like daycare are made available to families.

Concern is growing about the state of the environment in the maquiladora zone.

- Many of the factories use toxic chemicals. Manufacturers make little effort to destroy them properly after use.
- The increased population is overwhelming the sewage and waste-handling facilities.

Chemical and human waste threaten the environment in the maquiladora zone.

 1. Identify advantages and disadvantages of the maquiladora zone for Mexican workers, the country of Mexico, and transnational corporations. Record your ideas in a chart with these headings:

2. Explain how the maquiladora zone connects to the three main ideas covered in this chapter: industrialization, urbanization, and transportation. Write three sentences in which you state the connections.

	Advantages	Disadvantages
Mexican workers		
Mexico		
Transnational corporations		

Knowledge and Understanding

1 In your own words, define each of the following terms. Explain how each term is connected to urbanization, industrialization, or transportation.

   a) port renewal

   b) globalization

   c) transnational corporation

   d) megacity

2 This chapter is about the connections between industrialization, urbanization, and transportation. Draw a web organizer to show at least seven links between urbanization, industrialization, and transportation. Label factors that affect these areas on the connecting arrows. Your web organizer should begin like this:

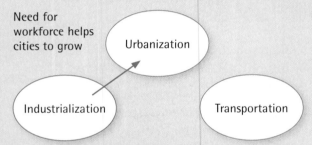

Need for workforce helps cities to grow

Urbanization

Industrialization

Transportation

Inquiry/Research and Communication Skills

3 Imagine you are a member of a family that has been living in a rural farming village in a developing country. Your family cannot make ends meet on your small plot of land, so you are talking about moving to a city to try to find work. You think about the good and bad points about your home in the rural area, and what you imagine the city will be like. Record your ideas in an organizer like the one below. Make sure that you have at least one point in each part of the square.

Good Points about Rural Areas	Bad Points about Rural Areas
•	•
•	•
Good Points about Urban Areas	**Bad Points about Urban Areas**
•	•
•	•

4 Investigate one megacity that is experiencing rapid growth. Choose from the following:

   • Mexico City, Mexico
   • Beijing, China
   • Shanghai, China
   • Mumbai, India
   • Cairo, Egypt

   a) Make up three questions about how rapid growth has affected this city.

   Use the Q-Chart (question chart) example at the bottom of this page to help you make up your research questions. Connect the W words on the left with the action words on the top to make up questions (for example, What is...? and What did...?).

   As you move down the column of W words and across the row of action words, you will create more open-ended questions. (How would...? and Why might...? are open-ended questions. What is...? and Who did...? are closed questions.)

   b) Research answers to your questions. Use an organizer to record details about the megacity.

   c) Share what you have learned about the city. Choose from one of the following options:

   • Make a PowerPoint presentation. Include visuals such as maps and graphs.

   • Write a news report about the challenges facing the megacity. Make sure to use the standard format for newspaper reports. (See the Literacy Tip on page 115.)

   • Create an informative poster summarizing your findings.

	is	did	can	would	will	might
What	→					→
Who						
When						
Where						
How						
Why						

Cities of 10 Million People or More, 1950, 1975, and 2000

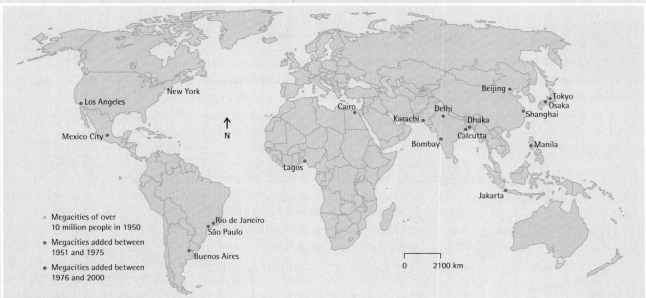

Figure 5.27

This map shows cities of 10 million people or more that existed in 1950, 1975, and 2000. Why might it be useful to identify the megacities of the world?

Map, Globe, and Graphic Skills

5 Examine the map in Figure 5.27 showing cities of 10 million people in the world in 1950, 1975, and 2000.

a) Record the number of megacities in each year, using a table like the one below:

Continent	1950	1975	2000
North America			
South America			
Europe			
Africa			
Asia			
Australia			
Total			

b) Describe the patterns of megacities that your table shows. You should be able to identify patterns where growth has taken place, and where there has not been growth.

c) Predict how many megacities there will be in 2025. To do this, draw a line graph using the total number of megacities for the three years shown. Put the years on the horizontal or *x*-axis of your graph: 1950, 1975, 2000, and 2025.

On the vertical or *y*-axis, use an interval of two: 0, 2, 4, 6, and so on. Extend the vertical axis so that you can determine the number of megacities for 2025. Plot the total number of megacities for each year on your graph. Use a ruler to connect the points and extend the line for the next time interval. Read the number of megacities that you predict on the vertical axis.

d) Use what you know about the connections between urbanization, industrialization, and transportation to explain the patterns that you identified in b), and the prediction you made in c).

Application

6 Imagine you are a world leader. The United Nations has asked you to design guidelines to help other leaders tackle the problem of rapid urban growth. You need five guidelines altogether. The first two are shown below. Make up three more.

Guidelines for Dealing with Rapid Urban Growth
- Protect the natural environment.
- Everyone should be able to find or make a safe home.

UNIT 2

Economic Systems

IN THIS UNIT

- describe the characteristics of different types of economic systems and the factors that influence them, including economic relationships and levels of industrial development
- use a variety of geographic representations, resources, tools, and technologies to gather, process, and communicate geographic information about regional, national, and international economic systems
- compare the economies of different communities, regions, or countries, including the influence of factors such as industries, access to resources, and access to markets

1 People do many different jobs to earn money. What are some of the jobs your friends and family do? Do they do them just to earn money?

2 Technology has changed the way we do things. What are some new technologies you use that were not available at the time this photograph was taken?

3 All people need clothes and other basic necessities. Where do many of the clothes we buy come from? Why do they come from these places? What other things do people need?

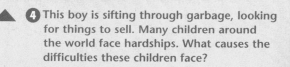

4 This boy is sifting through garbage, looking for things to sell. Many children around the world face hardships. What causes the difficulties these children face?

5 Not everyone in Canada enjoys the benefits of a good life. Why is there poverty in such a wealthy country? ▼

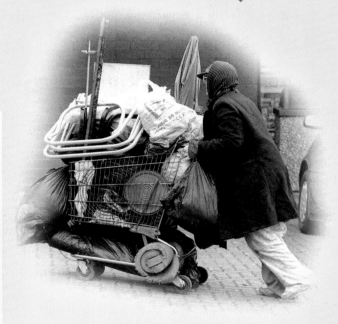

6 Everything is connected. How many businesses can you think of that were involved in producing the hamburger this boy is eating—from the very beginning to the point where it is ready to eat? How does producing the hamburger affect the environment, especially the rainforests? ▼

Imports to Canada, 2007

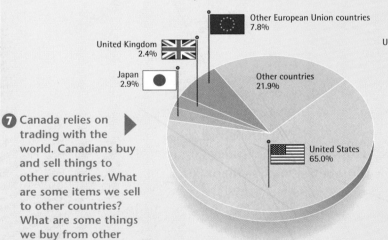

Other European Union countries 7.8%
United Kingdom 2.4%
Japan 2.9%
Other countries 21.9%
United States 65.0%

Exports from Canada, 2007

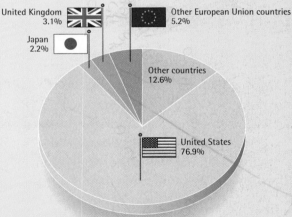

United Kingdom 3.1%
Japan 2.2%
Other European Union countries 5.2%
Other countries 12.6%
United States 76.9%

7 Canada relies on trading with the world. Canadians buy and sell things to other countries. What are some items we sell to other countries? What are some things we buy from other countries?

8 Research and development are important in all fields. How do high-technology industries that produce innovations like the Canadarm or new vehicles like the Smart Car help all Canadians?

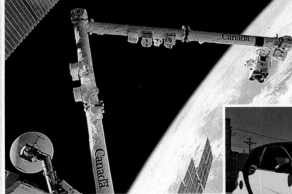

6 Economic Activity and Economic Systems

KEY VOCABULARY

agricultural revolution
capital
economic activity
economic system
factors of production
gross national product (GNP)
Industrial Revolution
material wealth
mixed economy
non-material wealth
quality of life
Stone Age

Living Better

1. Make a t-chart. Write the heading My Needs on one side, and My Wants on the other side. List up to seven items in each column. Then, compare your list with a classmate's.

2. What does the word *economy* mean to you? Look at the photographs in this chapter and select one photograph that best illustrates economy or economic activity to you. Explain why you chose this photograph.

Imagine what life would be like if people did not have to work. The idea of spending our days doing whatever we like might seem pleasant. However, in reality, life would be terrible if no one worked. There would be little or no food or shelter, and no computers, TV, or other things that make our lives comfortable. Humans must work to have a better **quality of life**. The work that people do is called **economic activity**. Economic activities include the following:

- extracting, refining, and using natural resources
- making goods such as household appliances for people to buy; providing services, such as legal and medical services

The purpose of economic activity is to meet our needs and wants.

Figure 6.1

Work is part of the human experience. It is also an economic activity. In what ways are these firefighters engaged in economic activity?

The Beginnings of Economic Activity

The earliest economic activity focused on getting food. The **Stone Age** lasted until about 11 000 years ago. During that time, humans wandered in tribal or family groups, hunting animals for food and picking nuts, berries, and fruits.

About 12 000 years ago, people began to grow their own food crops and raise their own animals. In other words, they began to domesticate plants and animals. This was the start of an **agricultural revolution**. Having a reliable supply of food improved people's lives. They spent less time looking for food, and had more time for other activities. The demands of growing crops and herding animals also encouraged people to remain in one location, so villages and towns began to develop.

Figure 6.2

Native American women herd sheep in Arizona, U.S.A. Herding domestic animals is an ancient form of agriculture. It is still done in some parts of the world. Can you think of an advantage and a disadvantage of this type of life?

Agricultural technology improved with the invention of the plough, the tractor, and better farming techniques, such as irrigation. (See Figure 6.3.) This led to even better lives for people. The new technology improved crop yields and food quality, and it also resulted in better methods for storing, transporting, and selling food.

Some Advances in Agricultural Technology

a) Foot plough

b) Simple plough

c) Iron plough

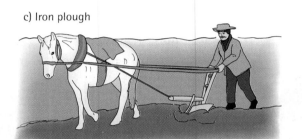

d) Plough pulled by tractor

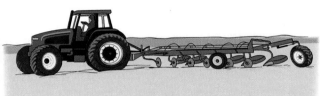

The technological changes gave people time to do other things besides produce food. They could become craftspeople, and work with metal, wood, or cloth. They could teach, develop laws, practise medicine, and lead their growing communities. This freedom led to key developments, such as the ability to write. People began to understand how technology could improve their lives.

Figure 6.3

Agricultural technology has improved over the years. It takes fewer people to produce food now than it did in the past. How have the advancements in agricultural technology *not* represented an improvement? (Think about use of fossil fuels, soil degradation, the employment of fewer people, and so on.) How might agricultural technology improve to address these concerns?

1. Why did the earliest forms of economic activity deal with food, rather than some other product or activity?

2. Examine Figure 6.3, which shows changes in how farmers prepared the land to plant crops. Use a chart like the one below to analyze the changes. In the Consequences column, suggest ways in which the change might have affected the farmer, farm life, and the nation.

Agricultural Change	Description of the Change	Consequences of the Change
From foot plough to simple plough		
From simple plough to iron plough		
From iron plough to plough pulled by tractor		

Modern Economic Activities

Modern economic activities started around 1700 CE. A second agricultural revolution took place at that time. Farmers began to apply new scientific ideas to producing food. They started to use new machines and equipment. This spurred the development of manufacturing. By the 1800s, the **Industrial Revolution** had started. This revolution dramatically changed economic activities. Fewer people were needed to produce food, so many moved to cities to find work in the new factories there.

Cities became the focus for economic activities during the Industrial Revolution. Urbanization occurred, as much of the population moved from the countryside to the cities. Cities that were built on manufacturing or transportation quickly grew. People found work not only in factories, but also in stores, banks, insurance companies, theatres and restaurants, and many other places.

Today, economic activities include many different types of services and professions. Few jobs now are directly linked to producing food or providing other basic needs, such as shelter and clothing.

Figure 6.4

In the early 1900s, manufacturing grew in Canada. Large numbers of people moved from rural areas to cities to work in factories. Suggest some advantages cities offered people at that time.

LITERACY TIP

Creating Flow Charts

A flow chart is a drawing that uses arrows to connect key events to their consequences. At the top, identify a main event. In the next boxes, summarize each consequence.

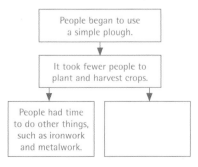

People began to use a simple plough.

It took fewer people to plant and harvest crops.

People had time to do other things, such as ironwork and metalwork.

1. Review the definition of *economic activity* on page 122. Name five economic activities that you have performed in the past few days. Explain why you consider each one to be an economic activity.

2. Using the information in this section, make a flow chart to show how the new technologies used in agriculture led to urbanization.

3. Identify two changes in economic activities that resulted from the development of technology.

Measuring Economic Activity

1. Read the subheadings in this section and create a statement in your own words to predict what you will be learning about.

Economic activity is meant to improve people's lives. Clearly, there have been great improvements over human history, beginning with the Stone Age. Your parents and grandparents can probably point to changes that brought improvements within their lifetimes. Geographers, economists, and sociologists are some of the scientists who study economic change. They need to measure what has changed and by how much. Understanding change in economic activity can lead to the following:

- more improvements in the future
- fewer negative impacts of economic activity, such as pollution and child labour

What Is the Value of Work?

The difficult part of measuring economic activity is deciding what to measure. Figure 6.6 shows many different types of economic activities. Not all of them can be measured in dollars and cents. It is fairly easy to measure formal economic activities. These are jobs where money is paid, usually as fees, wages, or profits. Governments spend a good deal of time and energy measuring these activities because they base taxes on these figures. It is harder to measure informal economic activities. Often people try to avoid having the government count and measure their activities. Informal economic activities include criminal activities, private yard sales, and bartering. Bartering occurs when people exchange things of value. An example would be trading car repairs for painting a house.

Figure 6.5

Economic activities have improved worldwide. However, people in some regions have not benefited as much as most Canadians. What economic activity does this child seem to be doing?

Figure 6.6

This chart shows the four categories of economic activities in a country. Private sector activities are those carried out by individuals and businesses. Public sector activities are paid for by governments. They include health care and education. Which of the four categories do you think creates the most wealth in Canada?

The Four Categories of Economic Activities

All the Wealth of a Country			
"Money" Economy			"Non-Money" Economy
Formal Economy		Informal Economy	Unpaid Activities
Private Sector (Businesses and corporations)	Public Sector (Governments, including education and health care)	(Crime, tax avoidance, yard sales, and so on)	(Child rearing, housework, volunteer work, shopping, and so on)

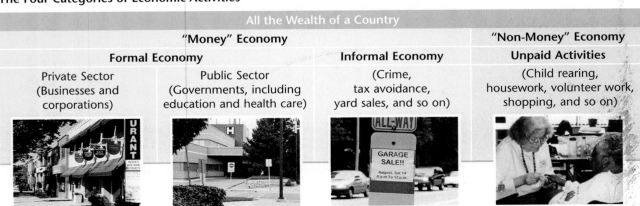

To learn more about volunteering in your community,

Go to Nelson
Social Studies

Unpaid economic activity is also hard to measure. What is the economic value of looking after a younger brother or sister, or an elderly grandparent? Many jobs people do around the home improve their living conditions. However, it is unpaid work, so its value is difficult to measure.

1. Use the information from this section of the chapter and what you already know about the economy to show how the activities for each pair of terms would be the same and different.

Economic Activities	Ways That the Economic Activities Are the Same	Ways That the Economic Activities Are Different
Money economy and non-money economy		
Formal economy and informal economy		
Private sector and public sector		

2. Explain why unpaid activities, such as volunteering and doing work inside the home, are considered economic activities.

What Makes a Better Life?

We often describe economic activity as producing more goods and services to make people's lives better. These goods and services are our **material wealth**. Without question, some of these goods and services help people to live longer, more comfortable lives. Automobiles, for example, are important because they give us more choices in how we live and what we can do. However, automobiles also have negative consequences such as pollution and traffic congestion.

Material Wealth of Canadians, 1990 to 2006

Appliance or Product	Ownership in 1990 (%)	Ownership in 1997 (%)	Ownership in 2006 (%)
Air conditioners	24.4	29.1	48.1
Dishwashers	42.0	48.5	57.7
Home computers	16.3	36.0	75.4
Microwave ovens	68.2	86.2	93.9
Telephones	98.5	98.6	94.1
Televisions	99.0	99.1	99.0
Video recorders	66.3	84.7	82.0

Figure 6.7

This table shows some products that made up the material wealth of Canadians from 1990 to 2006. Why might some appliances or products have little growth over time?

Expenditures per Household in Canada

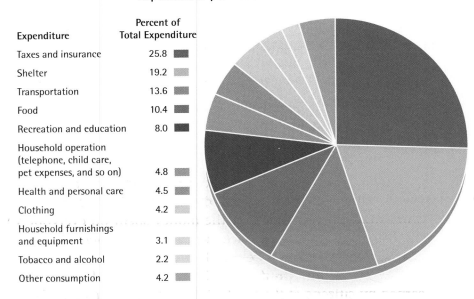

Expenditure	Percent of Total Expenditure
Taxes and insurance	25.8
Shelter	19.2
Transportation	13.6
Food	10.4
Recreation and education	8.0
Household operation (telephone, child care, pet expenses, and so on)	4.8
Health and personal care	4.5
Clothing	4.2
Household furnishings and equipment	3.1
Tobacco and alcohol	2.2
Other consumption	4.2

Figure 6.8

This circle graph shows how the average Canadian household spent their money in 2006. That year, the average household's income was $67 736. Identify two facts in this table that you find interesting.

LITERACY TIP

Reading a Circle Graph

A circle graph, also called a pie graph, shows the parts that make up a whole. When reading a circle graph, look for the following information:

• title

• individual sections and their sizes

• labels on each section (these tell what the section represents; they may include a percentage)

Circle graphs make it easy to compare the sizes of the sections.

Our lives can also be improved by **non-material wealth**. These improvements cannot be seen or measured as easily as goods and services. An example is the protection of human rights in a society. Human rights improvements may be important to our satisfaction with our lives, but it is hard to measure their economic value.

When measuring economic activity, we need to consider more than just material wealth. People are most satisfied when they have both material and non-material wealth. It is when we have both types of wealth that we can say we have a high quality of life.

DURING READING

1. Examine the categories that make up the parts of the circle in Figure 6.8. List the top three categories that contribute the most to people's material wealth. Explain your choices to another classmate. Compare lists with your classmate, and discuss any differences between them.

2. Identify three factors that contribute to your non-material wealth. Explain how these factors improve your quality of life.

Figure 6.9

Achieving and protecting equality in society is an important goal for many people in Canada. What are these First Nations people asking for? Why are they demonstrating with placards?

Fact File

In 2006, the lowest annual family incomes were in Newfoundland; the average there was $50 500. Families in the Northwest Territories had the highest annual incomes in Canada. The average was $88 800. However, the cost of living is very high in the Northwest Territories. This fact must be considered with the high annual income. What would make the cost of living so high in the Northwest Territories?

Figure 6.10

This table compares the average gross domestic product for people in selected countries. How might average incomes affect material and non-material wealth for people in different countries?

Measuring the Wealth of a Country

Most measures of economic activity look only at the formal sector of the economy. A number of ways are used to measure economic activity and wealth. One common way is to look at incomes—how much money people earn per year. This shows how much people have to spend on goods and services. In Canada, in 2006, the average income of households was $67 736 per year.

Two other ways are commonly used to measure economic activity:

- The gross domestic product, or GDP, measures the value in dollars of all the goods and services produced *in the country* in one year. Money earned outside the country is not counted. In other words, if you added up the money spent on everyone's rent, groceries, Internet service, dentists' fees, phone bills, and the like, the total would be the GDP.
- The **gross national product**, or **GNP**, measures all the wealth earned by citizens *of the country* in one year, no matter where it was earned.

These two measurements are often expressed as per capita values to make them more meaningful. For example, in 2007, Canada's GDP was $1 432 000 000 000. Our GDP per capita (per person) was $43 116.

The Average Gross Domestic Product for People in Selected Countries

Country		Gross Domestic Product (billions of US$, 2007 estimate)	Population (2008)	GDP per capita (US$, 2007 estimate)
Australia		$908.8	20 601 000	$44 114
Bangladesh		$72.4	153 547 000	$471
Brazil		$1 314.0	191 909 000	$6 847
Canada		$1 432.0	33 212 696	$43 116
China		$3 251.0	1 330 045 000	$2 444
Egypt		$127.9	81 714 000	$1 565
Spain		$1 439.0	40 491 000	$35 539
United Arab Emirates		$192.6	4 621 000	$41 679

1. Suppose you are an economics expert and someone has asked you to define the term *quality of life*. What definition would you give?

2. Look at Figure 6.10, which shows the gross domestic product for selected countries.

   a) China has the highest GDP, but it has a relatively low GDP per capita. Suggest how that is possible.

   b) The United Arab Emirates has a relatively low GDP, but it has a relatively high GDP per capita. Suggest how that is possible.

   c) GDP per capita provides clues about the quality of life in a country. Look at Canada's GDP per capita in Figure 6.10. How might your quality of life change if your country had a GDP per capita of only $471, as Bangladesh does?

GeoSkills

Creating a Comparative Bar Graph— Analyzing Countries' Earning and Spending Patterns

A comparative bar graph is a useful tool to compare economic activity and wealth of different countries. When creating a graph, remember TAPP—Title, Axes, Pattern, and Purpose. Use the following steps to create a comparative bar graph using the data below:

Step One

Read the *title* and the data in Figure 6.11 to begin to understand what you will graph.

Revenues and Expenditures for Select Countries, 2007

Country	Revenues— How Much a Country Earns in a Year ($ billions)	Expenditures— How Much a Country Spends in a Year ($ billions)
Australia	321.3	309.1
Bangladesh	6.8	9.8
Brazil	244.0	219.9
China	674.3	651.6
Egypt	35.1	44.9
Spain	589.2	556.5
United Arab Emirates	58.9	38.1
United States of America	2 568.0	2 730.0
Canada	569.3	555.2

Figure 6.11

Some countries do not earn enough money in a year to buy what they need for their people. They have to borrow money from other countries. Which countries are spending more than they earn?

Step Two

Using graph paper and a ruler, create your two axes, and label them.

- On the *x-axis* (horizontal), write labels for all the countries listed above. Each country will need two separate bars, so each country must be four squares wide. Leave one space before you begin your next country bar. You will need 44 squares.

- Label the *y-axis* (vertical) $ Billions. Start with a 0 at the bottom of the axis, and go up by 50s— 0, 50, 100, 150, 200, and so on—until you reach 700. At 700, draw a wavy line that goes up two squares. (A wavy line on a graph indicates that there is a large gap between the two numbers. If you were to continue to go up by 50s, you would not have enough room to complete the graph.) Then, start at 2550 and continue by 50s to 2750. You will need 20 squares.

Step Three

Create a legend for your graph.
- Blue = Revenues
- Red = Expenditures

Place a title at the top of your graph.

Step Four

Look at the data and begin to create your *pattern*. Start with Australia and the revenue data.
- Begin by drawing a horizontal line at approximately $321 billion on the *y-axis*. The line will be two squares wide.
- Use your ruler to draw two vertical lines down to the bottom of your graph. Colour your first bar blue to represent revenues.
- Now, draw a horizontal line at approximately $309 billion on the *y-axis*. This line should be two squares wide and directly beside the blue bar. This bar will represent expenditures and should be coloured red.
- Follow step four for the remaining countries.

Step Five

Determine the *purpose*. Ask yourself the following questions:
- What does this graph tell me about these countries' spending habits?
- What problems might a country like the United States or Egypt face if they keep spending this way?
- How might a country's spending patterns affect its material and non-material wealth?

GeoSkills

Creating a Comparative Bar Graph (continued)

Figure 6.12

Use the data in Figure 6.11 to begin creating your graph.

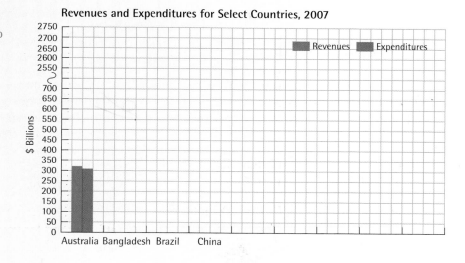

Revenues and Expenditures for Select Countries, 2007

Australia Bangladesh Brazil China

Economic Systems

BEFORE READING

1. a) Who in your household decides how money is going to be spent?

b) Describe your own role in deciding how the money is used.

c) What happens when family members disagree about spending money in your household?

2. In what ways are families and countries similar when considering how money is to be earned and spent?

Figure 6.13

What decisions have you made in the last month about how to use your limited resources?

People try to improve their quality of life through economic activities. There are many goods or services we would like to have to improve our lives. Unfortunately, we only have limited resources to obtain these goods and services. We have only so much time, energy, and money. Like a family that must decide what to buy with its income, a society must decide what to do with its limited resources. This is why we need **economic systems**.

Deciding on an Economic System

An economic system is the system of how goods and services are produced, distributed, and consumed in a country. Each nation must answer the following economic questions:

- What resources are available? Economic systems organize the economic resources that are available. These resources include land, **capital**, labour, and technology. These four resources are known as the **factors of production**. (See Figure 6.14.)
- What goods will be produced, and how much will be produced? Each country must consider its economic resources as it decides the answers to these questions.
- How will these goods be produced? To answer this question, each country must consider its factors of production.
- Who will produce these goods?
- For whom will the goods be produced?
- How will the finished products be distributed?

All economic decisions are really about how the society is arranged in order to use resources to produce goods and services that meet people's needs and wants. No two societies develop identical economic systems because the factors of production vary from place to place.

The Factors of Production

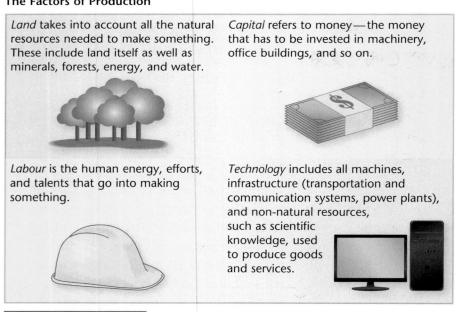

Land takes into account all the natural resources needed to make something. These include land itself as well as minerals, forests, energy, and water.

Capital refers to money—the money that has to be invested in machinery, office buildings, and so on.

Labour is the human energy, efforts, and talents that go into making something.

Technology includes all machines, infrastructure (transportation and communication systems, power plants), and non-natural resources, such as scientific knowledge, used to produce goods and services.

Figure 6.14

Because factors of production vary from place to place, economic systems around the world vary a good deal. In what ways does your school demonstrate these four economic resources?

Fact File

North Americans make up less than 5 percent of the world's population, but consume more than 30 percent of its resources. What does this tell you about the factors of production that are available to us?

Figure 6.15

The government of Canada, led by the prime minister, makes many decisions that affect the country's economy. How is the government of Canada chosen?

LITERACY TIP

Reading Complex Webs

In a complex idea web, look for titles or captions that will help you identify the main topic. Find the main web (often in the centre), and follow the arrows to the smaller webs. Then, follow the arrows from the subwebs to the outside bubbles. These bubbles contain specific information related to ideas in the smaller webs. Finally, in your own words, summarize all the information in the idea web.

Who Decides?

In different economic systems, different people and groups have a say in the decisions that are made. Decisions can be made by the following:

- the government in power
- industries and businesses in the country
- important institutions, such as religious organizations or environmental groups
- individuals

In each economic system, these groups play different roles. In one country, government may be very important; in another, business may be most influential. When we look at the differences in economic systems, we can learn much about societies and what they value.

Who Makes Decisions in Economic Systems?

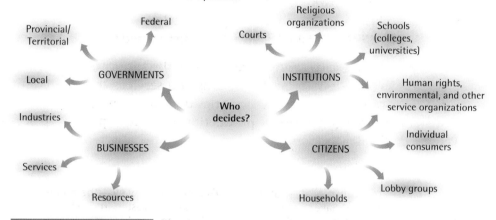

Figure 6.16

A wide range of groups and individuals help to determine a country's economic system. Where do you fit into your economic system?

1. The factors of production are land, capital, labour, and technology. Write out this list, and beside each item, write another label that means the same thing. Explain why you chose the labels you did.

2. Copy the chart below into your notebook. As you read the next section, complete the chart. Rank the four categories of decision makers for each type of economic system. Give the most important category a rank of 1, and the least important a rank of 4.

Economic Systems	Economic Decision Makers			
	Governments	Industries and Businesses	Institutions	Citizens
Traditional				
Command				
Market				
Mixed				

Types of Economic Systems

The world's economic systems can be grouped into four categories. These are shown in Figure 6.17.

The Four Categories of World Economic Systems

Type of Economy	Economic Decision Makers	Example
Traditional (no modern national example exists)	Decisions are based on what was done in the past. People organize their economic choices by following their custom and tradition.	Decision makers might consult Elders about constructing a new road. They would decide based on the traditions of the people.
Command (e.g., North Korea)	A central authority (such as a dictator or government) makes decisions. Citizens must accept these decisions; personal choices are few.	If the people in power decide that building a road will meet their needs, the road will be built.
Market (e.g., Singapore)	All members of the society make decisions, based on their own needs and desires. Citizens make economic choices buying and selling in the marketplace. Governments have only a small involvement in the economy.	A corporation would decide whether a road should be built, based on whether a profit could be made. Governments might or might not be involved.
Mixed (e.g., Canada)	The mixed economy has some characteristics of both command and market economies. Governments, businesses, and individuals are all included in economic planning and decision making.	Before deciding to construct a road, governments, businesses, and consumers would discuss it. The decision could be made by any or all of these groups.

Figure 6.17

These are the types of economic systems we find around the world. Which type of system gives individuals the most freedom in making economic choices?

Traditional Economies

Few traditional economies exist today. Those that remain are in remote areas where there are few outside influences. These societies are based on subsistence farming or hunting and gathering. They meet most of their needs by their own activities. Members have little economic contact with outsiders.

Traditional economic systems are slow to change. Since decisions today are based on what was done in the past, economic choices vary little from one generation to the next. It may be difficult for traditional systems to adapt to economic change. Contact with outsiders often leads to rapid change and conflict within the society. New economic ideas may not fit the old ways of life.

Figure 6.18

People in traditional societies often try to hang on to their ways of life. In 2008, this indigenous group in the Amazon travelled to protest a proposed hydro-electric dam on the Xingu River in Brazil. Why might the dam be seen as a threat to the people?

Figure 6.19

Robert Mugabe is the dictator who has ruled the African country of Zimbabwe for many years. He controls the economy of the country, and he has caused it to be one of the poorest on the continent. Many people have left Zimbabwe and called for other countries to help remove Mugabe. Who is the target of this protester's message? Why?

Command Economies

Cuba is an example of a command economy. The communist government in power makes all the economic decisions for the country. The decisions are supposedly for the good of all the people. Citizens are organized to accomplish the government's plans. The communist government decides the following:

- which natural resources to develop
- which manufacturing industries to emphasize and what should be produced
- how much money to spend on the military

The government owns all factors of production and controls all industrial sectors of the economy. Citizens have jobs, and it is the government's responsibility to look after their needs.

In reality, most command economies do not work very well since the citizens usually want more freedom and better human rights. In Cuba, the government restricts basic human rights, such as freedom of expression and the right to own property.

Market Economies

In market economies, the government has very little involvement. Factors of production are largely owned by individuals and businesses. Profit is the guiding force. Businesses make decisions about what to produce based on what they think consumers—the market—want to buy. If businesses make the right decisions, they make money. If they make the wrong decisions, they lose money. Consumers influence what gets produced in a market economy. The United States is an example of this type of economic system.

Poverty occurs in all economic systems, but profit-driven market economies create a greater division between those who make a profit and those who do not. The successful people become wealthy and meet their economic needs. Those who do not have the abilities, opportunities, or luck to be successful can have difficulty meeting even basic needs. These societies tend to be divided into "have" and "have not" groups. This division can cause conflict within a country.

Figure 6.20

In market and mixed economies, businesses use advertising to try to get consumers to buy their products or services. Look at the ads in this photo of Piccadilly Circus in London, England. Which business names do you recognize?

Mixed Economies

Most countries have a **mixed economy**. Mixed economies have some elements of both command economies and market economies. The goal of a mixed economy is to enjoy the benefits that both command and market systems offer, but to avoid their weaknesses. Elected government representatives, businesses, and citizens all have roles to play in managing factors of production.

The Continuum of Government Control in World Economies

The Range of Economies Around the World

Command Economy	Mixed Economy	Market Economy

Increasing Government Control

Example: North Korea, Cuba	Example: Canada, United Kingdom	Example: Singapore, United States

Figure 6.21

This diagram shows that there is a continuum of economies, with more or less government control. In which type of economy would you prefer to live?

In mixed economies, governments often own resources or businesses that serve the public good. The Canadian Broadcasting Corporation (CBC) is an example. We see national communication as so important that the government must have a key role in providing it. Governments also set policies for the public good that affect businesses and consumers. For example, they require packaging to be in both official languages. Privately owned businesses make decisions within those policies. Businesses' actions are based on their understanding of the market and what consumers want. Consumers make choices that influence the success of businesses. Canada is a good example of a mixed economy.

AFTER READING

1. Write a four-sentence paragraph in which you use the following words clearly to show their meaning: *labour, command, economic system, consumers, tradition.*

2. Answer five questions that compare market and command economies. Make a comparison chart like the one below, and complete it using ideas from this section. Two questions have been provided to get you started. Construct the remaining three questions. Consider the factors of production and the decision makers as you make up your questions.

Questions	Market Economies	Command Economies
Who makes economic decisions?		
What roles do consumers play in economic decisions?		

Figure 6.22

In mixed economies, one of government's roles is to make sure that products meet high standards of performance and safety. In Canada, government inspectors visit meat packing plants to ensure that all the meat we eat has been properly stored, processed, and packaged before it is shipped.

BE A GLOBAL CITIZEN

Made in Canada?

If someone were to ask you where your food came from, what would you say? Many people would respond, "It came from the grocery store." However, we need to look further. We need to ask more questions:

- Who grew the food?
- Who canned or packaged it?

These questions are growing more important as more Canadians want to support their local food producers and help reduce pollution caused by transportation.

What does "Made in Canada" mean? The provincial and federal governments recently tackled this question. They learned that many Canadians looked for the "Made in Canada" label when buying a product. They did so in order to support the local economy and keep their money in Canada...or so they thought. But the "Made in Canada" label actually meant that as little as 51 percent of the production costs were earned in Canada, while the ingredients could come from anywhere in the world. For example, manufacturers imported apple juice concentrate from China, for about one-fifth the cost of Canadian concentrate. By adding water to it in Canada, the manufacturer was able to label it "Made in Canada."

Labels are changing. As of January 1, 2009, food can only be labelled "Product of Canada" if all major ingredients and labour to produce it came from Canada. The apple juice concentrate mentioned above will have to use a label that says "Made in Canada from imported ingredients."

Ensuring proper labelling is one role of the government in a mixed economy like Canada's. Another role is to ensure that we have safe food. In 2006, Canadians ate $430 million worth of food from China. Food products coming from

Figure 6.23

In a mixed economy, advertising is used to influence consumers' habits. Many buyers want locally produced fruits and vegetables in order to support nearby growers.

China are not tested for contamination as carefully as Canadian products, and this can lead to trouble. For example, in the spring of 2007, thousands of dogs and cats fell ill or died after eating pet food that contained contaminated wheat gluten from China. Many people believe that the Canadian government needs to do more testing of these food products.

Canadians are trying to be more educated consumers. They do not want to buy fruit that travelled thousands of kilometres to get to their tables. Consumers are looking at ways to help the Canadian economy. They are also becoming more knowledgeable about food safety. By educating yourself and your family about labels and doing research into the sources of your food's ingredients, you will be a better consumer and make choices that are good for the environment and the economy.

CASE STUDY

North Korea—A Command Economy

North Korea has a command economy that is tightly controlled by a communist government led by a strict dictator. The government's policy has always been one of national self-reliance. That means that the country strives to meet all its economic needs on its own. These policies can be seen in several ways.

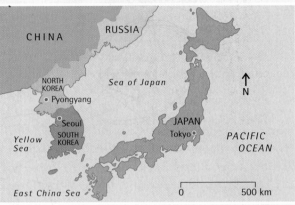

Northeastern Asia

Figure 6.24

North Korea is located in the northeastern part of Asia. What countries are its neighbours?

Comparing North Korea, South Korea, and Canada

Characteristics	North Korea	South Korea	Canada
Area	120 540 km²	98 480 km²	9 984 670 km²
Population (2008)	23 479 100	48 379 392	33 212 700
Life expectancy at birth	males 69.4 years females 75.1 years	males 75.3 years females 82.2 years	males 78.7 years females 83.8 years
Infant mortality rate	21.9 deaths per 1000 live births	4.3 deaths per 1000 live births	5.1 deaths per 1000 live births
GDP per capita (2007)	US$1900	US$25 000	US$38 400
Telephone lines in use	980 000	23 905 000	21 000 000

Fact File

North Korea spends about 32 percent of its GDP, or US$6 billion a year, on the military. It is the most militarized country in the world. Its standing army of active troops is the fourth largest in the world. Nearly one out of every four citizens serves in some military capacity.

Figure 6.25

This table compares North Korea, South Korea, and Canada. Using this information, how would you describe the quality of life in North Korea?

Agriculture

The government collectivized agriculture. This means that farmers no longer own the land. Farmers now work together on co-operative farms, pooling their time and resources. The government distributes the output from the farms to the rest of the country.

Industries

The government owns most industries. National planning committees decide which goods the factories will produce. They have given priority to building an industrial base to meet the country's needs for such items as machinery and transportation equipment. This industrialization strategy gives consumer goods a low priority, and few are available.

Military Spending

North Korea has long been suspicious of its neighbour South Korea. This has caused the country's government to spend a great deal of money on its military. North Korea considers a strong military the best defence against possible attack by South Korea or its allies. As a result, military equipment is one of the largest industrial sectors in the country.

CASE STUDY

North Korea — A Command Economy (continued)

Economic Problems Faced by North Korea

North Korea's farms have been unable to feed the country's growing population. Since the 1990s, crop failures and floods have resulted in widespread hunger and famine. The government has been reluctant to accept food aid from the rest of the world. More than 2 million people in North Korea have died of hunger since the 1990s.

Because of the government's focus on self-reliance, the North Korean economy has become isolated from the world. Manufacturing companies have not had to compete with other companies, and they are inefficient. The few products they make are of poor quality.

Much of North Korea's energy has come from imported oil. As the nation's wealth declines, it cannot afford to buy oil, and power supplies have become unreliable. The government's efforts to develop nuclear power caused other countries to fear that North Korea was trying to make nuclear weapons.

North Koreans recognize that their material wealth and quality of life are poor in comparison with their neighbours and other countries in the region. However, they can do little about it as long as the country is run as a command economy.

Figure 6.26

Political factors have caused hunger in North Korea.

Figure 6.27

This satellite image shows the Korean Peninsula. South Korea is in the lower half and North Korea is in the upper half. Because of unreliable energy supplies, few people in North Korea have electricity at night. How do you think this lack of power affects the country's economy?

The Future

Widespread famine, a very weak economy, and dissatisfaction among the people suggest that change is necessary in North Korea. However, the Communist Party that controls the country refuses to change its approach. The future for the command economy of North Korea does not look bright.

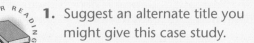
AFTER READING

1. Suggest an alternate title you might give this case study.

2. Imagine you are a farmer in North Korea, and the government has collectivized your farm. Write a diary entry describing your feelings and opinions about this event.

3. In your opinion, what is the greatest problem that North Korea faces with its command economy? Explain your choice in a short paragraph. Don't forget to use the 4 Cs of persuasive writing: *catch* the reader's attention; *commit* to your opinion; *convince* the reader, and *close* your argument.

Knowledge and Understanding

1. Identify two advantages and two disadvantages for each of the following types of economies:

   a) command economies

   b) market economies

   c) mixed economies

2. Suppose you have discovered a cure for the common cold. You want to make your cure available to as many people as possible. Describe how you would do this under each of the four economic systems described in this chapter.

3. Explain why Canada's economy can be called a mixed economy.

4. Draw a diagram to illustrate the difference between material and non-material wealth. Review the information about these two ideas on pages 127–128 before you begin.

5. Copy the following table into your notebook. Match the terms in column A with the appropriate terms in column B.

Column A	Column B
agricultural revolution	bartering
informal economic activities	national earnings
material wealth	based on custom
gross domestic product	domesticated plants
capital	investment money
traditional economy	goods and services

Inquiry/Research and Communication Skills

6. What are the world's wealthiest and most impoverished countries?

   a) Research to find the 10 wealthiest countries and the 10 most impoverished countries in the world, as measured by gross domestic product per capita. You can visit your school library and look for this information in encyclopedias, world almanacs, international atlases, and other reference books.

   b) Locate and label the 10 wealthiest and 10 most impoverished countries on an outline map of the world.

   c) Create a title for your map that explains its purpose to the reader.

   d) Create a legend for your map. Pick one colour to represent the 10 wealthiest countries and another colour to represent the 10 most impoverished countries. Colour your map.

   e) Look for patterns in your map. Describe the patterns you observe about the locations of these countries.

   f) Look at world maps such as Land Use and Oil Production in the Map Appendix. Look for patterns that relate to resources for the 10 wealthiest countries and for the 10 most impoverished countries. Describe the patterns you observe about the resources of these countries.

   g) How might resources influence economic success?

7. Which of the four types of economic systems do you think is the most effective way to organize an economy? In making your decision, think about questions such as the following:

   - In which system are resources shared most equally among citizens?

   - In which system is there the least waste of resources?

   - In which system is there the greatest freedom of choice?

   - In which system are citizens best able to meet their personal needs and wants?

   (Refer to GeoSkills on page 115 in Chapter 5 for information on making an informed decision.)

   Design a poster to advertise the system that you think is best. Your poster design should include a bold image and a brief and clear message that will leave a lasting impression on the reader.

Map, Globe, and Graphic Skills

8 How do you compare the quality of life in the three different types of economic systems? What factors would you need to look at? Examine the table in Figure 6.28. This table shows statistics that demonstrate the quality of life of people in countries with different types of economies: command, market, and mixed.

a) Use the information in Figure 6.28 to construct a comparative bar graph. (Refer to GeoSkills on pages 130–131.) Pick three different statistics to plot for all six countries. Remember to look at statistics that show material as well as non-material wealth.

b) Use the following questions to help you look for patterns on the comparative bar graph you created and record your observations:

- Why might command economies have no data or very little access to modern communication technologies?

- Is there any one country that stands out as very different from the rest? Why might this be so?

- Which countries are similar? Why might this be so?

c) What conclusion can you make about the quality of life in different types of economic systems?

Application

9 Review the economic questions that all societies must answer. (See page 132.)

a) Explain how Canada as a society has answered these questions.

b) Explain why Canada's economy can be called a mixed economy.

10 Choose a country that interests you. Do research to find out what type of economy it has. Use the following questions as a guide for the evidence you will need to decide if the country is a command, market, or mixed economy:

- Who makes the economic decisions? (See page 132.)
- Who owns the factors of production?
- What role do consumers play in economic decisions?
- What role do businesses play in economic decisions?
- What role do governments play in economic decisions?

You will have to base your decision on the evidence that you collect, so it is important to organize your evidence carefully. Use an organizing chart like the one below.

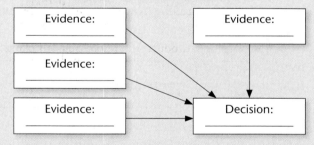

Figure 6.28

Use the data in this table to compare the quality of life in command, market, and mixed economies.

Comparing Quality of Life in Command, Market, and Mixed Economies

		Birth Rate/ 1000 ppl	Life Expectancy	Infant Mortality/ 1000 ppl	Cell Phones/ 100 ppl (2006)	Internet Users/ 100 ppl (2006)
Command economy	North Korea	14.61	72.2	21.86	n/a	n/a
	Cuba	11.27	77.27	5.93	1.2	2.1
Market economy	Singapore	8.99	81.89	2.3	109.3	39.2
	United States	14.18	78.14	6.3	77.4	69.1
Mixed economy	Canada	10.29	81.16	5.08	52.5 (2005)	67.9 (2005)
	United Kingdom	10.65	78.85	4.93	116.4	56.0

7 World Patterns of Wealth and Poverty

IN THIS CHAPTER

- explain how economic resources influence the economic success of a place
- use maps to identify economic patterns
- compare key characteristics of a number of developed and developing countries

KEY VOCABULARY

colonization
colony
commodity
desertification
export
foreign debt
Sahel

Who Is Wealthy and Who Lives in Poverty?

BEFORE READING

1. What does a person need to have in order to be considered wealthy? What does it mean when a person is considered to live in "poverty"? Discuss these two questions with a classmate. Together, write definitions for "wealth" and "poverty."

When you think of families who live in poverty, where do your thoughts go first? Do you think of families in developing countries? When the media shows images of poverty, do the people tend to live in developing countries? Around the world, people usually think of Canada as a "have" country—a country with a high standard of living and opportunities for all. However, it is important to remember that poverty is not only an issue for developing countries. It is also an issue for Canada and other developed nations. Measurements of standard of living present average scores. Many Canadians live below the average. In 2004, about 3.5 million Canadians lived in poverty. Why is it that some people have so little while others have so much? This chapter looks at patterns of wealth and poverty around the world. As you learn about the economic conditions that create these patterns and differences, think of how these conditions might apply to Canadians who live in poverty.

All countries have economic resources—land, labour, capital (money), and technology. However, not all countries have an equal share of these resources. Also, countries organize their economic resources in different ways. Some countries, like Canada, have been able to organize their economies to benefit most of their citizens. Many of their citizens have material wealth and non-material wealth, such as protection for human rights and the environment.

Figure 7.1

How does your family's quality of life compare to the quality of life of this family in Afghanistan?

Other countries have not been as successful. People living in these countries have a low quality of life. When looking at the world as a whole, we can discover some distinct patterns.

Avoiding Miscalculations

Before we can identify economic patterns, we must decide how we will measure a country's economy. We might use an economic measurement, such as gross domestic product (GDP) per capita. GDP is the average of all the wealth in the country created in one year divided by all the people. The problem is that this figure is an average. It cannot tell us how much of the population actually enjoys a decent life. Figure 7.3 shows how misleading averages can be. What we need is a measurement that takes into account both the material and the non-material wealth of countries.

Figure 7.2

Even in wealthy countries like Canada, some people live in poverty. Why do you think this is?

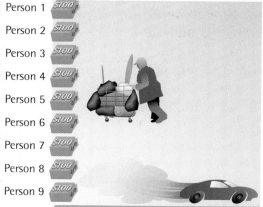

Incomes by Person

Person 1	$100
Person 2	$100
Person 3	$100
Person 4	$100
Person 5	$100
Person 6	$100
Person 7	$100
Person 8	$100
Person 9	$100
Person 10	$1100

Figure 7.3

This bar graph shows how averages can sometimes lead to misunderstanding about conditions in a country.

- There are 10 people in this society. The graph shows their incomes.
- The gross domestic product of this society (the sum of all the incomes) is $2000 (9 x $100 + $1100).
- The GDP per capita (per person) is calculated as GDP divided by the number of people, or $2000/10 = $200.
- According to our statistic, the average income in the country is $200, yet 9 out of the 10 people earn only half that amount. Averages can give a false measurement of conditions in a country.

Can you think of a situation in your life where averages do not tell the whole story?

Who Has the Good Life?

The Human Development Index (HDI) measures the average quality of life of a country's citizens. The United Nations introduced the HDI in 1990. It takes into account many factors, such as the following:

- people's ability to purchase food and other things they need to survive, such as clothing and shelter
- the availability and quality of education and health care

The best score a country can get in the Human Development Index is 1.0. This score would mean that a country is doing extremely well on all items measured by the HDI. Canada's score in 2005 was 0.961. This tells us that conditions were very good, but not perfect.

Fact File

For the decade from 1990 until 2000, Canada had the highest HDI score for eight of the years. Japan held the top spot the other two years. Based on what you know, why might Canada have slipped from its first place ranking? What could we do to improve our HDI ranking?

Highest- and Lowest-Ranked Countries Based on the Human Development Index

Highest-ranked Countries			Lowest-ranked Countries		
Rank	Country	HDI Score	Rank	Country	HDI Score
1	Iceland	0.968	168	Democratic Republic of the Congo	0.411
2	Norway	0.968	169	Ethiopia	0.406
3	Australia	0.962	170	Chad	0.388
4	Canada	0.961	171	Central African Republic	0.384
5	Ireland	0.959	172	Mozambique	0.384
6	Sweden	0.956	173	Mali	0.380
7	Switzerland	0.955	174	Niger	0.374
8	Japan	0.953	175	Guinea-Bissau	0.374
9	Netherlands	0.953	176	Burkina Faso	0.370
10	France	0.952	177	Sierra Leone	0.336

Figure 7.4

The chart shows the highest- and lowest-ranked countries on the Human Development Index in 2005. From which continent are the countries in the list of the lowest-ranked? From which continents are the countries in the highest-ranked? Why do you suppose no country has a perfect score of 1.0?

Fact File

The HDI is not just based on incomes. How do the following two examples prove this?

Country	HDI Score	GDP/Capita (US$)
Bahrain	0.866	$17 773
Chile	0.867	$7 073

GeoSkills

Creating a Circle Graph

Circle graphs show the different parts that make up a whole. When reading a circle graph, look at the title, the individual sections, and the labels to understand the information. When creating a circle graph, it is important to measure and label the individual sections correctly. To do this, you need a compass and a protractor. Follow the steps below to create a circle graph using the data provided.

Step One

Read the title and the data in Figure 7.5 so you begin to understand what you are going to graph.

Human Development Index (HDI)	Percentage of 177 Countries Ranked
High HDI	40%
Medium HDI	48%
Low HDI	12%

Figure 7.5

Use the data in this chart to create a circle graph.

Step Two

Using a compass, draw a circle on a sheet of paper. Draw an initial line from the centre point to the edge of the circle. Mark that line 0°/360°.

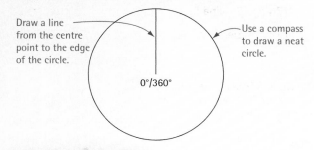

Figure 7.6

Always begin the first line for the first section of your circle graph at 0°/360°.

Step Three

Plot the data to create the sections of the circle graph.

- To plot the data, calculate the number of degrees within the circle for each of the three items. To find the number of degrees, multiply the percentage number by 3.6. This calculation will provide the correct number of degrees for each section.

  Circle = 360° = 100%
  Therefore 3.6° = 1%
  Calculate the sections:
  High = 40% × 3.6° = 144°

- Set your protractor on the line labelled 0°/360° and ensure the midline of the protractor is aligned with the centre point of your circle. Locate 144° on your protractor and mark it on the circle. Draw a straight line from the 144°-point to the centre of the circle. This is the first section of the circle graph. Shade this first section.

Repeat this step for the remaining two sections. Shade each section a different colour.

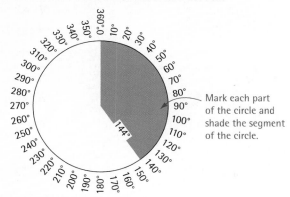

Figure 7.7

Mark each part of the circle and shade the segment of the circle a different colour, or a different shade of the same colour.

Step Four

To complete the graph, give it a title and add labels to identify each section of the circle and the percentage it represents.

Step Five

Determine the purpose of the graph. Ask yourself this question: What does this graph tell me about the countries of the world and how they are divided in terms of quality of life?

1. Calculate the range of scores for each of the lists in Figure 7.4. Why do you suppose the range is much larger for the lowest-ranked countries than for the highest-ranked countries?

2. Suggest two actions that a country could take to try to improve its HDI score. (Hint: Review the factors that are used to calculate the HDI, discussed on page 144.)

To learn more about HDI scores and rankings,

Go to Nelson
Social Studies

Figure 7.8

Average Human Development Index scores are shown for groups of countries for 2005. In what ways might low incomes help to produce low HDI scores?

Average Human Development Index Scores, 2005

HDI Category	HDI Average Score	Life Expectancy (years)	GDP per Capita (US$)
High (e.g., Canada, France, United States)	0.897	76.2	$23 986
Medium (e.g., China, Egypt, Jamaica)	0.698	67.5	$4876
Low (e.g., Rwanda, Sierra Leone, Zambia)	0.436	48.5	$1112

Figure 7.9

It takes more than just material goods to create a high quality of life. It also includes the expectation that life will be comfortable in the future, too. Having a strong education system is one way a society can help people ensure a high quality of life in the future. How does a strong education system contribute to strong economic resources?

Human Development Index and Selected Economic Statistics for Selected Countries, 2005

Country		HDI Score	Number of Physicians per 100 000 People	Number of Internet Users per 1000 People
Bangladesh		0.547	26	3
Brazil		0.800	115	195
Canada		0.961	214	520
Chad		0.388	4	4
China		0.777	106	85
Egypt		0.708	54	68
France		0.952	337	430
Jamaica		0.736	85	404
Russia		0.802	425	152
South Korea		0.921	157	684
Spain		0.949	330	348
Yemen		0.508	33	9

Figure 7.10

The Human Development Index and two other economic statistics are shown for selected countries for 2005. How do you think the two other statistics relate to the HDI score of a country?

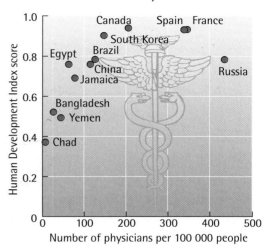

HDI Scores Compared to the Number of Physicians

Figure 7.11

This scatter graph is drawn using HDI scores and number of physicians for these selected countries. What pattern do you see in the graph?

AFTER READING

1. a) Using an atlas and an outline map of the world, locate and shade in green the 10 countries with the highest HDI rankings. (See Figure 7.4.) Shade in red the 10 countries with the lowest HDI rankings.

b) Add a title and legend to your map.

c) Describe the pattern of the countries shaded in green. Describe the pattern of the countries shaded in red. (Hint: Look at where these countries are found in the world.)

d) Based on this map, determine which regions of the world have a generally high quality of life. Which regions have a low quality of life?

2. Look at the Fact File on the bottom of page 144. Explain why a country with a high per capita income, such as Bahrain, and a country with a much lower per capita income can have similar HDI scores.

3. Use the scatter graph in Figure 7.11 to answer the following questions. With your finger, trace a "line of best fit." Refer to page 35 in Chapter 2 to review what the "line of best fit" tells geographers.

a) Is there a strong or weak correlation between the HDI scores and the number of physicians per 100 000 people?

b) Is there a negative or positive correlation between the HDI scores and the number of physicians per 100 000 people? Describe this correlation.

Explaining Poverty

1. a) With a partner, brainstorm for reasons why some people live in poverty. Consider people who live in poverty in all regions of the world. Share your ideas with another group and add any new reasons to your list.

b) In Chapter 6 on page 132, you learned that economic resources include the factors of production (land, capital, labour, and technology). Which reasons on your list relate to economic resources, or the factors of production?

c) How do you suppose the factors of production relate to how wealthy or impoverished people are in a country?

Many people live in poverty in the world. Figure 7.4 on page 144 shows countries with the highest and lowest scores on the HDI. It is important to remember that HDI scores measure the average quality of life of a country's people. Even in the countries with the highest HDI scores, many people live in poverty. There are many reasons why people may live in poverty:

- lack of educational opportunities
- lack of economic resources—land, capital, skilled labour, and technology
- lack of employment that will provide a living wage

A country must have economic resources in order for its people to enjoy high quality of life. Countries that receive the highest HDI scores also have strong economic resources. Those countries that receive the lowest HDI scores do not have the economic resources needed for economic success. Thus, most of their people live in poverty.

In this section, we will consider why most citizens of some countries do not share a high quality of life.

Looking at the Past

What happened in the past often affects what happens today. Most countries with a low quality of life, such as some countries in Africa and Asia, were once **colonies** of European countries. These European countries included England, Spain, Portugal, and France. They controlled the colonies.

The European countries set up governments and economies to suit their own purposes. Sometimes they made slaves of the local people. How were the Europeans able to do this? They had stronger technologies. In particular, their military equipment was more advanced and powerful. The Europeans controlled the colonies through military might.

LITERACY TIP . . . .

Mapping Important Information

When reading text with a lot of facts, you can use a web or concept map to identify and organize important information. For examples, see Figure 6.16 on page 133 in Chapter 6.

Fact File

An estimated 12 million African people were enslaved by Western countries between 1500 and 1865. Think about how many African people were enslaved. What would that number look like? Visualize almost the entire population of Ontario!

Figure 7.12

Figure 7.12

In the African slave trade, the young and strong were targeted by traders. Millions of young men and women were forced into terrible lives as prisoners. What might have been some impacts on African societies and economies?

LITERACY TIP

Cause and Effect

To understand why things happen, we need to look for cause/effect relationships. A cause is an action, event, or problem that makes something happen. The effect is the result of that action, event, or problem. Often an action, event, or problem can have many causes and many effects. Causes and effects can be both positive and negative.

Cause(s)   Problem   Effect(s)

Colonization changed local societies in many ways. The Europeans carried out these changes for the following reasons:

- to control the resources of the land
- to control the local people
- to "civilize" the local people by making them more like Europeans

The Europeans believed their culture was superior to the local cultures. Thus, they imposed their rule on others.

Figure 7.13

The slave trade was set up in a triangular fashion. Americans benefited from the captured labour force. Europeans benefited from the products that they bought and sold in the trade. How did the economic resources of the Europeans and Americans compare to the economic resources of the Africans? How did the Europeans and Americans use the Africans as an economic resource? (Think of the factors of production.)

The Triangular Pattern of the Slave Trade

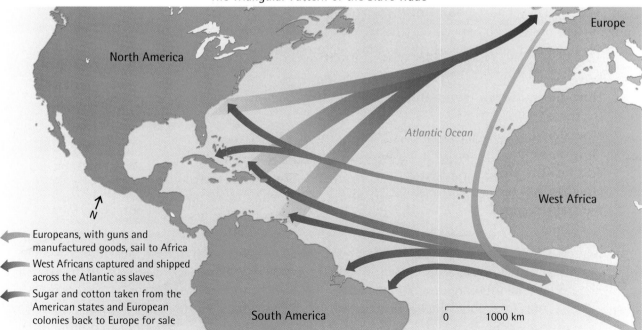

Europeans, with guns and manufactured goods, sail to Africa

West Africans captured and shipped across the Atlantic as slaves

Sugar and cotton taken from the American states and European colonies back to Europe for sale

Figure 7.14

This chart identifies how colonization by European powers affected people in the colonies. Why did the European powers work to create unequal distribution of land (including natural resources), labour, capital, and technology?

The Effects of European Colonization

Area of Change	Type of Change	Reason for Change	Impact of Change
Leaders	Old leaders, or leaders who resisted European expansion, were replaced by co-operative leaders. Or, no local leaders were allowed.	Europeans used their own leaders to take complete control of the people.	The people in the colonies had to develop skills in making political decisions when they began the movement to become independent countries.
Land and natural resources	The Europeans took the natural resources from the land in the colonies.	The Europeans wanted greater material wealth. They shipped the resources from the colonies back to industries in their own countries.	The people in the colonies did not develop their own industries.
Labour	The Europeans used people in the colonies as the labour force they needed to get and load natural resources for shipping from the colonies.	The Europeans wanted greater material wealth and power. They used people in the colonies as their forced labour. They gained control over the people and access to greater riches from the use of the colonies' natural resources.	The people in the colonies did not learn the skills or gain the knowledge they needed to create their own industries.
Technology	The Europeans used their more effective military equipment to control the people. The Europeans advanced their industrial technology in their homelands while they forced the people in the colonies to do their manual labour.	The Europeans wanted to use the colonies to gain more material wealth and power.	The people in the colonies did not have the opportunity to learn as the technology advanced in other countries.

When the colonies finally became independent, many had to begin from scratch. They had to build new social and political structures. Some of their old ways had been destroyed. Many newly independent countries have had difficulty organizing their economies. They faced questions such as the following:

- How do we use our own natural resources to produce products for trade?
- How do we get enough capital to build new factories?
- How do we get the farming technology we need to grow large and healthy crops?
- How do we get the technology we need to extract our own natural resources?

Fact File

Thirty-three African colonies became independent countries between 1956 and 1966.

1. What other questions would newly independent countries face? Create one question for each of the factors of production (land, labour, capital, and technology).

2. European powers went into other parts of the world, took over land for themselves, and enslaved the people. List two reasons they might have offered to explain why they thought they had the right to do that.

Weak Economies

European countries used the people in the colonies for unskilled labour. They needed workers to extract the natural resources and prepare them for shipping back to the European countries. The Europeans used their capital and technology to control the people in the colonies and take their natural resources to increase their material wealth. They did not invest capital or use their technology to develop industries or train skilled workers in the colonies. The Europeans used the colonies' economic resources of land and labour for their own profit.

European countries made no effort to build the economies of their colonies. Europeans felt that colonies had only the following economic purposes:

- to be sources of cheap raw materials for industries of the colonizing countries, including minerals, timber, spices, sugar, fish, and other foods
- to be buyers of goods manufactured in the colonizing countries, such as the tools to extract raw materials, fabrics, and farming equipment

People in the colonies had to sell to and buy from the colonizing country. They were not allowed to establish their own trade connections or develop their own industries.

No Trade Base

Because of colonization, many newly independent countries must rely on their natural resources. Their most important economic activity is extracting and selling natural resources such as sugar, timber, or minerals. Many countries are selling these **commodities**. Thus, there is a lot of choice for buyers. Tough competition means that prices remain low. This is good for the buyers of the raw materials. Who are the buyers? They are industries in the wealthier countries. They have the capital to buy the resources, and the skilled labour force and technology to manufacture these raw materials into products for trade.

Also, demand for resource commodities varies widely. Prices are unstable. One month prices might be high, but the next month they might be low. This makes long-term planning nearly impossible. Former colonies do not have industries and other economic activities to fall back on. While the European countries were profiting from the use of their labour and land, they were not developing their own economic resources. They now face great difficulties in building stable economies.

Figure 7.15

For the Costa Rican economy, bananas rank second only to tourism as the country's most important source of income. Which European country colonized Costa Rica and other countries in Central America?

No Manufacturing Base

Under European control, the colonies could not develop industries. When they became new countries, they had trouble setting up their own factories and businesses. They often did not have the capital or technical knowledge needed to compete with industrialized countries. With few manufactured goods to sell, these countries have few trade ties to the rest of the world. The following situations result:

- Their people earn lower wages.
- Their governments collect less money in taxes. Therefore, they have little to spend on things like education, hospitals, railways, and power plants.

Figure 7.16

This map puts countries into categories based on the amount of exports they have per capita. **Exports** are goods and services sold to other countries in order to earn income. Which countries have the highest exports per capita?

Country Exports per Capita

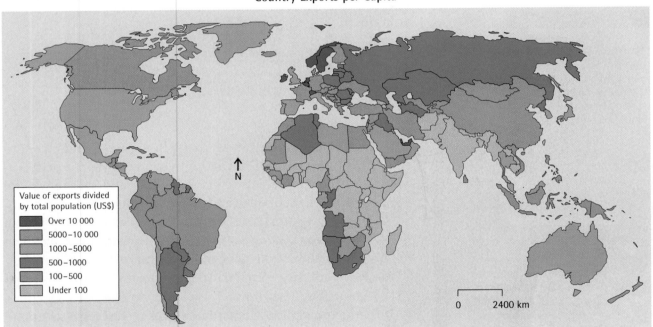

Value of exports divided by total population (US$)

- Over 10 000
- 5000–10 000
- 1000–5000
- 500–1000
- 100–500
- Under 100

0   2400 km

1. a) Use the following questions to help find the patterns in Figure 7.16:

- Which countries have the highest value of exports per capita?
- Which countries have the lowest value of exports per capita?
- What do countries need in order to produce exports to trade with other countries?

b) What can you conclude about the strength of the economic resources (the factors of production) in countries with the highest and lowest values of exports per capita?

c) Some countries in Africa have a wealth of natural resources, but the people still live in poverty. Based on what you have learned, why might this be the situation?

Paying Off the Debt

After independence, many former colonies tried hard to improve conditions for their people by doing the following:

- building schools and hospitals
- developing electricity
- developing factories
- improving roads

To do this, they borrowed large sums of money from wealthier countries. Everyone believed that these improvements would create new economic activity. They also believed that the **foreign debts** would be repaid in a few years. In some cases, countries borrowed money for less constructive purposes. For example, some used borrowed money to expand the military and build palaces for government leaders.

Unfortunately, many countries were unable to pay back their loans. In the 1970s and 1980s, world interest rates went up. The economies in the new countries did not grow as much as expected. Some countries had to borrow even more money just to keep their governments running. In the time since that money was borrowed, many countries have paid much more in interest than their original loans were worth.

The banks and other lenders pressure the borrowers to repay their loans. As they try to deal with their foreign debts, many countries have done the following:

- slashed spending on health and education—programs that would improve the quality of life for their people
- focused on producing goods they can export in more natural states (such as minerals, food, and forest products) to earn money, since they have not had the capital to develop manufacturing industries

These countries are struggling just to maintain their quality of life.

The Effects of Foreign Debt on Developing Countries

- Cuts to health care
- Reduced education spending
- Higher infant mortality rates
- Higher food prices
- More hunger
- Higher unemployment rates

Figure 7.17

As developing countries strive to repay their foreign debts, their people's lives are greatly affected. Which group in society will feel the effects of debt the most: the wealthy or those living in poverty? Explain your answer.

1. Explain how countries' weak economies led to high debts.

2. How do large foreign debts lead to even greater poverty in African countries?

Exploding Populations

Most countries with low qualities of life have rapidly growing populations. This occurs for the following reasons:

- There is a lack of education, especially for girls. Research has shown that educated women marry later and have fewer children. Without education, children do not develop the skills and knowledge to advance beyond unskilled labour.
- Children often work to help meet their family's needs. They may work on family farms, in factories, or on city streets. Often, families survive because of their children's incomes. In these cases, there is little reason to limit the number of children in a family.

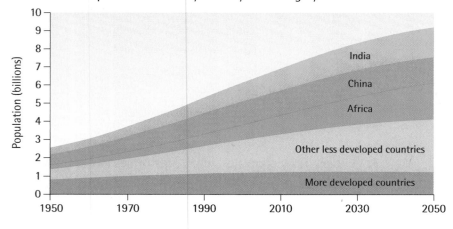

Figure 7.18

In many parts of the world, children must work to help support their families. This boy in Brazil is sifting through garbage, looking for items that can be reused or resold. What is the future for these children? What opportunities for economic success do these children *not* have?

World Population Growth by Country and Category

India

China

Africa

Other less developed countries

More developed countries

Figure 7.19

Over the next decades, most of the population growth of the world will be in India, African nations, and other developing countries. What will this population increase mean to the economic success of developing countries? How can they develop the economic resources they need to be successful in the global marketplace?

- Health care in developing countries is often poor. They do not have the capital, enough trained people, or the medical technology to provide the health care that is available in Canada. As a result, infant mortality rates are high. Because couples expect some children to die, they often have many children. These parents rely on their adult children to look after them in their old age.
- Birth control is often too expensive for couples in impoverished countries. Also, some societies and religions may forbid its use.
- In some countries, tradition and religious views encourage large families. Some governments encourage people to have more children because they can help create a strong military and economy in the years to come.

Rapid population growth is a challenge for developing countries. Not only do these countries have to try to meet the needs of more and more people, but they are also trying to overcome their history of colonization. They are struggling to develop their economic resources and to deal with foreign debt. On top of these challenges, they must share the economic resources they do have among a greater number of people. Lower quality of life often results.

The Cycle of Poverty

Figure 7.20

Limited economic resources contribute to all parts of the cycle of poverty. When families have limited economic resources, why do they often have many children? What future do children have who must work to support their families? How do limited economic resources contribute to poor health and high infant mortality rates? What might help break this cycle?

LITERACY TIP

Flow Diagrams

A flow diagram is a graphical method of presenting, describing, and analyzing a process. It includes small illustrations with explanations. These represent a series of steps. Arrows connect the illustrations to show the sequence of events.

1. How are economic resources (land, labour, capital, and technology) related to poverty and poor quality of life in developing countries?

2. Create a flow diagram to show how colonization, weak economies, foreign debt, and rapid population growth are linked together. Include at least five links in your diagram. (Refer to Figure 5.8 on page 103 in Chapter 5.)

BE A GLOBAL CITIZEN

Children Helping Children in Developing Countries

How would you feel if there were no school for you to attend? At first, you might be happy and enjoy the free time, but where would you socialize? What would you do all day? How would you learn to read, write, and think for yourself? What chores might your parents give you to do?

In many parts of the world, access to education is very limited. In fact, some children are not allowed to go to school because it costs too much, or because they are girls. Large numbers of children go to work instead of school because their families need the money.

One organization that is dedicated to helping children become educated is Free The Children. Free The Children is a worldwide organization. Canadian Craig Kielburger started it in 1995, when he was 12 years old. He organized 11 of his friends to begin to fight against child labour.

Today, Free The Children is the world's largest network of children helping children through education. More than 1 million young people are involved in 45 programs around the world. This organization has received the Children's Nobel Prize. It has formed partnerships with many school boards and with TV host Oprah Winfrey's Angel Network.

Free The Children knows that education can help children and their families break out of poverty. School is where social and economic development begins. Developing countries need strong education systems in order to keep improving economically. Free The Children uses its donations to build schools and education centres for communities that could never afford a school on their own. More than 50 000 children attend over 500 schools built by the organization.

Figure 7.21

Free the Children's partner organization Me to We offers International Volunteer and Leadership Trips to the Arizona–Mexico border region. Participants can experience life on the U.S.–Mexican border by volunteering at a primary school, a migrant shelter, and a fair trade coffee co-operative. What do you suppose are the most critical issues facing the people who live in this border region?

BE A GLOBAL CITIZEN

Children Helping Children (continued)

Figure 7.22

The Take Action! Summer Academies offer students the opportunity to develop leadership skills and explore social issues.

Your school or class could organize a fundraiser to help Free The Children build schools. Here are some of the costs involved in building a school:

- constructing the school building—$8500
- building a place for teachers to live—$1000
- buying textbooks—$100

Here are some other things you can do to help:

- Join Free The Children's partner organization Me to We
- Invite a speaker from the organization to talk to your class.

- Take part in Free The Children's leadership training program.
- Volunteer to help out overseas. Me to We takes young people on international volunteer and leadership trips in countries around the world. Groups travel to Ecuador, China, Kenya, India, and Arizona-Mexico.
- Take part in their Summer Academies offered across Canada.

To learn more about
Free The Children and Me to We,

Go to Nelson Social Studies

CASE STUDY

Poverty in the Sahel Region of Africa

Most parts of the Sahara Desert receive less than 100 millimetres of rainfall each year. This is about one-eighth the amount Ontario gets.

As you travel southward from the Sahara Desert, rainfall increases. At first, you would notice scattered clumps of grass and sparse shrubs. Soon the grass grows thicker, and scattered trees replace the shrubs. This vegetation zone is known as the **Sahel**, and it is one of the most impoverished parts of Africa.

Traditional Economic Activities

The Sahel region has a long history. In fact, civilizations existed in cities like Timbuktu (now in Mali) long before Europeans knew anything about the continent.

Early societies based their economic activities on the herding of goats, sheep, cattle, and camels. The animals grazed on grasses and small shrubs. Herds were moved throughout the year from one grazing area to another. The wet and dry seasonal cycles influenced their movements. This nomadic way of life ensured that no area was over-grazed. The vegetation in each area had time to renew itself before the herds returned. This sustainable way of life went on for thousands of years.

Because of their location on the edge of a great desert, the peoples of the sub-Saharan region became important traders. Camel caravans were formed in the communities for the long treks northward across the desert.

A New Way of Life

The traditional way of life in the region began to change with the arrival of Europeans in the late 1800s. To mark their land claims, the Europeans mapped out country boundaries. These boundaries prevented the nomadic people from travelling into neighbouring countries where they had gone for centuries. The national boundaries also made long-distance trading much more difficult.

Countries of the Sub-Saharan Region

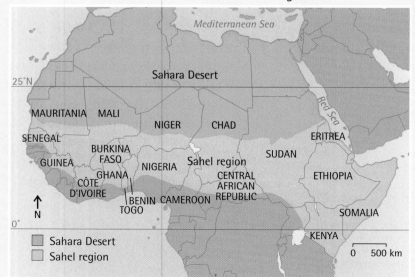

Figure 7.23

This map shows the countries of the Sahel region. Which countries have you heard about in the news?

CASE STUDY

Poverty in the Sahel Region of Africa (continued)

In addition, the Europeans encouraged farming. Arable lands were divided into small farms and plantations. The way of life changed. People became tied to particular locations. Herds began to overgraze this land and overuse water supplies. The result was food and water shortages in times of drought. The people drilled new wells to help solve the water shortages. These wells were sometimes funded by aid agencies like the Red Cross. With the improved water supply, people increased their herds. This led to more overgrazing.

Desertification

Overgrazing results in **desertification**. With plants eaten by herds, winds can easily blow away the thin soil. The lack of roots means that soil is washed away when it does rain. In the end, there is less vegetation and more infertile land that cannot grow crops or graze herds.

Searching for Economic Opportunities

Many of the economic problems of this area are caused by how the land is used. Most people are farmers. This is the case in the country of Chad. Even though only 3 percent of the land in Chad is arable, 80 percent of workers have jobs in agriculture. There are few other economic opportunities. Without jobs in industries or services, workers must remain farmers, earning very little and barely getting by from one year to the next.

It is difficult for industries to start in the area because of the very low income levels. Families have little money to spend on goods and services. As a result, few industries develop and workers do not develop the industrial skills that would help to attract factories making products for export. Corrupt governments and civil wars have also discouraged industries.

Conditions in the Sahel Region for Selected Countries

Country	Arable Land (% of total area)	Life Expectancy (years)	Population Below Poverty Line (%)	Literacy Rate (% of population who can read)
Chad	3	47.4	80	26
Ethiopia	10	55.0	39	43
Ghana	18	59.5	29	58
Kenya	8	56.6	50	85
Niger	11	44.3	63	29
Nigeria	33	46.5	70	68
Senegal	13	57.1	54	39

Figure 7.24

This chart shows statistics about conditions in selected countries of the Sahel. How do the life expectancy and poverty rates compare to those in Canada?

LITERACY TIP

Using Word Parts

When you come across an unfamiliar word, such as *desertification*, check to see if the word has a root word that you know. Then, check to see if a prefix or suffix has been added to the root word. Put the meanings of these two word parts together to create a definition of the new word. Often, you can use what you know about common root words, suffixes, and prefixes to help you figure out the meaning of new words.

continues...

Poverty in the Sahel Region of Africa *(continued)*

Figure 7.25

Aid agencies have helped construct wells in the Sahel to make the water supply more reliable. What effects might wells have on people's daily lives?

Looking to the Future

It is hard to be optimistic about the future of the Sahel region. The area desperately needs capital to invest in roads, electrical grids, schools, and health care. These factors are required for countries to industrialize and develop their economies. However, foreign agencies do not have much money to invest. The debt level is too high, and there are too many political problems in the area. The Sahel region is seen as a bad risk. In addition, governments in the wealthier countries have cut back on their foreign assistance programs. Thus, less aid is reaching African countries. This region faces a difficult future.

Figure 7.26

This schoolroom is in Mogadishu, the capital of Somalia. How would you describe conditions in this classroom?

CASE STUDY

Poverty in the Sahel Region of Africa *(continued)*

1. How has the lack of economic resources (land, capital, labour, and technology) contributed to the lack of economic success in the Sahel region of Africa?

2. A local organization has invited you to give a speech on the reasons for the poor economic success in the Sahel region. Write the speech, providing facts to support your ideas. (Refer to GeoSkills on page 246 in Chapter 11.)

3. The arrival of Europeans in North America caused many changes in the lives of Aboriginal peoples. Compare these changes with the changes experienced by the nomads from the Sahel due to European colonization. Record your ideas on a chart with the following headings: Changes That Are Similar; Changes That Are Different.

4. "The people of the Sahel region shouldn't expect us to help them with their problems. They should be able to look after themselves and not depend on charity." This is one opinion about giving assistance to other countries. Do you agree or disagree with this statement? Create a chart like the following to record your ideas:

Evidence Supporting the Opinion That We Should Give Aid to the People of the Sahel Region	Should We Give Aid to the People of the Sahel Region?	Evidence Supporting the Opinion That We Should Not Give Aid to the People of the Sahel Region
•		•
•		•
•		•
Decision:		
Reasons:		

Knowledge and Understanding

1. Make sketches, use cutouts from magazines and newspapers, or print pictures from the Internet to illustrate one of the following:

   - economic resources that give Canada a high quality of life compared to most other countries

   - lack of economic resources that contribute to the low quality of life of some people in Canada (for example, some Aboriginal peoples, homeless people, people living in ghettos, and so on)

   Add labels to your images and give your work a title. On the back of your work, explain why you chose each image.

2. Explain why colonization contributed to the poverty in African countries today.

3. In this chapter, you discovered that events in the past, such as slavery, allowed some countries to become wealthy while other countries became impoverished. Do wealthy countries now have a moral responsibility to help impoverished countries? Write a paragraph expressing your opinion. You could use the "point, proof, and comment" strategy. That is, introduce a point or idea, give proof such as facts, statistics, or examples, and end with a comment.

Inquiry/Research and Communication Skills

4. **a)** Tourism is a growing industry in some parts of the Sahel region. It has the potential to create good jobs. Using the Internet and other sources, name and describe five places in the region that are, or could be, important tourist destinations.

   b) On which economic resources would tourism be based in these five places?

   c) Suggest two actions that tourism leaders might take to encourage more tourists to come to the region.

   d) List two negative impacts that tourism could have on the Sahel region.

5. Research what has been done to try to help developing countries reduce their foreign debts. To guide your research, make up questions using the 5 Ws + 1 H strategy. (Refer to the Literacy Tip on page 41 in Chapter 2 and GeoSkills on page 246 in Chapter 11.) Choose two of your questions and research the answers. Organize your findings in a display, such as a poster or a PowerPoint presentation.

Map, Globe, and Graphic Skills

6. The Human Development Index describes the conditions for people in countries for a particular year. Conditions can change from year to year. Figure 7.27 shows how the HDI scores have changed for selected countries over time.

Human Development Index Scores for Selected Countries, 1975–2005

Country	1975	1980	1985	1990	1995	2000	2005
Canada	0.873	0.888	0.911	0.931	0.936	0.946	0.961
Greece	0.841	0.856	0.869	0.877	0.882	0.897	0.926
Mexico	0.694	0.739	0.758	0.768	0.786	0.814	0.829
China	0.530	0.559	0.595	0.634	0.691	0.732	0.777
Pakistan	0.367	0.394	0.427	0.467	0.497	0.516	0.551
Kenya	0.466	0.514	0.534	0.556	0.544	0.529	0.521
Rwanda	0.337	0.385	0.403	0.340	0.330	0.418	0.452

Figure 7.27

Human Development Index scores are provided for selected countries from 1975 to 2005. Why do most countries' scores rise over the time period?

a) Draw a multiple line graph to show the trends in the scores.

b) On the *x*-axis (horizontal) of your graph, label the years at five-year intervals, starting with 1975. You will need 30 squares.

c) The *y*-axis (vertical) should be labelled HDI Scores. Start with 0.0 at the bottom, and go up by 0.100s every 2 squares—0.0, 0.100, 0.200, 0.300, and so on—up to 1.0. You will need 20 squares.

d) Plot the points for each country and join the dots with a coloured line. Use a different colour for every country and add each one to your legend.

e) Describe the patterns or trends that you see in the lines. Note which countries have changed the most and which have changed the least. Identify countries that do not seem to fit the overall trends.

f) Offer two suggestions for why some countries have experienced reduced HDI scores over some time periods.

7 **a)** Use the data in the chart in Figure 7.10 on page 147 to construct a scatter graph relating the number of Internet users per 1000 people and the countries' HDI scores. (Review GeoSkills on pages 36–37 in Chapter 2 before you begin.) The vertical axis of the graph will show the HDI score. The horizontal axis will show the number of Internet users. Use Figure 7.11 as a model.

b) Write two conclusions that you can draw from the pattern you observe on your scatter graph. (Review Steps 7 and 8 on page 37 in Chapter 2.)

Application

8 A scale such as the Human Development Index is calculated using several factors. This type of scale gives a more accurate picture of a situation than just one measurement. What measurements would you include if you wanted to determine a Students' Quality of Life Index for Canadian students? List five items you would measure, and give reasons for your choices.

9 Suppose you are a government official in one of the countries in the Sahel region. How would you improve access to economic resources for people of the Sahel?

10 Free The Children uses the slogan, "Children helping children." Design an advertisement to encourage Canadians to donate tools and money to countries in the Sahel region. Your advertisement must persuade the reader to become involved. It has to get the reader's attention. You can try to make the reader emotionally involved, or you can use excitement or "star power." Another way to catch the reader's attention is by using facts and figures. Include an explanation for any symbols and images you use in your advertisement.

11 The Canadian government has just hired you to help improve the economies of developing countries. Make two suggestions. For each one, write a short paragraph explaining why your ideas would lead to better qualities of life in these countries.

8 The Structure of Economies

IN THIS CHAPTER

- explain how economic resources influence the economic success of a place
- identify and give examples of the three major types of industries —primary, secondary, and tertiary—and describe how these industries have developed
- compare the economies of some top trading nations and explain the reasons for their success
- describe how an industry affects the economy of a region
- compare key characteristics of a number of developed and developing countries

The More Things Change ...

1. Think about all the different vehicles that you see on the streets and roadways every day. Now, think about the different categories that we use to talk about these vehicles, such as minivans, pickup trucks, and so on. List as many categories as you can.

2. Why do you suppose we make up categories when we think about vehicles? How do categories help us make decisions?

3. Figure 8.1 outlines economic activities in Canada 125 years ago. How would you change each point to outline economic activities in Canada today?

Suppose you could travel back in time and see what your community was like in the past. You set the dial of your time machine for 125 years ago. When you emerge, the difference in your community's appearance surprises you. People are dressed in old-fashioned clothes. Buildings are smaller, and—this is most striking—there are no cars. You begin to focus on your mission. Your job is to learn about past economic activities in and around your community. You record your observations on your high-tech wristband computer.

Finally, you return to the present and analyze your data. You see that economic activities have changed greatly over the years. You need to understand these changes.

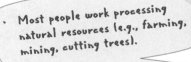

- Most people work processing natural resources (e.g., farming, mining, cutting trees).

- Most families are self-sufficient in food and buy only a few household items, such as sugar, tea, and cloth, at stores.

- There are few shops. My community has only a general store, an inn, and a few other smaller shops.

- Most goods are made by craftspeople in small workshops. There is a blacksmith, a cooper (barrel maker), and a cobbler (shoemaker) in this community.

Figure 8.1

Economic activities in Canada 125 years ago were much different from today's. What was the most important economic activity in your area 125 years ago?

Ask yourself the following questions:

* What caused such changes?
* Have all communities and societies gone through changes like these?
* Which economic activities decline over time?
* Which economic activities become important?

Answering these questions will take more research.

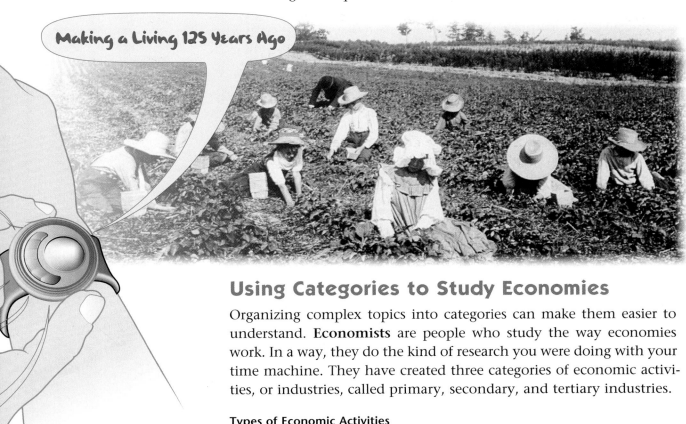

Making a Living 125 Years Ago

Using Categories to Study Economies

Organizing complex topics into categories can make them easier to understand. **Economists** are people who study the way economies work. In a way, they do the kind of research you were doing with your time machine. They have created three categories of economic activities, or industries, called primary, secondary, and tertiary industries.

Types of Economic Activities

Category	Descriptive Label	Definition	Examples
Primary industries	Extraction	Extract natural resources from the environment and make them into **semi-finished products**.	Fishing, farming, forestry, mining
Secondary industries	Manufacturing	Take semi-finished products from primary industries and manufacture them into **finished goods** for consumers' use.	Car manufacturing, furniture making, house construction
Tertiary industries	Services	Provide personal and business services to consumers.	Hairstyling, car repairs, teaching, government service, retail sales

Figure 8.2

All economic activities can be divided into three categories. Why would economists create categories when they study economic activities?

These categories are helpful, but some businesses or activities do not fit neatly into just one category. Consider multinational fast-food chains:

- Some own ranches that raise cattle for beef. Ranching is a primary industry.
- They also own meat packing plants, which process the beef into burger patties. Meat processing is a secondary industry.
- Then, the meat packing plants ship the burger patties to their retail outlets. There, employees cook them for customers. Cooking the patties is a service, which makes it a tertiary industry.

Is the multinational fast-food chain a primary industry? Is it a secondary industry? Is it a tertiary industry? Or, is it all three? In spite of these problems, the category method does help us analyze economic activities.

Figure 8.3

There are a lot of business activities that come together to serve you that hamburger. Can you think of other businesses that supply or service fast-food chains?

1. Make up sketches or diagrams that will help you remember the three categories of industries. Base your sketches on the descriptive labels and definitions for each category.

2. Explain the order of the categories: first (primary), second (secondary), and third (tertiary).

Primary Industries: From the Earth to the Mill

Primary industries are the first step in making goods. All of the goods we need and use must be made from raw materials found in the natural environment. All jobs related to getting and refining resources are primary industries.

Fact File

Close to 60 percent of Canada's total exports are based on natural resources. These exports include minerals, pulp and paper, lumber, wheat, and pork. Our rich natural resources, combined with our relatively small population, mean that we have plenty to sell to other countries. What finished goods might other countries make from our exports?

Figure 8.4

The Ekati Diamond Mine in the Northwest Territories is a good example of a primary industry. Describe what you see in the foreground (closest to the camera), middle ground (halfway between the camera and the horizon), and the background (farthest from the camera).

Primary industries generally do not produce goods that are sold directly in stores. Steelmaking is a good example. Iron ore, coal, and limestone are transported to a steel plant. The workers at the plant use these raw materials to make steel in various forms. They produce steel plates, sheets, bars, beams, and tubes. These semi-finished products need further work before consumers can use them. They will be made into finished goods such as cars, tools, and buildings.

Steel Processing and Production

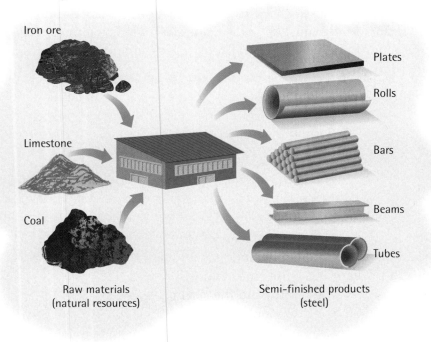

Iron ore

Limestone

Coal

Raw materials
(natural resources)

Plates

Rolls

Bars

Beams

Tubes

Semi-finished products
(steel)

Figure 8.5

It takes a small number of natural resources to make steel. However, we use steel to make many different products. What semi-finished products are made from other natural resources, such as forests or food crops?

Fact File

Minerals such as iron and copper often make up only 1 percent to 5 percent of the ore dug from the ground. Profitable deposits of precious minerals, such as gold or diamonds, occur in even lower percentages. What do the mining companies do with the leftover material, or tailings, after the minerals are extracted from the ore?

Most processing plants for primary industries are located near their sources of raw materials. Extracting natural resources usually produces a lot of waste material. Transporting this waste is costly and lowers profits. Transportation costs are lower for these industries when processing is done near their sources.

Figure 8.6

Before iron, nickel, and copper can be used in manufacturing, they must be smelted. At smelters, they are treated at very high temperatures to remove the metal from the raw ore. Here, the molten waste material is being dumped out of bucket cars. How might this process affect the environment?

Figure 8.7

Logging is another example of a primary industry. What semi-finished products might sawmill workers produce from these logs?

1. Create a web with the words "Primary Industries" in the centre bubble. Identify four characteristics of primary industries and record each one on a branch extending from the centre of the web. One characteristic is provided to help get you started.

Use raw materials

Primary Industries

2. What primary industries are found in your part of the province, or used to be there?

3. Identify some semi-finished products that might be produced from the following:
a) fishing industries
b) agriculture
c) mining industries

Fact File

Manufacturing processes are varied. They include the following actions:

cutting
shaping
bending
gluing
polishing
grinding

welding
assembling
stamping
drilling
sanding
packaging

Which manufacturing processes can you find in the bulleted text to the right?

Figure 8.8

The processing of semi-finished products into finished goods almost always changes the shape of the materials used. Processing also increases the value of the materials used. Think about three manufactured products you have used today. What semi-finished products were used to make them?

Secondary Industries: Making the Goods We Want and Need

The second step in manufacturing is to turn the semi-finished products of the primary industries into finished goods. For example, factory workers make auto parts from the steel produced at a steel plant.

Consider your desk. It went through the following manufacturing processes before it arrived in your classroom:

- At the factory, workers brought together semi-finished materials such as steel, wood, and plastic for assembly.
- The metal legs were stamped out of rolls of steel. Then, they were shaped and welded onto desk bases.
- Chipboard (a semi-finished wood product) was delivered from a wood mill and cut to size.
- The plastic desktop was glued onto the chipboard and trimmed.
- Then, top and base were joined together using steel fasteners.
- The finished desk was packaged and shipped to a warehouse, and then to your school.

Processing Semi-Finished Products

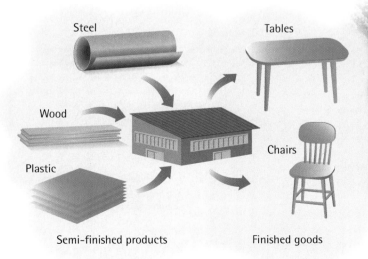

Figure 8.9

Construction activities are also a secondary industry. What semi-finished products are being used in this photograph?

Most secondary industries are located near the **market** where the finished goods are sold. Finished goods take up more space than the raw materials used to make them. (Think about the shape of your desk if the materials were shipped flat versus the shape of your desk once it is assembled.) Therefore, it costs more to ship finished goods. Also, finished goods are more fragile and require more care to ship than do semi-finished products. To increase profits, manufacturing is usually located near large cities such as Vancouver, Winnipeg, or Toronto.

DURING READING

1. Create a web with the words "Secondary Industries" in the centre bubble. Identify four characteristics of secondary industries and record each one on a branch extending from the centre of the web. One characteristic is provided to help get you started.

Located near markets

Secondary Industries

2. What secondary industries are found in your part of the province?

3. Why are secondary industries usually located around larger cities in the most populated parts of a country?

Tertiary Industries: Providing Services

Tertiary industries do not produce goods. They provide services to help us use and enjoy the manufactured goods we buy.

An automobile dealership is a good example of a tertiary industry. Before we can drive out of the showroom with our new car, we need a number of services:

- The dealer must order and display cars for consumers to look at and test drive.
- The dealer must get the car ready for sale (for example, by removing protective coverings).
- We need to get a licence plate.
- A bank lends us the money to buy the car.
- We must obtain insurance through a broker.

Once we have the car, we need even more services:

- We need fuel.
- The car will need regular servicing and repairs.
- Often, people buy accessories, such as sound systems, for their vehicles.
- Drivers buy auto club coverage for emergencies and breakdowns.

These are only some of the tertiary jobs needed just so we can buy and enjoy our car.

Figure 8.10

Auto mechanics provide an important service to car owners.

Tertiary industries are usually located near their customers. Customers must be able to reach their services easily, or they will go elsewhere. Companies that operate on the Internet are the exception to this rule. In "cyberspace," it does not matter where you are. Services are supplied electronically.

The tertiary industries category is very broad. It includes people who provide personal services such as cutting hair. It also includes those who provide business services such as bankers and stockbrokers. Doctors, teachers, prime ministers, and dogcatchers also belong in this category.

Some economists believe that the tertiary category is too broad. They argue that it should be divided into the following two subcategories:

- tertiary industries—services that are mainly concerned with *goods* (for example, retailers, who sell clothing, shoes, or sports equipment)
- **quaternary industries**—services that deal mostly with ideas and information (for example, teachers, who help students to understand the world around them and to think critically about new ideas)

The quaternary category fits in with the reality that we are in a new era—the Information Age.

Figure 8.11

Doctors are part of the quaternary category because they provide a service that involves the sharing of information and ideas with both patients and colleagues. People who work in quaternary industries usually require a long period of training.

AFTER READING

1. Create a Venn diagram to compare tertiary industries and quaternary industries.

2. List five examples of tertiary industries that you have used in the past month. It might be helpful if you start by thinking about some needs and wants that you have for health care, entertainment, nutrition, and personal grooming.

3. a) Explain why tertiary industries are almost always located near their markets.
    b) Give an example of a tertiary industry that would be located in remote or isolated parts of a province.
    c) Give an example of a tertiary industry that does not have to be located near its market.

4. Copy the chart below into your notebook and fill in the columns. In the bottom row, include examples of goods and services from each industry sector that you use in daily life.

Characteristics	Primary Industries	Secondary Industries	Tertiary Industries
Purpose			
Best location			
Key words to remember			
Examples			

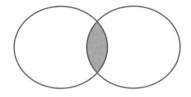

Figure 8.12

Hairstylists and barbers provide a personal service and so fall under the category of tertiary industries. Some hairdressers will come to your home to cut your hair. Can you think of other personal service providers who make house calls?

Global Patterns in Economic Structure

1. Primary, secondary, and tertiary industries are found in all countries. However, not all countries have the same amount of each type of industry. Based on your knowledge of primary, secondary, and tertiary industries, discuss and predict in groups the ratio of each type of industry in developed and developing countries. Use the following chart and the words "more," "less," and "equal" to show the amount of each type of industry. Be prepared to share your group's reasons for your choices.

	Primary	Secondary	Tertiary
Developed countries			
Developing countries			

We can learn a lot about a country by looking at how many jobs it has in each economic category—primary, secondary, and tertiary industries. The quality of life in a country is related to the strength of each economic category there.

Figure 8.13

These photographs compare some of the food choices for people in wealthy countries to those in developing countries. Which photograph depicts industrialization of the food supply? Does more processing imply better quality?

Quality of Life

Statistics show how economic categories relate to people's quality of life in a country. Note the difference in how countries earn their GDP.

- Countries with a high quality of life (for example, Canada)
  - earn a small percentage of their GDP from primary industries
  - earn a large percentage of their GDP from tertiary industries
- Countries with low quality of life (for example, Chad)
  - earn a large percentage of their GDP from primary industries
  - earn a small percentage of their GDP from tertiary industries

A high quality of life seems to be linked to having many services available in a country. Let us explore some reasons why this is the case.

Fact File

Developed countries become less dependent on primary industries while they expand their secondary and tertiary sectors. Canada has such rich natural resources that our primary sector has remained strong. Close to 60 percent of our total exports are based on natural resources. However, only 5 percent of our workforce is engaged in the primary industries. Thirteen percent of our labour force works in manufacturing industries, which process these natural resources for export. Processing includes polishing diamonds, making steel, sawing lumber, and processing food products. Which of Canada's economic resources can you identify in this Fact File? (Hint: Think of the four factors of production.)

HDI Scores and Percentage of GDP by Industry Sector for Selected Countries, 2007

Country	HDI Score	Percent of Gross Domestic Product from		
		Primary Industries	Secondary Industries	Tertiary Industries
High Quality of Life				
Canada	0.961	2.1	28.8	69.1
France	0.952	2.2	20.6	77.2
New Zealand	0.943	4.5	26.2	69.3
Medium Quality of Life				
China	0.777	11.3	48.6	40.1
Ecuador	0.772	6.7	35.1	58.2
Sri Lanka	0.743	11.7	29.9	58.4
Low Quality of Life				
Chad	0.388	21.5	47.8	30.6
Ethiopia	0.406	47.0	13.2	39.8
Nigeria	0.470	17.7	52.6	29.7

Figure 8.14

This table compares selected countries for 2007. An HDI score of 1.00 is perfect, which would mean that citizens living there have a very high quality of life. How do the percentages of GDP earned by tertiary industries vary among the countries?

LITERACY TIP

Reading a Statistical Table

Follow these steps to identify trends or patterns in a table with statistics:

1. Read the title to learn the purpose of the table.
2. Read the column headings to see what information is being compared.
3. Read the row headings to learn which countries or categories are being compared.
4. Read the data and look for patterns or differences.
5. Make concluding statements about the trends or patterns you observe.

Primary Industries

Jobs are scarce in many developing countries. To feed themselves and their families, many people must work in subsistence agriculture.

In Chapter 7, you learned that European colonization left developing countries with weak economies for the following reasons:

- People in the colonies became the labour force that extracted the natural resources from the land and prepared them for shipping to the industries in the colonizing country.
- People in the colonies had to buy the goods that were produced in the colonizing country.
- Colonies could not set up their own trade connections.
- Colonies could not develop their own industries.

Today, many developing countries still depend on exporting products from their primary industries. They export natural resources, such as timber, minerals, or sugar cane. In wealthier countries, workers have a wider choice of jobs in other sectors of the economy.

Secondary Industries

Wealthier countries have more capital to invest in manufacturing and construction. They tend to have strong secondary industries. However, they are losing many manufacturing industries to developing countries in the globalized world. The main reason is that labour costs less in developing countries.

Countries with poor qualities of life have little capital to invest. Their manufacturing industries have trouble competing in the global market. Asian and African countries pay lower wages than wealthier countries do. These lower wages attract international corporations that operate manufacturing industries. They want to keep labour costs low and profits high. Big transnational corporations invest in industries in developing countries. Then, these corporations take the profits out of the developing countries.

Figure 8.15

The data on primary, secondary, and tertiary industries in this graph are from Figure 8.14. Notice how the amount in each category varies for the countries. Which country has the lowest quality of life? How do you know this from the graph? What might be happening in Chad to account for the level of secondary industries?

Percent of GDP by Industrial Sector for Selected Countries, 2007

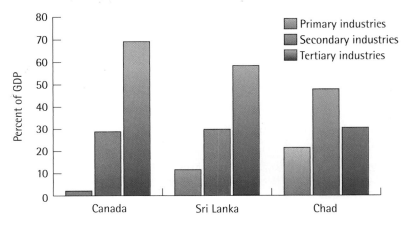

HDI Scores Compared to Percentages of GDP Earned by Primary Industries

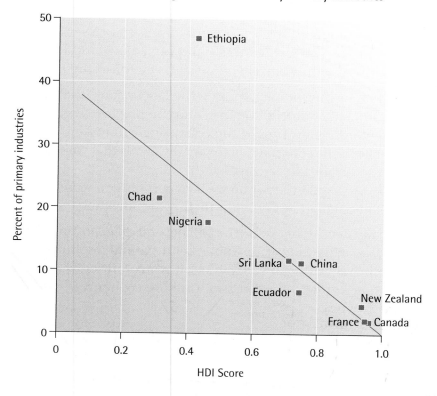

Figure 8.16

This scatter graph is drawn using HDI scores and percentages of GDP earned by primary industries. The data are from Figure 8.14. Using this graph as a model, draw a scatter graph to show HDI scores and tertiary industries. (Refer to GeoSkills on pages 36–37 in Chapter 2.) What is the correlation between HDI scores and percentage of GDP earned by primary industries? (Refer to page 35 in Chapter 2.)

Tertiary Industries

Many people in countries with lower qualities of life have low incomes. They do not have much money to spend on services. In wealthier countries, high incomes allow more people to demand many types of services.

Fact File

Equatorial Guinea, a country in Africa, earns only 4.6 percent of its GDP from tertiary industries. Monaco, in Europe, earns 95.1 percent of its GDP from this sector. How would Equatorial Guinea earn most of its GDP? What might Monaco's HDI score be?

1. Review the predictions you made about the amount of each type of industry in developed and developing countries in Before Reading question 1 on page 173. How close were your predictions to the reality?

2. a) Explain why developing countries often have more primary industries than developed countries.

   b) Explain why developed countries often have more tertiary industries than developing countries.

3. Why is it becoming more difficult to define whether developed or developing countries generally have more secondary industries? (Hint: Think of globalization and the cost of labour.)

GO GEO-GREEN

Climate Change and African Agriculture

Agriculture is one of the oldest primary industries in the world. Countries that rely largely on agriculture suffer the most from climate change.

In many African countries, agriculture is the most important sector of the economy:

- Agriculture earns up to 30 percent of Africa's GDP.
- 70 percent of Africa's population depends on agriculture.

Climate change is causing hardship in many African countries. It affects agriculture in this region in the following ways:

- Reduced crop yields—In many parts of Africa, the crop yields have reached their maximum. As the climate changes, the crop yields go down.
- More pest attacks on crops—As the temperature rises, it lengthens the breeding season for the insects that eat the crops.
- Less available water—The water supply in most parts of Africa is decreasing. In southern Africa and countries near the Mediterranean Sea, rainfall is also decreasing.
- More and longer droughts—This is the most serious side effect of climate change. It especially affects many countries in the Sahel region, including Ethiopia and Senegal. Most countries in Africa rely on rain to water their crops.
- Less fertile soil—As the temperature rises, soil loses its moisture. It also loses its ability to store moisture.

Many organizations are trying to help Africa. The United Nations Environment Programme (UNEP) realized that they had to involve young people in seeking solutions to the world's environmental problems. In 2003, UNEP formed the TUNZA Youth Strategy. TUNZA means "to treat with care" in Kishwahili, a language spoken in Eastern Africa. TUNZA engages young people around the world in efforts to "treat Earth with care."

Every two years, a Junior Board is elected at the TUNZA International Children's Conference

Figure 8.17

These young people attended the 2007 African Regional Children's Conference for the Environment, held in Cameroon. They prepared for the 2008 TUNZA International Children's Conference on the Environment, to be held in Stavanger, Norway. What topics do you think they discussed about Africa?

on the Environment. This board advises UNEP on how to involve young people in its work. In 2008, the TUNZA International Children's Conference on the Environment was held in Stavanger, Norway. Seven hundred children (10 to 14 years old) from 105 countries took part. They attended workshops and field trips related to the theme of Creating Change. That same summer, youth over 14 years old attended a retreat in Nairobi, Kenya. They discussed climate change and the role of young people.

You and your class can get involved with TUNZA. TUNZA believes that the world's young people are the makers of the future. Will you become a maker of the future? Behave in an environmentally responsible way and educate yourself and others about the problems facing our world.

· · · · · · · · · · · · · · · · · ·

To learn more about TUNZA,

Go to Nelson Social Studies

Creating a Multiple Line Graph

Line graphs are useful because they clearly reveal trends or patterns over time. You can compare similar items over the same period of time with a multiple line graph. When creating multiple line graphs, it is important to follow TAPP—Title, Axes, Pattern, and Purpose. Follow these steps to create a multiple line graph using the data below.

Step One

Read the title and the data in Figure 8.18 to understand what you are going to graph.

Gross Domestic Product in Millions, by Industry Sector, for Canada

	2003	2004	2005	2006	2007
All industries	1 091 378	1 126 802	1 160 024	1 193 905	1 223 949
Primary—Agriculture, forestry, fishing, and hunting	25 478	27 685	28 437	27 847	27 077
Primary—Mining, oil and gas extraction	54 979	55 849	56 044	57 174	58 342
Secondary—Manufacturing	181 349	185 504	188 478	186 631	184 712
Secondary—Construction and utilities	88 928	92 723	99 077	104 215	108 053
Tertiary—Service-producing industries	740 590	765 429	788 966	818 915	846 439

Figure 8.18

This table shows the amount each industry sector contributed to Canada's GDP for the years 2003 to 2007.

Step Two

Using graph paper and a ruler, create your two *axes*, and label them as follows:

- Label the *x*-axis (horizontal) with the years. Place your first year, 2003, on the second space, then leave 4 spaces before you label the next year, and so on. You will need 22 spaces.
- Label the *y*-axis (vertical) with $ Millions. Start with 0 at the bottom and go up by 25 000 for every square — 0, 25 000, 50 000, 75 000, 100 000, and so on. You will need 34 squares.

Step Three

Place a *title* at the top of your graph.

GeoSkills

Creating a Multiple Line Graph *(continued)*

Step Four

Look at the data set and begin to create your *pattern*. You will create an individual line graph for each of the sets of industries. Start with Primary — agriculture, forestry, fishing, and hunting. Place a dot where the year 2003 on the *x*-axis intersects with the number 25 000 on the *y*-axis. (Round the number to the nearest thousand.) Place the next dot where the year 2004 on the *x*-axis intersects with 28 000 on the *y*-axis. Continue this pattern until you have plotted the dots for all five years on the map. Use a coloured pencil to join the dots together to form a line. Create a legend for your graph that will identify the industries represented by each coloured line.

Step Five

Follow Step Four for the remaining sets of industries. Choose a different coloured pencil to represent each set.

Step Six

Determine the *purpose* of the graph by answering the following questions:
- Which industry sector makes up most of Canada's GDP?
- Which industries are contributing less to our GDP than they used to?
- How does the information on agriculture as a portion of Canada's GDP compare to what you have learned about the importance of agriculture to some countries in Africa?
- How does your completed line graph reflect what you learned in this chapter about the development, quality of life, and economic success of countries?

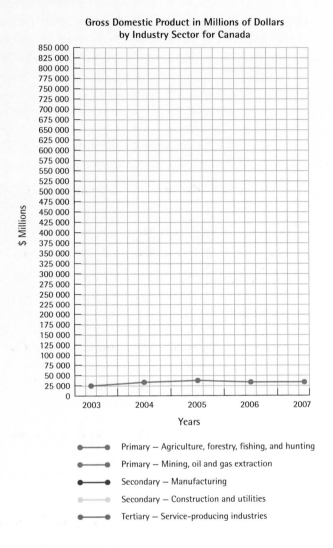

Gross Domestic Product in Millions of Dollars by Industry Sector for Canada

Legend:
- Primary – Agriculture, forestry, fishing, and hunting
- Primary – Mining, oil and gas extraction
- Secondary – Manufacturing
- Secondary – Construction and utilities
- Tertiary – Service-producing industries

Figure 8.19

This line graph shows data plotted for primary industries— agriculture, forestry, fishing, and hunting from 2003 to 2007. Plot this information on your own graph. Then plot the data for the remaining industry sectors in Figure 8.18.

Ways of Life

We have seen that quality of life varies with economic structure. Living conditions vary also. Primary industries are traditionally located close to the natural resources they use. Countries with a large number of primary jobs have fewer cities. More people live in small towns or villages. This is often true of developing countries. However, in industrialized countries, factories and jobs are plentiful. Most people live in cities. Tertiary industries also develop well in cities, since many customers demand their services. Figure 8.20 shows other differences in employment and quality of life.

The Effects of Economic Structures on Quality of Life

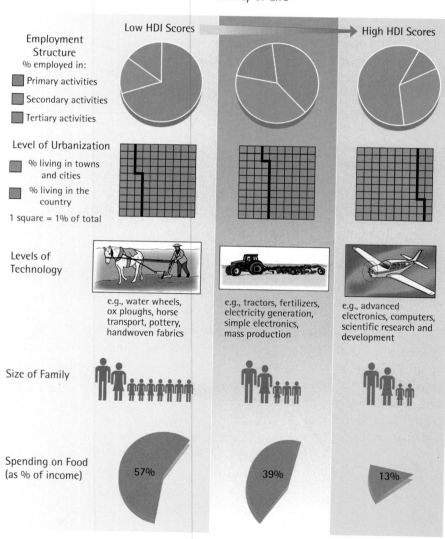

Figure 8.20

As countries develop, important changes occur in people's way of life. Why do you suppose the number of children a family has declines as a country develops? Why might the percentage of income spent on food decrease as a country develops?

LITERACY TIP

Reading Complex Figures

There are many parts to Figure 8.20. Read this figure as you would a simple table. This table uses graphs instead of words and numbers. Each row shows a different feature that affects quality of life. Each column shows how these features vary among countries, depending on their HDI scores. Read one row at a time and identify patterns you observe.

1. How is the economic success of a country influenced by its HDI score? To answer this, use the following questions and the information in Figure 8.20 to write point-form characteristics of countries with low HDI scores and with high HDI scores. Use a chart like the one below to organize your jot notes.

Countries with Low HDI Scores	Countries with High HDI Scores
•	•
•	•
•	•

a) Read the circle graphs and determine what happens to a country's workforce as countries develop. How does the percentage employed in each of the industry sectors change?

b) Read the 100-square charts that show the percentage of people who live in urban and rural settings. What switch occurs?

c) Examine the pictures that show levels of technology. How does the level of technology change?

d) Read the pictographs that show the number of children in an average family. How does the number of children change?

e) Look at the circle graph sections in the bottom row. What happens to the amount of money people spend on food?

f) Think about the economic resources of land, labour, capital, and technology. Explain how the point-form characteristics in your chart connect with the economic resources that influence a country's economic success.

Figure 8.21

Manufacturing in developing countries — like this weaving co-operative in the Philippines — often starts small because there are few sources of investment capital. Small, local community industries are often seen to have the following advantages over huge megaproject industries:

• more effective
• more sustainable
• benefit the local economy more

What might be another name for megaproject industries? Why would small, local community industries have these advantages over huge megaproject industries?

Development of Countries

A century ago, Canada's economic structure and way of life were largely agricultural. Most people lived in rural areas and worked in primary industries. Over the years, our economic conditions improved. Our way of life changed, too. Our quality of life now ranks among the best in the world.

We use the term "development" to describe the changes that take place in economic structure. Developing countries have the following characteristics:

- They are becoming less dependent on primary industries.
- They have growing secondary and tertiary industrial sectors.

Many countries in Africa and Asia fit this category.

In developed countries, such as Canada, tertiary industries form a large part of the economy.

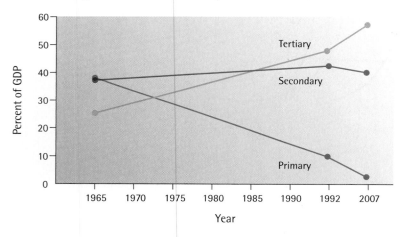

Changes in Economic Structure for South Korea, 1965–2007

Figure 8.22

This graph shows changes in economic structure for South Korea. Which economic category has changed the most? What can you conclude about South Korea's development?

Development and Happiness

Canadians enjoy a very high quality of life. Does this make us happier than people in other countries? It is easy to think that people in places with a lower quality of life must be unhappy. This is not true. We all find happiness in many forms. We find it in our family and friends, our work and personal accomplishments, and our spiritual beliefs. People in developing countries can live happy, productive lives. On the other hand, people in developed countries can be very unhappy. Living in a developed country does not guarantee happiness.

Figure 8.23

Two Tibetan exiles pray in a refugee camp in Leh, India. Material wealth is important to health and happiness. It does not guarantee them, however. How much material wealth do you need to be happy?

AFTER READING

1. Explain why countries that depend on primary industries are also rated as having lower economic success and qualities of life.

2. Make a sketch or diagram that illustrates the differences between developing countries and developed countries. In your sketch, include three characteristics that are shown in the chart in Figure 8.20 on page 180.

3. Suppose you are in charge of an agency that gives aid to a developing country. You have a limited amount of money. In what area of the country's economy would you invest to do the most good? Explain your answer in a paragraph. Remember the four Cs of persuasive writing:

- *Catch* the reader's attention.
- *Commit* to your opinion.
- *Convince* the reader by making a point and supporting it with proof.
- *Close* your paragraph. (Refer to page 70 in Chapter 3.)

CASE STUDY

E-Commerce

Tertiary economic activities include selling goods and services. These activities often take place in retail outlets, such as shopping malls or stores. People can also sell goods and services door-to-door and by mail. Now there is a fast-growing method of selling—through the Internet. This fast-growing sales method is called "e-commerce."

The Internet

The Internet links governments, universities, schools, factories, offices, and homes around the world through a high-speed telecommunications network. In 1994, 3 million people used the Internet. By 2008, 1.4 billion people around the world were using it. E-commerce has become a key part of the global economy.

Businesses began using the Internet to buy and sell products and services in the 1990s. Many people find Internet shopping fast and convenient. By 2006, e-commerce was worth more than $132 billion. Many of the services people buy online are related to travel. The travel industry makes up about 44 percent of all e-commerce transactions.

Delivery of Information and Goods

Most e-commerce is in one of the following two forms:

- electronic delivery of information—software programs, newspapers, and music
- retail sale of goods and services — computers, cars, books, CDs, and flowers

Figure 8.25

E-commerce has a number of advantages for consumers. Which advantage is most important for you and your family?

Advantages of E-commerce

Advantage	Explanation
Choice	People can buy from sellers anywhere in the world. They are not limited to stores within walking or driving distance.
Better information	Consumers can research products online before they buy.
Lower prices	Buyers can choose from many sources. This means sellers have to compete harder for their business. Booksellers and other Internet sellers often offer discounts to attract buyers.
Customization	Internet sellers can tailor some products to meet buyers' personal preferences. For example, they can send online magazine readers only the specific articles they want to read.

Percentage of Population with Internet Access by World Region, 2008

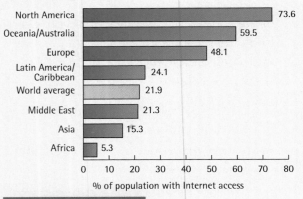

North America — 73.6
Oceania/Australia — 59.5
Europe — 48.1
Latin America/Caribbean — 24.1
World average — 21.9
Middle East — 21.3
Asia — 15.3
Africa — 5.3

% of population with Internet access

Figure 8.24

This graph shows the percentage of the population that had access to the Internet in different regions of the world in 2008. Why do you suppose North America has such a large percentage of Internet users?

To learn more about Internet use,

Go to Nelson
Social Studies

CASE STUDY

E-Commerce *(continued)*

Challenges of E-Commerce

E-commerce has raised the following issues:

- Personal security and invasion of privacy—To buy something on the Internet, you usually have to give a credit card number and other personal information to people you do not know. Could they later use that information in ways that you do not know about? Canada is working to put laws in place to ensure fair trade practices in e-commerce. However, the Internet operates on a global scale. That makes it difficult to enforce laws.

- Pornography and violence—More and more people have easy access to the Internet. They can be exposed to pornographic, violent, and hate materials.

- Internet crime—Criminals are finding new ways to use the Internet and e-commerce for personal gain. Each advance in communications opens new opportunities for everyone. That includes criminals.

Figure 8.26

Call centres, such as this one in Delhi, India, are important to the success of e-commerce. The call centres take orders from customers around the world. They also provide support services for products. What would be some advantages and disadvantages to working in a call centre?

1. Brainstorm three endings to the following: "An important advantage that the Internet has for me as a consumer is ..." Write each sentence in your notebook.

2. Suppose you work for a store owner who has asked for your advice about setting up a website to sell her goods. Using the following outline, plan and write a paragraph setting out the advantages and disadvantages of e-commerce for your employer.

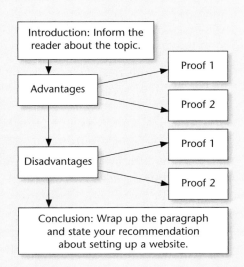

Introduction: Inform the reader about the topic.

Advantages → Proof 1

Advantages → Proof 2

Disadvantages → Proof 1

Disadvantages → Proof 2

Conclusion: Wrap up the paragraph and state your recommendation about setting up a website.

Knowledge and Understanding

1 You have been asked to give a speech about the importance of all categories of industry in a strong economy—primary, secondary, and tertiary. Write an outline of the main points that you will make. Be sure to include information from this chapter to support your opinion.

Use this graphic organizer to help create an outline for your speech.

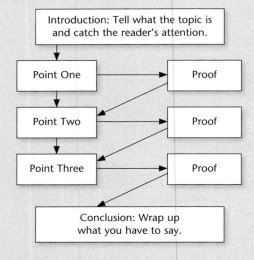

2 Decide which of the following statements is true or false. Write each of the true statements in your notebook. Change each of the false statements to a true statement, and write the true one in your notebook.

a) Over the last century, the Canadian economy has grown more dependent on primary industries.

b) Tertiary industries are all about providing services, such as growing food and making cars.

c) Primary industries are usually located in rural areas, and tertiary industries are usually located in urban areas.

d) People who live in places with low qualities of life are constantly unhappy, while people who live in places with high qualities of life are always happy.

3 In this chapter, you learned about how the economic structure of a country changes as the country develops its economic resources. We see these changes when we examine primary, secondary, and tertiary industries. Complete a chart like the one below in which you identify the following:

- changes that take place as a country develops
- reasons for each change
- consequences or impacts of each change

One change has already been completed to get you started. Add three more changes.

Changes	Reasons	Consequences/Impacts
The country's economy depends less on primary industries.	People can find work in other parts of the economy.	Rural residents move to urban places.

4 Explain why people in countries with low HDI scores usually live in rural areas, while people in countries with high HDI scores usually live in cities.

Inquiry/Research and Communication Skills

5 Collect pictures from the Internet and other sources showing people in countries in which a high percentage of the population works in primary industries. Most countries in Africa fit this description.

a) List five terms that describe the quality of life of the people in the pictures.

b) Using information from this chapter, explain why these countries have kept their ties to primary industries and have not developed strong secondary and tertiary industries.

6 a) Research the economic structure of one country in Africa to find out:

- why it has not developed more secondary and tertiary industries
- what economic resources it has or does not have that have influenced the economy

To begin, think about what you want to find out, and record questions to guide your answers.

If you use the Internet to search for answers, use keywords from your questions as possible search strings. You can use a KWHL organizer like the one below to plan your research and organize your notes.

K	W	H	L
What do I **K**now about this topic?	What do I **W**ant to find out about this topic?	**H**ow can I find this additional information?	What did I **L**earn?
• • •	• • •	• • •	• • •

b) Report your research results using a poster or written report.

Map, Globe, and Graphic Skills

7 Examine Figure 8.27, which shows the number of Internet users by region of the world.

a) Draw a circle graph or a bar graph to show this information. (Refer to GeoSkills on page 130 in Chapter 6, and on page 145 in Chapter 7.)

b) On the back of the graph, explain why you decided to draw the graph that you did.

Number of Internet Users by World Region, 2008

World Region	Number of Internet Users (millions)
Asia	578.5
Europe	384.6
North America	248.2
Latin America and the Caribbean	139.0
Africa	51.1
Middle East	41.9
Oceania/Australia	20.2

Figure 8.27

This table shows the number of Internet users by world region in 2008. Why do you suppose Asia has more Internet users than North America?

c) Make three observations about the information in your graph. You can describe patterns that you see, interesting relationships or connections, or items that do not fit the patterns.

Application

8 a) Percentages of GDP earned by each sector of the economy for three unnamed countries are given in Figure 8.28. Using an atlas and your knowledge of world patterns, identify two possible countries that each could be. Give reasons for your choices.

b) What can you infer about the economic resources of land, labour, capital, and technology for each country in Figure 8.28?

Percentage of GDP by Industry Sector and HDI Scores for Selected Countries, 2007

Country	Primary Industries (%)	Secondary Industries (%)	Tertiary Industries (%)	HDI Score
A	36.9	21.7	41.4	0.452
B	13.7	31.4	54.8	0.771
C	1.0	20.5	78.5	0.951

Figure 8.28

This table gives the percentage of the GDP earned by each industry sector for three countries that have not been named. What information will you use to try to identify the actual countries?

9 Canada's Economy

KEY VOCABULARY

European Union (EU)
free trade
North American Free Trade
   Agreement (NAFTA)
productivity
protectionism
structural adjustment
tariff
trading bloc

Different Voices, Many Choices

1. Canada is a wealthy country, compared to many other places in the world. Suggest three reasons why it is considered a wealthy country. Compare your reasons with a classmate.

2. Draw visual symbols to represent the meaning of the following terms, which you have already learned: mixed economy, primary industries, secondary industries, tertiary industries.

   Check how well your visual symbols match the definitions in your notebook or in the Glossary on pages 325–328.

Canadians have one of the highest qualities of life in the world. Yet, if you listen to the news or hear people talk, you might get a different picture. "Taxes are too high," some people complain. "We need more money for health care and education," others protest. "Our businesses are moving away to countries where wages are lower." "We need to work harder to compete with developing countries in Asia." "We aren't developing our high-tech skills or our green technologies fast enough." "We need to focus more on the development of the energy sector of our economy." Everyone seems to criticize Canada's economy. However, criticism does not have to be a bad thing.

Canada's future ble[a]
Economic think tank report

Exports up, tr[a]

Health care [

Canadian brain dra[
Professionals flock to U.S.

Figure 9.1

Many views exist on the economy. What do you think your future in Canada will be like? Why?

In Canada, we have a mixed economy. Decisions about how our taxes are spent and what businesses can and cannot do, for example, are influenced by many groups in society. These include

- governments
- businesses
- consumer groups
- environmental groups
- other organizations

Every day, many different voices give very different views about the economy and what we should do about it. This is a democratic process. It is time-consuming and sometimes confusing. Not everyone will be happy with the economic system that results. Still, this process allows the greatest input for Canadians to shape their economy.

From Goods to Services

Figure 9.2

Canada's economic structure is shown by percentage of workers in different sectors from 1951 to 2001. What trends do you notice in the data?

Percentage of Workers in Different Industrial Sectors, 1951–2001

Year	Primary Industries (resources)	Secondary Industries (manufacturing)	Tertiary Industries (services)
1951	22.8%	33.3%	43.9%
1961	14.2%	30.2%	55.6%
1971	9.1%	28.3%	62.6%
1981	6.2%	28.8%	65.0%
1991	5.5%	21.3%	73.2%
2001	4.1%	20.6%	75.3%

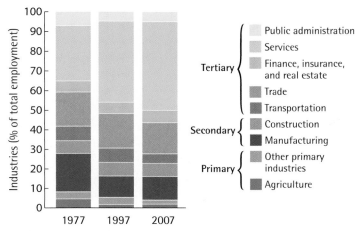

Canadian Employment by Industry, 1977, 1997, and 2007

Figure 9.3

This graph shows Canadian employment by industry for 1977, 1997, and 2007. What are the most significant changes in jobs over the 30 years covered in the graph?

(sidebar, left margin)

High taxes keep industries away

Canadians lack high-tech skills: More college programs needed

...ture bright

...ers to strike

LITERACY TIP

Reading a Stacked Bar Graph

A stacked bar graph compares two or more sets of information at the same time. Stacked bar graphs are used to

- show patterns and trends over time
- compare patterns or trends for different locations

When reading these graphs, remember to follow TAPP—Title, Axes, Pattern, and Purpose. Refer to the legend to see what each colour represents.

This graph shows provincial employment by industrial sector for 2007. Which provinces have strong primary industries? Using your knowledge of Canada's physical geography, why do you think they developed where they did?

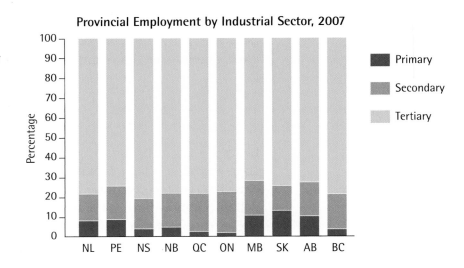

Provincial Employment by Industrial Sector, 2007

Legend:
- Primary
- Secondary
- Tertiary

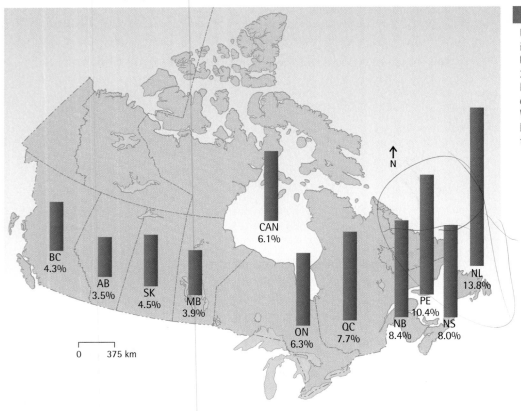

Unemployment Rates in Canada by Province, August 2008

CAN
6.1%

BC
4.3%

AB
3.5%

SK
4.5%

MB
3.9%

ON
6.3%

QC
7.7%

NB
8.4%

PE
10.4%

NS
8.0%

NL
13.8%

N

0   375 km

Unemployment rates in Canada are shown by province for August 2008. Which regions have the highest levels of unemployment? Which have the lowest levels? Why do you think this is so?

DURING READING

1. Using the data in Figures 9.2, 9.3, 9.4, and 9.5, make three true statements about the structure of Canada's economy. In other words, what can you conclude from these figures about how Canada's economy is organized?

2. Suppose you want to take three photographs, or draw three images, that show how the structure of the Canadian economy has changed over the years. What images would you choose? Explain your choices.

Canada's Exports and Imports

Figure 9.6

This table shows Canada's exports and imports over a 70-year period, from 1937 to 2007. Which countries are Canada's most important trading partners? What patterns do you see in the data? Why do you think these patterns developed?

Canada's Exports and Imports, 1937–2007

	Exports			Imports		
Year	To USA	To UK	To Others	From USA	From UK	From Others
1937	36%	38%	26%	61%	18%	21%
1950	65%	15%	20%	67%	13%	20%
1975	66%	6%	28%	68%	4%	28%
1997	68%	2%	30%	82%	1%	17%
2007	77%	3%	20%	65%	2%	33%

Figure 9.7

This circle graph shows exports from Canada for 2007. What challenges might Canada face when so many of our exports are to the United States?

Figure 9.8

This circle graph shows imports to Canada for 2007. Why do you suppose we import so much from the United States?

Exports from Canada, 2007

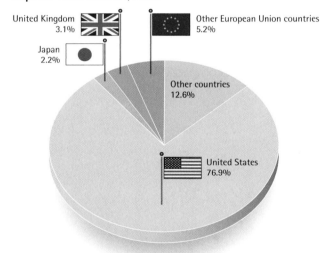

Imports to Canada, 2007

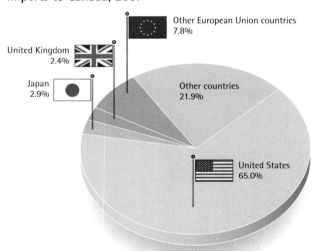

Canada's Exports and Imports by Category, 2007

Exports ($ billions)	Category	Imports ($ billions)
34.4	Agriculture and fishing products	25.5
91.6	Energy products	36.6
29.3	Forest products	3.0
104.4	Industrial goods and materials	85.1
71.1	Machinery and equipment	85.0
22.3	Industrial and agricultural machinery	31.6
53.0	Automotive products	43.8
24.3	Motor vehicle parts	36.2
18.7	Other consumer goods	54.7

Figure 9.9

This table shows Canada's exports and imports by category for 2007. Which categories are Canada's top exports? Which categories are Canada's top imports? Why do you think we both export and import machinery? Why do you suppose we do not make all the machinery that we need here in Canada?

1. a) Which countries are Canada's most important trading partners?

b) For each of our most important trading partners, suggest a reason why they are important.

2. Some people argue that Canada's economy depends too much on the economy of the United States. Give evidence from this section that could support this argument.

3. Examine the goods that Canada exports and imports, as shown in Figure 9.9.

a) What evidence tells you that primary industries are important to the Canadian economy despite their decrease in employment over the years?

b) What evidence tells you that secondary industries are important to the Canadian economy?

GeoSkills

Reading an Editorial Cartoon

Cartoonists often comment about Canada's economy in editorial cartoons. Editorial cartoons are humorous drawings that present an issue or event and make a comment about it. They are visual tools used to express an opinion and present a message. They are meant to get you thinking about the topic presented. Cartoonists may add words to help you understand the message (for example, titles, captions, name tags, balloon comments, or dialogue). Cartoonists often use stereotypes as symbols for more complicated ideas.

Step One

Look at the cartoon below.

Figure 9.10

This editorial cartoon is from the *Toronto Star*, September 2007. The cartoonist is commenting on the strength of the Canadian dollar compared to the American dollar at that time.

GeoSkills

Reading an Editorial Cartoon *(continued)*

Step Two

Use the graphic organizer below to help you read and understand this editorial cartoon.

Source: *Toronto Star,* September 20, 2007	**Artist:** Patrick Corrigan	**Emotional response (how you reacted on first viewing this cartoon):** I giggled.

Describe the setting in the cartoon. A running track	**Describe the symbols and characters in the cartoon. Draw on your knowledge of local and world events and things.** Uncle Sam: symbolizes the United States The Loonie: symbolizes the Canadian dollar

Examine the characters. Describe facial expressions, body expressions and appearance, clothing, exaggeration of physical characteristics.

Facial expressions: Uncle Sam looks worried and tired; the Loonie has a confident smile.

Body expressions: Uncle Sam is behind the Loonie.

Exaggeration of physical characteristics: Uncle Sam looks very thin and weak. The Loonie is large and strong. He has dust clouds behind him.

Identify the issue the cartoon is illustrating. Consider both the image and words.

This cartoon shows a race between Uncle Sam (the American dollar) and the Loonie (the Canadian dollar). The Loonie is winning the race. He appears to be stronger than Uncle Sam in this race. Uncle Sam says the Loonie must be using steroids to win the race.

State what you think the cartoonist is trying to say.

The cartoonist is commenting on how strong the Canadian dollar was in the fall of 2007. The Canadian dollar was worth more than the American dollar for a short period that year. The Uncle Sam character is saying that the Canadian dollar is using steroids. The cartoonist might be saying that some Americans believe the Canadian dollar's strength came about unfairly.

Find another editorial cartoon (look in a newspaper editorial section), and practise what you have learned.

Why Is Our Economy Changing?

1. a) Work with a classmate to brainstorm ways that Canada is connected economically to other countries in the world.

b) Organize the items in your list into categories.

c) What statements can you make about Canada's economic connections?

All economies change over time. Sometimes the changes are good. They can create a better quality of life for people. In Canada, over the last 60 years, tertiary industries (including personal services, software development, and retail sales) have grown. This growth has been a good change that has created more jobs. However, changes in a country's economy can create bad consequences. For example, in recent years, many Canadian companies have moved their factories to developing countries. There, wages are lower so profits will be higher. Canada has lost many manufacturing jobs because of this change.

Whether economic changes are good or bad, it is important to analyze what causes them. As we do, we can make the economy work better for Canadians. The following two forces have been important in recent years:

- globalization
- the creation of special trade agreements among countries to form **trading blocs**

A trading bloc is a partnership among countries that makes exporting and importing goods and services cheaper, easier, and more efficient.

LITERACY TIP

Brainstorming and Categorizing

When you brainstorm, let the ideas come without judging them. You want as many ideas as possible. Stop the brainstorming session when a minute has passed without a new idea being added to your list. Then, look at your list of ideas to see how they are similar and different. Group ideas that are related. Name each group to show how the words are connected.

Figure 9.11

These containers of trade goods will be loaded onto ships at Vancouver's harbour. Canada has long been a trading nation. Globalization of the world's economy makes our trade relations even more important. Why is world trade so important to Canadians?

LITERACY TIP
. . . .

Using Word Parts

Use what you already know about suffixes, or word endings, to help you understand new vocabulary. "Globalization" has two suffixes: *–ize* means "to make," and *–ation* means "the result of." "Globalization" means "the result of making something global." "Protectionism" also has two suffixes: *–ion* means "being" or "the result of," and *–ism* means "act" or "condition." Therefore, "protectionism" means "the act of being protected."

One Big World

Globalization is a trend toward increasing trade among the world's countries. In the past, many countries protected their local industries by limiting competition from outside the country. This is called **protectionism**. The countries intended it to ensure jobs and a good economic future for their citizens. Two ways of protecting local industry include the following:

- reducing foreign imports (that is, not letting goods made elsewhere into the country)
- imposing taxes, or **tariffs**, on imported goods

Tariffs make imported goods more expensive than domestic goods (items produced locally). For example, imports of milk and cream into Canada have tariffs of 7.5 percent of their cost added to the price, up to a certain amount; after that amount is reached, the tariff jumps to 241 percent. Tariffs encourage consumers to buy products made in their own countries.

Protectionism can help local industries grow and create jobs. However, it also reduces competition, which businesses need to stay productive. Less competition can result in the following:

- poor-quality, expensive consumer goods
- inefficient, out-of-date local industries

In recent years, most countries have moved toward **free trade**. The "free" in free trade means there are no taxes on imported goods. Also, there are no conditions on imports, such as unnecessary labels or tough safety standards. Countries have reduced or removed tariffs and other rules about foreign goods. As a result, goods and services produced in one country can be sold in almost any other country around the world. Free trade results in more competition between industries here in Canada and industries in other countries. It also increases competition between industries from all around the world.

Figure 9.12

On January 1, 2003, the Canadian government announced that people in Canada would be able to buy clothing products from the world's less developed countries without a tariff. As a result, there has been a shift away from trade with the United States to other countries such as China and India. What are some ways that globalization has affected your life?

Benefits of Globalization

People who support globalization and free trade believe that competition is good. They say that it makes businesses and industries more efficient. In order to compete successfully with businesses from around the world, a business must become very good at what it does. That is, it must do the following:

- reduce its costs
- increase the quality of its products
- develop better production methods

These actions benefit consumers. They can buy cheaper, better-quality products and services.

In the global market, countries produce only those items that they are best at producing. They use the money they earn from selling these items to buy what they need. Each country specializes in economic activities in which they excel. Countries with highly educated populations, like Canada, focus on high-tech industries. Exports from these industries include aerospace and telecommunications products and services. Countries with low wage rates, like Mexico, produce lower-tech goods. They export goods such as textiles, or fabrics, and car parts.

. . . .
To learn more about the effects of globalization on people and the economy,

**Go to Nelson
Social Studies**

Figure 9.13

The Smart Car is produced by a German automaker. Many Canadians prefer to buy cars that are produced in other countries, or cars that are produced in Canada by foreign-owned companies. How does importing products like these without trade protections help consumers?

Figure 9.14

The Canadarm was designed and built in Canada for the U.S. space shuttles. With free trade, countries specialize in those activities they do best. In what other industries, besides aerospace, do you think Canada has an advantage?

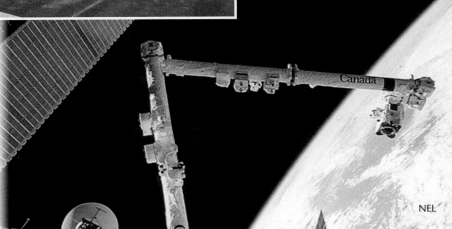

Problems with Globalization

Not all countries are able to compete successfully in the global marketplace. For example, the countries of the Sahel region of Africa (refer to the Case Study in Chapter 7 on pages 158–161) face the following problems:

- few natural resources
- locations that are not good for manufacturing
- low literacy and skill levels
- a history of colonization that has left them with poor economies and unstable political systems

Developing countries in Asia and the Americas face similar problems.

The countries that are best able to compete are those that are already doing well. Japan, the United States, and Canada are successful in the global marketplace. Globalization is widening the gap between rich and poor countries.

Globalization also causes unemployment. This occurs even in industrialized countries like Canada. Increased competition forces industries that are not working well to shut down. Workers lose their jobs. Some workers may find new jobs with businesses that are successful and growing. However, many workers do not have the skills needed to do the new jobs. Others cannot move to places where jobs are being created. The unemployment and closing of businesses that goes along with globalization is called **structural adjustment**.

In a global marketplace, countries need to keep costs of production, including labour wages and raw materials, low and profits high. To achieve this, they may cut back on their efforts to improve people's quality of life. Consider these examples:

- A government may refuse to take a tough stand on environmental problems. Lower environmental standards can mean lower production costs for companies, but higher health and cleanup costs over time.
- A government may refuse to protect the rights of its workers in order to keep labour costs low.

All citizens may suffer as a result of country leaders trying to stay competitive in the global economy.

Figure 9.15

Rows of tombstones representing job losses at Canadian manufacturing facilities are lined up on the front lawn of Parliament Hill as part of a protest organized by labour unions in 2007.

DURING READING

1. Using the headings shown below, complete a t-chart comparing the benefits and problems of globalization. (Refer to the Literacy Tip on page 58 in Chapter 3.)

Benefits of Globalization	Problems of Globalization
• •	• •

Trading Blocs

Some countries get together to form a private trading club called a bloc. They make special rules to help them trade with each other more easily. A trading bloc links the economies of the countries together. This has two advantages:

- The linked economies of the countries are much larger and more powerful on the global scene.
- The countries can exchange resources more easily and efficiently.

Important Trading Blocs of the World, 2008

Trading Bloc	Number of Countries	Total Population	GDP per Capita (US$)
North American Free Trade Agreement (NAFTA)	3	445 000 000	35 491
European Union (EU)	27	497 000 000	28 213
Association of Southeast Asian Nations (ASEAN)	10	566 500 000	5 541
Caribbean Community (CARICOM)	15	14 600 000	4 409
Union of South American Nations (UNASUR)	12	370 200 000	7 749

Figure 9.16

This table shows five important trading blocs of the world for 2008. How does NAFTA compare to the other trading blocs?

The European Union

Of all free trade agreements, the **European Union (EU)** takes the idea of a trading bloc the furthest. Goods and services move freely among the 27 member countries, as does capital (money). Each country in the EU has its own national government. However, representatives from each country in the EU form the European Parliament, which makes rules about economic and political matters. These rules apply to all countries in the trading bloc. Most EU countries also use a common form of money called the euro. This makes business transactions even easier.

Member Countries of the European Union, 2008

Fact File

The euro was launched in 1999 and became the official currency of the European Union in 2002. How might NAFTA benefit from the creation of a common currency?

Figure 9.17

Twenty-seven member countries make up the European Union in 2008. What advantages might these countries enjoy by being part of this trading bloc?

The North American Free Trade Agreement

In 1994, Canada, the United States, and Mexico created a trading bloc with the **North American Free Trade Agreement (NAFTA).** The agreement did not create the same close links as the European Union. However, it did encourage greater economic co-operation among the three countries. Here are the main points of the agreement:

Member Countries of the North American Free Trade Agreement, 2008

- to get rid of barriers to trade, such as tariffs, and to speed the movement of goods across borders
- to increase investment opportunities
- to create steps to resolve disputes quickly
- to look for ways to expand the benefits of the agreement, including bringing other countries into it

There has been talk about expanding NAFTA to form a Free Trade Area of the Americas. This would add some countries from Central and South America to NAFTA. So far, there have been lengthy talks but few results.

Figure 9.18

In 2007, Canada conducted US$542.9 billion worth in trade with its NAFTA partners. Since the agreement came into effect in 1994, NAFTA has created 4.1 million jobs in Canada. The numbers tell a success story, but many Canadians would argue that there are problems with NAFTA. Ask adults you know for their opinions of NAFTA.

AFTER READING

1. Make a t-chart to show the similarities and differences between the EU and NAFTA. (Refer to the Literacy Tip on page 58 in Chapter 3.)

2. Explain how trading blocs help their members become more successful in a world where globalization is a powerful force.

Similarities Between the EU and NAFTA	Differences Between the EU and NAFTA
•	•
•	•
•	•

GO GEO-GREEN

Switching to Green— The Good and the Bad for Ontario's Economy

Figure 9.19

Automakers such as General Motors and Honda are in the process of testing hydrogen-powered fuel–cell cars. How does Ontario benefit from manufacturing a new car?

Do you ever hear your parents or other family members complain when the price of gas increases? Do people in your family change their driving habits when gas costs more? Have people in your family changed their driving habits because they are concerned about the environment? Many families are switching to smaller, more fuel-efficient cars, or cars that run on alternative energies.

There is a downside to this switch. General Motors is the largest vehicle manufacturer in Oshawa, Ontario. General Motors closed factories and laid off workers as the demand for trucks and SUVs plunged. In spring of 2008, the company decided to close some of its truck plants. The Oshawa plant was slated to close in the fall of 2009. Two thousand plant workers were to be laid off, and parts plants were to cut about 1000 more jobs. This would hurt the economy of Oshawa, as well as Ontario. These jobs paid well. As these people lost their jobs, they had less money to spend. With fewer people shopping in local department stores, eating in restaurants, and buying other goods and services, the overall economy was hurt. These economic losses are a sign that the vehicle industry is very important to the economy of Ontario. The industry employs hundreds of thousands of workers in hundreds of plants. Closing car assembly plants sends harmful ripples all across the economy of Ontario and Canada.

There is a possible bright side to this situation. Experts say that Ontario should see these auto plant closures as a wake-up call. They suggest that Ontario should begin to focus on manufacturing "clean" cars and clean car technology. The province has invested in hydrogen and fuel-cell technology. However, it needs to create the plants and systems for these types of cars to be built, serviced, and fuelled.

Hymotion is an Ontario company that converts conventional hybrid electric vehicles into plug-in models. Hymotion could not find the investment or government support in Ontario that it needed to succeed. It was only when an American firm bought this company that it could continue its work. If Ontario wants to become a leader in developing and producing these new technologies, we need to gain strong public support for them here. We have to make the government aware that we need this type of manufacturing in Ontario if we want to keep our economy strong.

The future of our economy is changing. We must attract more green jobs to Ontario. Government, business, labour organizations, and environmental scientists must work together to make this happen. "Green-collar" employment is the future for the Ontario economy. How can you get involved?

- Alert your local government to the need to switch to green jobs.
- Research green companies and make your local politician aware of what these companies do.
- Research local green employers and see what they manufacture.
- Is your family thinking of buying a new car? Discuss fuel-efficient options.

As consumers switch to green options, we will find new opportunities to keep Ontario's economy strong.

CASE STUDY

Canada's Car Makers

Here are some facts about the automobile industry in Canada as of 2006:

- Canada is the world's ninth-largest producer of automobiles.
- The auto industry is Canada's largest manufacturing sector.
- Automobiles make up 24 percent of our manufacturing trade.
- More than 158 000 Canadians work in jobs producing cars and trucks.
- Another 336 000 Canadians sell cars and work in related sales and service jobs.

World Motor Vehicle Production, 1996 and 2006

Country		1996	2006
Japan		10 346 000	11 484 000
United States		11 832 000	11 260 000
China		1 240 000	7 280 000
Germany		4 843 000	5 820 000
South Korea		2 354 000	3 840 000
France		2 359 000	3 147 000
Spain		2 412 000	2 777 000
Brazil		1 813 000	2 611 000
Canada		2 397 000	2 571 000
Mexico		1 222 000	2 046 000
India		541 000	1 958 000
United Kingdom		1 924 000	1 650 000
Russia		1 029 000	1 502 000
Rest of the world		5 730 000	10 588 000
World total		50 042 000	68 561 000

Figure 9.20

This statistical table shows world motor vehicle production for 1996 and 2006. Which countries saw an increase in the number of vehicles produced from 1996 to 2006? Which countries saw a reduction in the number of vehicles produced?

Auto Manufacturing and NAFTA

The Canadian auto industry links closely with the auto industries in the United States and Mexico. Canada receives 80 percent of its total automotive imports from the United States and Mexico. It sends 98 percent of our automotive exports back to these two countries. How was this pattern of imports and exports created? NAFTA is partly responsible. It removed tariffs on North American trade. If foreign car companies wanted to sell cars in Canada without the added cost of tariffs, they had to manufacture cars in Canada.

What resulted?

- Thousands of jobs were created for Canadians.
- Japanese and European companies produced more cars in North America.
- Non-NAFTA imports declined. These are vehicles made outside of North America.

Fact File

In 2006, Canadians bought 1.7 million vehicles but produced 2.6 million vehicles. That year, Canadians spent $75 billion on new vehicles.

However, in 2000, the World Trade Organization ruled that NAFTA broke fair trade rules because it required automakers in Japan and Europe to pay tariffs of 6 percent if they wanted to sell in Canada. Canada had to remove all tariffs on vehicles in 2001. Foreign-made vehicles cost slightly less as a result, so more Canadians bought them.

continues...

CASE STUDY

Canada's Car Makers *(continued)*

Value of Motor Vehicles Imported into Canada, 1998–2007

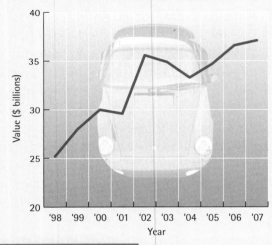

Figure 9.21

This graph shows the value of motor vehicles imported into Canada from 1998 to 2007. How did removing tariffs affect automobile imports in 2001?

Fact File

On average, Canadians spend more at new car dealerships each year than they spend at grocery supermarkets. In 2006, for every $100 Canadians spent at retail outlets, they paid $19.12 to car dealers and $18.35 to supermarkets.

Reasons for Canada's Success

Three main factors helped Canada become a strong player in the North American automobile market:

- *Lower wage rates.* Canadian auto workers have earned about 25 percent less than American auto workers. This has increased profits for auto plants north of the border. It is true that wages in Mexico are much lower than in Canada. However, not all jobs can be done in Mexico because the labour force there lacks the technological skills of Canadian workers.
- *Better productivity.* **Productivity** is the efficiency with which inputs (labour, technology, capital) are used to produce outputs (vehicles). Time after time, Canadian automobile plants have produced more than those in the U.S. and Mexico. A highly skilled workforce in Canada is the main cause.
- *A good business environment.* Canada's trade policies encourage manufacturing. They support new ideas, invention, and investment. For example, companies that do research pay lower taxes.

Challenges for the Future

Sales of vehicles in Canada grew steadily until 2008, when a global economic slowdown hit the industry hard. Sales of vehicles slumped. A disturbing trend in sales made the slowdown even worse. Canadian manufacturers are selling fewer vehicles. Canadians are buying more imported cars and trucks. Between 1996 and 2006, vehicles made overseas took 20 percent more of the Canadian market. What caused this change?

- Imported cars were smaller and more fuel efficient.
- Consumers thought the quality of foreign-made vehicles was higher.

North American companies are struggling to make the switch from larger fuel-guzzlers to the fuel-efficient vehicles that consumers are demanding. More importantly, North American companies are having trouble convincing buyers that their products can match the imports in design and quality.

CASE STUDY

Canada's Car Makers *(continued)*

The great importance of this manufacturing sector means that their failure to rebuild a successful industry could have lasting harmful effects on the Canadian economy.

The North American automobile industry must also become more environmentally friendly. Cars powered by fossil fuels have contributed a lot to global warming. Designs for vehicles with lower emissions have been tried. However, few models have become important in the market. The pressure to be more environmentally friendly will continue. The automobile industry will have to respond.

LITERACY TIP

Reading a Multiple Line Graph

It is important to remember TAPP — Title, Axes, Pattern, and Purpose. Look at individual lines on the graph first. Pay attention to what each colour represents and the pattern that each line makes. Then, compare the three lines to make a conclusion about the trend shown by the graph.

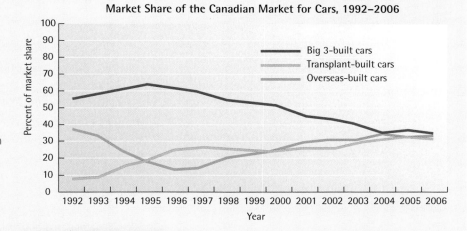

Market Share of the Canadian Market for Cars, 1992–2006

- Big 3-built cars
- Transplant-built cars
- Overseas-built cars

Figure 9.22

This graph shows where cars sold in Canada from 1992 to 2006 were produced. "Overseas-built" refers to cars made outside North America. "Big 3-built" means cars made by General Motors, Chrysler, and Ford in North America. "Transplant-built" identifies cars made in North America by companies owned in other countries. What impacts do you think these patterns have had for workers in Canada?

LITERACY TIP

Creating Slogans

A slogan is a short phrase that captures an important idea. It clearly communicates a message and gives people a reason to remember it. Effective slogans are simple, but they contain key words that evoke emotions, present benefits, or call people to action (for example, "Made in Canada" shows pride in Canada!).

1. Design a bumper sticker encouraging people to buy Canadian-made automobiles. Make sure that your bumper sticker gives a reason for "buying Canadian." Bumper stickers often use slogans to make their point.

2. Identify two important challenges facing the Canadian automobile industry. For each challenge, explain why it is happening and offer one suggestion to help deal with it.

3. What type of vehicles do you think Canada will be producing in 2020?

4. What type of vehicle do you want to drive in the future? Why do you want to drive this type of vehicle?

Knowledge and Understanding

1 You have been asked to give a speech to foreign businesspeople about the advantages of doing business in Canada. What are three important points about Canada's economic resources you would make in your speech? Explain why you have chosen each of these points. Organize your ideas using a chart like the one below.

Key Points in Speech	Reasons for Key Points
•	•
•	•
•	•

2 **a)** Review the Key Vocabulary list on page 188. Three of the terms in this list have been used as the beginning of an ideas web about globalization. Add the remaining five terms to complete this web.

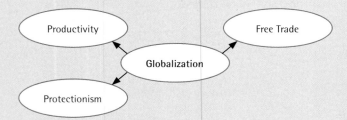

b) Write a short paragraph in which you explain how you connected the five remaining terms to the ideas web, and why you made these connections.

Inquiry/Research and Communication Skills

3 You have an opportunity to interview the president of one of the large automobile companies about how the auto industry affects the economy of a region in Ontario. Make up five questions about the auto industry that you want answered during the interview. Use the following guidelines:

- Use the 5 Ws and 1 H questions.
- Aim for open-ended, higher-level thinking questions.
- Avoid questions that have one-word or simple statistical answers. (Refer to the Literacy Tip on page 41 in Chapter 2.)

4 **a)** Collect two newspaper, magazine, or Internet articles about Canada's economy. Use a three-column chart like the one below to record the point of view for each article. Look for "judging words/phrases" such as *ineffective, too late, too slow, harmful for families, supports big business,* and so on. Words such as these provide clues about whether the writer views Canada's economy positively or negatively. They will help you determine the writer's point of view.

Article (include title, author, source, and date of publication)	Point of View Expressed	Words or Phrases That Show the Point of View

b) Share your articles and chart with two classmates. Discuss the differences in the articles and their points of view.

c) Identify two ways that the articles connect to what you have been learning about economic resources, industry sectors, mixed economies, trade agreements, globalization, and so on.

5 The North American Free Trade Agreement has shaped our trade patterns since it was signed. Has it been good for Canada? Use the Internet, as well as classroom and library resources, to find out more about NAFTA.

a) Organize what you learn from your research about Canada's involvement in NAFTA in an advantages and disadvantages chart. You should be able to list five items under each heading.

Advantages of NAFTA for Canada	Disadvantages of NAFTA for Canada
•	•
•	•
•	•
•	•
•	•

b) Write an opinion paragraph to support the view that NAFTA has been, or has not been, good for the Canadian economy. Plan your paragraph and organize your evidence to follow the 4 Cs of persuasive writing. (Refer to page 70 in Chapter 3.)

Map, Globe, and Graphic Skills

6 Figure 9.20 on page 201 lists the top 13 automobile-producing countries in the world.

a) Using an atlas and an outline map of the world, locate and label these countries.

b) Shade all of these countries the same colour.

c) Give your map an appropriate title. Also, include a legend and a compass.

d) In a paragraph, describe the pattern you see on your map, and identify the factors that you think created this pattern. Remember that a paragraph must begin with a topic sentence that states the main idea (for example, "World automobile production is located …"). Follow the topic sentence with supporting sentences that explain the factors that created this pattern (for example, "These locations have automobile production because …"). End your paragraph with a concluding statement that wraps up your main idea.

Application

7 Is globalization a good trend for Canadians and Canadian economic activity? Write an opinion paragraph that answers this question, using facts and ideas from this chapter to support your opinion. Organize your evidence using a chart like the one below. (See page 70 in Chapter 3.)

Evidence Supporting the Opinion That Globalization Is a Good Trend for Canada	Is Globalization a Good Trend for Canada?	Evidence Supporting the Opinion That Globalization Is Not a Good Trend for Canada
•		•
•		•
•		•
Decision:		
Reasons:		

8 Select one of the roles listed below. Write for the audience listed, in the format identified, and on the topic provided.

Role	Audience	Format	Topic
The president of a large corporation	Canadian government officials	Letter	Encouraging more exports to countries in Asia
A forest worker from Newfoundland and Labrador	Voters in a provincial election	Letter to the editor	Limiting the importing of foreign-made forest products into Canada
A Canadian auto worker	Protesters outside an auto plant that is going to be shut down	Speech	Efforts to stop the loss of jobs due to plant closures
Canada's prime minister	The presidents of Mexico and the United States	Dialogue	Encouraging the expansion of NAFTA

IN THIS UNIT

- identify factors that affect migration and mobility, describe patterns and trends of migration in Canada, and identify the effects of migration on Canadian society
- use a variety of geographic representations, resources, tools, and technologies to gather, process, and communicate geographic information about migration and its effects on people and communities
- connect the real experiences of Canadians to information about the causes and effects of migration

③ Canada has not always treated migrants well. This Japanese internment camp during World War II is one example. Can you think of any other examples?

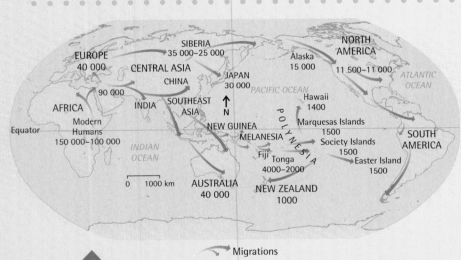

Migrations

① The numbers on the map show approximately how many years ago people settled in different places around the world. How long ago did people first move into North America?

④ Sometimes environmental disasters force people to move. Why might these people need rescuing? What immediate problems might they face? ▼

② Why do people move? Many, like these West Africans, take great risks to flee to other countries in the hope of making a better life.

NEL

5 Before 1970, most immigrants to Canada came from Europe. Which world regions do most immigrants to Canada come from today?

CANADA					
Countries of Origin		Numbers of Immigrants, 1995	Countries of Origin		Numbers of Immigrants, 2004
1. Hong Kong		31 700	China		37 280
2. India		16 200	India		28 183
3. Philippines		15 100	Philippines		13 900
4. China		13 300	Pakistan		13 011
5. Sri Lanka		8 900	Iran		6 491
6. Taiwan		7 700	United States		6 470

6 What are some ways in which modern Canadian culture has affected these Inuit girls? How might their traditional culture be affected?

7 Many cultural celebrations take place in Canada. What are some cultural events that are celebrated in your community?

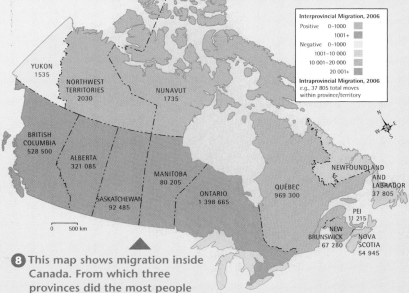

Interprovincial Migration, 2006
Positive 0–1000
1001+
Negative 0–1000
1001–10 000
10 001–20 000
20 001+
Intraprovincial Migration, 2006
e.g., 37 805 total moves within province/territory

YUKON 1535
NORTHWEST TERRITORIES 2030
NUNAVUT 1735
BRITISH COLUMBIA 528 500
ALBERTA 321 085
SASKATCHEWAN 92 485
MANITOBA 80 205
ONTARIO 1 398 665
QUÉBEC 969 300
NEWFOUNDLAND AND LABRADOR 37 805
PEI 11 215
NEW BRUNSWICK 67 280
NOVA SCOTIA 54 945

0 500 km

8 This map shows migration inside Canada. From which three provinces did the most people leave in 2006? Do you think the most people leave the same three provinces today?

9 This is a Grade 3 and 4 class in London, Ontario. Does this class have a similar cultural makeup to the classes in your school?

10 Migration

IN THIS CHAPTER

- identify the push and pull factors that influence people to move
- describe how technology has improved human mobility
- formulate questions to guide and analyze research on migration and mobility
- use thematic maps to identify patterns in migration
- use a decision-making model to select an ideal place to live, and present this decision to other members of the class
- investigate the migrational roots of the members of the class and relate them to Canada's cultural development

KEY VOCABULARY

forced migration
mass migration
migrant worker
migration
point system
preferred treatment
pull factor
push factor
refugee
refugee status
squatter settlement

People on the Move

BEFORE READING

1. In one minute, list as many things as you can think of that migrate. Share your list with a partner and add any new items to your list.
2. With your partner, examine your list and identify a reason why each item migrates.

Figure 10.1

The NASA satellite images show the Three Gorges Dam project in 2000 and 2006. In the satellite image from 2000, the grey area is all the land where buildings were torn down prior to flooding the area for the reservoir. You can see this area is covered by water in 2006. The photo shows the last buildings being demolished in Kaixian County in 2007 to make way for more flooding. More than 1 million people were forced to leave their homes and resettle in other locations. How would you feel if you had to move from your home because the land it was on would be flooded for a power project?

Earthlings Get Out!

North America has been taken over by aliens from outer space. They like it here. They want Canada all to themselves. They pass a law that all human life forms must leave Canada within one week. The aliens are providing ships and planes. Each family will be allowed three bags of belongings, but the total weight must not be more than 150 kg. The aliens have taken control of the banks, the road systems, and all telephone, Internet, and other communications services. Suddenly, you have no country, no home, no money, and no clear future. Where in the world will you go? Which place would be best? What will you take with you?

This is not likely ever going to happen. However, each year, millions of people in the world do face similar situations and decisions. Geographers study these upheavals of people, called **migrations**. They look at the movements, their patterns, and the reasons why these migrations occurred.

DURING READING

1. Compare your list of things that migrate and the reason for each migration with what you read in the next two sections. How is your list similar to what you read? How does your list differ?

Fact File

The Three Gorges Dam power project is China's greatest construction project since the Great Wall of China.

- Situated on the Yangtze River, the main dam is 2.4 kilometres wide and about 200 metres high.
- The reservoir for the dam is deep enough and long enough (more than 600 kilometres) for ocean-going freighters.
- The dam's hydropower turbines will generate as much electricity as 18 nuclear power plants!
- The reservoir flooded over 600 square kilometres of land, covering more than 100 towns.
- Fertile farmland that has been cultivated for hundreds of years is now under water.

Some wonder if the relocation of more than 1 million people and the cost to China's environment is worth the energy this dam will produce for the country. What do you think?

What Is Migration?

Migration is the movement of people, animals, or things from one place to another. Migrations take place for a variety of reasons.

- Animals migrate at different seasons of the year. They change their environments in order to have ample food, favourable weather, and a safe place to mate and raise their young.
- In Canada, most Aboriginal peoples were, at one time nomadic, or moved from place to place. They moved with the changing seasons to ensure good hunting and gathering of food.
- People often move to new locations to find work or to be closer to family. Most adults and many children have lived in more than one house during their lifetime.
- Sometimes entire industries migrate from one location to another. They move to be closer to the source of their raw materials, their markets, or available workers.
- In the 1950s, the whole town of Iroquois, Ontario, had to be moved. The building of the St. Lawrence Seaway flooded the original town site under many metres of water. Recently, more than 1 million Chinese people had to relocate as a result of the Three Gorges Dam power project on the Yangtze River.

Why Migrate?

People move for many reasons. Can you imagine what the people faced in the following examples from the past?

- Many people moved to obtain free or cheap land. Consider the challenges faced by the people who settled the Canadian Prairies.
- Others moved with the dream of becoming wealthy. Think of all the people who joined the gold rushes in California, the Yukon, and Brazil—all dreaming of striking it rich!
- Sometimes, people moved to get a new start and better economic opportunities. Imagine the hard work endured by many Asian people who came to help build the Canadian Pacific Railway through the western mountains. (See Figure 10.2.)
- Some groups moved to find freedom to practise their religions. Think of the Mennonites, Doukhobors, and Jews who moved to escape persecution. (Persecution is harassment or hostility directed at someone, often because of their religious or political beliefs, or because they belong to a certain ethnic group.)

However, moving has its price. Those who migrate have to leave familiar surroundings for a new and strange place. Migration can involve loss and gain, leaving and arriving, ending and beginning. As you learn about migration, keep in mind the turmoil and upheavals that migrants face.

Fact File

Before Canada took over the land in the West, immigrants had to buy land for their houses or farms. In 1872, Parliament passed the Homestead Act. This made land in Western Canada free to Europeans willing to settle there. In 1874, 1400 Russian Mennonite families settled in Manitoba. Between 1896 and 1914, more than 170 000 Ukrainians came to Canada. From which other countries did large numbers of immigrants come to settle in Canada?

LITERACY TIP

Analyzing a Historical Photograph

When viewing a historical photograph such as the one in Figure 10.2, ask yourself these questions:

- Who is in the photograph?
- Who might have taken the photograph?
- Why do you think this photograph was taken?
- How might the people in the photograph have felt about having their picture taken?
- What has changed since this photo was taken?
- In what ways does this photo summarize what was happening at the time it was taken?
- How do you feel about what you see in the photo?

Figure 10.2

From 1881–1885, more than 16 000 Chinese workers were hired to help build the western section of the Canadian Pacific Railway through the mountains. Many died doing this hard, dangerous work. Chinese workers were paid $1 a day—half the wages that non-Chinese workers were paid. Why do you suppose so many Chinese workers were hired for this work? Why would this unfair work situation not happen today?

Figure 10.3

The Great Rift Valley extends about 6000 km from northern Syria in Southeast Asia to Mozambique in East Africa.

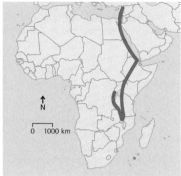

Figure 10.4

This map shows the earliest movements of people from their point of origin in Africa. The arrows show the point of origin and the point of destination of each of these movements. It also shows how many years ago people first settled in regions of the world. About how many years did it take for the earliest people to reach Australia?

The First Migrations

Our earliest ancestors moved to find food, shelter, freshwater, and safety. Scientific evidence shows that the first movements of people in history were out of Central Africa. People followed natural valleys, like the Great Rift Valley in Africa, to move northward. Over thousands of years, small groups of early humans moved to Asia and Europe. Humans reached the Americas last. The spread of people around Earth took about a million years. Locate the point of origin in Africa on the flow map in Figure 10.4. Then, trace the flow arrows to follow the early migration routes.

Early Migrations

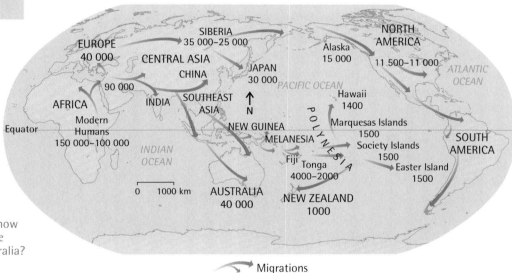

1. Use Figure 10.2 to answer the questions in the Literacy Tip—Analyzing a Historical Photograph—on page 210.

2. Suggest two ways people would travel over land during the early migrations, as shown in Figure 10.4.

3. Oceans created huge barriers to movement. How do you suppose early humans got across the bodies of water shown in Figure 10.4?

4. Besides ocean barriers, what other barriers limited people from spreading over Earth's surface faster than they did?

Fact File

Modern humans have existed for only about 150 000 years. However, fossils found in the Great Rift Valley suggest that our early ancestors lived there 2 to 3 million years ago.

Building Empires

In more recent times, nations created migrations to satisfy different national needs. Some countries wanted to reduce their populations at home. Others wanted to extend their power, conquering new lands and creating new wealth for themselves.

Using sailing ships, the French and British moved people into eastern North America, Australia, India, and the South Pacific. The Spanish and Portuguese moved people into Central and South America. The Dutch established settlements and trade in all parts of the world. The flow map in Figure 10.5 shows major migrations over the past 500 years. As you look at the migrations represented by the coloured arrows, also look at the points of origin and destination. What might have been the reasons for each of these migrations?

Fact File

In 1908, nearly all immigrants came to Canada aboard ships that took two weeks or more to complete the journey across the ocean from Europe or Asia. In 2008, most immigrants arrive by airplanes. Some travel by trains, ships, and automobiles. Most of the journeys start and end the same day. Advances in technology make travelling times shorter for many immigrants. Would technological advances help all immigrants?

Figure 10.5

The coloured arrows on this flow map represent major migrations of people since 1500 CE. Read the legend first to understand what the numbers and coloured arrows represent. Each number and colour corresponds with a specific migration. The arrows show the countries of origin and destination for each migration. Note that some arrows have multiple destinations. What is an important difference in the words used to identify migrations 12 to 17? How is migration 11 similar to migrations 12 to 17?

Major Migrations since 1500 CE

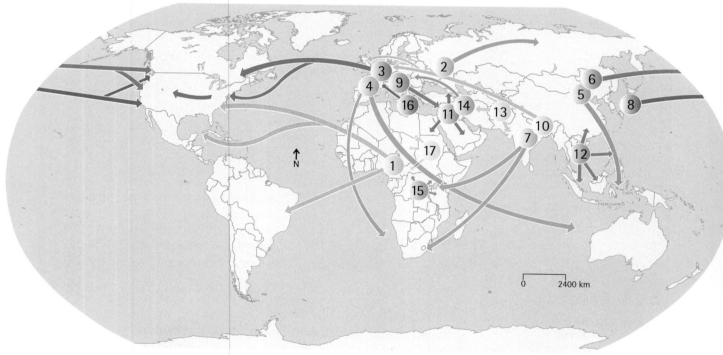

1500–1950

1	Slaves from Africa are taken to the Americas	1500–1850
2	Russians settle Siberia	1850–1950
3	Europeans settle North America	1820–1920
4	Europeans settle southern Africa and Australasia	1840–1960
5	Chinese migrate to Indo–China	1880–1910
6	Chinese migrate to the Americas	1860–1950
7	Indians move to Africa	1860–1910
8	Japanese migrate to North America	1870–1910
9	Jewish people move to Israel	1949–

Since 1950

10	Asians migrate to Europe	1950–1970
11	Palestinian refugees move out of Israel	1950–1970
12	Indo–Chinese flee to southeast Asia and China	1970–1980
13	Afghans flee to Pakistan and Iran	1970–1980 and 2000–2004
14	Iraqis flee to neighbouring countries and to Europe	1990–
15	Rwandans flee to neighbours in Africa	early 1990s
16	Kosovars flee to Europe and beyond	1999–2001
17	Western Sudanese flee Darfur, Sudan, to neighbours in Africa	2003–

Reaching the Ends of the Earth

By the start of the 1900s, there were few places left on Earth that were untouched by immigration. Today, the pace of migration shows no signs of slowing down. Not long ago, people living far from oceans had to travel for days before they could even begin to journey across the oceans. However, with advances in transportation, especially air travel, more people than ever before can move long distances in short time periods.

1. a) List three reasons why people have migrated.

  b) Which of these reasons do you think is most important today? Why?

2. Which areas of the world were the last to have settlements? Why?

GeoSkills

Creating a Flow Map—Immigration to Canada

A flow map shows the movements of people or goods. Lines or arrows show these movements. The arrows (or lines) begin at the source of the movement and end at the destination. You learned how to read a flow map in GeoSkills on pages 88 and 89 in Chapter 4. Figures 10.4 and 10.5 are also examples of flow maps.

  For this activity, you will create a flow map that shows the regions of birth of Canada's immigrant population in 2006. You will use the data listed in Figure 10.6 to create proportional arrows on your flow map. The width of the arrows will represent the number of Canadian immigrants in 2006 that were born in each of the regions.

Regions of Birth for Immigrant Population in Canada, 2006

Region of Birth	Number of Immigrants from that Region
United States	250 535
Central and South America	381 165
Caribbean and Bermuda	317 765
Europe	2 278 345
Africa	374 565
Asia and the Middle East	2 525 160
Oceania and other countries	59 410

You will need a blank outline map of the world, an atlas, pencil crayons, a pencil, and a ruler.

Step 1

Decide on a title for your map. Consider the purpose for your map and the data it will show.

Step 2

Create a legend. This legend needs two parts, as you can see in Figure 10.7.

- Arrow Width and Number of Immigrants: You will draw proportional arrows for this map. The width of these arrows will represent the number of people who immigrated from each region. The wider the arrow, the more people immigrated.

- Region and Colour: Decide on a different colour to shade each of the seven regions. (Keep blue for shading water.) Show these colours beside the names of the regions.

Figure 10.6

This table shows the number of Canadian immigrants in 2006 who were born in each of the seven geographic regions of the world. From which two regions did the most immigrants originate?

continues...

GeoSkills

Creating a Flow Map—Immigration to Canada *(continued)*

Step 3

Use an atlas to identify and colour the seven geographic regions. Use the colours you chose in your legend for each region.

Step 4

Draw your proportional flow arrows. Begin by drawing a line from the point of origin to Canada. Then, measure the appropriate width and draw the second line. Add the point at the end. Refer to Figure 10.7 to see how the first flow arrow is drawn. When all arrows are complete, shade them all the same colour because they represent one thing—the number of people who immigrated from each region. For Oceania and other countries, use Australia as the point of origin for your arrow.

Step 5

Check that your map is complete. Does it have a title, legend, and compass? Is it shaded correctly? Do the arrows show the correct widths?

Step 6

Examine your completed flow map. What do the size and point of origin of the flow arrows tell you about recent trends in Canadian immigration?

Regions of Birth for Canadian Immigrants, 2006

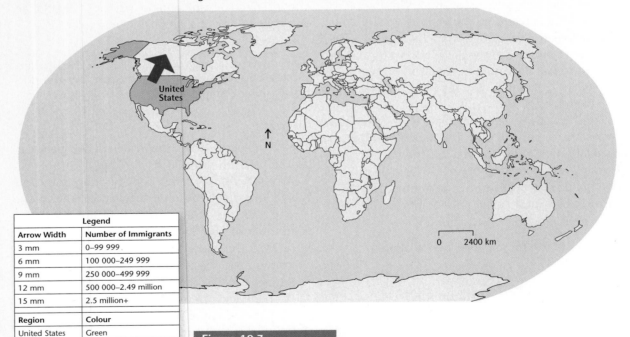

Legend	
Arrow Width	**Number of Immigrants**
3 mm	0–99 999
6 mm	100 000–249 999
9 mm	250 000–499 999
12 mm	500 000–2.49 million
15 mm	2.5 million+

Region	Colour
United States	Green
Central and South America	
Caribbean and Bermuda	
Europe	
Africa	
Asia and the Middle East	
Oceania and other countries	

Figure 10.7

This map shows the shading of the United States and the proportional arrow representing the number of United States–born immigrants to Canada in 2006. The table in Figure 10.6 shows that the number of Canadian immigrants born in the United States in 2006 was 250 535. The legend shows that the width of the arrow beginning in the United States and moving toward Canada should be 9 mm. What is the next region on the list in Figure 10.6? What colour did you choose to represent this region? How wide should the arrow be to represent the number of immigrants from this region?

Why Do People Move?

1. Have you ever moved to a new home, or do you know someone who has moved? What were the reasons for the move? Share these reasons with a small group, and make a list of reasons for moving to a new home or community.

LITERACY TIP

Organizing Information

When reading text that has a lot of information, use a chart to organize your notes and help you remember the key points. Use subheadings from the text as headings for your chart. Categorize the reasons why people migrate within each subsection as push or pull factors.

	Push Factors	Pull Factors
Social factors		
Economic factors		
Political factors		

Have you watched or read news reports about boatloads of people who endured terrible travelling conditions in order to reach the shores of Canada or some other country? Why do people take such big risks? Why are they so desperate to risk everything to make a new start? Why do they feel they must leave their homes for a new country?

In general, people move because of social, economic, or political factors. Usually, more than one factor influences their decision. Factors that influence people to move away are called **push factors**. These can include

- persecution
- lack of freedom
- poor living conditions
- war
- drought or other environmental disaster
- lack of employment

Pull factors attract people to new places. These factors can include
- opportunities for better education or good jobs
- security and the chance to live in a peaceful country
- better living conditions
- good climate

Figure 10.8

Thousands of people have taken big risks fleeing to other countries in hopes of making a better life. What might influence you to flee from your home, risking your life?

1. Use a chart like the one shown in the Literacy Tip on this page to organize your answers to the following questions:

a) Which push factors would influence you to move away from your home and community?

b) Which pull factors would influence you to move to another place?

Social Factors

Family ties are one of the most important ingredients in migration. During the war in Kosovo in 1999, over a million people fled their homes. (See Figure 10.11 on page 217.) Displaced because of war, these people became **refugees**. They usually stayed in refugee camps until they could be taken care of elsewhere. Many European countries, as well as Canada, the United States, and Australia offered temporary homes for these refugees. When families were given the chance to move out of the camps to better conditions, many were split up. Children and parents were separated. Brothers and sisters were separated. Imagine how you would feel if you were suddenly separated from your family. You would have no idea where they had gone or whether you would ever see them again. When these refugees had the chance to move back to Kosovo, they dreamed of reuniting with loved ones.

From War to Independence

The war in Kosovo brought with it grief, turmoil, and a search for refuge. However, most Kosovo refugees returned home and re-established their homes and family life. In 2008, Kosovo became an independent country.

Fact File

More than 5000 refugees were flown from Kosovo refugee camps to Canada. Every effort was made to keep family groups together. Refugees stayed at Canadian Forces bases, such as those in Trenton and Camp Borden, Ontario.

Figure 10.10

Kosovo became the world's newest country on February 17, 2008. Kosovo has a population of 2 million. Its capital city is Pristina. Locate Kosovo on the map in Figure 10.11. Which countries are Kosovo's immediate neighbours?

Figure 10.9

Kosovo refugees staying in Canada faced difficult decisions. Should they return home to Kosovo? Should they stay to start a new life in Canada? This family decided to return to Kosovo. What problems might a refugee family face if they decided to stay in Canada?

Figure 10.11

Kosovo refugees were evacuated to many different countries. Based on what you observe on this map, which two countries took in most of the refugees fleeing Kosovo? To which countries were refugees then evacuated? How many Kosovo refugees did Canada agree to accept?

Refugee Flows from Kosovo, 1999

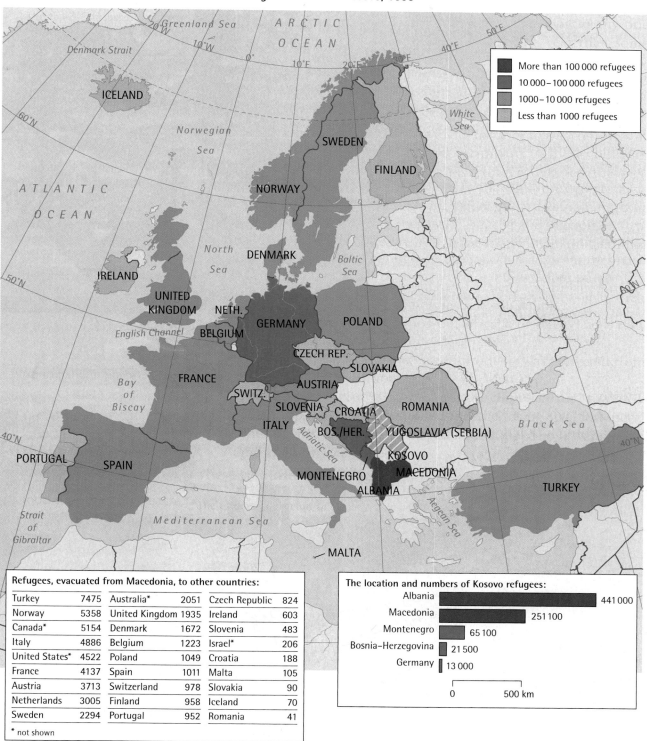

| More than 100 000 refugees |
| 10 000 – 100 000 refugees |
| 1000 – 10 000 refugees |
| Less than 1000 refugees |

Refugees, evacuated from Macedonia, to other countries:

Turkey	7475	Australia*	2051	Czech Republic	824
Norway	5358	United Kingdom	1935	Ireland	603
Canada*	5154	Denmark	1672	Slovenia	483
Italy	4886	Belgium	1223	Israel*	206
United States*	4522	Poland	1049	Croatia	188
France	4137	Spain	1011	Malta	105
Austria	3713	Switzerland	978	Slovakia	90
Netherlands	3005	Finland	958	Iceland	70
Sweden	2294	Portugal	952	Romania	41

* not shown

The location and numbers of Kosovo refugees:

Albania	441 000
Macedonia	251 100
Montenegro	65 100
Bosnia–Herzegovina	21 500
Germany	13 000

0   500 km

For the Sake of the Children

Whether people choose or are forced to migrate, they usually place the welfare and safety of their children above all else. Often, when a family decides to migrate, one parent will go first to get established and then send for the family.

Those who choose to migrate often select countries with high-quality education systems. They want to move to countries like Canada, the United States, Japan, Australia, France, and Britain. We sometimes take the quality of our schools and our education system for granted. How often do you grumble about having to go to school? How often do you complain about your teachers, your classes, or your homework?

Do your parents expect you to finish high school and go on to technical training or university education? In many parts of the world, high numbers of children never complete elementary school. In some places, like rural Brazil, some of the teachers have only completed Grade 5. When you read about this imbalance in education for children in the world, what questions come to mind? Use these questions to find answers through further research.

Fact File

One of the United Nations Millennium Development Goals is making equal rights to education a reality by 2015. However, more than 115 million children of primary school age were not in school in 2008. More than half of all children who were out of school— 61.6 million—were girls. Why do you suppose so many children are not in school?

Figure 10.12

These children are in a classroom in Sudan. How do the conditions shown here differ from those in your school? Consider the differences in technology available.

Figure 10.13

This table shows the primary school completion rate for selected countries in 2005. That is, it shows the proportion of students who started primary school around 1999 who had completed Grade 6 in 2005. Canada has a rate of 100 percent. In more than 25 African countries, less than 20 percent of both girls and boys are enrolled in secondary school. Some countries in the world do not allow girls to go to school past Grade 3 or Grade 4. Why might this be the case?

Primary School Completion Rate Percentage for Selected Countries, 2005

Country		Male	Female	Total
Afghanistan		46	18	32
Argentina		97	100	99
Bangladesh		74	79	76
Burkina Faso		32	24	28
Cambodia		94	90	92
Central African Republic		29	16	23
China		97	96	96
Egypt		100	93	97
India		94	86	90
Indonesia		100	100	100
Israel		100	100	100
Jordan		100	100	100
Mexico		98	100	99
Netherlands		100	99	99
Nicaragua		73	80	76
Niger		34	22	28
Norway		100	98	99
Romania		94	93	93
Rwanda		40	38	39
Spain		100	99	99
South Africa		99	99	99
South Korea		100	100	100
Turkey		89	83	87
Venezuela		87	91	89

Economic Factors

People most often move for economic reasons, for example, to find employment and to achieve a higher standard of living. Demographers predict that more people will move for employment reasons in the future than for any other reasons.

Jobs, Jobs, Jobs

People move to find and to keep jobs. The nature of some jobs causes people to migrate. For example, a miner may move many times from mining town to mining town in order to follow the job opportunities. Sometimes, a mine closes because it cannot make enough money to stay open. Sometimes, a mine just runs out of minerals.

1. Work with a partner to create a list of as many other jobs you can think of that might cause people to migrate to follow job opportunities. Then, share your list with another pair of students and see how many jobs you can add to your list.

2. Has your family moved to take advantage of job opportunities? Do you know someone who has moved because of work? What challenges do individuals and families face when they migrate for employment reasons?

Figure 10.14

This carpenter is working on a housing subdivision in Fort McMurray, Alberta. Many people from Newfoundland, including a large number of tradespeople, have moved to Alberta to take jobs created by the oil boom. What will this migration mean for Newfoundland?

Figure 10.15

Finite resources, like the uranium used for nuclear energy, eventually run out. Uranium City, Saskatchewan, had no other means to survive after its mine closed. Nearly everyone moved away. It was a "ghost town" when this picture was taken in 1957. After a brief comeback in the 1970s, the town has been closed since the early 1980s. Some think another comeback is possible soon. What do you suppose might make that possible?

People hold various attitudes toward jobs, and they choose their jobs based on a variety of reasons. Many people migrate for better jobs that require high education, special skills, or both. These high-paying jobs are often in professions and trades such as the following:

- medicine
- computer science
- engineering
- tool-and-die making
- business management
- high-end technology and communications

People who want to immigrate to Canada to work must earn enough points to pass the **point system** that is illustrated in Figure 10.16.

Figure 10.16

Most immigrants to Canada must pass the point system like this one for independent skilled workers. Sixty-seven points is a pass. If you know only one language and have no experience, is it possible to get enough points to be considered for immigration?

Needed Points for Independent Skilled Workers to Immigrate to Canada

Factor	Maximum Points	Your Score
1. Education Secondary School Diploma = 5 points Ph.D or Master's degree with 17 years of full-time study = 25 points	25	
2. Language First language skills = 16 points Second language skills = 8 points	24	
3. Experience Four years of work experience required for maximum points.	21	
4. Age To receive maximum points, applicant must be 21 to 49 years old.	10	
5. Arranged employment	10	
6. Adaptability Includes 5 points for a family tie in Canada	10	
Total	100	

Age:
People aged 21 to 49 get the full 10 points. Applicants lose two points for every year younger than 21 or older than 49. Why?

Adaptability:
People with family connections in Canada have greater success when they apply to immigrate. Family already in Canada can help new immigrants get used to new systems and lifestyles, and may also provide a place to live. The closer the family tie, the easier it is for a person to immigrate. A person joining a spouse or a common law partner will get higher preference than someone joining a second cousin. This is called **preferred treatment.**

Fact File

In 1908, Canada had few requirements like the current point system. Canada advertised for farmers, particularly young farm families, to come and settle in the Canadian West. Immigrants to cities were discouraged. In 1908, 143 326 people immigrated to Canada.

In 2008, Canada wanted business class people and entrepreneurs, as well as highly skilled workers and professionals. People with knowledge and technical skills, as well as money to start businesses, were favoured. Over 90 percent of the 250 000 immigrants entering Canada in 2008 settled in cities.

Number of Skilled and Unskilled Workers Arriving in Canada, 1998–2006

	1998	2000	2002	2004	2006
Skilled — Managers and professionals	21 979	37 934	37 933	35 714	30 671
Skilled — Technical and clerical	12 348	12 735	13 804	11 380	11 660
Unskilled — Labourers and inexperienced	42	33	37	16	38

Figure 10.17

This table shows the number of skilled and unskilled workers arriving in Canada from 1998 to 2006. During that period, the total immigration to Canada averaged more than 200 000. Note that only a small proportion of the total number of immigrants to Canada is included in this table. In 2006, what percent of workers arriving in Canada were managers and professionals? What percent were unskilled? What can you conclude about successful immigrants to Canada?

Two types of migration are increasing due to globalization:

- Executive migration: Business executives move around the world as part of their career training. These people and their families may spend a few years in each of several different countries over their careers.
- Contract migration: Other professionals, skilled technicians, and managers gain contracts to go to other countries and work on specific projects. They stay in these countries until the projects are finished, and then move on to other projects elsewhere. (See Figure 10.18.)

Figure 10.18

Canada has a worldwide reputation for talented, highly skilled, well-educated people. Many Canadians do contract work in different parts of the world. What technological skills do you think Canadian contract workers have that enable them to work around the world?

Rural Job Decline

The biggest migration in history was, and still is, the flood of people moving from rural to urban areas. This **mass migration** began in the 1800s with the Industrial Revolution. Fewer jobs were available on farms, so people left for the towns and cities to get work in the new factories. This flow continues today. (See Figure 10.19.) In many countries, this urban shift is creating huge problems.

As millions of people move into cities, governments cannot keep up with the demand for services. Sanitation systems cannot be built fast enough because of lack of money. Basic human needs such as clean water are not available. There is often a lack of affordable housing. Slums and **squatter settlements** develop, which are neighbourhoods where people build makeshift shacks for shelter. There are no services for people in these settlements, such as water, sewers, and electricity, which creates an environment for diseases to spread. Extreme poverty forces many people living in these settlements to beg, steal, and scrounge what they can to survive. (See Figure 10.20.) Can these people afford to move to Canada or even be eligible in the point system?

Fact File

Over 1 million homeless people live on the streets in each of the cities of Mumbai and Calcutta in India. Many spend their entire lives on the streets. One prediction is that 31 villagers will show up in an Indian city every minute from now to 2050—that is more than 700 million people! What will result from this migration trend if solutions are not found?

Percent of Urban/Rural in Developed and Developing Countries

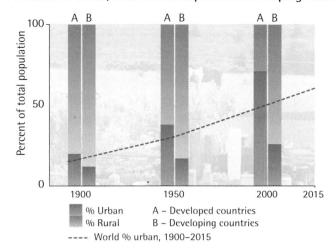

Figure 10.19

This bar graph shows the move from rural to urban areas in developed and developing countries, from 1900 to 2015 (estimated). The year 2008 marked the first time that the world was more urban than rural. Is your community more urban or more rural? Are there signs it is changing? What signs do you notice?

■ % Urban   A – Developed countries
■ % Rural   B – Developing countries
---- World % urban, 1900–2015

Fact File

Squatter settlements have different names around the world. They are called *bustees* in India, *favelas* in Brazil, and *barrios* in the rest of Central and South America.

Figure 10.20

This squatter settlement is in Corinto, Colombia. Living conditions are poor. The houses are made of wood and plastic, with zinc roofs and dirt floors. Why are no streets visible? What challenges would people face living in settlements like these?

Political Factors

In some countries, the government denies certain citizens their rights.
The politicians make new laws that reduce or eliminate the freedoms
that we take for granted in Canada.

1. a) What rights and freedoms are
you guaranteed as a citizen of
Canada?

b) In this section, you will learn about political
factors that push people from their homes and
communities in countries around the world.
Use the following organizer to note these
political push factors and the rights and
freedoms that guarantee this will not happen
to you as a Canadian citizen. Use the first entry
as a model for your own entries. Note that
you will enter the text from the Charter that
guarantees your protection from this kind of
unfair treatment.

Political Factors That Push People to Leave Their Homes in Other Countries	My Rights and Freedoms Guaranteed by the Charter

• persecution because of religion	• Everyone has the following fundamental freedoms:
	  – freedom of conscience and religion (2. a)
	  – freedom of thought, belief, opinion and expression, including freedom of the press and other media of communication (2. b)

• persecution because of skin colour, nationality, and language	• Every individual is equal before and under the law and has the right to the equal protection and equal benefit of the law without discrimination and, in particular, without discrimination based on race, national or ethnic origin, colour, religion, sex, age, or mental or physical disability. (15)

Persecution

For centuries, people have migrated to escape persecution because of
the following:

- their religion
- their skin colour
- their nationality
- their language

Persecution has often forced people to flee to find freedom, peace,
and acceptance.

Religious persecution and conflict are long-standing problems.
Many devastating examples have occurred in recent times. Major
events that caused large-scale migration include the following:

- the movement of Jewish people to Israel (see Figure 10.21)
- the movement of "breakaway" Christian groups, such as the
Mennonites and Quakers
- the conflict between Hindus and Muslims, which led to the
partition, or division, of India in 1947, and the migration of
more than 11 million people

Many of the world's major religions are hundreds, even thousands, of years old. Christianity started during the time of the Roman Empire. At that same time, Hinduism, Judaism, and Buddhism were already well established. The religion of Islam developed in what is now Saudi Arabia during the 700s CE. At times, many followers of these religions have been persecuted for their beliefs. Many groups had to either defend their faith or seek new and safer homes.

Figure 10.21

Jewish immigrants arrive in their new homeland in 1949. The United Nations approved the division of Palestine into a Jewish state and an Arab state in 1947. Israel became an independent homeland for Jews in 1948. Most of the Jewish people who moved to Israel came from Europe at this time. What major persecution had Jewish people suffered during the same decade?

Decision to Split

Sometimes, conflict between religious groups has been so deadly and ongoing that governments decide to divide the country and move people of one group away from the other. In 1948, India was divided into three countries to try to end the conflict between Hindus and Muslims. (See Figure 10.22.)

Division of India, 1948

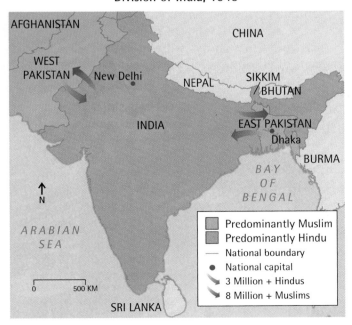

Figure 10.22

In 1948, India was divided into three countries—India, and East and West Pakistan. Hindus moved to the part that remained India, and Muslims moved to be in East and West Pakistan. Today, East and West Pakistan exist with different names. Check your atlas and identify the names that these countries are known by today.

Fact File

In terms of religion, India is 83 percent Hindu, 11 percent Muslim, 2 percent Christian, 2 percent Sikh, and 2 percent other. Pakistan is 97 percent Muslim. If India was divided into three different countries to end the conflict between Hindus and Muslims in 1948, why do you think Muslims still live in India today?

Canada's Past, Not All Rosy!

In Canada today, we think of ourselves as multicultural and accepting of immigrants. However, our past record shows that this was not always the case. What words would you use to describe the following government orders and actions? When did Canada begin to change its actions regarding immigrants?

1876—The *Indian Act* was the first act directed toward a race of people—Aboriginal peoples in Canada, then referred to as "Indians." It defined who had Indian or treaty status, and it made Indians legal wards of the government. This act gave individual Indians the right to seek Canadian citizenship if they gave up their rights and privileges as status Indians. It also denied Indians the right to vote in an election.

1906—The *Immigration Act* prevents "undesirable people" from immigrating to Canada (mostly people with mental or physical disabilities).

1910—The *Immigration Act* gives the government power to restrict any group from immigrating for any reason.

1911—The government orders all African-Americans entering Alberta from the United States to be turned back.

1914—Officials refuse entry to 352 of 376 people from India arriving in Canada at Vancouver Harbour. They are forced to leave.

1919—The new *Immigration Act* after World War I states that immigrants can be excluded from Canada if their beliefs are considered unacceptable.

1923—The government passes the *Chinese Immigration Act*, banning almost all Chinese from entering Canada.

1938—The government declares that all Jewish refugees must have at least $20 000 in cash before being allowed into Canada.

1946—After a major debate about allowing refugees into the country, Canada welcomes more than 22 000 orphaned children from Europe.

1947—The *Chinese Immigration Act* is repealed. Chinese people are to be treated like all other immigrants to Canada. They will no longer face quotas and controls on immigrating.

1947—The *Canadian Citizenship Act* makes it official that people can become Canadian citizens whether they were born in Canada or not.

1952—The new *Immigration Act* allows the government to discriminate against people it decides are not suitable to live in Canada.

1956—Following the revolution in Hungary against the communist government, Canada accepts 37 000 Hungarian refugees.

Figure 10.23

In May 1914, a group of 376 passengers—340 Sikhs, 12 Hindus, and 24 Muslims—sent to test Canada's exclusionary immigration policies, sailed to Vancouver on the *Komagata Maru*. For two months, the passengers and the authorities of British Columbia were involved in a heated legal battle. In the end, only 24 passengers were given permission to stay in Canada.

1962—The *Immigration Act* changes to remove racial discrimination from Canada's immigration policy. Qualified people can be considered for immigration, regardless of skin colour, race, or ethnic origin.

1967—The Immigration Appeal Board is set up to give immigrants the right to fight government deportation orders.

1967—The point system is established. Applicants receive points in categories such as education, age, personal characteristics, English or French language ability, and job opportunities in Canada. Applicants who receive more than 50 points are allowed to immigrate.

1971—Prime Minister Trudeau announces that Canada will embrace a policy of multiculturalism. Canada will welcome people of different ethnic backgrounds. Immigrants are welcome to keep their heritage and cultural traditions in Canada.

1988—Canada officially apologizes to Japanese Canadians for the poor treatment they received during World War II. Survivors receive payment for their suffering, and $12 million is used to set up a Japanese community fund.

1990—Canada opens its doors to 220 000 immigrants a year for five years.

2002—The *Immigration and Refugee Protection Act* emphasizes the social and economic importance of immigration to Canada. This act stresses the value of creating a culturally diverse society.

2004—Immigration hits a high of 261 000 people in one year.

2006—The Canadian government apologizes to the Chinese people of Canada for the Head Tax (a charge on Chinese people entering Canada between 1885 and 1923), and for the poor treatment received due to the *Chinese Immigration Act*. Twenty survivors and their spouses receive compensation.

2008—Canada reviews its immigration system so that it can move to get rid of a backlog of 900 000 immigration applications.

1. a) Review the timeline of Canada's immigration record. How many examples of discrimination before 1960 can you identify?

b) Since 1960, what two changes worked toward more positive immigration policies?

2. Should groups that were discriminated against receive official apologies from the government? Discuss this question in a small group. Choose a leader to keep the discussion on track and to make sure that everyone has a chance to speak. Choose a recorder to keep track of the main arguments for and against the need for official apologies. Choose a reporter to share your opinion(s) and your supporting reasons with the rest of the class.

BE A GLOBAL CITIZEN

Doctors Without Borders, Médecins Sans Frontières

Imagine that you wake up one morning and your parents tell you that you will be leaving your home. You can only take one suitcase with you, and you must be able to carry it on your own. You will be leaving in one hour. What would you take with you? How would you feel?

As far back as history has been recorded, people have been forced to leave their homes in a great hurry. They have to leave most of their belongings behind, taking only what they can carry. They may be fleeing from a war, persecution, or an environmental disaster. These people need help when they leave. One organization that works with displaced people is Médecins Sans Frontières (MSF), or Doctors Without Borders.

Médecins Sans Frontières was created by doctors and journalists in France in 1971. MSF provides help to those most in need. They do not take sides or associate themselves with any political, military, or religious organizations. They remain neutral in armed conflicts and offer assistance to all who need it. MSF speaks out on behalf of the neglected, and they challenge abuses of the aid systems. They promote improved medical treatments for dislocated people. In 1999, MSF received the Nobel Peace Prize.

In 1975, MSF began to work with refugees. They helped Cambodians fleeing from the Khmer Rouge. By the mid-1980s, MSF was helping refugees on many continents. They also brought the stories of the horrors these people faced to the media. They worked in Ethiopia, where the government forced people to flee and took aid away from the people who needed it most. In Central America, they helped refugees from Nicaragua and El Salvador. In 1991, they provided care to the Kurds who were displaced by the Gulf War. They also cared for refugees in Turkey, Iran, and Jordan. Since 2000, MSF has expanded their program even further.

MSF Canada was established in 1991. Their national office is in Toronto. Your class or school might want to help raise funds for MSF. You could organize small fundraisers in which all students, staff, and parents could participate. As a class, you could educate other students in your school about the problems that displaced people face worldwide, and how MSF helps to alleviate these problems.

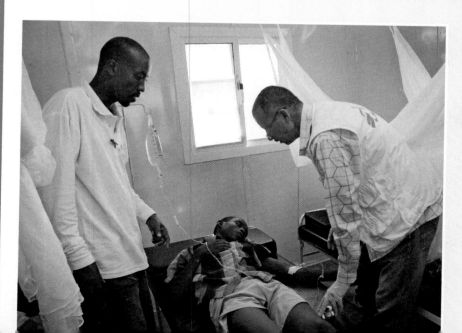

Figure 10.24

A doctor from Médecins Sans Frontières treats a young patient in a refugee camp in Ahwar, Yemen. Thousands of Somalis risk death crossing the Gulf of Aden to Yemen to escape civil war in their own country. What challenges do these doctors face in locations such as this?

Human Rights and Migration

In 1948, the United Nations proclaimed the Universal Declaration of Human Rights. It identified the key rights and protections that everyone in the world should have. All people are entitled to rights and freedoms such as

- the right to life, freedom, and security
- freedom of thought and opinion
- freedom of religion
- freedom of speech
- freedom from wrongful imprisonment
- freedom from slavery
- freedom from mistreatment and torture

Unfortunately, some world leaders still do not follow this International Bill of Human Rights. They continue to violate the rights of many of their citizens and force some to flee their country. These people go wherever they feel they can find safety. Eventually, if they cannot safely return to their homes, they try to gain **refugee status** in some other country. Government officials hear their case and decide whether they will be allowed to stay in the country. There have been times when Canada was not open to immigrants. However, Canada now has an excellent humanitarian record and has welcomed many refugees.

When Will the Aims of the United Nations Declaration Be Met?

Our world has a great need for tolerance and understanding among peoples. Each year, we see many examples of people's inhumanity to one another. Prejudice exists in every culture. No one should be discriminated against because of his or her race, religion, language, social class, or gender. There is no room for these acts of violence and intolerance. It will take time for all governments to meet the aims of the Universal Declaration of Human Rights. Still, there is something you can do. You can start by treating all people in your community fairly, equally, and respectfully.

Fact File

Between 2003 and 2007, Canada took in 147 000 refugees. On average, Canada accepted nearly 30 000 refugees each year. Recently, the top 10 sources of refugees have been: Afghanistan, Colombia, Ethiopia, Burma, Sudan, Congo, Somalia, Iran, Eritrea, and Iraq. How does this list compare with what you learned about world patterns of wealth and poverty in Chapter 7?

1. Discuss the following questions with a partner or a small group.

a) You have been reading about political factors that push people to leave their homelands. In which parts of the world do many of these forced migrations seem to happen?

b) Think about the history of North America. When have people been forced to migrate on our continent? (Hint: Think of the First Nations peoples.)

Forced Migration

You have been reading about examples of **forced migration** —people leaving their homelands against their will. Whatever the causes, the results are almost always the same: danger, hardship, unhappiness, and economic loss for the migrants.

Slavery

One example of forced migration is the most brutal in history. Between 1500 and 1850, millions of Black Africans were captured, herded onto ships, and transported to the Americas. Their captors stripped them of all their social, human, and political rights. They were sold as slaves at auctions and forced to live and work in inhuman conditions. (See Figure 10.26.) Families were split apart. Their cultural heritages and languages were suppressed. Yet, pride, music, religion, and storytelling kept many of the Black African cultures alive through those terrible years of slavery.

Figure 10.25

Since 2003, more than 400 000 people have been killed in the Darfur region of Sudan, and another 2.5 million have fled the region. The situation has been grave, as the government has not taken steps to stop the ethnic violence. In this conflict, Arabs are using an armed militia, the Janjaweed, to attack African tribespeople. Tens of thousands must live in refugee camps with little food and clean water. What organizations could you contact to find ways to help with this situation?

Figure 10.26

Slaves were sold at auctions and treated as the property of the landowners who bought them. Some slaves from the southern U.S. states escaped to freedom via the "Underground Railroad." This secret network of safe havens provided food and shelter along the way. Many slaves escaped to Ontario. Can you locate where many went on the map? Is slavery a thing of the past, or does it still exist in the world today? How can you find out?

The Underground Railroad

Forced Dislocations

In North America, European settlers forced many First Nations peoples to move from their lands and onto reserves. These lands were of little value for farming and contained few natural resources. They were lands that no settlers wanted. What the settlers did want was the rich farmlands and forests that were the homes of the First Nations peoples. In Chapter 2, you also read about the forced dislocation of Aboriginal children to residential schools. This had one of the greatest impacts on Aboriginal people in their history. It destroyed their cultures, languages, societies, and ways of life.

As more and more Europeans moved to North America, greater numbers of First Nations peoples were forced onto reserves. This forced migration created many issues that societies continue to face today. Pay attention to current news stories and reports. Can you identify problems faced by First Nations today that stem from those forced migrations?

First Nations were not the only peoples to be dislocated in Canada. Japanese Canadians were also dislocated due to government policies. Japan attacked the United States at Pearl Harbor on December 7, 1941. Canada and the United States were allies in World War II. That attack meant that Canada was at war with Japan. Early in 1942, the Canadian government decided to take away the property of all Japanese people living in Canada. Most of the Japanese people lived in British Columbia. The government sent the Japanese to internment camps. (See Figure 10.28.) Families were divided, and the government disposed of whatever property the families could not carry.

Figure 10.27

Living conditions on reserves have been a major problem. Recently, flooding and contaminated water supplies caused major problems in northern Ontario. In the low-lying settlement of Kashechewan, high water levels overloaded the old local sewage systems, which then polluted the drinking water. The villagers had to move away to places like Hearst, Thunder Bay, and Stratford, Ontario. Can you suggest one action that may prevent further dislocations for the people of Kashechewan?

Figure 10.28

Conditions were harsh in the Japanese internment camps in British Columbia. Some families lived together in flimsy shacks. Others were split up into separate dormitories for males and females. In 1988, the government of Canada apologized for this treatment. What did we learn from this forced migration?

To learn more about Japanese internment camps,

Go to Nelson
Social Studies

The Going Gets Faster

Migration around the world shows no signs of slowing down. The pressures that encourage migration continue. These push factors include

- drought and starvation (for example, in Africa, south of the Sahara desert)
- political conflicts (for example, in Afghanistan and Iraq)
- environmental damage and loss of natural resources (for example, the destruction of the Congo rainforest)
- lack of jobs (for example, in many highly populated rural areas, such as parts of India)
- social and economic problems (for example, religious conflicts or the closure of fisheries in our Atlantic Region)

Where do people migrate? They are pulled to the more developed countries, like Canada. Canadians' lifestyle and the things we have attract many migrants. Through television, movies, the Internet, and other media, people in developing countries see how people in the developed countries live. (See Figure 10.29.) They see the quality of our lives compared to their standard of living. When they recognize the possibilities, many want to immigrate with the hope for a better quality of life.

Fact File

An average Canadian consumes 10 to 15 times more than an average person in Argentina, the Philippines, or Egypt. (The average Canadian produces much more waste, too!) The average Canadian household has 10 000 "things," yet only about 200 are basic necessities. What do these statistics tell you about the gap in wealth that exists in our world?

Who Consumes the Most?

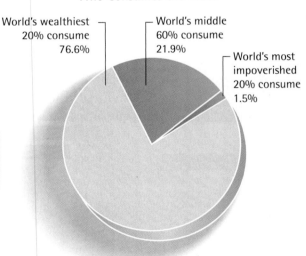

World's wealthiest 20% consume 76.6%

World's middle 60% consume 21.9%

World's most impoverished 20% consume 1.5%

Figure 10.29

Eighty percent of the world's people live on less than US$5 per day. Fifty percent live on less than US$3 per day. The gap between the wealthiest and most impoverished groups is widening. Of the goods and services available to buy in our world, the most impoverished 20 percent of the population can only purchase 1.5 percent. The wealthiest 20 percent consume over 75 percent of the world's goods and services. How do these statistics relate to migration?

It is natural for people to want to look after their basic needs and to have some pleasures in their lives. In many developing countries, people are unable to meet their basic needs, and they struggle to survive. Unless people can live securely in their own countries, they will continue to migrate.

Moving to Another Country—How Do You Decide?

Whether or not to migrate to another country is a tough decision for families. Imagine your family has to move to another country. Your choice comes down to two countries. How will you decide where to go? One decision-making model uses the following steps:

- *Select criteria*: Which pull factors are drawing your family to migrate to another country?
- *Pose questions*: What does your family want to know about each pull factor within the countries you are considering?
- *Research the answers*: Use all possible sources (for example, the Internet, embassies, government departments, people who have been to the countries, newspapers, magazines, and so on) to gather information to answer the questions your family has.
- *Analyze the answers*: Examine the information you gathered. Ask yourself if the answers meet the needs of your family.
- *Make a decision*: Based on the information you gathered, decide which country provides the most satisfying answers to your questions. Which country meets your criteria best?

Every day around the world, thousands of people make decisions about where to move. Most immigrating families have time to research and analyze information before making the decision. Unfortunately, refugees do not have the luxury of time to make such choices.

Criteria and Questions to Help Decide Where to Move

Criteria	Questions to Research	Answer Country A	Answer Country B
Job availability	What is the employment rate?	• 3 percent unemployment	• 7 percent unemployment
Education quality	Can my children get a good education?	• 90 percent of males/females complete secondary school	• 85 percent of males/females complete secondary school
Health care system	Will we be able to get a family doctor easily?	• 20 doctors/1000 people	• 17 doctors/1000 people
Government stability	Is the country safe and is the government stable?	• 10 demonstrations by citizens since 1990	• 25 demonstrations by citizens since 1990
Economic well-being	Is the quality of life good?	• $35 000 GDP/person	• $38 000 GDP/person
Religious freedom	Will we be free to practise our religion?	• many practising religions	• one state religion

Figure 10.30

Analyze the answers in this chart and decide: Would you move to Country A or B?

AFTER READING

1. Why is having family ties in a country very important for a new immigrant?

2. Re-examine Figure 10.29. Suggest three things you could give up, at least in part, that would help reduce your demand for resources. Suggest one solution to help reduce the gap between the wealthy and the impoverished.

3. How has technology affected migration?

CASE STUDY

Migrant Workers

A new form of migration has emerged in the developing countries of the world. Advances in technology, like computers and the Internet, have allowed people in need of **migrant workers** to advertise globally. Our transport systems allow workers to travel to the regions of need. Each year, migrant workers from developing countries travel to more industrialized countries for seasonal or even longer work periods. Many people and companies hire these workers to do low-level jobs.

In 2007, nearly 66 000 migrant workers came to Canada. They worked in low-skilled, temporary jobs. (For example, migrant workers come to Ontario from the Caribbean to help with the tobacco, tomato, and apple harvests.) Of the 66 000 who came to Canada, 54 percent worked as babysitters, nannies, and parent helpers. Twenty-five percent were general farm workers. The rest were kitchen

help, cleaners, construction workers, and food and beverage processing workers.

Most foreign workers go to Europe, the United States, and Japan. They often feel that having any job is far better than being unemployed in their own countries. Sometimes, strict immigration restrictions make it difficult for them to enter other countries. They might try other, perhaps illegal, ways of entering a country in order to get a job. Some employers take advantage of these illegal immigrants and pay them very low wages.

Persian Gulf Migrant Workers

Amin Sharif, age 30, and his brother Ahmed, age 24, live in Lahore, Pakistan. They work 11 months a year in the oil fields of Saudi Arabia. They live in a compound with over 500 other workers. These workers migrate from countries around the region, including India, Bangladesh, and Egypt. (See Figure 10.31.)

Estimated Sources of Foreign Workers

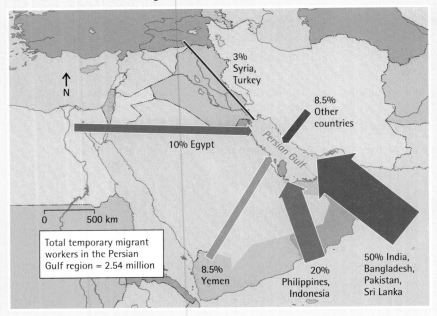

Figure 10.31

Thousands of people leave developing countries each year to work elsewhere. The oil-rich countries around the Persian Gulf attract many migrant workers. More than 11 million international workers are in this region. Note how the proportional arrows represent the percentage of migrant workers from different countries. Why might so many of the migrant workers come from India, Bangladesh, Pakistan, and Sri Lanka?

CASE STUDY

Migrant Workers *(continued)*

Amin and Ahmed help install oil pumping equipment. They work at an oil shipment centre on the shore of the Persian Gulf. For them, the US$700 they receive each month is high pay. Their accommodation and meals are provided. They spend very little money on themselves. Instead, they send most of what they earn back to their families in Pakistan. This money sent back is called migrant remittance. It is an invisible gain to Pakistan's wealth, since it is money added to their economy from outside their country. (See Figure 10.32.)

Amin is married. He and his wife have three children—two little girls, ages seven and five, and a one-year-old son. His wife and children live in his parents' home in Lahore with his two younger sisters. Ahmed has plans to be married soon.

Amin and Ahmed work long shifts—10 to 15 hours every day. Yet, jobs like these are essential to the well-being of their families back home.

**Sending the Money Home—
Migrant Remittance Totals, 2006**

Countries		Migrant Remittance (US$ billions)
1. India		25.7
2. Mexico		24.7
3. China		22.5
4. Philippines		14.9
5. Bangladesh		5.5
6. Pakistan		5.4
7. Morocco		5.0
8. Egypt		5.0
9. Lebanon		4.9
10. Vietnam		4.8

Figure 10.32

The top 10 countries in migrant remittance dollars receive one-third of the world total. The Philippines is fourth on the list. Recently, they trained 80 000 nurses to "export" to jobs in other countries. Why would the Philippines train so many nurses to work in other countries?

1. Identify three reasons why people leave their homelands to work in distant countries.

2. Most migrant workers in Canada come from the Caribbean. Compare their travelling distance to that of Amin and Ahmed.

3. In your own words, explain how a migrant remittance is an invisible gain to a country's wealth.

Fact File

In 2007, migrant remittances were valued at US$318 billion worldwide. Over 70 percent of this money went to developing countries. If migrant remittances are invisible gains to the economies of developing countries, how do you suppose these statistics are gathered?

Knowledge and Understanding

1 Five key terms in this chapter deal with migrants or migration. Explain each term in your own words and provide an example that will help explain the meaning. An example is provided for you.

Key Term	Meaning (in your own words)	Example
Migration	Migration is when people move for social, economic, political, or environmental reasons.	• A family moves to a new community because of the mother's new job.
Mass migration		
Forced migration		
Migrant worker		
Migrant remittance		

2 The 1948 United Nations Universal Declaration of Human Rights identified the key rights and protections that everyone in the world should have.

a) Identify three push factors that violate these rights and protections.

b) Explain the rights that each of these push factors violates.

3 a) How has technology affected migration?

b) How has technology affected where immigrants to developed countries are coming from?

4 The following poem is very old. It expresses the emotions that flow through the hearts and minds of immigrants. Immigrants today experience the same emotions. Read the poem and answer the following questions:

a) What emotions is the poet experiencing?

b) What will the poet miss?

c) What is so difficult about leaving?

d) What is the poet's wish?

e) How do you suppose the poet left his homeland and travelled across the ocean?

f) How might the poem change if it was written by an emigrant today? Think about how technology has improved human mobility.

Goodbye rivers, goodbye springs
Goodbye little streams
Goodbye view from my eyes
I don't know when we will see each other again

Goodbye glory, goodbye happiness
I leave the house where I was born
I leave the village that I know so well
For a world I have not seen
Goodbye also my loved ones
Goodbye forever, perhaps
I say this goodbye with tears in my eyes
Whenever I am overseas
Do not forget me, my love
If I die of solitude
So many leagues across the ocean
O for my little house my home

Figure 10.33

This is known as The Poem on the Emigrants' Monument. It is located in La Coruña, a city in northwest Spain. The poem was translated from Gallego, the language of Galicia, by Russell King.

Inquiry/Research and Communication Skills

5 The Acadian Odyssey is an example of a forced migration in North America.

a) Make up four questions you want answered about the Acadians. Two of your questions should deal with factors that caused their forced migration and major events that occurred during and after their migration.

Use the Q-Chart (question chart) on page 237 to help you make up your research questions. Connect the W words on the left with the action words on the top to make up questions (for example, What is …? and What did …?) As you move down the column of W words and across the row of action words, you will create more open-ended questions. (How would …? and Why might …? are open-ended questions. What is…? and Who did …? are closed questions.)

	is	did	can	would	will	might
What						
Who						
When						
Where						
How						
Why						

Go to Nelson Social Studies

b) Read the following sections about the Acadian Odyssey to find answers to your research questions: Acadia, Acadian Roots, Life Prior to 1755, Acadians in Exile, Acadian Life After 1763.

c) Where do most Canadians of Acadian ancestry live today?

Map, Globe, and Graphic Skills

6 **a)** Survey your class to find out about their geographic origins. Ask each student where her or his family came from and when they arrived in Canada. Some may have arrived fairly recently. Others may have been here for several generations. Every Canadian family has a migration history. The migration theory suggests that First Nations peoples and Inuit migrated to North America thousands of years ago. (See Figure 10.34.) Compile a list of the countries and times of arrival.

b) Plot the countries on a world outline map and calculate the percentage of arrivals from each continent.

c) Draw proportional arrows from the continents to Canada to show the flows. (Refer to GeoSkills on page 213.)

d) Using the data in Figure 10.34, compare the countries of origin of your class to the most recent flows of immigrants to Canada. How many of the top 10 countries are represented in your class?

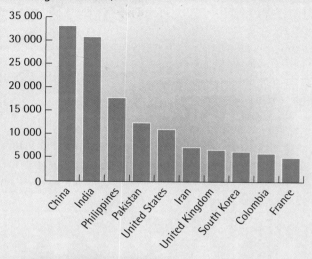

Top 10 Source Countries for Immigrants Coming to Canada, 2006

Figure 10.34

This bar graph shows the countries that most of Canada's immigrants originated from during 2006. How does this list compare to the countries of origin of students in your class?

Application

7 Suppose you plan to move within your community or region.

a) Identify five criteria, or pull factors, that will help you decide where to go (for example, the availability of mass transit (buses, trains), housing, schools, or recreation facilities).

b) Select two possible places as choices for your move (for example, other neighbourhoods or nearby communities).

c) Complete a chart like the one below that follows the model: select criteria, pose questions, research the answers, analyze the answers, and make a decision.

d) Analyze your answers for Choices A and B.

e) Make your decision. Will you choose A or B? Which pull factor was most important to you?

Criteria/ Pull Factors	Questions to Research	Answer Choice A	Answer Choice B
For example, availability of mass transit	Can I use public transportation to get to school?	• Buses provide transportation to all schools. Buses travel each route every half hour.	• Bus and subway transportation is available. Buses and subways travel each route every 15 minutes during the busiest times of the day, and every 30 minutes at other times.
1.			

11 Barriers to Migration

IN THIS CHAPTER

- identify barriers to migration
- describe how technology has improved human mobility
- use thematic maps to identify patterns in migration

KEY VOCABULARY

Berlin Wall
emigrate
exit tax
immigrate
quota

Barriers of All Shapes and Sizes

1. a) What is a barrier? What are some examples of barriers?

b) Why are barriers used?

c) Based on what you know, what might barriers to migration be?

Imagine that you want to leave your country, but everywhere you turn, people are stopping you. Would you be frustrated? What would you do to overcome the barriers you face?

Many types of barriers prevent people from migrating:

- political barriers—laws prohibiting people from leaving the country
- physical barriers—distance, oceans, mountains, or walls/fences
- economic barriers—not having enough money to move
- legal barriers—limits to the number of people the new country will let in
- procedural barriers—getting passports and visas

Is migration a basic human right? Most people have no trouble supporting a person's right to **emigrate**, or leave a country. However, some people debate the right to **immigrate**, or enter a country. Many people want to control the flow of immigrants into their countries.

Figure 11.1

Some people, like this young woman in Kosovo, have spent much of their lives in the midst of conflict and war. If they want to leave the country of their birth, what could stop them?

Fact File

In the former Soviet Union (Russia and its neighbours today), people wishing to migrate had to pay nearly US$50 000 to move away. Almost no one had that much money. The exit tax stopped migration.

Fact File

After World War II, the East (the communist countries of Eastern Europe controlled by the former Soviet Union) and the West (the democratic countries of Western Europe and their allies, such as the United States and Canada) had a tense relationship. Former British Prime Minister Winston Churchill gave the sealed border between the East and the West its name—the Iron Curtain. This barrier was a defended zone that kept two worlds apart and prevented any movement of people between the East and the West.

DURING READING

1. Immigration refers to the migration of people moving into a new country. Emigration refers to the migration of people moving out of their home country. Work out an easy way to remember which term is which and how to spell them. (Hint: Look at the prefixes and the root word.)

2. Is migration a basic human right? What is your opinion? Discuss this question with a small group. Make sure that everyone has a chance to express their opinions and the reasons why they feel as they do. Remember to listen to each other and that each person in the group is entitled to his or her own opinion.

Political Barriers

Governments may set up different ways to stop people from leaving. Sometimes nations make it difficult for their citizens to emigrate by making them pay large sums of money to leave. These fees are known as **exit taxes**. Some countries close their borders completely, and allow only those people the government trusts to go in and out of the country.

When the Iron Curtain Fell

After World War II, the communist-controlled countries in Europe closed their borders. (See Figure 11.2.) It became illegal to emigrate. In fact, those who tried were often shot or imprisoned. In what was then East Germany, the authorities built a wall—the **Berlin Wall**—to keep their citizens in and foreigners out.

Figure 11.2

The map shows Europe as it was divided in 1950. The red line shows the Iron Curtain, the division between the communist-controlled countries of Eastern Europe and the countries of Western Europe. Since then, this map has changed dramatically. Using your atlas, identify which countries of Europe are the same, and which have new names or borders.

Europe, 1950

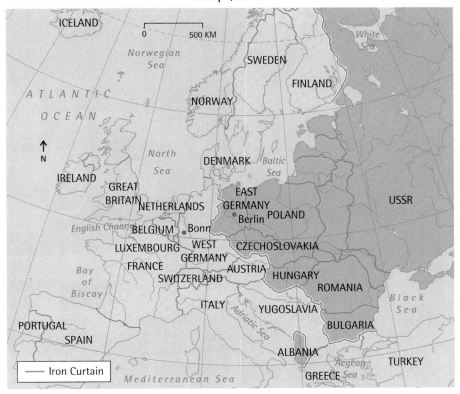

Figure 11.3

An East German soldier leaps to freedom over a checkpoint at the Berlin Wall. The Berlin Wall and the heavily guarded border between Eastern and Western Europe became the focal point for many Hollywood movies and spy stories, such as *The Spy Who Came in from the Cold*. What did this soldier risk by his action? Why was getting to West Berlin seen as a "leap to freedom"?

Figure 11.4

Some people cheered, but others cried as the Berlin Wall fell in 1989. East German citizens knocked it down after the government ordered it down. Soviet Union control had collapsed. One night, people were prisoners in their own country, and the next, they could freely move between East and West Berlin, and East and West Germany, to visit family and friends and to rejoin relatives. Why do you suppose there were concerns about this sudden movement of people?

Fact File

Before the Berlin Wall fell, many Eastern Europeans did defect (escape) to the West. Hockey players, musicians, and dancers slipped away from their teams and groups while on special visits to Canada and the United States. They sought asylum, or freedom from political persecution. Ballet dancer Mikhail Baryshnikov defected while on tour in Toronto. Why do you suppose he escaped while he was on tour?

Organizing Information

When reading text that has a lot of information, use a chart to organize your notes and help you remember key points. Use subheadings from the text as headings for your chart.

Type of Barrier	Explanation	Example(s)
Political	set up by the government	exit taxes, closed borders
Physical		
Practical		
Legal		
Quotas		
Procedural		

1. a) Why might some governments not want to let their citizens emigrate?

   b) How would you feel if you lived in a country where you were not allowed to leave or cross the border to go on a holiday or to visit friends and relatives?

2. If possible, ask some adults about their memories of the Iron Curtain and how they felt when it came down. Record their comments and share them with the class.

Physical Barriers

At one time, physical barriers blocked or slowed migration a lot. Mountains stopped people's movements. Deserts forced people to go long distances out of their way to get around them, or prevented migration completely. Large bodies of water were barriers, too. People did not want to risk long trips across open water, so they stayed close to the coastlines.

Such physical barriers slowed the pace of migration. However, advances in transportation technology changed all this. Over time, millions of immigrants crossed the ocean to populate continents such as the Americas and Australia. Modern transportation systems easily and safely took people over mountains, across deserts, and over oceans. Communities even sprang up in mountain and desert regions.

Figure 11.5

This family sailed from China to British Columbia in 1889. The voyage would have taken two months. What do you suppose the conditions on the ship would have been like for this family? How might an immigrating family travel between China and British Columbia today? How long would the journey last?

It's a Long Walk!

In the 1970s, desertification expanded in the region of Africa called the Sahel. (See Figure 11.6.) Long-term drought, overgrazing, and removing woodlands led to these desert-like conditions. Several million people in this region died from starvation. Others packed up their few belongings and began treks to distant cities. Some of these cities were hundreds of kilometres away. Many died along the way. They had no money to buy food. Their local governments could not help.

Many people worldwide donated money to help these people. The United Nations, World Vision, Oxfam, and the Red Cross sent food, shelter, equipment, and volunteers. Unfortunately, help came too late for most of these migrants. Hundreds of thousands of children and adults died from starvation and disease. Those who survived did not see their lives improve. They stayed in and around towns and cities, mainly living on the support of others. Their living conditions were horrible, but few found ways to leave. In order to emigrate, people need some money to get started. The people emigrating from the Sahel were further limited because they had no access to transportation like cars, and public transport like railways cost money.

LITERACY TIP

Using Word Parts

When you come across terms such as "immigration," "emigration," "desertification," and so on, look for familiar word parts and use them to predict the meaning. For example, "desertification" has the root word "desert." You can predict that this word has something to do with deserts.

Fact File

Desertification of the Sahel forced many people to walk hundreds of kilometres to find new places to live. Their trek was similar to walking from Windsor to Kingston, Ontario. Find Windsor and Kingston on a map of Ontario. Imagine having to walk this distance. How long do you suppose it would take to walk that far?

African Regions at Risk of Becoming Deserts

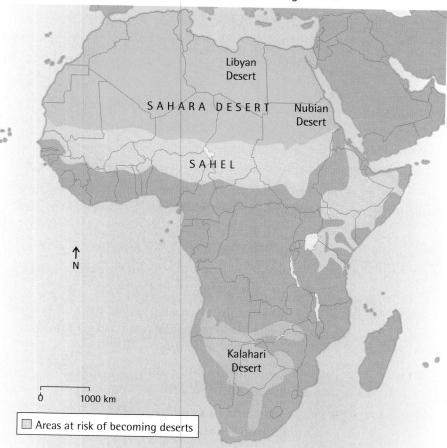

N

0   1000 km

☐ Areas at risk of becoming deserts

Figure 11.6

The Sahel region is one of the regions in Africa that is at risk of becoming a desert. More frequent, longer-lasting low-precipitation periods, along with poor management of the land, made these regions unable to sustain life. Use the map in Figure 7.23 on page 158 to identify the countries that are part of the Sahel. As desertification continues, where will the people of the Sahel be forced to migrate?

Figure 11.7

Shadows define the ridges on sand dunes in the desert of Niger in the Sahel. What force creates the dunes? What human activities would allow this force to have a greater influence in this region?

Fact File

People migrate between countries. They also migrate within countries. In 2007, more than 12.8 million people were internally displaced. They were forced to move from one place to another within their own countries.

Severe flooding in Bangladesh affected 28 million people and displaced over 2 million people within the country. What other events might cause people to be internally displaced?

Figure 11.8

When people move under such conditions, they have to live on what they can find along the way. That is usually very little. Why do you think their governments cannot do more to help them?

Many Canadian organizations provide help to people who are forced to move. Some organizations are working to help prevent problems such as flooding, soil erosion, and overuse of land. Which do you think provides the most help to people in developing countries: programs aiming to prevent problems, or programs aiming to ensure that people meet their basic needs? Is it a question of one type of help being more useful than another? What kinds of assistance are needed to truly improve things over the long term?

Figure 11.9

Canadian International Development Agency (CIDA) promotes interplanting programs like this one in India. Different crops are planted together in a field at the same time (interplanting or intercropping). Each type requires different nutrients and amounts of moisture. Some grow faster than others and help protect neighbouring plants from wind erosion. Such practices mean that the soil needs less fertilizer and will hold moisture longer. Do you think Canada should pay for more programs like this in other countries? Why?

AFTER READING

1. Due to advances in transportation technology, migrants can travel long distances over physical barriers in short periods of time. How might the role of technology be different in the forced migration of people from the Sahel in Africa? (Hint: Did technology help the people move to a new place to live? Did technology play a role in the reason they had to move?)

2. Using a climate map from an atlas, compare the climate conditions in the Sahel region to those areas in southern North America that receive 10 to 50 millimetres of precipitation yearly. Why do these areas in North America not face major migration problems?

GO GEO-GREEN

Forced Migration due to Desertification

Desertification is a major issue that threatens the people of Africa. In the last 20 years, the expanding desert has forced more than 20 million people to move. As these people move into other regions, conflicts over land arise.

After decades of desertification in the Darfur region in western Sudan, one of the bloodiest wars in African history began. The war in Darfur is a complex situation, but the root cause is conflict over scarce resources. After decades of drought, thousands of nomadic people from northern Darfur were forced to move south in search of water and grazing land for their herds. This movement brought them into conflict with the farmers who were already living in this area and needed the land to grow their crops. People began to fight as they tried to protect what little land and water they had. Conflict between rebel groups and the government made a bad situation worse. It is estimated that 500 000 people have died in the Darfur region on account of these conflicts, and about 2.5 million people have been displaced.

By 2020, 60 million people are expected to move from the new desert areas of Sub-Saharan Africa toward North Africa and Europe. This huge movement of people poses a big problem for nearby countries. The North Atlantic Treaty Organization (NATO) sees the northward movement of people from the Sahel region as a security threat. Millions of people migrating northward will place a burden on the region's water and land. Again, conflicts will arise as people try to protect their water and land resources.

How has desertification occurred? Human activities are the main causes:

- People let their herds overgraze the land. When the plant growth is gone, the wind erodes the topsoil.
- Farmers grow crop after crop in the soil without adding any nutrients.
- Farmers overwork the soil with machinery.
- Too much logging leads to soil erosion by removing trees that hold the soil in place. Trees also conserve soil moisture.
- People burn bushlands and forests to make more room for farming. This leaves the soil unprotected.

What happens when you add severe drought, brutal storms, and high winds due to global warming? The result is deadly. Desertification is linked to almost every other major problem on Earth. It is connected to

- poverty
- starvation
- epidemics
- conflicts
- forced migration

Therefore, stopping desertification will help solve these problems, too.

How can you help? Tell people about desertification. Look for news stories about the affected regions. Discuss the issues in class or with an environmental club. Create posters that raise awareness about the problems created by desertification. The United Nations Convention to Combat Desertification states "Desertification is a problem that humans have created. Desertification is a problem that humans can solve." Be a part of the solution and make your school aware!

Figure 11.10

Volunteers in Somalia hope to slow desertification by planting vegetation.

. . . .

To learn more about desertification,

Go to Nelson Social Studies

GeoSkills

Creating Research Questions That Work

Your teacher has assigned a topic for a research project. Where do you start? Begin by creating questions about the topic. Why is this step so important? Questions will help you focus and direct your research. Instead of collecting information about a general topic, you will research to find answers to your questions. Learning how to develop effective research questions is a skill that you can use for essays, written projects, debates, website creation, persuasive arguments, and so on.

Step One

Start with the 5 Ws and 1 H questions. The chart below shows possible research questions on the topic of desertification.

The 5 Ws and 1 H questions are a good place to start, but they do not direct your research enough. Use these questions as a jumping-off point, and refine the purpose of your research with Step Two.

Step Two

The types of questions you use will depend on the topic or problem being considered. A well-researched project should try to address all of these questions. (See Figure 11.11 below.)

With effective questions, you will use your research time more productively. You will not waste time finding information you do not need.

Question Starter	Question
Who	Who might be affected by desertification?
What	What happens to the land when a desert grows?
Where	Where is desertification happening?
When	When did desertification begin?
Why	Why is desertification increasing around the world?
How	How do we stop desertification from continuing?

Question Type	Explanation	Example
Factual	• asks for details that you need to know about the topic or problem	Which countries are people leaving because of desertification?
Definitional	• clarifies the meaning of the terms that are important to understanding the topic or problem	What causes desertification?
Comparative	• explores differences or similarities related to the topic or problem	How has desertification affected different groups of people in the Sahel?
Cause and effect	• looks at reasons why a problem is occurring	Why is desertification increasing in the Sahel region of Africa?
Decision making	• explores actions that could be taken to deal with the topic or problem	What actions might help to stop desertification in rural Africa?
Speculative	• considers what might be an outcome or a conclusion	What might happen if desertification continues to take over the Sahel region and spreads even farther into Africa?
Ethical	• explores the rights and wrongs of a topic or problem	Do environmentalists have the right to tell African farmers how to farm their land?

Figure 11.11

Use these question types to help you develop research questions that focus your investigation of a topic or problem.

Environmental Migration: A Problem in the Making

1. a) Think about what you read in Go Geo-Green on page 245. What aspects of this forced migration make it a type of environmental migration?

b) How does the second part of the heading of this section—A Problem in the Making—suit the main part of the heading—Environmental Migration?

Over the last few decades, environmental factors that caused migrations include

- long-term drought
- severe flooding
- tsunamis
- hurricanes

Environmental disasters will continue to happen. As they do, they will force people to migrate.

Today, people are more and more concerned about global warming and its impacts on where people live. Environmental migration will get worse. Experts make the following predictions:

- Sea levels are rising. Coastal areas could disappear under the oceans. By 2020, 200 million people will be forced to move to higher ground. (See Figure 11.14.)
- Today, half a billion people live with chronic water shortages. By 2025, 3 billion people will live in countries without enough water. Millions of people will be forced to move. (See Figure 11.14.)
- By 2050, famine will cause the migration of 50 million people. Climate change will be the underlying cause.
- More frequent extreme weather events such as hurricanes and tornadoes will force many to move.

Imagine the problems that will erupt with so many people on the move. Think of what would be involved if everyone living in Ontario were forced to leave—and we only have 12 to 13 million people!

LITERACY TIP

Cause and Effect

To understand why things happen, remember to look for cause–effect relationships. (See the Literacy Tip on page 149 in Chapter 7.)

Figure 11.12

Rescue team members evacuate residents after heavy rain flooded part of the city of Kuala Lumpur in Malaysia.

Figure 11.13

A police officer in Venice, Italy, directs people over temporary scaffolding after canals flooded St. Mark's Square. Rising sea levels have caused widespread damage in places like Venice. Are our lifestyles part of the problem?

Fact File

Between 2004 and 2008, two enormous areas of the Antarctic ice cap, as large as the Greater Toronto Area, broke off. The Arctic Ocean ice is thinning, and there is more open water than there used to be. Why does the fear of rising sea levels cause worry in low-lying countries such as Bangladesh, and in cities such as Venice and New York, which are at, or close to, sea level?

LITERACY TIP

Making Inferences

Sometimes answers to questions are not stated clearly in the reading. You have to infer the answer by connecting what you read and what you already know about the topic. Try making an inference to answer the question at the end of the Fact File above.

Regions Predicted to Experience Drought and Flooding by 2050 due to Climate Change

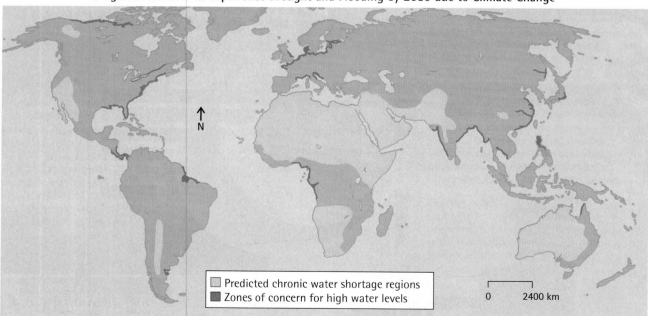

☐ Predicted chronic water shortage regions
■ Zones of concern for high water levels

0　　2400 km

Figure 11.14

If climate change continues to occur at the same rate, this map shows areas where drought and flooding due to rising sea levels are most likely to occur. Which parts of Canada are affected? When drought and flooding occur, in which directions will people be forced to migrate?

DURING READING

1. Environmental disasters force large numbers of people to migrate to safety.

   a) What will these people need when they reach a safe place?

   b) What challenges face aid workers who want to help migrants?

   Discuss these questions with a partner or a small group. Be ready to share your ideas with the class.

Practical Barriers to Migrations

Many practical problems arise when large numbers of people move into one area at the same time. No matter where people are, they still need food, housing, clean water, clothing, health care, and other basic services.

Services for Everyone

When masses of people migrate to one area, tremendous stress is placed on that area. Such large-scale migrations raise questions such as the following:

- Where will the doctors, nurses, social agencies, and other services come from?
- Will there be enough jobs available for the immigrants to earn a living?
- Will there be enough housing available for the immigrants?
- Will the transportation systems be able to meet the needs of more people?
- Will the sewer systems be capable of meeting the increased demand?
- Will the schools be able to hold all the new students?
- Are there language teachers available to help the newcomers adjust to their new language?

When you consider all the requirements, the list seems endless.

Ensuring safe water supplies is always a concern when environmental disasters happen and people are displaced. We often take safe water supplies for granted. However, on a global scale, many people do not have access to clean water that is safe to drink.

Figure 11.15

The Louisiana Superdome in New Orleans is the largest domed stadium in North America. In 2005, it was damaged badly and threatened by flooding during Hurricane Katrina. Despite the damage, more than 30 000 people took shelter in the Louisiana Superdome for six days after the hurricane. The people in charge were not able to provide enough food, sanitation, fresh water, and other services for the crowd. What other problems might these displaced people have faced during this time?

To learn more
about water issues,

**Go to Nelson
Social Studies**

Figure 11.16

Members of the Myanmar Fire Department and
army soldiers unload fresh water supplies from
U.S. Air Force cargo planes that transported
relief goods from Thailand to Myanmar after a
deadly cyclone in May, 2008. More than a week
after the cyclone killed thousands of people,
the government in Myanmar finally requested
aid. Fresh drinking water, mosquito netting, and
blankets were on the first aid flight to Myanmar.
Why is clean drinking water so important to
survivors of environmental disasters?

Figure 11.17

After the cyclone of May, 2008,
Germany's federal disaster relief
agency sent six water treatment
plants and 17 specialists to
Myanmar to help provide much
needed clean water for tens of
thousands of people displaced
by the cyclone. Why are water
treatment plants needed, as
well as bottled water supplies?

A Place to Live for Everyone

Migration occurs quickly after a war or natural disaster. In these
instances, migration causes serious social problems.

- Shelters must be built quickly.
- Money is needed to provide these shelters.
- Space must be found for shelters, which can be difficult. Often,
  areas into which migrants flow are already crowded.
- Access to clean water is essential, as is sewage treatment.

A sudden inflow of refugees creates problems for local communities. Outside help is often needed. International organizations
and governments are asked to send tents and other supplies to help
the migrants. Governments may need transportation help to move
migrants to shelters.

Figure 11.18

Nearly 2000 squatters live in a tent ghetto in Kandahar, Afghanistan. They are part of the country's 90 000 internal refugees. How long do you think most refugees end up living in refugee or squatter camps? What challenges might they face on a daily basis?

1. In your own words, define an environmental refugee.

2. Which services are in most demand when large numbers of refugees arrive to an area?

3. Why might water be the most important resource needed by a large group of refugees?

4. With a partner, brainstorm ways in which technology can play a part in environmental migration. Think of how technology can be involved before, during, and after migration caused by environmental disasters. When you are finished brainstorming, meet with another group to share your ideas and compile a master list.

Legal Barriers

1. When you see the word "legal," what comes to mind? Using what you know about the words "legal" and "barrier," how would you define "legal barriers"?

2. a) What legal barriers to migration might exist?

   b) What reasons might exist for legal barriers to migration?

How many countries would welcome the large-scale arrival of immigrants? Governments pass laws to control the flow of immigrants. They use political barriers to keep people out. These barriers can be

- border closings
- tight **quotas**, or limits on the numbers of immigrants

Some countries encourage groups from different cultures to live together peacefully. These nations support multiculturalism. Most Canadians appreciate what immigrants add to our country.

Where Do Most Immigrants Go?

Some countries provide more opportunities for immigrants to come than others. This influences where people choose to migrate. These countries gain many more people from immigration than others. North America is the world's major host for immigrants.

Top Four Desirable Immigrant Destinations, 1995 and 2004

UNITED STATES

Countries of Origin		Numbers of Immigrants, 1995	Countries of Origin		Numbers of Immigrants, 2004
1. Mexico		89 900	Mexico		175 411
2. Ex-Soviet Union		54 500	India		70 151
3. Philippines		51 000	Philippines		57 846
4. Vietnam		41 800	China		55 494
5. Dominican Republic		38 500	Vietnam		31 524
6. China		35 500	Dominican Republic		30 506

FRANCE

Countries of Origin		Numbers of Immigrants, 1995	Countries of Origin		Numbers of Immigrants, 2004
1. Algeria		8 400	Algeria		27 629
2. Morocco		6 600	Morocco		22 176
3. Turkey		3 600	Turkey		9 047
4. United States		2 400	Tunisia		8 766
5. Tunisia		1 900	Congo		4 104
6. Ex-Yugoslavia		1 600	Haiti		3 010

CANADA

Countries of Origin		Numbers of Immigrants, 1995	Countries of Origin		Numbers of Immigrants, 2004
1. Hong Kong		31 700	China		37 280
2. India		16 200	India		28 183
3. Philippines		15 100	Philippines		13 900
4. China		13 300	Pakistan		13 011
5. Sri Lanka		8 900	Iran		6 491
6. Taiwan		7 700	United States		6 470

UNITED KINGDOM

Countries of Origin		Numbers of Immigrants, 1995	Countries of Origin		Numbers of Immigrants, 2004
1. Pakistan		6 300	India		11 870
2. India		4 900	Pakistan		10 225
3. United States		4 000	Serbia/Montenegro		9 605
4. Bangladesh		3 300	Philippines		8 250
5. Nigeria		3 300	South Africa		7 805
6. Australia		2 000	Nigeria		4 845

Figure 11.19

These tables show the top four immigrant destinations for 1995 and 2004. Which host country showed the greatest change in immigrant sources from 1995 to 2004? From which countries do the most immigrants originate? Canada and the United States accept more immigrants each year than the whole of Europe. Why do you think that is?

$a^2 + b^2 = c^2$

1. Use Figure 11.19 to answer the following questions:

a) From which new country did a large number of U.S. immigrants originate in 2004?

b) From which continent did most French immigrants originate in 2004?

c) From which continent did most Canadian immigrants originate in 2004?

d) Which host country shows the most continuity in countries of origin between 1995 and 2004?

e) From which countries did the number of immigrants more than triple between 1995 and 2004?

Quotas as Barriers

Governments set limits on immigration by setting quotas. A quota on immigrants is the maximum number allowed to enter the country. Under a quota system, the government gives a source nation only so many immigration spots. If more than that number of people applies to enter, they are refused.

For many years, some countries used quota systems to support racist policies.

- At one time, Australia had a "whites-only" immigration policy.
- Canada also once had quotas on the number of people entering from countries outside Europe and the United States. World opinion and world problems helped to alter many of these policies for the better.
- Even today, it is almost impossible for any immigrant to Japan to become a citizen there. Japan's policy is to keep Japan "Japanese."

Figure 11.20

The Oath of Citizenship must be recited by all Canadian citizen applicants over the age of 14. What is the significance of the swearing-in ceremony?

Procedures as Barriers

When people want to immigrate to Canada, they apply through one of our international embassies. They must complete application forms and be measured on our point system. These procedures take a lot of time. They often frustrate and frighten applicants. Yet, these procedures are in place for a reason. They establish the person's suitability for entry according to our rules.

DURING READING

1. Remember to complete your chart about the types of barriers. (Refer to the Literacy Tip on page 241.) Explain and provide an example of each type of barrier.

Figure 11.21

In 1956, people revolted against the communist government in Hungary. Many Hungarian refugees applied for permission to immigrate to Canada. (See the photo above.) Today, the main function of many embassies is dealing with immigration concerns. In the photo to the right, the First Secretary at the Canadian Embassy in Manila, Philippines, is giving instructions to Filipinos who are applying for visas to Canada. Compare the two photos. What similarities and differences can you identify?

There are 190 million migrants and 23 million refugees around the world. Governments need ways to deal with them. Many arguments exist for both tightening and loosening controls on immigration. (See Figure 11.22.)

Figure 11.22

Have you heard arguments like these for tightening or loosening controls on immigration? Where do you stand on this issue?

The Immigration Debate

Arguments for Tightening Controls on Immigration	Arguments for Loosening Controls on Immigration
• Many countries and individuals argue that they cannot provide enough services for their own people. Thus, they cannot take more, and they tighten controls.	• Many people realize that we need to share our wealth and standard of living with those who are struggling and need to migrate to find a better quality of life.
• Others argue that the economy will not support a large number of new people. There would not be enough jobs. Many would have to be supported by the government.	• People argue that Canada and other developed countries have such a low natural increase that their economies will not grow if they do not take in more immigrants.

Figure 11.23

The border between the United States and Mexico is a major concern to many Americans. Patrols try to control entry, but thousands continue to cross illegally. The U.S. government spends more than $500 million a year to keep illegal migrants in jail. Why do you think many people who have been caught and returned to Mexico keep trying to cross back into the United States?

Illegal Migration

When people are desperate, some turn to illegal actions. Families forced out of one region and not allowed into others often try to sneak into another country. The result is a world problem with illegal migration. Thousands of "illegals" pay thousands of dollars to be taken to other countries. In the 1980s and 1990s, several boatloads of illegal immigrants were left on Canada's shores. Many prohibited migrants try to enter the United States along its southern borders and coasts. Each year, the United States tries to prevent hundreds of thousands of people from entering illegally.

Figure 11.24

In 1999, one Korean ship and four Chinese ships attempted to smuggle people into British Columbia. Most of these people were refused entry. How do you think they were caught? Why do you suppose some were refused entry and others were allowed to stay?

AFTER READING

1. Population growth is often a reason why countries impose legal barriers. If a country's population growth is too great, and population density is very high, the government will likely restrict entry to immigrants. Could population growth ever cause a country to reduce its legal barriers to migration? Explain your answer.

2. a) Why do you think any country would want to keep some immigrants out?

   b) Do you think it is right to allow some immigrants into a country and to refuse others? Why or why not?

3. Why might immigration application procedures be so frustrating and frightening to many applicants?

CASE STUDY

Urban Migration in India—The Pushpak Express

Every day, on average, about 45 000 Indians move from rural village life to the cities. Most people struggle to earn a living in rural India. The majority of the country's rural communities do not have services such as running water, electricity, and sanitation (water and sewage treatment). As a result, many young people, mainly young men, are leaving. They want a better life. They dream of finding a good job or becoming a Bollywood star. Unfortunately, the dreams of nearly all migrants are quickly changed.

These migrants soon run into many barriers:

- practical—Where will they live? Where will they find a job?
- economic—With little money, how will they meet their needs? How long will it take to find a job?
- social—How will they fit in?

Most are heading to the biggest cities, such as Calcutta and Mumbai. They have very little money and few belongings. Thousands crowd onto the Pushpak Express train heading to Mumbai. Most ride in third

Route of the Pushpak Express, India

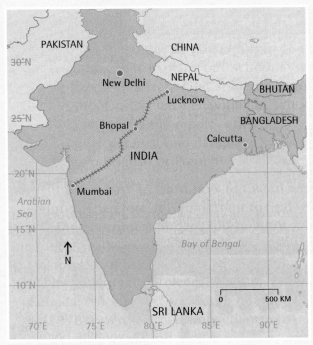

Figure 11.25

Pushpak means "the flying chariot of Ravana" in Hindu mythology. Use an atlas to follow the electric-powered train's route in greater detail.

class and are sealed off from the luckier ones in first and second class.

Figure 11.26

Third-class passengers pay $6 for the 24-hour train ride from Lucknow in the northwest to Mumbai on the coast. This may sound inexpensive to us, but it is three days' pay for many who live in India. ((In comparison, Toronto to London by passenger train is a two-hour ride for $52.) Can you suggest why the Pushpak Express is so inexpensive compared to travelling by train in Canada?

CASE STUDY

Urban Migration in India *(continued)*

Fact File

In one of Mumbai's most impoverished neighbourhoods, there is one toilet for 200 families and one water tap for 75 families. How does this compare with where you live?

The migrants face discrimination from the time they step on the train. Third class compartments are barely serviced. Comfort is not possible in the densely packed cars. Many leave their homes as heroes who will help their poverty-stricken families. They are the young people on the train. The older people on the train have been to places like Mumbai before with little success. They are heading back to try again. "I don't live for myself," said Newshad Ali, who has travelled to Mumbai 15 times to work in a bakery. Each month, Newshad sends part of what he earns back to his family in his former village.

When many arrive in Mumbai, they have nowhere to live and no contacts to help them get started. Very few have jobs lined up.

They may wait many days to get a job. They might eventually join the taxi drivers who treat their cars as homes, or take temporary construction jobs that pay $2 a day.

In the big cities, the higher classes hold the power and money. These classes are remnants of India's outlawed caste system of social classes. The migrants who come to the cities receive little assistance when they arrive. They survive in whatever way they can, often living on the streets or in squatter settlements. Another train full of people will arrive the next day.

All over the world, large cities must face the challenge of this great global migration from rural to urban. Rising urban population densities are creating big problems for cities. How do they find space and provide services for all these new people? These problems present barriers to continued migration. Despite these barriers, it is predicted that 75 percent of all people in the world will live in big cities by 2050.

Fact File

Shanghai: 96 200 people per km²
New York: 53 000 people per km²
Mexico City: 43 000 people per km²
Toronto: 4000 people per km²

Can you imagine what these population densities will be by 2050?

AFTER READING

1. Identify a practical, a social, and an economic barrier facing these migrants.

2. Most of the migrants who travel to cities like Mumbai end up living in squatter settlements, or *bustees*, as described in Chapter 10. Why do they not just return home to their rural villages?

3. Is it possible that rural-to-urban migration will cause similar problems in Canada?

Knowledge and Understanding

1. Summarize, in point form, examples of the barriers that some people face when they try to migrate. Use these headings to organize your points:
   - Political Barriers
   - Physical Barriers
   - Practical Barriers

2. a) What is a quota system for immigration?

   b) Explain one argument for having a quota system.

   c) Explain one argument against having a quota system.

   d) Should Canada have a quota system? Why or why not?

3. What are the top four qualities you think immigrants should have to enter Canada? Give a reason for each quality.

4. What is the difference between an immigrant and a refugee?

Inquiry/Research and Communication Skills

5. Should Canada place fewer restrictions on refugees and immigrants entering Canada? Write an opinion paragraph that answers this question, using facts and ideas from this chapter to support your opinion. Organize your evidence using a chart like the one shown below.

Go to Nelson Social Studies

6. What is Canada doing to help refugees resettle in this country? To learn more about Canada's refugee programs, read "Citizenship and Immigration Canada—What Canada Is Doing to Help Refugees." Select two actions that you think are most helpful to refugees resettling in Canada. Explain what the actions are and your reasons for choosing them.

Map, Globe, and Graphic Skills

7. Read, watch, or listen to the news for one week. Note the trouble spots around the world that are, or may become, sources of refugees.

   a) Locate these places and mark them with a letter or number symbol on an outline map of the world.

   b) In a legend, record the following information for each place on the map:
   - the main problem in that location
   - the reason why this problem has caused (or will cause) people to become refugees
   - where the refugees are going, or will likely go

   c) Suggest two barriers that may face the refugees in one of the locations you mapped. For each barrier you suggest, explain why you think it may apply in this location.

Evidence Supporting the Opinion that Canada Should Place Fewer Restrictions on Refugees and Immigrants Entering Canada	Should Canada Place Fewer Restrictions on Refugees and Immigrants Entering Canada?	Evidence Supporting the Opinion that Canada Should Keep Restrictions on Refugees and Immigrants Entering Canada
•		•
•		•
•		•
Decision:		
Reasons:		

Application

8 Read the newspaper article below. (Refer to the Literacy Tip on page 115 in Chapter 5.)

a) Do you think many of Kosovo's 2 million people will migrate from their new nation? What push factors do you see?

b) What are two positive things you can see about Kosovo's chances of success as an independent country?

c) If you were the country's leader, would you create any legal barriers to prevent emigration? Why or why not?

9 Look back at the photographs of the young woman from Kosovo in Figure 11.1 on page 238 and the soldier at the Berlin Wall in Figure 11.3 on page 240. Suppose you could interview the woman or the soldier. Make up four questions that you would ask. Two of your questions should deal with the following:

- the conditions in his or her homeland
- feelings about migrating

(For help to make up your questions, refer to the Q-Chart in Chapter 10 on page 237.)

Impoverished Kosovo faces many daunting challenges

It's noon on a weekday, and Kosovo fashion designer Krenare Rugova's sewing machines are strangely silent.

Rugova, young and U.S.-educated, is trying to build an upscale clothing business in her homeland. But she can't work because the power has gone out for the second time this morning.

"These blackouts are killing me," she said, fussing over fabrics at her studio in Vucitrn, a drab and dusty town north of the capital, Pristina.

"They just shut me down. I'm thinking, 'OK, I'll get all these wedding dresses finished in an hour,' and then 'zap.' It's very frustrating."

Her predicament illustrates just one of the daunting economic challenges confronting Europe's newest country—an impoverished, underdeveloped corner of the continent that experts warn could be a handout-dependent hardship case for years to come.

As Kosovo seeks international recognition of its declaration of independence, the round-the-clock rumble of thousands of portable power generators threatens to drown out the celebratory fireworks. And its problems go far beyond an electricity grid so unreliable that just keeping the lights on can be a daily struggle.

Roads are badly rutted or unpaved. Joblessness runs close to 50 percent, and much of the workforce is uneducated. The average monthly salary is a paltry $220.

By virtually every measure, Kosovo joins the family of nations with the dubious distinction of being one of Europe's poorest.

It doesn't even have its own international telephone country code: Kosovo shares Monaco's, a holdover from the days when French Foreign Minister Bernard Kouchner was the top U.N. administrator here and French-owned Alcatel was chosen to develop the phone network.

"Everyone knows it's going to be hard," said Alex Anderson, Kosovo project director for the Belgium-based International Crisis Group, which keeps tabs on trouble spots in the Balkans. "No one has the idea that it's going to be the land of milk and honey overnight."

Kosovo's late leader Ibrahim Rugova used to present visitors with crystals and other gems as proof of its untapped mineral wealth. Many snickered, but Rugova—a distant relative of the fashion designer—may have been on to something, said Shpend Ahmeti, executive director of the Policy Analysis Group, a think tank in Pristina.

Geologists conducting a thorough survey of Kosovo's resources say it has vast amounts of high-quality lignite coal. They say it also has deposits of nickel, lead, zinc, bauxite and even small seams of gold that could be tapped. "Kosovo is richer than we thought," Ahmeti said.

But officials caution Kosovo needs to improve its shoddy infrastructure—battered by its 1998–1999 war between Serb forces and ethnic Albanian rebels—if it is to have a decent shot at an economic future for its 2 million people.

The government has been reviewing bids for a $4 billion contract to build a lignite coal-fired power plant officials say would end outages. But the plant won't be fully operational until at least 2012.

Eight in 10 business owners, Ahmeti said, point to the lack of reliable energy as their biggest obstacle—bigger than high taxes or rampant corruption.

For the foreseeable future, an independent Kosovo will remain dependent on handouts from the U.N. and the European Union, which plans to convene an international donors' conference in June.

12 How Culture Is Affected by Migration

KEY VOCABULARY

assimilation
cultural diffusion
culture
deportation
enclave
ethnoburb
mainstream population
racism
xenophobia

What Is Culture?

1. What comes to your mind when you see the word "culture"? Brainstorm for ideas with a partner and be ready to share them with the rest of the class.

2. a) How would you define "culture"?

b) Keep reading and see how your definition of "culture" compares with what you read.

A **culture** is a way of life shared by a group of people. It is composed of a number of things, such as the way people obtain their food, the way they raise their children, and the values they believe in. Cultures change over time. Imagine your grandparents' way of life when they were your age. Think about how your culture has changed since then.

Culture gives us our identity and helps us sustain it. Culture helps people define who they are in many ways. People in a cultural group

- use a shared language to communicate with each other
- share religious beliefs
- are members of families and communities
- share activities, such as celebrations and holidays
- produce goods and provide services in distinctive ways
- educate their children about their way of life
- use stories, art, music, and dance to express who they are

Often, culture is connected to a specific place. This location becomes a symbol for people of their "belongingness" within a group. For example, many people of Irish descent who live in North America still feel a strong bond with Ireland.

LITERACY TIP

Making Connections

Before you start reading a text or answering a question, always connect the topic with what you already know about it. Think about what you have already read, seen, or heard about the topic. For example, what do you already know about culture?

Figure 12.1

Cultures change, as these two photographs of Toronto's skyline show. The top photo was taken 100 years ago. A current photo of Toronto's skyline is below it. Compare these photographs. What changes can you see? What can you infer about changes in people's way of life?

Figure 12.2

This map shows the world's cultural realms. Each realm has similarities that distinguish it from others. These similarities include economics, politics, language, religion, and ethnic origins. How does Canada fit into this picture? What is your cultural realm? Do you have only one?

The World's Cultural Realms

NORTH AMERICA

EUROPE

NORTHERN ASIA

EASTERN ASIA

NORTH AFRICA–MIDDLE EAST

SOUTH ASIA

SOUTHEAST ASIA

LATIN AMERICA

CENTRAL AND SOUTHERN AFRICA

AUSTRALIA AND OCEANIA

N

0   2400 km

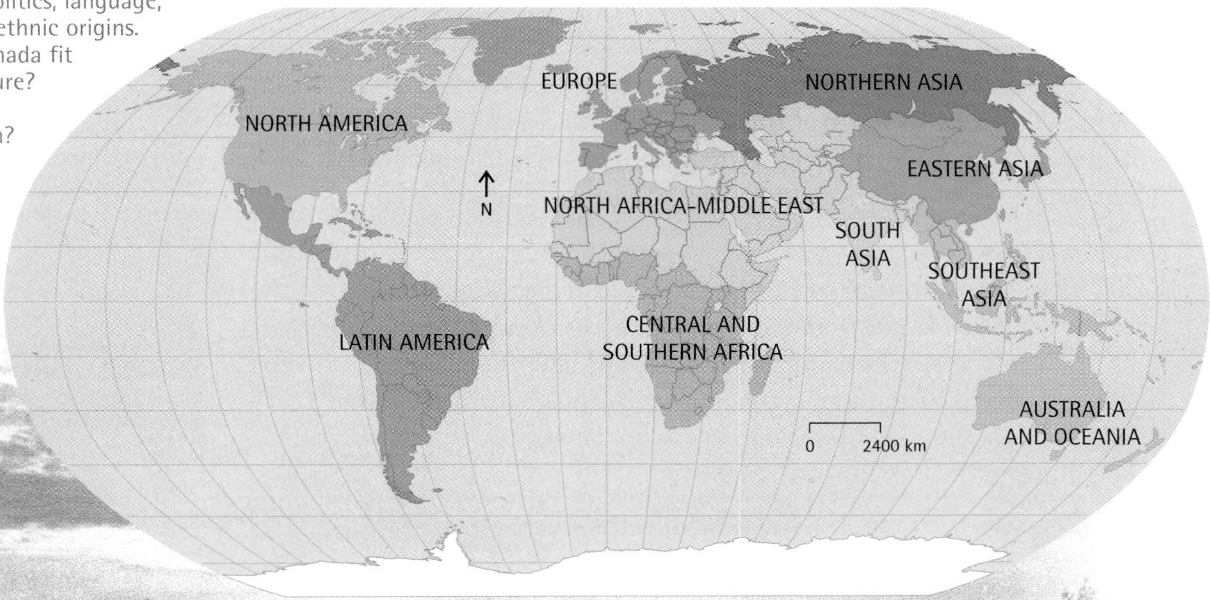

Language

Language is often considered the most important part of a culture. When you share a language with others, you can communicate and understand their values. You may also come to share what is important to them. Throughout history, leaders have used language to gain power. Forcing a people to stop using their language has been an effective way to control them. In Canada, Aboriginal people who attended residential schools were not allowed to speak their native languages. They were forced to use English or French.

1. Suppose you are not allowed to speak your own language and you are forced to speak the language of your new leader. This language is completely unfamiliar to you, but it is the only language you are allowed to use. In fact, you are punished if you are caught using your original language. How might you be affected?

2. Compare the map in Figure 12.3 to the map in Figure 12.2. What similarities do you see?

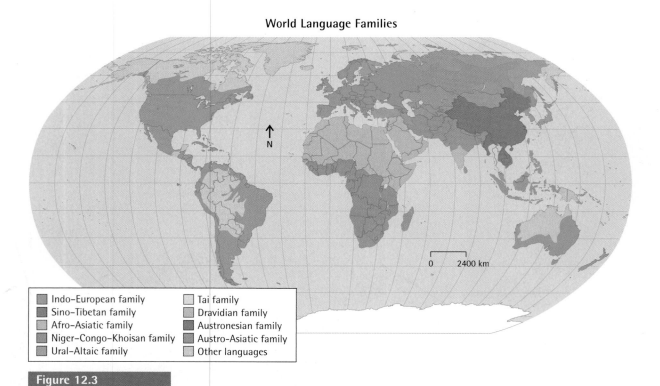

World Language Families

- Indo–European family
- Sino–Tibetan family
- Afro–Asiatic family
- Niger–Congo–Khoisan family
- Ural–Altaic family
- Tai family
- Dravidian family
- Austronesian family
- Austro–Asiatic family
- Other languages

0   2400 km

Figure 12.3

This map shows the world language families. A language family is a group of similar languages that developed from a common parent language. Can you find other areas of the world that are in the same language group as you? Think about what you have learned about migration in the last two chapters. Why is the Indo-European language family in so many areas of the world?

Religion

Beliefs are another important part of culture. People often decide to migrate because of their beliefs. Some people are persecuted because of their religious beliefs. To escape persecution, they decide to migrate. Other people want to live in a community where they can share their religious beliefs with a larger group of people.

World Religions

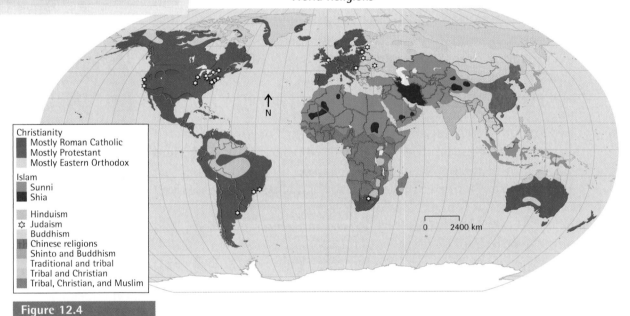

Christianity
  Mostly Roman Catholic
  Mostly Protestant
  Mostly Eastern Orthodox
Islam
  Sunni
  Shia

  Hinduism
✡ Judaism
  Buddhism
  Chinese religions
  Shinto and Buddhism
  Traditional and tribal
  Tribal and Christian
  Tribal, Christian, and Muslim

0   2400 km

Figure 12.4

This map shows the major world religions. People are free to practise the religion of their choice in Canada. Does your family belong to one of the major world religions shown on the map? Which one? Compare this map to the map in Figure 12.3. How is the pattern similar?

Figure 12.5

The *Canadian Charter of Rights and Freedoms* guarantees freedom of religion in Canada. Thus, Canadians practise many of the world religions. The Muslim community is part of the Canadian religious mosaic. This community is culturally very diverse. Muslim immigrants have come from the Arab world and from Pakistan, Bangladesh, Turkey, Iran, Eastern Europe, East Africa, and the Caribbean. Which cultural realms do these groups represent? (See Figure 12.2.)

When Cultures Meet

Beginning in the 1400s, explorers and conquerors moved from Western Europe into North, Central, and South America, Africa, and elsewhere. They made contact with cultural groups that lived on those lands. Since the 1500s, the cultural map of our world has been changing quickly. As people became more mobile, they migrated from different cultures. (See Figure 10.5 on page 212.) This movement brought more people from different cultures together. Migration and mobility influenced cultural change.

As cultures moved together, people shared ideas and information. Often, very different cultures were thrown together suddenly. In many cases, one culture imposed or forced its ideas and ways of life on the other cultural groups. This changed many cultures that had existed for a long time. Some cultures were destroyed.

The history of Canada is filled with stories of what happens when cultures meet. Canada became a country in 1867. Before that, it had been a colony of France and Britain. Even earlier than that, Aboriginal peoples inhabited the land. When Europeans arrived, they interacted with Aboriginal communities, who shared their knowledge and taught them how to survive in this new land.

As more settlers arrived, the various Aboriginal peoples were forced to change their traditional ways of life. Formal treaties were signed, and many Aboriginal peoples were moved onto reserves. They could no longer live the life they had lived for thousands of years.

As you read in Chapter 2, Aboriginal children were forced to go to residential schools. There, they had to speak French or English. Their traditional languages and cultures were forbidden. Residential schools operated across Canada from the nineteenth century until as late as 1996. The lives of many generations of Aboriginal children were dramatically affected. As each generation of children was taken from their families to live in residential schools, they lost more of their traditional languages and cultures.

LITERACY TIP

Making Connections with Question Circles

Use question circles to help you connect more deeply with what you are reading. As you read, think about how Text, Self, and World interconnect. How does the text connect with you (self) and the world?

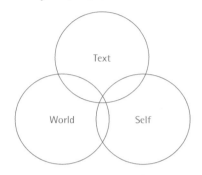

Fact File

Residential school survivors may now apply for compensation to the Federal Government. In 2005, the Supreme Court of Canada awarded a survivor $300 000 for the abuse he suffered and its impact on his life. Can money compensate for the impact of abuse and the loss of language and culture?

Figure 12.6

Students at a residential school in Moose Factory, Ontario, in 1945.

1. Answer the following questions by writing or drawing and labelling your response.

a) If you lost your culture, what would you lose?

b) How might losing your language and your culture affect you?

European Voluntary Migrations, 1815–1914

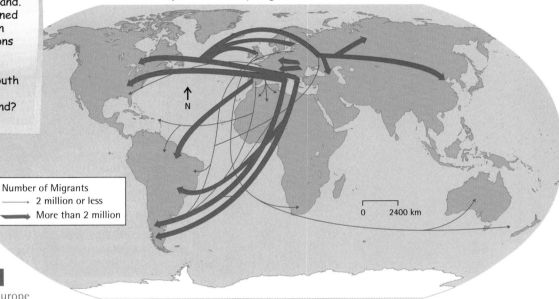

Figure 12.7

Millions of migrants left Europe between 1815 and 1914. How many of your classmates trace their family roots in Canada to these European migrations before World War I?

Cultural Isolation

Outside groups did not influence some cultures greatly until more recent times. Japan, the Koreas, China, and Mongolia had official policies designed to keep foreigners out. These countries did not welcome contact with outsiders. The great distance between these countries and Europe or the Americas allowed them to stay isolated. Westerners who wanted to reach these Eastern countries had to face either a long journey over land or a dangerous ocean voyage. The cultures of countries such as Japan, the Koreas, China, and Mongolia remained protected from the influences of other cultures.

1. In the next section, you will learn about how cultures change due to migration. As you read, complete the following organizer to help you understand and remember each change. The first entry is done for you:

How Migration Changes Cultures	Examples
The living conditions of a cultural group change.	The Bantu people forced the !Kung to move and adapt to living in the Kalahari Desert.

Why Cultures Change

Cultures change for many reasons. Sometimes, the living conditions of a group change. For example, when the Bantu people of Africa moved south, they forced the people who were already there, the !Kung, to move toward the Kalahari Desert. To survive, the !Kung had to change their way of life. They needed new tools, new methods of getting food, and new survival skills. Their culture changed to match their new living conditions.

The Forced Migration of the !Kung People

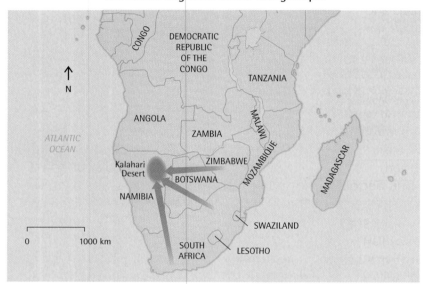

Figure 12.8

The !Kung once lived throughout a large area of Southern Africa, but the Bantu pushed them into the Kalahari Desert. The !Kung developed new skills to survive in this severe desert habitat. Which Aboriginal group in Canada survives and thrives in our coldest, harshest environment?

Figure 12.9

!Kung hunters hunt with traditional weapons in the Kalahari Desert (above). Cape Province was the original home of the !Kung (left). How do the two landscapes differ?

I'm so bored!

1. Imagine that you have to start life anew in the Arctic—Canada's cold desert. How would your way of life change? What adjustments would you have to make? Write, sketch, or dramatize your ideas.

The Spread of Ideas

Sometimes, different cultures borrow from one another. The early Lapps of Norway were hunters. Some of them moved south and met other groups who were farmers. From them, the Lapps learned how to grow grain and raise domestic animals. They began to live a more settled life. Some Lapps lived along the seacoast. They learned how to build boats from their Norwegian neighbours. They became such excellent boat builders that they even sold boats back to their teachers! This peaceful movement of cultural ideas from one group to another is called **cultural diffusion**.

The meeting and sharing of cultures can result in a win-win situation. Everybody can win or gain something from the relationship. Often, tools and technology make their way from one cultural group to the next. The canoe was an Aboriginal invention. Voyageurs used it during the fur trade. Aboriginal peoples also invented snowshoes and moccasins. Voyageurs quickly learned the benefits of using these items. Likewise, Europeans brought rifles with them. Aboriginal hunters soon mastered hunting with rifles rather than bows and arrows.

Fact File

European fur traders brought horses, saddles, firearms, and metal tools to North America. First Nations people gave Europeans canoes, snowshoes, moccasins, corn, squash, and tobacco. What have you borrowed from other cultures?

Figure 12.11

Examples of cultural diffusion can be found in mall food courts. What foods from other cultures do you enjoy eating?

Figure 12.10

Frances Anne Hopkins created this painting of Canadian fur traders called *Canoes in a Fog, Lake Superior*, in 1869. How does this painting show cultural diffusion?

Destruction of Cultural Groups

Throughout history, some cultures have been destroyed or lost. Others have been forgotten or have become unimportant. Some cultures had stronger, more advanced weaponry. They often overran other cultures and destroyed them. This was especially true of the Europeans. In their quest for riches, they tried to control or destroy most cultural groups they encountered.

As well, the minor diseases of one group can become deadly killers of another. This happened with the native peoples in Australia and North America. (See Chapter 1, Case Study, on page 18.) It also happened in Amazonia, which is the area drained by the Amazon River and its tributaries. When the first Europeans went to Amazonia, they brought diseases with them. These included smallpox, tuberculosis, measles, and even the common cold. The native people had never been exposed to these diseases before, so they had no resistance to them. As a result, thousands of Amazon Indians died of these diseases. Today, there are few surviving Indians of Amazonia, and they live mainly in non-native settlements.

In Canada, similar events took place with the First Nations. The First Nations peoples on the Prairies depended on the bison herds. As more European settlers moved west, the bison were slaughtered almost to the point of extinction. Their traditional way of life disappeared, forcing First Nations to sign treaties with the government. As they were moved onto reserves, their traditional way of life had to change.

Traditional Inuit culture has also suffered. The demand for Arctic oil and gas increased through the 1970s. Large companies moved their drilling rigs into the Canadian North. This greatly affected Inuit culture. Many Inuit left their traditional ways of living to work on the oil rigs. They learned the skills needed for their new life, and began to change to fit into modern North American society. Then, oil prices dropped. Oil companies stopped most of the drilling in the Arctic. Many Inuit lost their jobs. They had little money to look after their needs and little hope of quickly finding new jobs in the North. Some Inuit even lost the skills needed to live off the land.

Figure 12.12

The Trans-Amazonian Highway opened the Amazon Basin to settlement and Western-style development. It went right through natives' reserve lands. This has caused great damage to the rainforest and drastic cultural changes for the people living there. What are some of the changes that these people might be forced to accept?

Fact File

The Canadian government dismissed and even forbade traditional spiritual and cultural practices of Aboriginal peoples. For the first half of the twentieth century, many spiritual practices were outlawed. If people cannot use their language or practise their traditions, what happens to their culture?

Figure 12.13

What evidence do you see of outside cultural influence (cultural diffusion) in this Inuit community?

LITERACY TIP

Using Context Clues

If you read terms that you do not know, try doing the following:

- Look for clues in the sentence.

- Read the surrounding text to get an idea of how the word is being used.

- Look for clues in the pictures or diagrams.

Toward Assimilation

Some cultures are dominant or overpowering. When they encounter another culture, they often leave little room for the original culture to survive. The new, more modern culture makes the older way of doing things seem less important. Many young people in the less dominant culture turn away from their traditional lives. They want to try to join the more modern culture. This changing to fit into another culture is called **assimilation**. It is not always very successful. Young people from the older culture seldom have the skills required to get good jobs in the new culture. Even when they do have the skills, they often face strong resistance from the new culture. This resistance takes the form of prejudice and **racism**. In Australia, Aborigines were treated as second-class citizens and given the lowest-paying jobs. As a result, they had to rely on the government for assistance. Canadian government policies in the past and present are directed at assimilation of Aboriginal people into the mainstream society.

Fact File

U.S. immigration policy encourages all migrants to assimilate into the dominant culture. This is referred to as the "melting pot." In Canada, different cultural groups are encouraged to hold on to their ethnic traditions. This policy is compared to a "mosaic."

AFTER READING

1. What happens when cultures meet? Identify four ways that cultures can change. Provide an example of each cultural change.

2. The Fact File on this page refers to a melting pot in describing U.S. immigration policy. Think of what happens to individual cooking ingredients when you put them into a pot and add heat. The Fact File describes Canada's policy toward immigrants as a mosaic. To create a mosaic, the artist sets small coloured pieces such as stones, tile, or glass onto a surface to form a larger picture.

a) What do "melting pot" and "mosaic" tell you about each country's migration policies?

b) Would you rather live in a melting pot culture or a mosaic culture? Design a poster that expresses your point of view. Your poster should use images and a slogan to communicate the type of culture you prefer to live in. (Refer to the Literacy Tip—Creating Slogans on page 203 in Chapter 9.)

From Roots to Routes

1. When people think about where to move, what would they need to know about possible destinations? Brainstorm for ideas with a partner, and be ready to share your ideas with the rest of the class.

What influences a migrant's choice of destination the most? The greatest influence is the strength of the cultural connection to that destination. Are the people there like me? What language do they speak? Will I be able to practise my religion there? The answers to these and similar questions strongly influence a person's decision about where to emigrate. Often, the connections between the two places may date back to colonial times. For example, many people from the Caribbean and India were educated in English schools. The British established schools in these countries in the seventeenth and eighteenth centuries. Consequently, people from the Caribbean and India frequently choose the United Kingdom as a destination. Or, there may be more modern ties between countries. For example, many people in the Philippines have chosen to move to the United States. They became familiar with American culture after American navy and air force bases were established in the Philippines in World War II.

Figure 12.14

Britain's ethnic minorities make up less than 5 percent of the country's total population. The ethnic population is concentrated in the inner cities. There, poverty and social problems persist. Why do you think many people have migrated to Britain from places like Jamaica and India?

Coming to Canada

When you travel to a strange city or community, what makes you feel more comfortable? Is it seeing signs in your own language? Is it hearing music with which you are familiar? Is it visiting stores similar to those you find at home? Many Canadians who travel a great deal remark that they feel best when their airplane touches down in Canada or when they cross back over our border. Your comfort with your cultural identity, and the place where that identity is welcomed, gives you a feeling of relief when you return home.

Most immigrants look for that same level of comfort. They try to go to countries that share some of the things they are familiar with. It could be a place with a similar physical environment. For example, many northern Europeans settled in Ontario, west of Lake Superior. There, the physical setting is much like their former homes in Finland, Sweden, or Norway.

Others look for a common cultural connection such as language, religion, music, or history. People who move to Canada from the countries of West Africa generally go to Montréal. The language of colonialism in West Africa was French. In Montréal, West Africans can communicate more easily with Canadians. Most migrants who move to Canada from the Caribbean islands, like Jamaica, settle in Toronto. The English roots of this city make life more comfortable for them.

Within many large cities, there are clusters of people who come from the same cultural background. Immigrants new to a country often move near these cultural clusters, or **enclaves**. They can find personal support, eat familiar foods, and acquire friends more easily within the districts where these groups live.

Figure 12.15

These ethnic neighbourhoods, or enclaves, provide support to immigrants. They also attract the broader community for ideas and celebrations. What are some of the ways in which immigrants enrich Canadian culture?

DURING READING

1. a) What are two advantages for migrants who settle in ethnoburbs?

   b) What are two disadvantages for migrants who settle in ethnoburbs?

   c) Should migrants be encouraged to settle in ethnoburbs? Why or why not?

Figure 12.16

In recent years, many suburban developments have centred around one cultural focus, like a church or mosque. These result in **ethnoburbs**, suburbs with a large number of a particular ethnic population. Thus, an ethnoburb is an enclave that develops in a suburban area. What attracts people to live in ethnoburbs?

BE A GLOBAL CITIZEN

Settlement Workers in Schools

Choosing to leave your home and move to a new country is a difficult and emotional decision. Think of how it would feel to leave your home, your job, and even members of your family. Imagine the challenges you would face when you arrive in the new country. Consider how hard it is for a newcomer to figure out our education system and how our schools work. What questions would they have?

Many families come to Canada to provide a better education and future for their children. On arrival, new families often find it difficult to understand the Ontario school system and to figure out how to help their children. Schools are one of the first services with which these families connect in the community. It is important to make that connection strong and positive.

In southern Ontario, thousands of immigrants arrive every year. Settlement agencies, boards of education, and Citizenship and Immigration Canada have created a program to help newcomers when they arrive in Canada. It is called Settlement Workers in Schools (SWIS). Right now, six communities are involved in the program: Hamilton, Peel, Kitchener, Ottawa, Toronto, and York.

Settlement Workers in Schools knows that the first few years in Canada can be difficult. SWIS helps new families in the following ways:

- connects new families to school and community services and resources to help them settle in (housing, employment, health and legal services, as well as information about arts and culture community groups, library services, forms of media and international programming available, finding a place of worship, sports and recreation facilities)

- offers programs for parents on how to use computers and the Internet, so that they can help their children in school
- provides guides and handouts in 18 languages that explain our school system (how to register, what students learn in school, expected behaviour in schools, how to read the report cards)
- helps parents find language classes to learn English or French

It is not easy to learn how to live in a new country. Therefore, it is important to find ways to help newcomers understand how the community works. Only then can they begin to feel a sense of belonging.

If your family recently immigrated to Canada, who helped you settle into your new life? What were your first experiences?

As a class, you can look into the programs your school board has for new students and their families. Your class could also find out what settlement agencies work in your community outside of the school. As Canada's need for immigrants continues, so will the need for people who will help them settle into a new life in our country. Might you be one of these people?

Figure 12.17

Can you volunteer with any existing programs in your school or community to help newcomers feel welcome?

Figure 12.18

Professional athletes like Alexander Ovechkin use their talents as a way to move out of poor economic conditions. Their salaries often help their families in their homelands. Do you think high-profile professionals should get special treatment when they enter Canada?

Fact File

Since 1930 in the United States, more women than men have worked as migrant workers. Most work in the western coastal states. How might female migrant workers' experience be different from that of male workers?

AFTER READING

1. Name two high-profile migrants not mentioned in this text. Identify where they came from, where they went, and their professions.

2. Why might many migrant workers be mistreated and abused?

Changing Times, Changing Migrants

Today, there are new types of migrants. An increasing number are professionals—including musicians like singer Shakira, and athletes like hockey player Alexander Ovechkin and basketball player José Calderón. These high-profile people change countries to further their careers.

Modern, fast transportation systems, such as those in Europe, have given us the "commuting migrant." This is someone who may work one or more days each week in a neighbouring country, returning home at the end of each day or week. These workers have not given up their country. They merely work in another land.

Women as Migrants

Before 1980, most migrants were men. These were the long-distance migrants, often pioneers in new areas. Women used to be short-range migrants. They moved to low-risk areas along well-established routes. For example, women moved to other regions within their own countries for harvest time work, or to cities for work as housekeepers or nannies. This has all changed. More women now move more often. Since 2005, women have become half of all migrants from many Asian countries. Many female migrants find work on farms or in urban settings in three main areas: domestic work, food services, and health care.

Protection for Migrants

Concerns have been raised about the safety and rights of migrant workers. Many are mistreated and abused. In 2003, the United Nations passed the International Convention on the Protection of the Rights of All Migrant Workers. The guidelines help countries to ensure that migrant workers have adequate living conditions, are legally protected from sexual abuse, and do not work long hours for low wages. Ontario has been making efforts to protect migrant workers in agricultural activities. In 2008, Ontario allowed farm workers to form a labour union. Its purpose is to protect farm workers in large greenhouse and agricultural companies that employ thousands of migrant workers.

Migrant Numbers

Since 2000, the number of migrant workers in the world has increased by 15 million. The numbers have skyrocketed because little work is available in their home countries. This is especially true in developing countries where there are very high percentages of people under 30 years of age. Today, more than 191 million people, or 3 percent of the world's population, are living and working in a country other than their own. Of these, 60 percent live and work in Europe and North America. Most of the other migrant workers are in Kuwait, Saudi Arabia, Jordan, Bahrain, United Arab Emirates, Japan, and Australia.

In the Mainstream

1. In a small group, discuss whether immigration is mainly positive or negative for a country. Share your group's main ideas with one other group in your class.

The major cultural group in a society is called the **mainstream population**. Outside of Québec, the mainstream population for nearly all of Canada's recent history has been white, Anglo-Saxon, and Protestant. In Québec, it has been white, European, and Catholic. When newcomers arrive, they bring both social and economic changes to their new country. Most people in the mainstream group react to these changes. In some instances, the reactions are favourable. In others, they are not.

Using Immigration to Foster Racism

Some people are threatened by people migrating from different cultures. Many do not want their culture to be changed. Some people within some cultural groups mistrust strangers. They fear people who look and act differently from themselves. This fear is called **xenophobia**, and it often results in racism.

There are groups that promote racism. Some use immigration and its problems to gain supporters. Within some countries, the idea of "racial purity" is strong. People in these countries do not want their cultures to have to change. They do not want to accept people from other cultures as their equals. Even their laws reflect this thinking as they are designed to make it very difficult for immigrants to become citizens. Immigrant families have lived in some countries for more than 200 years, but they still are not citizens. In Japan, many Koreans who were born in the country still do not have voting rights as Japanese citizens do.

Some groups throughout the world misuse religious teachings to encourage racism. They argue that all citizens must strictly follow the teachings of their faith to keep their culture intact. These groups do not want to allow others with different beliefs and values into their country. They fear their identity as a culture will suffer. Such countries harbouring these groups are feeling the pressures of our twenty-first century world, which brings different cultures together so easily. These countries continue to follow the laws of the past. For example, a group like the Taliban in Afghanistan misuses their religion. They persecute and create fear among their own citizens in their attempt to have their beliefs and values control the region.

Figure 12.19

Two hundred marchers from the Hungarian National Front demonstrate in Budapest. This organization has related groups in many countries. Like Hitler's Nazis, they believe that the Aryan (white European) race is superior to all others. Should racist organizations like this one be allowed? Why or why not?

Closing Cultures

In some countries, groups within a nation want to be independent. They wish to have their own land with their own cultural identity. This is the reason for the separatist movement in Québec. Many parts of the former Soviet Union became independent for the same reasons. Aboriginal groups in Canada as well as in Central America, Mexico, and Central Africa also want their own lands. They want to be able to protect their cultures from outside influences.

Often, these groups are reacting to the control other groups have on them. They may be restricted in their human rights or language, and may want to have equity and be included fully in the society. If they cannot see a good chance of this happening, they opt for independence. They feel their culture will be lost without it.

The Basques in Spain

One group that wishes to establish its own independent country is the Basques in Spain. The Basques live in northern Spain, mainly around the Pyrenees Mountains. They have maintained their distinct culture, including their own language, since the time of the early Romans. Modern DNA testing of blood groups has shown that the Basque people probably had very different ancestors from other Europeans.

The Basque separatist group ETA has been fighting for independence from Spain for 40 years. During that time, it has been blamed for causing more than 1000 deaths. The Basques took responsibility for the Madrid airport bombing in 2006.

Figure 12.20

Basque separatists demonstrate in Spain. Keeping an identity and heritage strong is a difficult task for many minority groups. Why do some groups feel it is important to have their own country in order to maintain a strong heritage?

LITERACY TIP

Supporting Your Opinion

When you want to convince someone of your opinion, you must present arguments that are logical and based on facts. A simple way to organize your argument is to use the "point, proof, and comment" strategy. Introduce a point (the idea), give proof (facts, statistics, examples, or experience), and wrap up the point with a comment.

1. Discuss the following question with a partner or a small group: Do groups within a nation have the right to take extreme measures (for example, acts of violence) to protect their culture because they want to become independent? Why or why not?

Immigration Helps

For many, immigration is a positive force. Canada's government encourages immigration for the following reasons:

- Immigrants contribute to our culture and economy. They make Canadian life more vibrant.
- The natural increase of the Canadian population is very low. In 2008, Canada's natural increase was 0.27 percent. (See page 26 in Chapter 2.) Immigrants are wanted to add to our workforce and domestic market for goods. When we add to the workforce, we add value. The new immigrants in our workforce spend money in our local economy. They also pay taxes that help support our country's services, including health care, education, and new roads. Immigrants also hire people to work in their businesses, and they create more jobs for Canadians than they take.

How Does Immigration Create Wealth?

Countries' economies grow when skilled workers and professionals immigrate. When immigrants arrive in their new countries, they need all sorts of new products—stoves, refrigerators, clothing, furniture, TVs, and toys. Meeting these new demands for products and services creates new jobs. In addition, some newly arrived immigrants start new business and hire many workers to help them.

Immigrants also increase the number of workers that are available to work at skilled, unskilled, and professional jobs in every sector of the economy. Studies show that, over the long term, immigrants increase a nation's wealth.

Immigrants Add to Our Culture

Immigration adds new spirit to a country's cultural life. Celebrations such as Caribana in Toronto or Mardi Gras in Rio de Janeiro add excitement to a community. Immigrants bring wealth, new foods, music, literature, dance, and ideas with them. We learn to share with and appreciate other people, and we learn about their history and way of life. This adds to world understanding and co-operation.

To learn more about immigrating to Canada and the categories of immigrants that are accepted,

Go to Nelson Social Studies

Fact File

In 2005, 1.75 million foreign workers were in Germany's workforce. These Gastarbeiters (guest workers) or foreign migrant workers were mainly Turkish and Polish. How do you think many Germans might have felt when more than a million foreign workers came to their country for the first time?

Figure 12.21

Caribana is Toronto's celebration of Caribbean music and dance. This cultural festival draws 1 million people annually from all over North America. What cultural festivals are celebrated in your area?

1. Re-examine the Immigration Timeline from Chapter 10 on pages 226–227. Find two pieces of evidence that Canada was nationally racist.

2. a) Why should we work toward eliminating xenophobia?

b) What is one thing that you can do to help?

3. How does immigration help Canada?

Worldwide Good Will

Canada has a policy of openness to immigrants and refugees. The world sees Canada as a leader in humanitarian aid. Canada works with many organizations that help people around the world. Our country has worked with the United Nations since it began in 1945. The United Nations operates special agencies such as the following:

- International Children's Emergency Fund (UNICEF)
- Educational, Scientific and Cultural Organization (UNESCO)
- World Health Organization (WHO)

Canada is involved with the work of these agencies. They work to ensure human rights, the end of poverty, and health for all people in the world.

Canada has also played an important role as peacekeeper in many countries. Our nation is quick to provide help in relief operations such as the 2005 hurricane in New Orleans and the 2004 Indian Ocean earthquake. All of this international activity benefits Canada. It helps Canadians when they travel abroad. Because Canada has a good reputation, our businesspeople can set up business opportunities more easily overseas.

Figure 12.22

Many travellers—even non-Canadians—wear the maple leaf when they travel abroad because it seems to gain them acceptance more easily. Do you sometimes wear items to gain acceptance at school? Which items do you wear and why?

Fact File

The first United Nations peacekeeping mission was proposed by a Canadian. Former Prime Minister Lester B. Pearson was awarded the Nobel Peace Prize for his work to resolve the Suez Crisis of 1956. He suggested the formation of this peacekeeping force to oversee the end to the conflict when Britain, France, and Israel tried to prevent Egypt from seizing control of the Suez Canal.

1. Discuss the following questions with a partner and be ready to contribute to a class discussion.

a) Canada has a reputation as a leader in humanitarian aid and peacekeeping. How does this reputation fit with its policy of openness to immigrants and refugees?

b) Should Canada continue to help others in the world and be open to immigrants and refugees? Why or why not?

GeoSkills

Evaluating Websites

The Internet is a source of information, but some information on the Internet is inaccurate or complete lies. As you research, you need to evaluate the information you find at individual websites. Use the questions below as a guide to evaluating websites.

Assessment Category	Background Information	Questions to Ask
Who? Who is the author of this information?	• Most websites will identify the author(s) or the institution responsible for creating the website. Look for contact information at the bottom of the home page. You can use this if you have further questions not answered by the web page. • If it is not clear who owns the information, question why that is so. Might there be something wrong with the website's content, so that no one wants to be connected to it?	• Who created this information? • Are the author and publisher of the website clearly identified? • What qualifies the author or the institution to provide this information? • Does the site contain contact information?
Objective? • What is the purpose of the website? • Is the information biased?	• Knowing the website's objective is especially important when you are researching controversial topics. Ask yourself why the site was created. Is its aim to – promote a particular group or belief? – inform readers about the topic? – entertain readers? • To decide if information is fact or opinion, look for facts or statistics that back up what the author is saying. If it is written in first person (using "I" statements), it is giving the author's opinion. • If the website has ads on it, perhaps you need to question if the information supports the company's ideas. • To decide if the website is free of bias or stereotyping, look for information that discusses cultural or gender groups in a negative way.	• Is the information fact or opinion? • Is the sponsor of the website clearly identified? • Does the sponsor have ads on the website? • Is the website free of any bias or stereotyping? • Does the information present only one point of view?
Accurate and reliable? Where does the information come from?	• Websites should identify the sources of their information by giving links and/or having a bibliography. • Look for clues in the website address that tell you that the information comes from a reliable source: – **.gov** tells you it is a government site – **.ca** tells you it is a Canadian site – **.org** tells you that the website belongs to an organization – **.edu** tells you that the website belongs to an educational institution (school, college, university)	• Where does this information come from? • Has the information been reviewed by others to make sure that it is true? • Is the information from a reliable, established organization? • Can I find two other sources that back up what is being said at this website?
Current? Is the information up to date?	• Most websites have a date of publication at the bottom. Some also indicate when the site was last updated. • Some topics need to be updated frequently because research is continuing in these areas. For example, climate change and its effects on the Arctic is a topic currently being studied.	• How current are the sources and links? • Does information on this topic have to be current?
Efficient? Is the site worth the effort?	It is important that a website be well organized and easy to use.	• Does the website have a table of contents, index, menu, or site map? • Is the information easy to find and navigate through? • Do the website's graphics add to the information or get in the way?

When Countries Lose Their Young

1. You and your classmates are part of Canada's youth. As a class, discuss how youth are important to the country.

The populations of many countries that are losing people to migration have a very high percentage of people under 20 years old. They choose to migrate because they have few prospects where they are. In many developing countries, millions of young people know that they are a burden for their families. Sometimes, young people migrate for better opportunities. Some emigrate to seek adventure and excitement.

Figure 12.23

Examine the population pyramids for Germany and Nigeria for 2008. Nigeria has 146.3 million people, and Germany has 82.4 million. Calculate the percentage under 20 years old for each country. Which country has the highest percentage under 20 years old? Is it a developed or developing country? What problems might this high percentage of youth create? Suggest two economic or social problems each country will face.

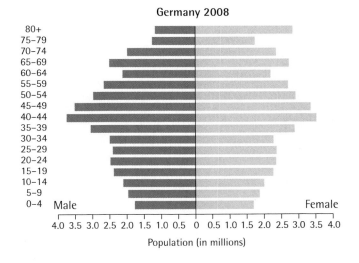

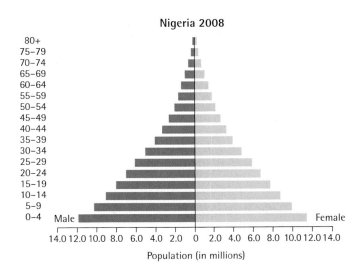

Parents are glad to know that, by migrating, their children will have a chance for a better future. However, the young people's departure is also a loss to their local community. When most of a small rural community's youth migrate, either to big cities or to other countries, the character of the community changes. Some regions see such a big decline in their population that whole villages disappear. Only a few elderly are left behind. The traditions of these communities—possibly even their language—will die with the elders.

Fact File

Between 1996 and 2008, the population of these Ontario cities declined by more than 1000 people.

Sudbury	-7479
Sault Ste. Marie	-5106
Thunder Bay	-4522
Timmins	-4502
Elliot Lake	-2039
Cornwall	-1438
Kenora	-1188

Which communities do you know that have declining populations? Why are people leaving these communities?

Figure 12.24

Communities are emptying quickly, especially in rural regions of the world. Canada has many communities that have become places for the elderly. Can you suggest examples?

AFTER READING

1. a) What are your plans after you complete high school? Where will these plans take you?

b) Share your plans with the class. How many students in your class plan to leave your community? How will your migration affect your community?

Fact File

In 2007, nearly three of every four migrants in the world were under age 35.

CASE STUDY

Dilemmas of Host Countries: The Pros and Cons of Immigration

As you learned in this chapter, countries can have different approaches and concerns about immigration. New Zealand and Greece are two countries with contrasting approaches and concerns about immigration. New Zealand has been advertising for more immigrants. Greece has been feeling the effects of too many immigrants.

▲▽▲▽▲▽▲▽▲

In 1990, to try to strengthen trade ties, New Zealand decided to advertise a more open immigration policy. It hoped immigrants from Asia-Pacific countries would come, and this would help to improve trade. Like Canada, New Zealand also needed more workers. Its slow population growth rate (0.97 percent) meant that, as older workers retired, there would not be enough younger ones to take their place. Immigration could fill this need.

When the new policy began, immigration grew rapidly. Between 1991 and 1996, 173 000 Asian immigrants entered New Zealand. It is a small nation of 4.2 million people. The proportion of immigrants in the population went up quickly, and the new arrivals were eager to start their lives in their adopted country. However, they were soon met with an attitude that said "we don't really want you here." Immigrants could not get high-paying jobs. Professionals who were qualified in their own countries could not get jobs in their fields. Many official roadblocks were put in their way.

Changing the Rules

About 50 percent of recent immigrants to New Zealand are from Asian countries. Thousands more Asian university students

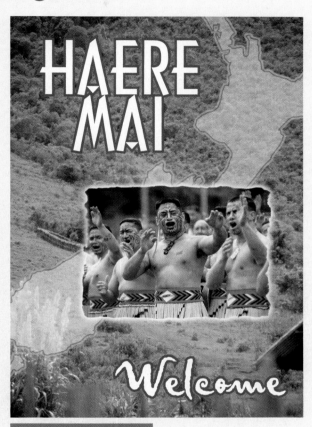

Figure 12.25

"Haere mai" means "welcome" in Maori, the language of New Zealand's indigenous people. For many new immigrants, the welcome seemed false as they struggled to get the jobs they were trained for.

and temporary workers have also come. The public demanded that the policy of open immigration be changed. Most people born in New Zealand are of British origin. They were not ready to accept this sudden diversity in their population. Some changes have since been made to the country's immigration policy. For example, immigrants now need higher English skills than before to qualify to immigrate. This requirement reduces chances for many Asian migrants.

continues…

CASE STUDY

Dilemmas of Host Countries: The Pros and Cons of Immigration *(continued)*

Main Flows of Migrants to New Zealand, 2004

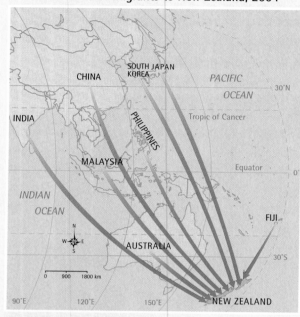

Figure 12.26

The map shows the main flows of migrants to New Zealand in 2004. Can you think of a strategy to help New Zealand change negative attitudes toward Asian migrants?

New Zealand needs more people in their workforce. However, public attitudes will need to change for the country to reach its goals.

▲▼▲▼▲▼▲▼▲

Greek culture and history date back over 5000 years. Greece has always attracted immigrants. Today, it faces many difficult problems stemming from immigration.

Greece is a small country by Canadian standards. Its population is nearly 11 million, which is about the same as that of Ontario. However, Greece is only one-sixth of Ontario's size. The country has a very long coastline (59 200 kilometres), including its many islands. It is also mountainous. These conditions make it hard for Greek authorities to stop the illegal flow of people into the country.

Where Do They Come From?

Communism ended in Eastern Europe (the countries of both the former Soviet Union and Yugoslavia) at the end of the 1980s. Since then, many immigrants have flooded into Greece from these countries. By 2000, Greece had received more than 1 million refugees. Most were from nearby Albania and Kosovo. Large numbers also came from Iran, Iraq, Turkey, Ethiopia, and Somalia.

Public Concern

Greece's economy did not grow much during the 1990s. The Olympic games of 2004 improved conditions for a while, but economic growth slowed down again afterwards. This made it difficult for the country to provide for the great numbers of people flowing in. Jobs were difficult to find. Immigrants held 20 percent of the jobs in 2007. Some people who had lived in Greece all their lives were upset by all the arrivals. Many Greeks encouraged the government to "shut the door"—to stop the flow of migrants.

To complicate matters, human smugglers are transporting people for a fee and dumping them illegally on Greece's shores. The long coastline and many islands make it difficult for the government to control the flow of illegal immigrants. Thousands of illegal immigrants continue to enter Greece.

CASE STUDY

Dilemmas of Host Countries:
The Pros and Cons of Immigration *(continued)*

Main Flows of Migrants to Greece, 2004

Figure 12.27

The map shows the main flows of migrants to Greece in 2004. Recently, the flows have mainly been from Albania and parts of the former Soviet Union. Why do you think Greece has had so many immigrants from countries like Albania, Croatia, and their neighbours in recent years?

AFTER READING

1. Could New Zealand's immigration system be considered national racism? Why or why not?

2. Choose one source region from Figure 12.27. Research to find out why people leave this region—for example, civil war, poor economy, or an environmental disaster.

Knowledge and Understanding

1 Identify three ways in which migration changes culture. Create a drawing to illustrate each change. You can use symbols to represent each culture and what can happen when they meet. Explain how your symbols illustrate each change.

2 Why do many people want to keep their culture from changing?

3 What are two ways that immigration helps Canada?

4 List three ways in which immigration is visible in your community.

Inquiry/Research and Communication Skills

5 In this chapter, you saw how First Nations were affected by the coming of the Europeans. Use the Internet and library resources to research an example of what happened when cultures met in a country other than Canada. For example, you might research the following events:

- Portuguese arrival in the Amazon region
- Spanish arrival in Mexico or Peru
- Chinese arrival in Malaya
- British taking control in India

a) Select a location to research.

b) Gather information about the nature of each culture before the contact with a new cultural group: their way of life, religion, language, and other cultural characteristics.

c) Research to find out what occurred during contact with the new culture. Compile a list of things that changed. For instance, did they share ideas and information? Did one group take control and force its ways on the other?

d) Based on your research, identify the main positive and negative effects of the two cultures meeting.

e) Present your findings using your choice of the following:

- t-chart comparing the positive and negative effects
- cartoon sketch(es)
- PowerPoint presentation
- videotape or audiotape presentation

6 The immigration policy in the United States has been described as a "melting pot." Canada's policy of multiculturalism is described as a "mosaic." William Kaplan disagrees with this multicultural approach in his book *Belonging: The Meaning and Future of Canadian Citizenship*. "Whatever may come after multiculturalism will aim not at preserving differences, but at blending them into a new vision of Canadianness … where every individual is Canadian, undiluted and undivided." Do you agree or disagree that immigrants should be Canadian first? Write an opinion paragraph to express your point of view. (Refer to page 70 in Chapter 3 to review the 4 Cs of writing opinion paragraphs.)

Map, Globe, and Graphic Skills

7 **a)** On a large sheet of paper, prepare a summary showing cultural themes that reflect your personal cultural roots. Use an organizer like the one below. Include sketches, symbols, or pictures to make your summary colourful.

My Cultural Roots	
Language(s) Which languages are spoken in your home?	
Religion(s) Which religions are practised? What are your family's spiritual beliefs?	
Celebrations and Holidays What cultural celebrations and holidays do you share with your family and community?	
Foods/Dietary Practices What are some main foods in your culture's diet? Are there unique customs related to eating/diet?	
Stories, Art, Music, and Dance How do you express yourself?	
Economic Activities How does your family earn a living in order to satisfy your needs and wants?	
Other Lifestyle Traits Are there other unique cultural traits?	

b) Include a world outline map that shows the locations of your family's cultural roots. Label the countries to which your family is connected. As a class, combine all the locations to show the class pattern on a larger map.

c) Combine all the cultural roots summary pages on the bulletin board to form a "cultural mosaic" of your class. Examine the mosaic. Consider that migration brought these cultures together. Write a paragraph that summarizes how culture is affected by migration.

Application

8 **a)** Define the following terms in your own words, illustrate them with your own sketches, or find pictures from magazines or the Internet to illustrate their meaning:

- assimilation
- cultural diffusion
- enclave
- mainstream population

b) Find and describe evidence of each term in your community or region.

9 **a)** How does the spread of cultural traits, such as U.S.-based fast-food chains, the popularity of Chinese foods, or the use of English as a business language in many world regions help to bring cultures together?

b) Does spreading material goods and trends from our society to others around the world really change other people's cultures? Explain your answer.

10 **a)** Suggest two ways to reduce discrimination toward immigrants.

b) Choose one of your ideas from a) and create a poster to communicate your message.

This ice cream outlet is located in Ho Chi Minh City, Vietnam. How does it look compare to ice cream outlets in your community or region?

13 | How Migration Affects Canada

IN THIS CHAPTER

- explain how culture can be affected by migration
- describe the effects that migration has had on the development of Canada
- use thematic maps to identify patterns in migration

KEY VOCABULARY

cosmopolitan
interprovincial migration
multiculturalism
net migration
visible minority

Fact File

Between 1928 and 1971, more than 1 million immigrants entered Canada through Halifax. All were processed at Pier 21, which has been restored as a museum of immigration. When did members of your family immigrate to Canada? Do you know their immigration stories?

A Country of Immigrants

BEFORE READING

1. What are your family's countries of origin?

2. Think about the following question and record your ideas: How does the title of this section fit what you know about Canada? Share your ideas with a partner or in a small group.

Canada is a land of immigrants. Everyone's ancestors got here one way or another. Many experts believe that the Aboriginal people walked across a land bridge between Asia and North America more than 20 000 years ago. Starting around 1600, new settlers arrived from Britain or France in Eastern Canada. Migrants from Europe came here after the two world wars. Refugees from disasters in other lands arrived in Canada throughout the 1900s. This trend shows no signs of slowing.

Many different cultural groups entered Canada after 1850. Some settled in and around places that were already established. Others settled in frontier areas such as the Canadian West. Often, these groups settled in parts of Canada that looked much like their homelands. People from the grassland steppes of Ukraine settled on the Prairie grasslands. Swedes and Finns settled on the Canadian Shield lake country west of Lake Superior. By settling in a familiar landscape, newcomers could keep some of their ways of living. Their memories of home would also stay with them.

Figure 13.1

While early immigrants to Canada came mainly from Europe, most immigrants to our country today come from Asia. How might the immigration stories of these families be similar? How might they differ?

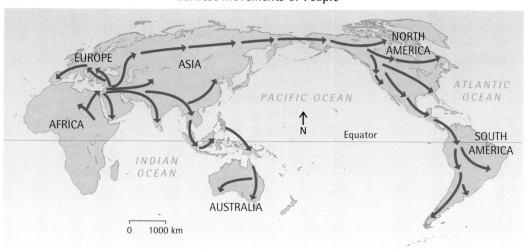

. . . .
To learn more about the experiences of new immigrants arriving in Canada,

Go to Nelson Social Studies

Fact File

Some experts believe in the Beringia Theory, which proposes that the Aboriginal people came to North America over a land bridge. Others believe that the Aboriginal people migrated from across the ocean. However, Aboriginal people from all nations believe that they were put on this continent by the Creator. Their creation stories and oral traditions support this belief. How could the beliefs of experts and Aboriginal people mesh together?

Earliest Movements of People

Figure 13.2

Some people think that the original settlers into North America arrived some 20 000 years ago, when they crossed from Asia at the end of the last Ice Age. At that time, sea levels were lower. Many other indigenous people on other continents have their own creation stories. Which creation stories do you know?

Love It or Hate It?

Canadian culture has developed and changed over time. In early Canada, the French and the English were the first European cultures to live with the First Nations peoples. As time passed, the population grew. New immigrant waves from Europe, and then from Eastern and Southern Asia, influenced Canadian culture.

Migration continues to influence Canada. New arrivals bring new ways of doing things. They bring different values, religions, languages, and customs. Our culture becomes more diverse and exciting. The speed of cultural changes makes it difficult to describe Canadian culture.

Many people have strong feelings about the effects of migration on our society and economy. When people talk about migration, prejudice and discrimination are sometimes evident. Some say that immigrants include criminals and that Canada is asking for trouble when more immigration is allowed. In fact, immigrants are involved in less of our nation's crime than people who were born in Canada. Others say that immigrants are taking jobs that Canadians need. In fact, immigrants bring skills and trades that Canadians need.

Some attitudes are based on mistaken ideas that have little evidence to support them. A newcomer can be rejected because of these false ideas. For example, differences in language or appearance can create barriers to acceptance of newcomers. It is against the law to discriminate against people because of their race or language. However, it has been quite common for people to refuse to rent apartments or housing based on these factors.

DURING READING

1. a) Think about your attitudes about immigrants. Are they positive or negative?

b) On what ideas about immigrants, or experiences as an immigrant, do you base your attitudes?

Figure 13.3

What do students in your school do to help to eliminate prejudice and discrimination? What do you do?

How Many Is Enough?

Do you think Canada has too many people? In 2008, Canada's population was over 33.2 million. Our population density was 3.7 people per square kilometre. To compare, France has nearly twice our population, but they have about 10 percent of our land area.

Canada's Future Population: 2008–2050

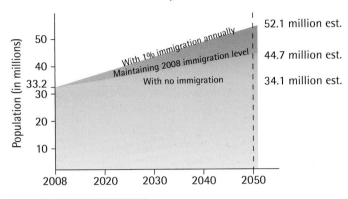

Figure 13.4

If Canada maintains its 2008 level of immigration, the population will grow to 44.7 million by 2050. In 2032, Canada's death rate will exceed the birth rate for the first time. What do you think Canada should do—raise the immigration rate to 1 percent of our population annually, maintain the 2008 level of immigration, or reduce immigration? Why?

In 2007, Canada's rate of natural population increase was 0.3 percent. At that rate, Canada's population would double in 233 years. However, demographers predict that our natural rate of increase will drop to zero by the year 2030. Our population would then start to decrease. Our workforce would shrink. Fewer working adults would mean increasingly higher taxes per person. These taxes would be needed to sustain government programs. A decreasing population would mean fewer consumers of Canadian products and services. Canadian companies would have to rely more on world markets.

However, the total numbers of births and deaths in Canada are not the only numbers that show population growth. Immigration is the hidden factor in all these numbers. Encouraging more immigration can help solve the problems of a shrinking population. New immigrants mean higher birth rates. If birth rates increase, Canada can be less dependent on new immigration for population growth.

If the number of immigrants is higher than the number who emigrate, or leave the country, positive **net migration** results. Net migration plus natural increase equals our total population growth. These numbers influence the demand for schools, housing, health care, and recreation. Planners use estimates of future changes to calculate how many workers, consumers, and taxpayers will be active in coming years. Planners need this information to plan for development to meet our society's future needs.

Total Population Growth

= **Natural Increase** (Number of births – number of deaths) + **Net Migration** (Number of immigrants – number of emigrants)

As our population grows, changes happen around us. However, it often takes time for these changes to become noticeable. You might notice changes to highway population signs outside communities, many new housing projects, or more traffic around the community.

Figure 13.5

This table shows Canadian population statistics for 5- and 10-year time spans, from 1851 to 2006. Demographers combine natural increase (births minus deaths) and net migration (the difference between immigration and emigration) to calculate population growth. Each year, about 1 percent of Canada's population, or about 200 000 people, enter the country as immigrants or refugees. From what census year has Canada averaged more than 200 000 immigrants annually?

Population Growth Components for Canada, 1851–2006 (Thousands of Persons)

	Population Growth	Natural Increase		Net Migration		Census (population at end of period)
		Births	Deaths	Immigration	Emigration	
1851–1861	793	1281	670	352	170	3 230
1861–1871	459	1370	760	260	411	3 689
1871–1881	636	1480	790	350	404	4 325
1881–1891	508	1524	870	680	826	4 833
1891–1901	538	1548	880	250	380	5 371
1901–1911	1836	1925	900	1550	739	7 207
1911–1921	1581	2340	1070	1400	1089	8 788
1921–1931	1589	2415	1055	1200	971	10 377
1931–1941	1130	2294	1072	149	241	11 507
1941–1951	2141	3186	1214	548	379	13 648
1951–1956	2072	2106	633	783	184	16 081
1956–1961	2157	2362	687	760	278	18 238
1961–1966	1777	2249	731	539	280	20 015
1966–1971	1553	1856	766	890	427	21 568
1971–1976	1492	1755	824	1053	492	23 518
1976–1981	1382	1820	843	771	366	24 900
1981–1986	1304	1872	885	677	360	26 204
1986–1991	1907	1933	946	1199	279	28 111
1991–1996	1848	1935	1027	1170	230	29 959
1996–2001	1410	1705	1089	1217	376	31 021
2001–2006	592	1661 (est)	1240 (est)	1110	200 (est)	31 613

1. Refer to Figure 13.5 above and describe the trend for each column of data. Use the following questions to help you identify the trend:

a) Total Population Growth: Has our population been consistently rising?

b) Natural Increase: Have the birth rates been rising/falling?

c) Natural Increase: Have the death rates been rising/falling?

d) Net Migration: Has immigration been growing steadily?

e) Net Migration: Has emigration been increasing/decreasing?

Figure 13.6

These pie graphs show source regions for Canadian immigrants over a 93-year period. What changes do you notice in the source regions for Canadian immigrants from 1911 to 2004? What effects do you think these changes have on Canadian society today?

Source Regions for Canadian Immigrants, 1911–2004

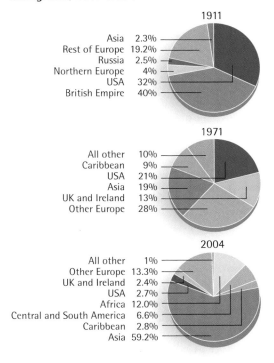

1911
Asia 2.3%
Rest of Europe 19.2%
Russia 2.5%
Northern Europe 4%
USA 32%
British Empire 40%

1971
All other 10%
Caribbean 9%
USA 21%
Asia 19%
UK and Ireland 13%
Other Europe 28%

2004
All other 1%
Other Europe 13.3%
UK and Ireland 2.4%
USA 2.7%
Africa 12.0%
Central and South America 6.6%
Caribbean 2.8%
Asia 59.2%

Visible Minorities

According to *Canada's Employment Equity Act*, **visible minorities** are "persons, other than Aboriginal peoples, who are non-Caucasian in race or non-white in colour." Persons belonging to visible minority groups include Chinese, South Asian, Black, Arab, West Asian, Southeast Asian, Filipino, Latin American, Japanese, and Korean, among others. Our population is not only changing in number. It is also changing by ethnic and cultural background, especially in the last 40 years. Some Canadians take more notice of migration when they see people belonging to visible minority groups in their daily lives.

Until the 1960s, most new Canadians immigrated from Europe. Canada now receives large numbers of people from Hong Kong, the Philippines, China, India, the Caribbean, South and Central America, and Africa. The effects of these immigration patterns can be seen most clearly in large urban centres. For example, in large cities, schools often have very diverse student populations, with increased numbers of students belonging to visible minority groups. Communities also have many new places of work and worship.

Figure 13.7

Immigration changes the way we view our country, its connections to other countries, and our basic values. The 2006 census showed that 6.1 million Canadians were born outside Canada and made up 24 percent of our population over 15 years of age. What do these statistics say about what is valued in Canada?

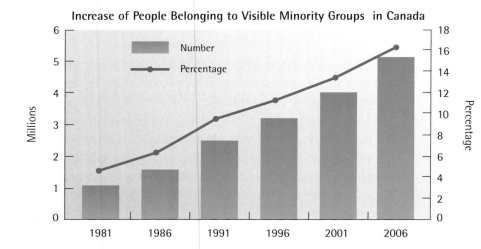

Increase of People Belonging to Visible Minority Groups in Canada

Legend: Number, Percentage

In 2006, 75 percent of all immigrants to Canada were people belonging to visible minority groups. Since the 1986 census, people belonging to visible minority groups have increased 500 percent to more than 5 million, or 16 percent of the population.

Cosmopolitan Canada

In Canada, migration has created an ethnically diverse society. Nearly 20 percent of Canada's population was born in a different country. Some of Canada's cities are among the world's most **cosmopolitan**. That is, many different ethnic groups live together in one urban area as enclaves or in multiethnic neighbourhoods. Not just the big cities are changing. Many smaller communities are changing, too. Migration has not affected all communities equally, but it has affected *all* communities.

Fact File

Nearly half of new immigrants to Canada settle in Toronto, Vancouver, or Montréal. Thus, these cities are becoming increasingly cosmopolitan. Why do you suppose such a high percentage of immigrants settle in these three cities?

Figure 13.9

The older ethnic neighbourhoods and enclaves in large cities are often cultural and business centres that attract visitors from other neighbourhoods, as well as tourists. Why do these enclaves attract visitors? Have you visited ethnic neighbourhoods that differ from your family's cultural background? What did you learn?

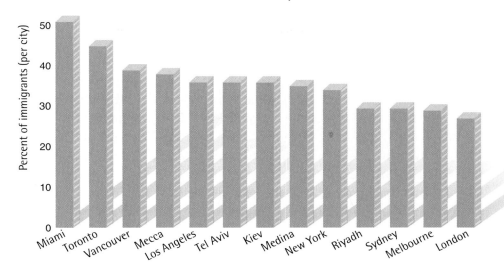

The World's Most Cosmopolitan Cities

Figure 13.10

This bar graph shows the world's most cosmopolitan cities (Toronto ranks second and Vancouver ranks third). Jobs, families, and friends pull migrants to big cities. The city's reputation for tolerance and diversity is also an important pull factor. Find Mecca, Medina, Riyadh, and Tel Aviv in your atlas. Which pull factor likely has the most influence on migrants in these cities?

Figure 13.11

In 2006, 11 ethnic groups passed the 1 million mark in Canada. Based on what you have learned so far, what ethnic groups do you think are decreasing as a percentage of Canada's population? What ethnic groups do you think are increasing as a percentage of Canada's population?

LITERACY TIP

Summarizing

Summarizing means choosing the most important ideas in a text. Follow these guidelines:

- Read a section of the text to get a general understanding.

- Read the first paragraph and look for the main ideas.

- Look away and identify the main ideas. If you cannot remember them, reread the text.

- Record these ideas in your own words.

- Follow the same guidelines for the rest of the paragraphs and figures in the section.

Canadians' Roots: The Origins Claimed Most Frequently

Ethnic Group	Total Number of Canadians Claiming This Origin (millions)
Canadian	10.0
English	6.6
French	4.9
Scottish	4.7
Irish	4.4
German	3.2
Italian	1.4
Chinese	1.3
Aboriginal	1.3
Ukrainian	1.2
Dutch	1.0
Indian	0.8

1. In your own words or with a combination of sketches and labels, summarize how the cultural makeup of immigrants to Canada has changed in recent decades.

2. Canada is one of the largest countries in the world. Its population density is one of the lowest in the world. (See Figure 1.6 on page 8 in Chapter 1.) Despite its vast area, why might Canada be close to its limits for supporting population?

Discuss this question with a partner or a small group. Be ready to share your conclusions with the rest of the class.

BE A GLOBAL CITIZEN

A Taste of Bangladesh in Toronto

Have you ever visited the following enclaves: Little Italy? Chinatown? Greektown? The Indian Bazaar? All of these places have one thing in common. They were created by immigrants who came to Canada and settled in an area with people who shared a common background. As the source regions for Canadian immigrants change, so do the faces in these communities.

More immigrants are coming to Canada from the Indian subcontinent—India, Bangladesh, Pakistan, and Sri Lanka. They often move into communities of people who share their own ethnic background. One community being studied is the area known as Little Bangladesh in the east end of Toronto. The study is focused on the Crescent Town community.

What makes this area unique is that it is also a vertical village. There is a whole community in the seven high-rise apartment buildings that make up Crescent Town. The Mecca Restaurant is one of many that serve food the traditional way. Markets sell fish that comes from Bangladesh. One Bengali man bought the local Hasty Market. He started to sell items that the people of the community wanted—long and short grain rice, halal meats, DVDs in Bengali, and other specialty products. Another family runs a tiny bookshop that sells imported Bengali books.

Many of the residents no longer have to leave their community to find what they need. Many services are available:

- mosque and weekly Qur'an classes
- daycare
- at-home beauty parlours
- Bengali language classes for children

The hub of the community is the Crescent Town Club. This large recreation centre is open to all residents of the towers. It has a pool, fitness facilities, gyms, day camps, and many programs that run all year. The other hub is Crescent Town Public School. This large school of more than 800 students, from Kindergarten to Grade 5, is inside the apartment complex.

Recently, a community health centre opened its doors in this community. The Bengali Cultural Society in Crescent Town helps immigrants get settled.

Little Bangladesh is a vibrant community in Toronto. Many other ethnic communities exist in large Canadian cities. As immigration continues to change the face of Canada, find ways to learn about new cultures. Here are some suggestions:

- Plan a class trip to an ethnic community.
- Try a new type of ethnic food. Learn about the people and the culture.
- Watch a film from a different culture.
- Plan a multicultural potluck lunch.

Brainstorm with your class for other ways to learn about the various cultures in Canada.

Figure 13.12

Crescent Town is made up of seven high-rise apartment buildings and some townhouses. The population of this area is about 16 000 people. Recent immigrants make up 41 percent of the population. How might living in Crescent Town help new immigrants adjust to their new lives in Canada? How might it act as a barrier to becoming an active member of Canadian society?

The Richness of Multiculturalism

LITERACY TIP

Practising Effective Listening

Follow these guidelines when you listen to other people share their opinions and ideas:

- Be patient and let the speaker complete her or his ideas.
- Maintain eye contact with the speaker.
- Keep your mind open to gain new information. Do not just look for points that support your ideas.
- Avoid negative language. You do not have to agree with what the speaker is saying, but if you disagree with supporting evidence, do it in an agreeable, respectful way. Think about what the speaker is saying before you respond.

1. Discuss the following question with a partner or a small group: Should immigrants assimilate into Canadian culture so that all Canadians have the same culture? Or, should immigrants be able to maintain their ethnic cultures when they settle in Canada?

Remember to respect opinions that may differ from yours. Listen to the reasons that others offer to support their points of view. Record the main points of view that arise from your discussion and be ready to share them with another group or the rest of the class.

Immigrants choose Canada for many different reasons. These pull factors include the following:

- Job opportunities—In their home countries, immigrants may be able to get only low-paying jobs, or they may not be able to get jobs for which they have training. They seek better-paying jobs suited to their abilities and skills. Canada advertises for immigrants to fill many roles, from skilled workers to professionals.
- Environmental factors—Immigrants may experience problems such as frequent widespread flooding or drought in their home countries. They move to escape these problems.
- Political stability—In many countries, governments have changed often. Dictators and armies have taken control. Armed conflict sometimes erupts between political groups. People immigrate to Canada to keep their families safe from violence.
- Democratic elections—In many countries, millions have never been able to vote. People have no say in who runs their country, how it operates, or what freedoms they have. They hope to have those privileges when they move to Canada.

Immigrants choose Canada for two other important reasons:

- The *Canadian Charter of Rights and Freedoms* protects the rights of individuals. Canadians have freedoms such as freedom of speech, freedom to practise religion, and freedom of assembly. Our rights include the right to vote, to own property, and to have our privacy protected. Rights and freedoms such as these are limited or unavailable in many countries. Many immigrants did not have the rights in their home countries that we are guaranteed in Canada. Some were mistreated in their home countries; they may not have been allowed to meet in groups with others, or they may have had to observe evening curfews. Immigrants cherish the rights and freedoms we have grown to expect as Canadians.

Figure 13.13

The *Canadian Charter of Rights and Freedoms* is part of Canada's Constitution—the supreme law of Canada. Do you have a document similar to the Charter at your school, for example, a code of conduct? What rights and freedoms does it protect?

• Canada's government has a policy of **multiculturalism**. The *Canadian Multiculturalism Act* of 1971 stated the following:

> It is hereby declared to be the policy of the Government of Canada to recognize and promote the understanding that multiculturalism reflects the cultural and racial diversity of Canadian society and acknowledges the freedom of all members of Canadian society to preserve, enhance, and share their cultural heritage.

In Canada, we want to understand each others' heritages, and to celebrate our diverse cultures together.

Canada's multicultural policy supports people of different ethnicities, religions, and ethnic groups that settle in Canada. It speaks to all Canadians, promoting appreciation and acceptance. Canada's laws protect everyone from racial prejudice and hate. However, it takes more than laws to make these ideas real. We must all practise them each day—in our communities, at school, at work, and in our attitudes and interactions.

1. The wording of the *Canadian Multiculturalism Act* is difficult, and you may need to read it several times to understand what it promises to all Canadian citizens. Work with a partner to identify its key points. Discuss what these points mean, and do one of the following:

• Explain this policy in your own words.
• Illustrate the meaning of this policy.
• Dramatize what this policy means.

Fact File

More than 4000 websites are dedicated to human rights. Many groups work to protect and improve human rights around the world. Who are these groups? What kinds of work are they doing?

Figure 13.14

This Moroccan family is receiving their citizenship at a ceremony in Montréal. Immigrants become citizens of Canada when they qualify through a process called naturalization. Citizenship is an important part of feeling that you belong in a society. In what other ways can immigrants find a sense of belonging in Canada?

Cultural Identity

When people move, they do not forget their roots and traditions. These things are important to identity and well-being. Food, celebrations, and entertainment often provide our first impressions of other cultural groups. Contact with a variety of cultural groups also opens the doors to cross-cultural understanding. Their presence can enrich our lives.

In the past 30 years, immigrant groups have constructed new buildings in communities across Canada. These include mosques, synagogues, temples, shops, and ethnic community centres.

Figure 13.15

The buildings of different cultural groups are found in nearly all Canadian towns and cities. Which cultural groups are in your community? Which buildings in your community display the cultural roots of immigrants?

Cultural Celebrations

Across Canada, cultural events and celebrations honour the past of many cultures. Cultural festivals celebrate the food, music, dance, traditions, and customs of the many cultural groups that live in Canada. They also bring people closer together in understanding. Such events include the following:

- There are celebrations of immigrant arrivals in Canada at Pier 21.
- Oktoberfest is the German Harvest Festival. Many Canadian communities celebrate this festival.
- Dreamspeakers is the Aboriginal arts and film festival in Edmonton.
- Chinese New Year celebrations are held in Vancouver, Toronto, and Montréal.
- Caribana is the popular Caribbean celebration in Toronto.
- Sunfest is the Celebration of World Cultures in London.

Figure 13.16

Counterclockwise from left, these photos show Oktoberfest in Kitchener, Chinese New Year celebrations in Montréal, and Sunfest in London. All cultural festivals contribute to Canada's cultural identity. These festivals also help to blend all our cultures. Which cultural festivals have you attended? Why are people from other ethnic groups attracted to such events?

Myth Busting

People sometimes think that immigrants harm their host countries. Some believe they take jobs from the local people. They think immigrants place a strain on social services such as welfare, children's programs, education, health care, and police. They are wrong. In fact, the opposite is true.

Immigrants increase economic growth in the following ways:

- They create employment by investing money and starting new businesses.
- They buy products such as furniture, clothes, vehicles, and food. The buying they do increases business.
- They use services such as banks, restaurants, and car repair shops.
- They add skills, knowledge, new ideas, and labour to the workforce.

All of these activities contribute directly to the local economy. In addition, like all Canadians, immigrants contribute to the economy by paying taxes.

To learn more about the "Racism. Stop It" National Video Competition for students and youth, and to watch winning videos,

Go to Nelson Social Studies

Figure 13.17

The Supreme Court of Canada ruled that Sikh police officers in Canada can wear turbans, as required by their faith, rather than hats. How does this show that Canada accepts new ideas?

Fact File

In 2006, half of the people in Canada who held a doctorate degree and 40 percent of those who held a master's degree were immigrants.

The Nature of Immigrants to Canada

Immigrants to Canada are usually well-educated and prepared for life in this country. According to the 2006 census, most immigrants could speak English or French. As well, most newcomers have higher levels of education than the majority of people born in Canada. In 2006, more immigrants had university degrees than Canadians in the same age groups. Half of the 2001–2006 immigrants held university degrees.

Most recent immigrants to Canada are classified as *economic immigrants*. These are skilled tradespeople, professionals, technical workers, and entrepreneurs. Another group of immigrants are *family class*. Their entrance is based on bringing family members together. These family members add more consumers to the domestic market, which increases the country's wealth. They enter schools and the workplace, and help meet the needs of a shrinking workforce. The remaining group of immigrants is the *refugee class*. These people are fleeing hardships such as war and environmental disaster elsewhere. Canada provides refugees with the opportunity to start over.

Figure 13.18

This pie graph shows the classes of immigrants who came to Canada in 2007. Look at the segment that represents economic immigrants. Since 1998, the percentage of skilled workers has stayed the same. In 2007, the number of entrepreneurs declined by 65 percent. Only 581 of 131 248 total economic immigrants were entrepreneurs. What is an entrepreneur? Why does Canada need entrepreneurs?

Types of Immigrants to Canada, 2007

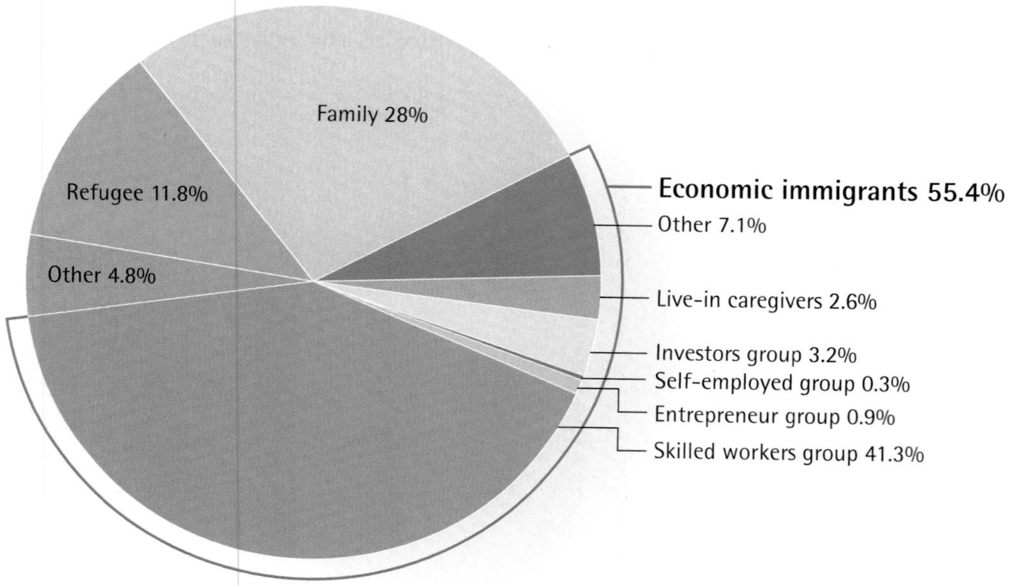

Family 28%
Refugee 11.8%
Other 4.8%
Economic immigrants 55.4%
Other 7.1%
Live-in caregivers 2.6%
Investors group 3.2%
Self-employed group 0.3%
Entrepreneur group 0.9%
Skilled workers group 41.3%

1. a) Why do you think Canada's largest cities attract the most immigrants?

b) One in every three people in Canada's large cities is an immigrant who is also a university graduate. Suggest why this might be so.

2. What negative statements have you heard people making about immigrants coming to Canada? Based on what you have learned about the immigrants who enter Canada, what would you tell these people? Dramatize your conversation.

Canadian Attitudes to Immigrants

The word "mosaic" has been used to describe Canada's policy toward immigrants. (Refer to page 269 in Chapter 12.) The poll conducted by The Strategic Counsel for the *Globe and Mail* and CTV (see Figure 13.19) suggests that Canadians are abandoning the "mosaic" approach to multiculturalism. Recent polls show that 7 in 10 Canadians say immigrants should be encouraged to integrate and become part of Canadian society, rather than maintaining their ethnic identity and culture. That means that more mainstream Canadians want immigrants to become part of the broader society. Despite this trend, most Canadians think immigrants make a positive contribution to Canada.

Figure 13.19

Review these results of a 2005 survey conducted by The Strategic Counsel for the *Globe and Mail* and CTV on Canadians' attitudes toward immigration. Why is it important to involve all Canadians in discussions about current and future immigration?

Immigration Attitudes Survey

Q: Do you think Canada accepts too many, too few, or just about the right number of immigrants per year?	
Don't know	12%
Too few	10%
Too many	32%
About the right amount	46%
Q: What approach should Canada take with new immigrants?	
Don't know	11%
Should encourage immigrants to maintain their identity and culture	20%
Should encourage immigrants to integrate and become part of the Canadian culture	69%
Q: Do you think immigrants from some countries/regions make a bigger and better contribution than immigrants from other countries/regions?	
Don't know	9%
Immigrants from some countries/regions make a bigger and better contribution	41%
There is no difference in the kind of contribution immigrants make based on their country/region origin	50%
Q: What kinds of contributions do immigrants from certain countries/ regions make? **Percentage saying very positive/positive contribution:**	
Europe	76%
Asia	59%
India	45%
Caribbean and West Indies	33%

Figure 13.20

Governor General Michaëlle Jean was born in Haiti. She and her family immigrated to Canada in 1968. She is interested in issues of racism and how our society must work to end them. How can she influence Canadians' views of immigrants and newcomers' views of Canada?

What Immigrants Say

It does not take long for immigrants to decide what they like and dislike about Canada. Our government surveys immigrants four years after their arrival in Canada.

What They Like

- the climate and physical environment (19 percent)
- cultural aspects like freedom and human rights (14.4 percent)
- safety for self and family (11 percent)
- peace and a stable government (10.4 percent)
- educational opportunities (9.9 percent)
- the opportunity to achieve the lifestyle they desire (9.2 percent)
- social programs such as health care (7.5 percent)

What They Dislike

- the climate and physical environment (26.7 percent)
- lack of employment opportunities (17.4 percent)
- high taxes (11.1 percent)
- health care system (5.3 percent)
- people's attitudes (3.9 percent)
- cultural aspects such as freedom and human rights (3.2 percent)

AFTER READING

1. Answer the survey questions in Figure 13.19. To which percentage of the Canadian population do you belong for each question?

2. a) In the survey of what immigrants like and dislike, high percentages picked climate and environment as their top like *and* top dislike. Why do you think that climate and environment made the top of the list in both likes and dislikes?

   b) You have read that many immigrants come to Canada for better jobs. However, the survey shows that immigrants rank "lack of employment opportunities" as the second highest dislike. Based on what you know, why do you think so many immigrants select "lack of employment opportunities"?

3. Refer to Figure 13.19. What term from an earlier chapter means the same as "immigrants should integrate and become part of the Canadian culture"?

GeoSkills

Persuasive Writing

The purpose of persuasive writing is to express your ideas about an issue. Clear persuasive writing will convince people to accept your point of view. In order to create a clear and concise piece of persuasive writing, follow the 8 Cs: Catch, Commit, Concede, Counter, Convince, Clinch, re-Commit, and Close.

Immigration and the Future of Canada

Catch

Can you imagine a Canada without any immigrants? You are either an immigrant, or the descendant of one. Immigrants have shaped Canadian culture. If we want to keep a variety of cultures in Canada, we need to allow more immigrants in. Newcomers have always helped Canada's economy. With our economy facing serious problems, the flow of new Canadians must be increased. The Canadian government should increase the number of immigrants allowed into the country each year. Simply put, Canada needs more Canadians.

Commit

Concede

Some may say that we have enough people in Canada already. These people point out that we have enough workers today to keep our economy strong. This is not true. The average age of Canadians is increasing. Many Canadians are nearing the age of retirement. Canada will soon face a shortage of workers. The Conference Board of Canada stated, "Canada will have to increase its number of immigrants from the existing 250 000 to 360 000 annually by 2025." Canada will need this increase to stay competitive.

Counter

Many immigrants have made important contributions to Canadian culture. Dr. Vincent Lam, the son of Asian immigrants, is an emergency room doctor. He wrote an award-winning novel, *Bloodletting and Miraculous Cures*. Somali-born Canadian Kanaan Warsame, better known as "K'naan" is a talented musician. He is one of many musicians who came to Canada and brought new musical styles with them. Immigrants like Dr. Lam and K'naan have enriched Canadian culture.

Convince

Immigration is good for Canadian businesses. New customers create new business opportunities. Many newcomers also set up businesses that deal with goods and services for their communities. Examples include ethnic restaurants, newspapers, fashion shops, and grocery stores. The *Toronto Star* reports that immigration is expected to be "key to fuelling sales" of homes in Canadian cities, as older Canadians sell their houses and move into smaller homes. If Canada's economy is to keep growing and our cities are to continue to be exciting, liveable places, more immigrants are needed.

Clinch

Re-Commit

Canada needs immigration for continued growth and success. Immigrants provide Canada with new energy, new culture, and economic strength. What do we have today because of immigrants in the past? What might we lose if Canada should fail to allow more immigrants in the future?

Close

Figure 13.21

Read the piece of persuasive writing above, and note the 8 Cs.

Catch: This is the first sentence in your first paragraph. It is the most important sentence because it is the one that will grab the reader's attention. You must find a way to introduce your topic so that the reader will want to keep reading. You might try by starting with a question, a quotation, or an interesting fact.

Commit: This is the last sentence in your first paragraph. Its job is to state the topic and your opinion clearly.

Concede: In this sentence, you state an opposing opinion to your own.

Counter: In this section, you use one of your strongest points to prove that the opposing idea is weak.

Convince: This is where you prove your point and support your opinion. You can use information from research and from your prior knowledge and experience to write this section. Make sure that your points are clear and concise.

Clinch: This is the last part of the body of your writing. Here, you place one of your strongest pieces of supporting information.

Re-Commit: This is the first sentence of your last paragraph. Its job is to restate your topic and opinion clearly.

Close: This is your conclusion. It may be one or two sentences long. This is where you leave the reader wanting to find out more about the topic, to continue to think about the topic, or to get involved with the issue.

The Effects of Migration within Canada

1. Do you know people who have moved to another province or territory in Canada? Have you read or heard about people moving from one province or territory to another? On an outline map of Canada, use arrows to show as many of these migrations as you can. Label each arrow to answer the following questions:

- Who migrated?
- Why did he/she/they migrate?

Share information about these migrations with your class or in a small group. Compile a master map of migrations within Canada.

International migration, movement of people from one country to another, affects our society. So does **interprovincial migration**. The prefix "inter" means between. Thus, interprovincial migration is migration between provinces, or from one province or territory to another. Over time, every country experiences changes due to the movement of people within their own borders.

Economic Migration

Economics is one of the main causes of internal migration. What is one word that captures the reason why people migrated in the following examples?

- In Canada, an industrial boom occurred in southern Ontario and Québec after World War II. This boom caused a major movement of people from other provinces to those areas.
- During the boom in the oil business in the late 1970s through the 1980s, people flocked to the West. Most people went to Calgary and Edmonton. This region experienced another economic boom recently due to oil and gas development.
- The Atlantic provinces lost the East Coast fishery. Slowdowns in the forest industry contributed to the slow growth overall in this region. Many people, mainly young, left the Atlantic provinces for other parts of Canada, especially the oil sands of Alberta.

Figure 13.22

The advertisements for all the jobs in demand in Alberta and Saskatchewan say "Come West!" The oil sands and other oil and gas resources have seen tremendous growth. Calgary is Canada's newest city with 1 million people. The province still cannot get enough labour to meet the demand. How could an oil boom create jobs that are not directly related to oil and gas development?

Migration Inside Canada, 2006

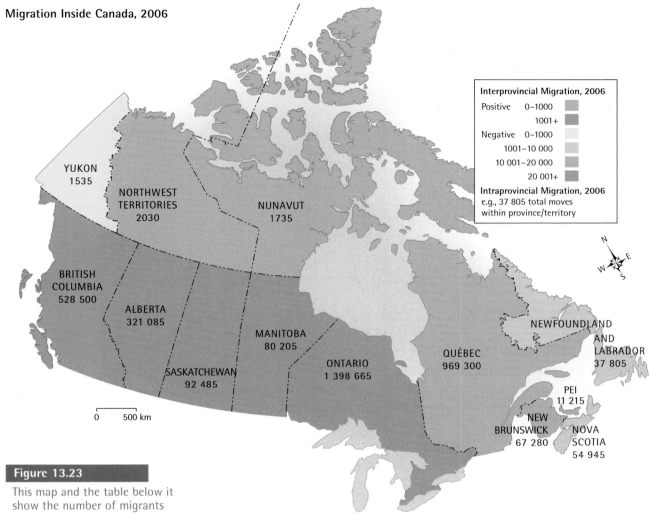

Interprovincial Migration, 2006

Positive 0–1000
          1001+
Negative 0–1000
          1001–10 000
          10 001–20 000
          20 001+

Intraprovincial Migration, 2006
e.g., 37 805 total moves
within province/territory

YUKON 1535

NORTHWEST TERRITORIES 2030

NUNAVUT 1735

BRITISH COLUMBIA 528 500

ALBERTA 321 085

MANITOBA 80 205

SASKATCHEWAN 92 485

ONTARIO 1 398 665

QUÉBEC 969 300

NEWFOUNDLAND AND LABRADOR 37 805

PEI 11 215

NEW BRUNSWICK 67 280

NOVA SCOTIA 54 945

0   500 km

Figure 13.23

This map and the table below it show the number of migrants within and between provinces for a single year, 2006. Which province gained the most people? Which lost the most? Why do you think that is?

Province/Territory	Intra	Inter-in	Inter-out	Net
Newfoundland and Labrador	37 805	25 780	32 020	−6240
Prince Edward Island	11 215	8300	7690	610
Nova Scotia	54 945	48 035	56 045	−8010
New Brunswick	67 280	31 570	42 185	−10 615
Québec	969 300	73 555	85 205	−11 650
Ontario	1 398 665	185 785	212 705	−26 920
Manitoba	80 205	36 585	57 330	−20 755
Saskatchewan	92 485	38 930	64 315	−25 385
Alberta	321 085	226 870	138 690	88 180
British Columbia	528 500	164 710	142 575	22 135
Yukon	1535	3665	3105	−560
Northwest Territiories	2030	6360	7040	680
Nunavut	1735	2425	2770	345

Regions Losing People

Experts predict that some parts of Canada will keep losing population. Atlantic Canada will be the most likely region. This part of the country was going through difficult times before the economic crisis of 2008. That crisis resulted in disaster for many people. In 2008, New Brunswick lost more than 20 000 forestry jobs. Many mills closed and operations slowed down dramatically. These losses seem small compared to the more than 100 000 manufacturing jobs that were lost in Ontario. When you consider the loss of 20 000 jobs in such a small province, though, it is comparable to the massive layoffs in Ontario's auto industry.

The lobster industry is valuable to the economy in Prince Edward Island, New Brunswick, and Nova Scotia. This industry faced very low prices in 2008. People had to sell their boats and equipment to make ends meet. Without work opportunities at home, young people are forced to leave.

In the 1990s, Newfoundland and Labrador was the province that was losing the highest percentage of its population to other regions in Canada. Now, thanks to the development of offshore oil and gas, the island has become more prosperous.

This ongoing loss of population from Atlantic Canada has cultural effects. More and more properties in many communities have "For Sale" signs. People see their neighbours leave, and no one moves in to take their place. Some communities may even die completely. It saddens many to witness such changes. They see their futures and their children's futures become limited. Their identity has always been linked to resources such as the fishery and forests. This identity and their traditional ways might be lost. How will this loss affect the Canadian identity and culture?

Fact File

During the 1990s, Newfoundland and Labrador lost 1 percent of its population each year. This trend, known as "The Emptying of the Rock," continued. The 2006 census showed a population of 512 500. This was a loss of more than 1 percent. However, in 2007–2008, Newfoundland and Labrador's net interprovincial migration showed a growth of 1299. More people migrated into the province than left the province. This growth reflects the improved oil and gas economy there. Instead of "The Emptying of the Rock," what could you name the trend now?

Figure 13.24

The government closed the northern cod fishery in the 1990s because so few cod were left. These fishers in Bonavista, Newfoundland and Labrador, survived by catching crab. Many young men and women had to leave the province to make a living. Recently, the oil and gas boom in Newfoundland and Labrador has meant more jobs and prosperity. What changes might this boom cause to the culture of the province? Areas of Ontario are also dependent on resources such as forestry and mining. They are suffering job losses and closures, too. Which areas in Ontario are affected by these losses?

DURING READING

1. Check Figure 13.23. How many people did British Columbia and Alberta gain in 2006?

2. If the map in Figure 13.23 were redrawn for 2008, what changes would you see? Consider what you have learned about changes in interprovincial migration in this section.

Fact File

More than 100 million people worldwide are without homes. Many big cities have more than a million homeless people. In Mumbai, India, 5 million people are homeless. There are 1.5 million homeless people in Cairo, Egypt.

Regions Gaining People

British Columbia and Alberta are gaining people. Many of the people arriving are new immigrants. This movement is changing the culture in many communities. New immigrants cause urban densities to rise. Higher population densities in cities change how people interact and get along. As more people live within the same area, society tends to become more impersonal. Many migrants feel isolated from the mainstream population. They need help getting settled.

Homeless Canadians

Homelessness also causes people to migrate. The numbers of homeless men, women, and youth who live on city streets affect communities greatly. Residents encounter street people asking for help or money every day. Nearly 20 000 homeless people live either in Vancouver or Toronto. They are part of Canada's "urban poor" who require a great deal of government and community help. Few cities have come to grips with solving the problems faced by the homeless.

The homeless face many disadvantages:

- limited health care
- limited access to education
- high risk of experiencing violence or abuse
- discrimination and difficulty getting work
- reduced access to financial services

The homeless move frequently from one refuge to another. They might be found in parks, vacant lots, broken-down structures, public places such as train stations, and abandoned underground havens such as tunnels or maintenance spaces. Canadian cities have homeless shelters, but not enough to meet the need.

Figure 13.25

During one severe winter in Toronto, the city opened its Moss Park Armoury to keep people from freezing on the streets. Homeless people find it hard to get jobs. Some try to make a living by panhandling (asking for donations or spare change) or cleaning windshields. Few people know what to do about this complex social problem. What suggestions do you have?

AFTER READING

1. Re-examine Figure 13.23 on page 305. Suggest two reasons people migrate within their province. If Ontario had approximately 12.7 million people in 2006, what percentage of the population moved within Ontario in 2006?

2. Discuss the following question with a partner: Why do governments spend money to attract industries to areas of the country experiencing population loss? Be prepared to share your ideas with another group or with the rest of the class.

CASE STUDY

Changing Population, Changing Schools

London, Ontario, has witnessed major changes in its population mix over the past 50 years.

Location of Lord Elgin Public School, London, Ontario

Lord Elgin Public School

- 10–15% non–European
- More than 15% non–European

Figure 13.26

This map shows the location of Lord Elgin Public School in London, Ontario. The map shows concentrations of non-Europeans by place of birth prior to 2001. Fifty years ago, less than 2 percent of London's population was non-European.

London is a centre for migration, both for refugees and for immigrants. This has many effects on the schools in the community. Schools have greater cultural diversity. Many teachers of English as a Second Language (ESL) are needed. Of the approximately 32 000 elementary students in London's schools, about 6 percent, or 1700, are in an ESL program.

Lord Elgin Public School: A Mini United Nations

The population of Lord Elgin Public School has changed. At one time it was nearly all English-speaking; today, 21 different first languages are spoken. In 2008, 80 percent of the school's 297 students spoke a first language other than English. The spoken first languages include

- Arabic
- Assyrian
- Bengali
- Bosnian
- Cambodian
- Cantonese
- Dutch
- English (dialect)
- German
- Kiswahili
- Kurdish
- Mandarin
- Oneida
- Persian
- Serbian
- Spanish
- Tagalog
- Tigrinya
- Urdu
- Uyghur
- Vietnamese

For many students, Lord Elgin is their first school experience in their new homeland. The 18 teachers have exciting days supporting and educating students from so many backgrounds. Communicating with parents can be a big challenge as language is sometimes a major barrier.

Students from other lands bring the following to share with their Canadian classmates:

- cultural diversity
- a wide array of new experiences
- different customs
- new ideas

As new immigrants learn about Canada, Canadian students learn about the world.

CASE STUDY

Changing Population, Changing Schools (continued)

Figure 13.27

When Lord Elgin Public School was built in the 1960s, it was the centre of a new suburb in which nearly everyone spoke English. If you were to visit this community now, what changes would you expect to see? Think of stores and food, as well as people.

Figure 13.28

Meet the Grades 3 and 4 students at Lord Elgin Public School in 2008.

In 2007–2008, the school held its first Cavalcade of Cultures, a community potluck dinner featuring entertainment from various cultures. More than 400 people took part. Celebrating their different cultures helped to bring the community together.

In some regions of the world, there are people who want to put up obstacles to cultural diversity, continued immigration, and education. There are some people in Canada, as well, who oppose cultural diversity and immigration. These people should visit Lord Elgin Public School. There, they would see a happy, safe, and nurturing environment where students get along and support one another. This school can be a model for the future.

Fact File

In 2008, students in ESL at Lord Elgin Public School were from the following countries: Afghanistan, Bangladesh, Bosnia, Cambodia, China, Croatia, Egypt, El Salvador, Eritrea, Germany, Ghana, Guatemala, Iraq, Jamaica, Jordan, Kenya, Liberia, Mexico, Pakistan, the Philippines, Somalia, Sudan, Syria, Turkmenistan, and Vietnam. How does the description "a mini United Nations" suit Lord Elgin Public School?

1. Is your community cosmopolitan? If not, provide an example of a cosmopolitan community near you. What signs are there to show this diversity?

2. a) What can communities do to help newcomers feel welcome?

b) What can you do to help newcomers feel welcome?

3. Using a blank world outline map, shade in the countries listed in the Fact File above. Compare the source countries shaded on your outline map with the cultural realms on the map in Figure 12.2 on page 261 in Chapter 12. Which cultural realms do most students in ESL at Lord Elgin Public School come from?

4. What might change in your school if the student population were suddenly as diverse as it is at Lord Elgin Public School?

Knowledge and Understanding

1 List four ways that movement of people can change the character of a community. Think about what you can see that tells you that change is happening.

2 **a)** Each year, people are born, people die, people migrate in, and people migrate out. What term applies to this statement?

b) Explain how positive net migration is important to Canadians.

Inquiry/Research and Communication Skills

3 Create a poster to attract immigrants to Canada. Imagine that your poster will assist Immigration Canada with recruiting new immigrants.

a) Brainstorm a list of the pull factors about Canada you think would attract newcomers. Look for groups of pull factors that go together. Categorize each group using your own headings. Reflect on your groups of features and choose the best ones.

b) Aim your poster at particular groups of immigrants you think Canada needs, such as entrepreneurs or skilled tradespeople. Include an enticing heading for your poster, for example, "Canada Wants You!"

c) Search magazines and newspapers for images showing the features of Canada that will especially interest the immigrants you are aiming to attract.

Remember, posters communicate a message using images and a small amount of written information. An effective poster delivers a clear message and leaves a lasting impression on the reader.

4 How would you persuade an immigrant to move to your community?

a) Think about the reasons people are pulled to migrate to Canada and the information about immigrants you have learned in this unit. List all of the positive things that your community has to offer a new immigrant.

b) Review the survey findings of what immigrants like and dislike after living four years in Canada, found on page 302. How might your community give immigrants more of what they like about Canada? How could your community help them with some of the items they dislike about Canada?

c) Use your answers to a) and b), and follow the 8 Cs of persuasive writing to answer this question: How would you persuade an immigrant to move to your community? (Refer to GeoSkills on page 303.)

5 **a)** The English language can be confusing to those who do not speak it as their first language. Identify and list English language words and phrases that might be misleading or puzzling to newcomers when they first hear them.

b) Provide the meaning of each word and phrase you identified, and explain why it might be misleading or confusing.

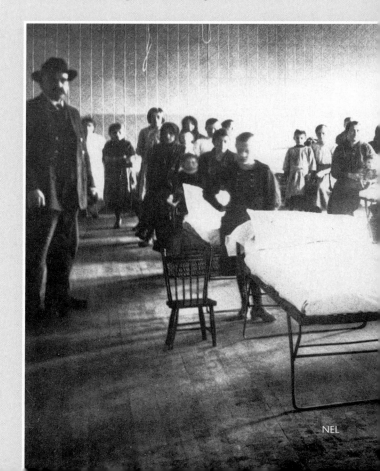

Figure 13.29

This photo was taken at the women's immigration dormitory in Saint John, New Brunswick, around 1920. Similar dormitories also existed in major ports such as Halifax and Québec City. Why do you suppose this is a women's immigration dormitory, and not a family immigration dormitory?

Map, Globe, and Graphic Skills

6 Use a road map of Ontario or another province of your choice. Identify place names that represent at least six cultural groups other than English. Ontario examples include Neustadt, which is German, and Belle River, which is French. Use an Internet search engine to find out which cultural groups your selected place names represent. Try search strings such as *place name Ontario history* or *place name Ontario origin of name.*

Application

7 **a)** What is your school doing to improve cultural understanding and acceptance of all cultural groups?

b) Discuss what your class can do to improve cultural understanding in your school. Plan a class project to help improve acceptance and understanding.

8 **a)** Create a photo display of buildings in your community that reflect cultural differences. Consider religious buildings, community centres, stores, restaurants, or other building types.

b) Create labels for the photos that explain how migration has affected your community.

9 Look carefully at Figure 13.29. This was the women's dormitory at the Immigration Building in Saint John, New Brunswick, around 1920.

a) How many adults do you see? How many children do you see? What do these numbers tell you?

b) Where do you think most of these immigrants came from? How can you tell?

c) Who might have taken the photograph?

d) Why do you think this photograph was taken?

e) How might the people in the photograph have felt about having their picture taken?

f) Imagine you are the child in the foreground of the photograph. How would you feel if you spent your first night in Canada in these surroundings?

g) In what ways does this photo summarize what was happening at the time it was taken?

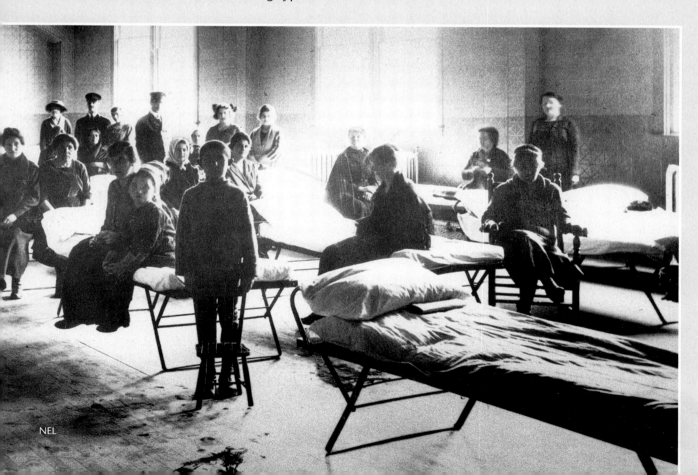

The World — Political

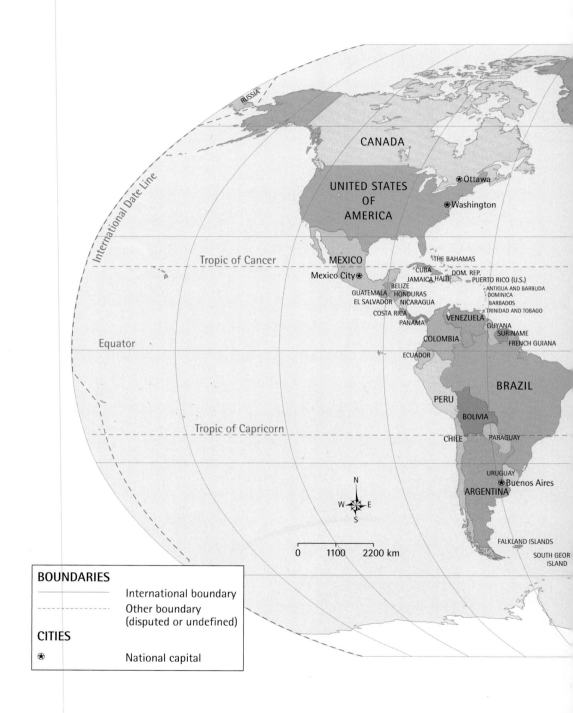

RUSSIA

CANADA

International Date Line

UNITED STATES
OF
AMERICA

⊛ Ottawa

⊛ Washington

Tropic of Cancer

MEXICO

THE BAHAMAS

Mexico City ⊛

CUBA
JAMAICA HAITI

DOM. REP.

PUERTO RICO (U.S.)

BELIZE
GUATEMALA HONDURAS
EL SALVADOR NICARAGUA
COSTA RICA
PANAMA

ANTIGUA AND BARBUDA
DOMINICA
BARBADOS
TRINIDAD AND TOBAGO

VENEZUELA

GUYANA
SURINAME
FRENCH GUIANA

COLOMBIA

ECUADOR

Equator

BRAZIL

PERU

BOLIVIA

Tropic of Capricorn

CHILE

PARAGUAY

URUGUAY
⊛ Buenos Aires

ARGENTINA

N
W ⊛ E
S

FALKLAND ISLANDS

SOUTH GEOR
ISLAND

0   1100   2200 km

BOUNDARIES

———————— International boundary

- - - - - - - - Other boundary
(disputed or undefined)

CITIES

⊛   National capital

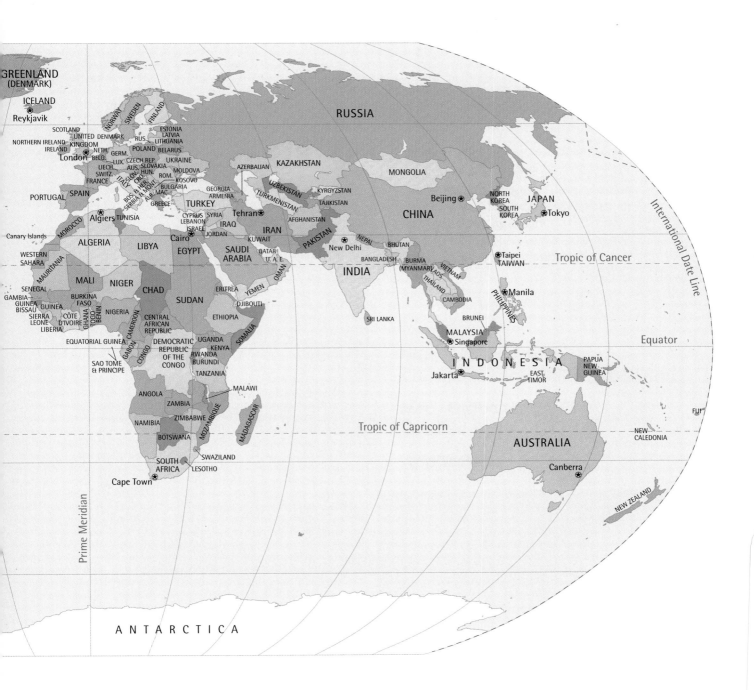

World Population Density

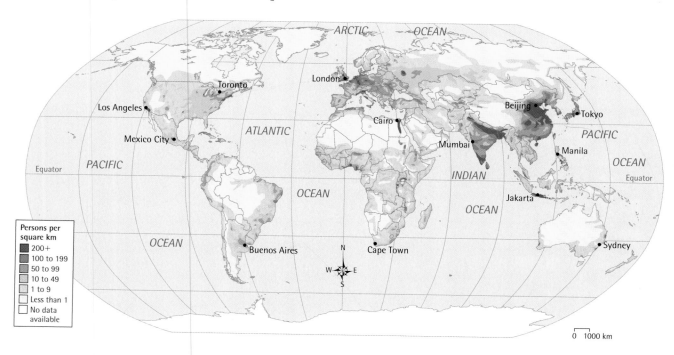

Persons per square km
- 200+
- 100 to 199
- 50 to 99
- 10 to 49
- 1 to 9
- Less than 1
- No data available

0 1000 km

Time Zones

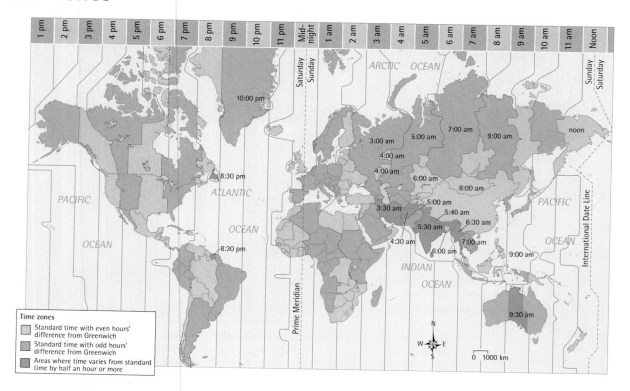

Time zones
- Standard time with even hours' difference from Greenwich
- Standard time with odd hours' difference from Greenwich
- Areas where time varies from standard time by half an hour or more

0 1000 km

Land Use

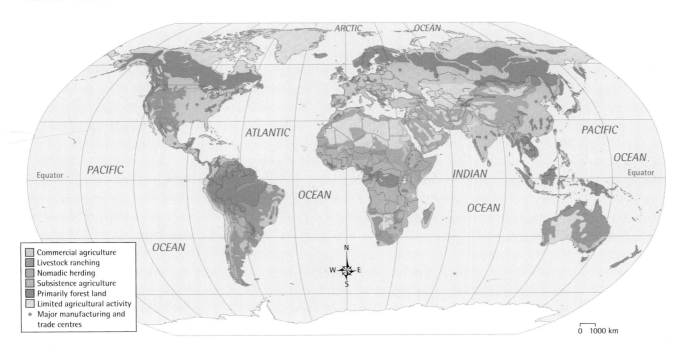

Legend:
- Commercial agriculture
- Livestock ranching
- Nomadic herding
- Subsistence agriculture
- Primarily forest land
- Limited agricultural activity
- Major manufacturing and trade centres

0   1000 km

Irrigated Land and Hunger

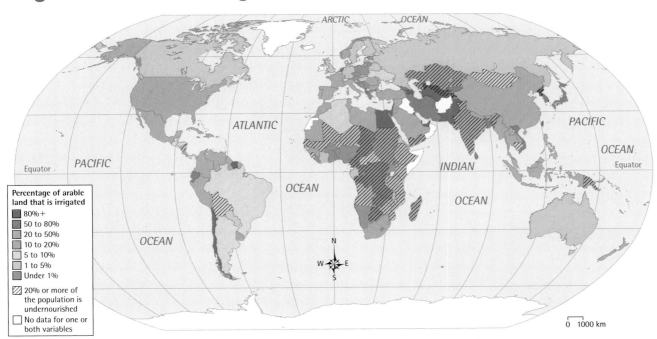

Percentage of arable land that is irrigated
- 80%+
- 50 to 80%
- 20 to 50%
- 10 to 20%
- 5 to 10%
- 1 to 5%
- Under 1%

- 20% or more of the population is undernourished
- No data for one or both variables

0   1000 km

The World's Big Cities

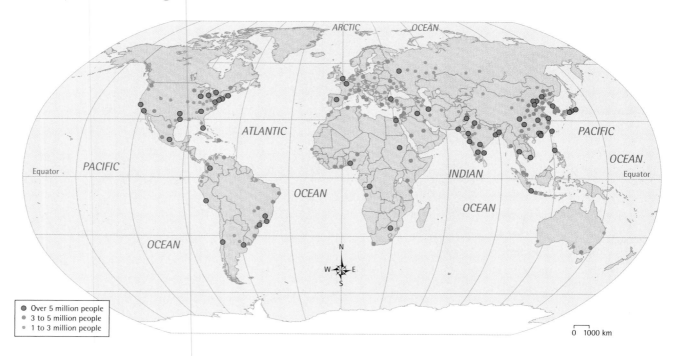

Over 5 million people
3 to 5 million people
1 to 3 million people

0   1000 km

Population Growth

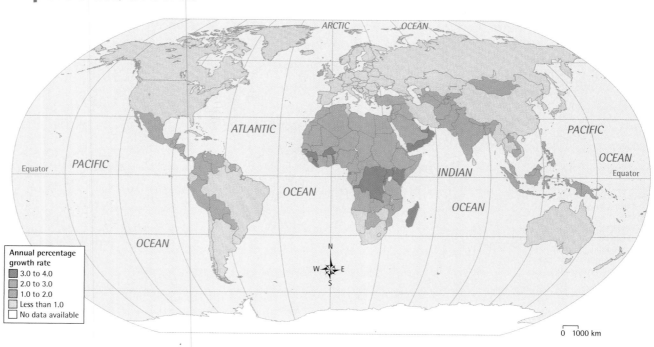

Annual percentage
growth rate
3.0 to 4.0
2.0 to 3.0
1.0 to 2.0
Less than 1.0
No data available

0   1000 km

Life Expectancy

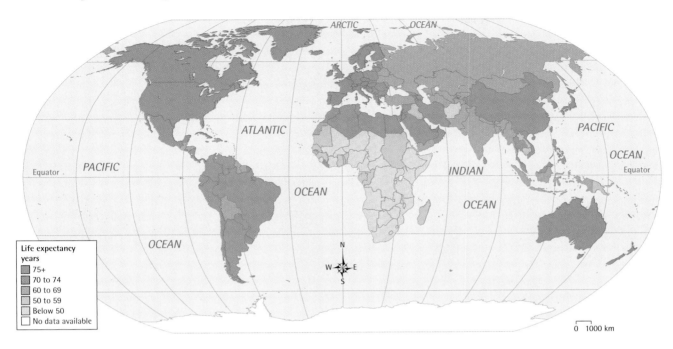

Life expectancy
years
- 75+
- 70 to 74
- 60 to 69
- 50 to 59
- Below 50
- No data available

0   1000 km

Fertility Rate

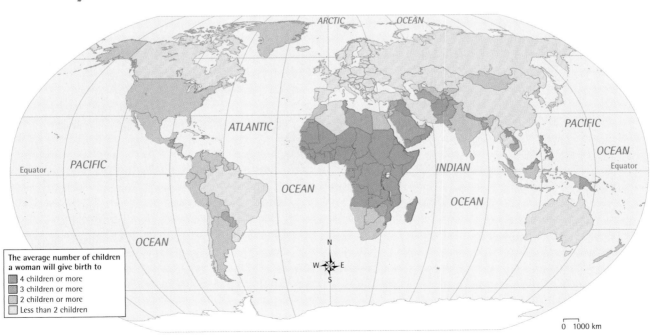

The average number of children
a woman will give birth to
- 4 children or more
- 3 children or more
- 2 children or more
- Less than 2 children

0   1000 km

Literacy

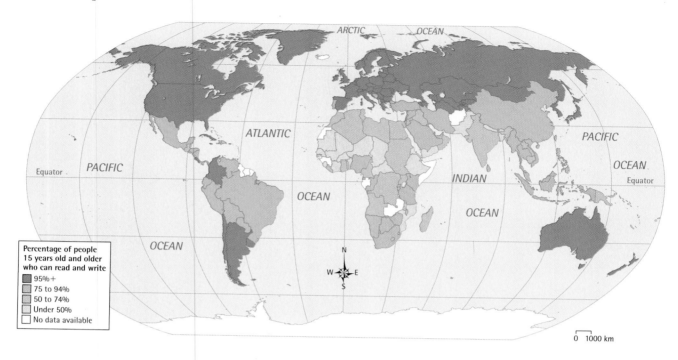

Percentage of people
15 years old and older
who can read and write
- 95%+
- 75 to 94%
- 50 to 74%
- Under 50%
- No data available

0   1000 km

Gross National Product per Person

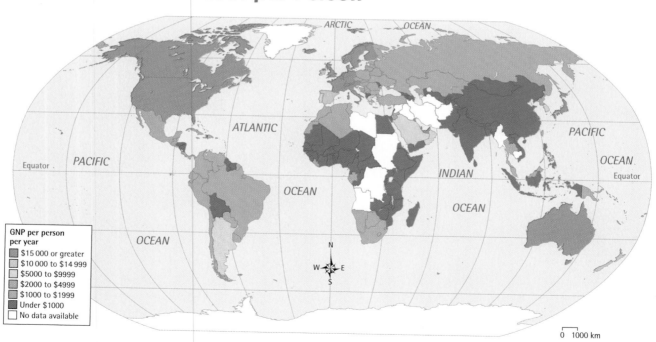

GNP per person
per year
- $15 000 or greater
- $10 000 to $14 999
- $5000 to $9999
- $2000 to $4999
- $1000 to $1999
- Under $1000
- No data available

0   1000 km

HIV/AIDS Deaths

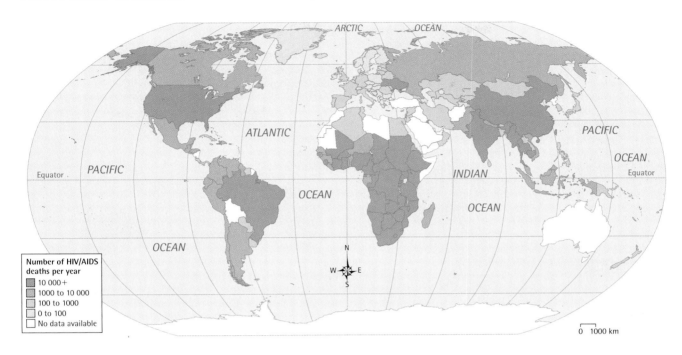

Number of HIV/AIDS deaths per year
- 10 000+
- 1000 to 10 000
- 100 to 1000
- 0 to 100
- No data available

0 1000 km

Food Availability

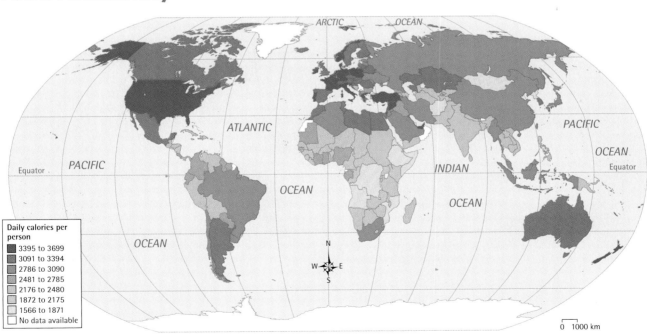

Daily calories per person
- 3395 to 3699
- 3091 to 3394
- 2786 to 3090
- 2481 to 2785
- 2176 to 2480
- 1872 to 2175
- 1566 to 1871
- No data available

0 1000 km

Access to Safe Drinking Water

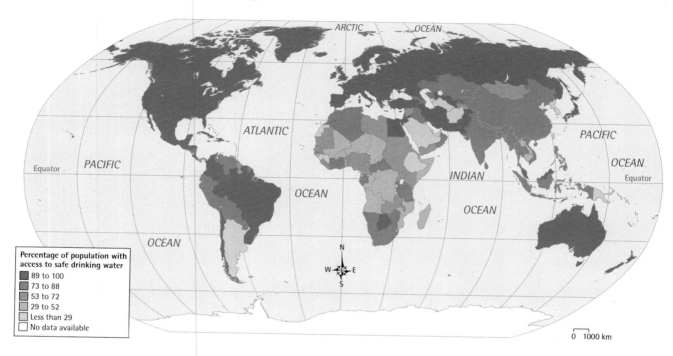

Percentage of population with access to safe drinking water
- 89 to 100
- 73 to 88
- 53 to 72
- 29 to 52
- Less than 29
- No data available

0   1000 km

Employment in Agriculture

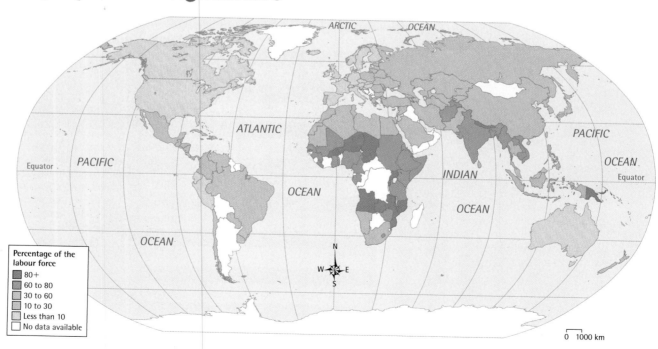

Percentage of the labour force
- 80+
- 60 to 80
- 30 to 60
- 10 to 30
- Less than 10
- No data available

0   1000 km

Employment in Manufacturing

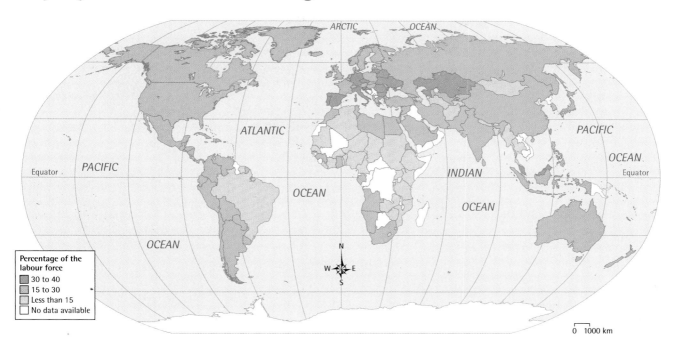

Percentage of the labour force
- 30 to 40
- 15 to 30
- Less than 15
- No data available

0   1000 km

Number of Internet Service Providers

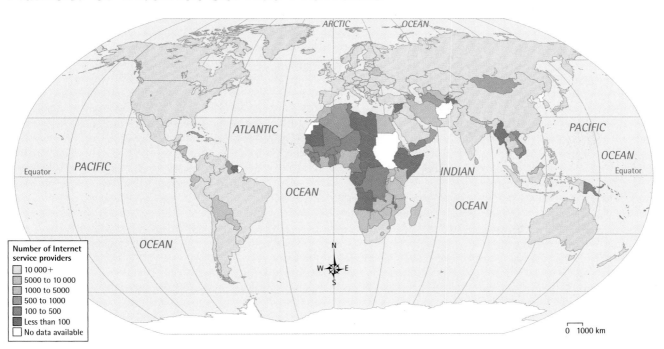

Number of Internet service providers
- 10 000+
- 5000 to 10 000
- 1000 to 5000
- 500 to 1000
- 100 to 500
- Less than 100
- No data available

0   1000 km

Oil Production

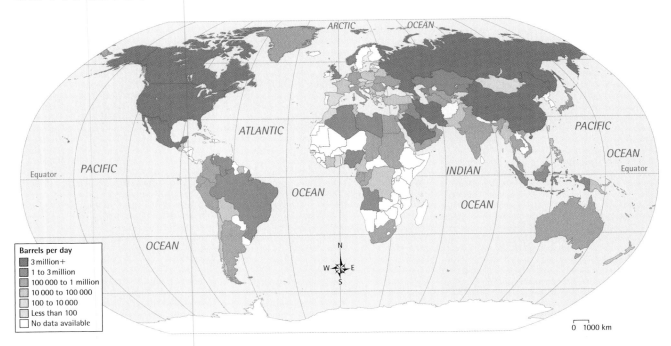

Barrels per day
- 3 million+
- 1 to 3 million
- 100 000 to 1 million
- 10 000 to 100 000
- 100 to 10 000
- Less than 100
- No data available

0   1000 km

Oil Consumption

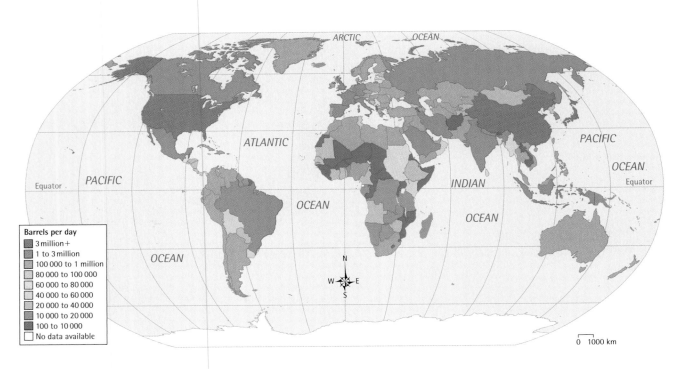

Barrels per day
- 3 million+
- 1 to 3 million
- 100 000 to 1 million
- 80 000 to 100 000
- 60 000 to 80 000
- 40 000 to 60 000
- 20 000 to 40 000
- 10 000 to 20 000
- 100 to 10 000
- No data available

0   1000 km

Balance of Trade

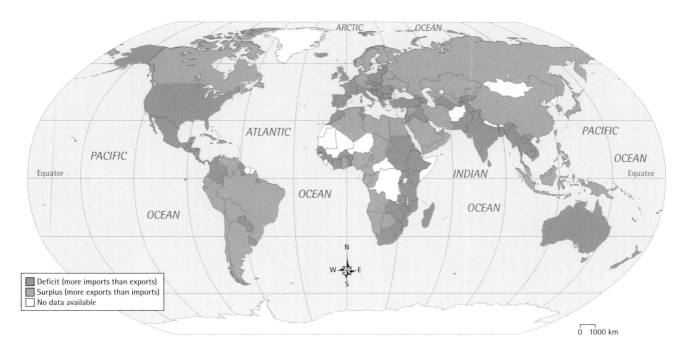

Deficit (more imports than exports)
Surplus (more exports than imports)
No data available

ARCTIC OCEAN

PACIFIC OCEAN

ATLANTIC OCEAN

PACIFIC OCEAN

Equator

INDIAN OCEAN

Equator

0 1000 km

Canada — Political

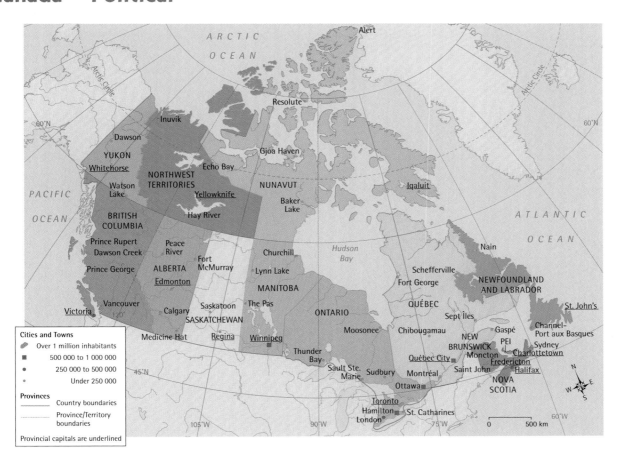

ARCTIC OCEAN

Alert

Resolute

Inuvik

Dawson

YUKON

Whitehorse

Gjoa Haven

Echo Bay

NORTHWEST TERRITORIES

NUNAVUT

Watson Lake

Yellowknife

Iqaluit

Baker Lake

BRITISH COLUMBIA

Hay River

ATLANTIC OCEAN

PACIFIC OCEAN

Prince Rupert
Dawson Creek

Peace River

Churchill

Nain

Prince George

Fort McMurray

Lynn Lake

Schefferville

NEWFOUNDLAND AND LABRADOR

ALBERTA

Edmonton

MANITOBA

Fort George

QUÉBEC

Vancouver

Calgary

Saskatoon

The Pas

ONTARIO

St. John's

Victoria

SASKATCHEWAN

Sept Îles

Channel-Port aux Basques

Medicine Hat

Regina

Winnipeg

Moosonee

Chibougamau

Gaspé

Sydney

NEW BRUNSWICK

PEI

Thunder Bay

Québec City

Moncton

Charlottetown

Fredericton

Halifax

Sault Ste. Marie

Sudbury

Montréal

Saint John

NOVA SCOTIA

Ottawa

Toronto

Hamilton

St. Catharines

London

Hudson Bay

Cities and Towns

Over 1 million inhabitants
500 000 to 1 000 000
250 000 to 500 000
Under 250 000

Provinces

Country boundaries
Province/Territory boundaries

Provincial capitals are underlined

0 500 km

North America — Population Density

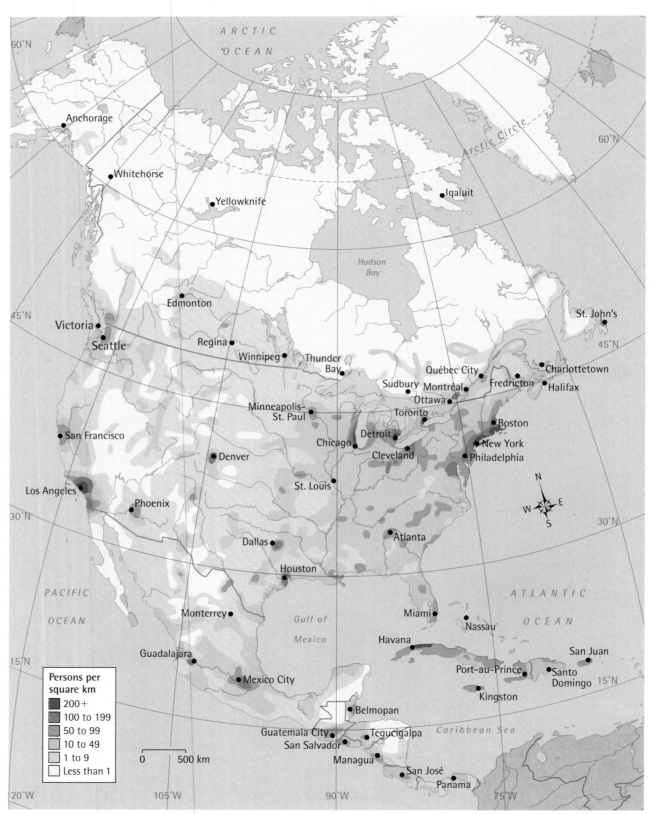

Persons per square km

- 200+
- 100 to 199
- 50 to 99
- 10 to 49
- 1 to 9
- Less than 1

0   500 km

Glossary

· ·

Aborigine — Aboriginal person of Australia

agricultural revolution — advances in technology that dramatically change our ability to grow, process, and distribute food; the first agricultural revolution occurred when people domesticated plants and animals 12 000 years ago; in the 1700s CE, farmers applied scientific ideas and new machines to produce more food

arable — describes land with fertile soil in a moderate climate with adequate water supply that can be used to grow crops

assimilation — the result of one culture changing to fit, or to be more like, another

Berlin Wall — a patrolled, high wall built by the USSR in the 1950s through the centre of the city of Berlin to prevent people from escaping to the West; the wall came down in 1989

biofuel — fuel made from plant biomass (e.g., corn and grain)

birth rate — the number of babies born each year for every 1000 people in a country

capital — money used to promote economic activities (for example, to build machines or to construct buildings)

census — the survey of a country's population to collect information about age, ethnic background, language, family size, and other facts

choropleth map — thematic map of a place that shows one type of data (or values); it clearly shows patterns of distribution using graded colour series to represent groups of data (numbers or percents); a population density map is an example

cluster — a term related to population distribution; describes a settlement pattern in which people settle closely together in groups rather than being evenly distributed over an area

cohort — a group of people born within a particular time span (for example, the baby boomers who were born in the time span from 1947–1960)

colonization — the process of one country controlling another country, either by military means or by populating the lands, for the purpose of acquiring natural resources

colony — a place that is controlled by a more powerful country; from the 1400s through the 1800s, European countries, including England, Spain, Portugal, and France, had colonies in the Americas, Africa, Asia, and Australia

commodity — anything that is bought or sold; the term most often refers to products made from natural resources

cosmopolitan — describes a place that is ethnically and culturally diverse, where many different ethnic groups live together

cultural diffusion — the peaceful spreading of cultural ideas from one group to another

culture — a way of life shared by a group of people, including the way they obtain food, the way they raise their children, their values, beliefs, language, customs, and religion

death rate — the number of people that die each year for every 1000 people in a country

demographic trend — factor that describes a change in the general population

demography — the study of human populations

dense — referring to high population density, where people live and work packed closely together; there is a high ratio of people to land area

deportation — the process of sending an illegal immigrant back to his or her country of origin

desertification — the expansion of deserts into surrounding areas, usually from the effects of human activities

developed country — a country that has a high proportion of its workforce in tertiary industries, with a small percentage in primary industries; incomes are usually high (for example, Canada)

developing country — a country that has a high proportion of its workforce engaged in primary industries and a small proportion working in the tertiary sector; incomes are usually quite low (for example, Haiti, Bangladesh)

diversified — having a wide variety of economic activities

downsize — to lay off large numbers of workers as a cost-saving measure

economic activity — the work that people do to improve their lives; includes all things that people do to get, refine, or use natural resources; also describes anything that people do to increase their wealth

economic development — the growth and improvement of the ways of creating wealth in a country or region; refers to how wealthy and industrialized a nation is

economic system — the way that a society makes economic decisions about what to produce and how to distribute it

economist — a person who studies the way economies work, often collecting data about how people make economic decisions

emigrate — to move away from one's country

enclave — an area, often within a large city, with a concentration of a particular cultural group

ethnoburb — an enclave that has developed in a suburban area

European Union (EU) — trading bloc among 27 member European countries; goods, services, and capital move freely among the member countries; a European Parliament makes rules about economic and political matters that apply to all countries; a common form of currency, the euro, is used

exit tax — a large sum of money, or fee, that the government requires a citizen to pay in order to emigrate

export — a good or service that is sold to other countries in order to earn income

factors of production — economic resources, which include land, capital, labour, and technology

fertility rate — the average number of babies born in a woman's lifetime in a country; to find the fertility rate, add up all the known births in a country (those reported in medical records) during one year for women aged 15 to 44, and then divide the total births by the number of women in that age group

finished goods — goods produced by secondary industries that consumers can use, such as automobiles, furniture, or food products

food conglomerate — a large corporation that owns a number of smaller companies dealing in a wide variety of products; food conglomerates are usually transnational corporations

forced migration — a mass movement of people who leave their homes against their will

foreign debt — money that a country owes to banks and lending agencies in other countries

free trade — trade between countries that takes place without tariffs or other barriers; Canada has a free trade agreement with Mexico and the United States

globalization — the increasing trend of doing business on an international scale; companies operate on a global scale, buying raw materials in some countries, manufacturing products in other countries, and selling their goods around the world; trading companies must consider all the forces at work around the world in order to compete

Greenbelt — green space that is permanently protected from urban development by legislation; it can only be used for farming, recreation, forests, wetlands, and watersheds

gross domestic product (GDP) — measures the total value of all the goods and services produced within a country in one year; does not include money earned outside the country; often expressed as GDP per capita, which is the GDP divided by the population

gross national product (GNP) — the sum of the wealth generated by all the economic activities of the citizens of a country in one year, no matter where the money was earned; may be expressed as GNP per capita, which is the average per person earnings

Human Development Index (HDI) — a combination of statistics about living conditions in a given country; the United Nations considers factors that measure how well each of 177 countries is doing in three areas of human development — health, knowledge, and standard of living

hydroponics — a system of producing plants without soil in a fertile water medium in greenhouses

immigrate — to move to a new country

imprint — mark on the physical environment

industrialization — the rapid development of manufacturing in a society; workers usually move out of a declining agricultural sector into an expanding industrial sector

Industrial Revolution — the period in the 1700s and 1800s that saw the changeover from a mainly farm-oriented society to a mainly industrial society

infant mortality —the number of deaths of infants (one year of age or younger) per 1000 live births

infrastructure — structures and systems built to enable a society to work well, such as roads, bridges, hospitals, electricity, clean water systems, schools, access to adequate housing, and access to food

interprovincial migration — the movement of people from one province or territory in Canada to another

knowledge worker — a person working in one of the information industries, such as computer software development

life expectancy — the number of years that a baby born in a certain year in a country can be expected to live

land use conflict — points of disagreement over the way land is used

linear — describes a settlement pattern in which groups of houses or communities form a line, which can be straight (usually along a road or railway) or wavy (as found along the edge of a river or lake, or in a long, narrow valley); sometimes called *strings*

literacy rate — the percentage of a country's population over age 15 that can read

mainstream population — the major cultural group in a society; in Ontario, the mainstream population has been white and Protestant, but that is changing

market — the consumers who buy a good or purchase a service; where the finished products are sold

mass migration — the movement of large numbers of people out of an area over a fairly short time period (for example, the flow of people out of Europe after the world wars)

material wealth — goods and services that we can see, touch, and measure that make our lives better, such as refrigerators and haircuts

megalopolis — a super-city that forms when cities grow into one another

migrant worker — a person who travels from one country to another for seasonal or even longer periods of employment

migration — the movement of people (or animals or things) from one place to another for political, economic, or environmental reasons

mixed economy — an economic system in which decisions are made by a combination of consumers, businesses, and government; includes elements of both command economies and market economies; Canada has a mixed economy

monoculture — growing only one crop on a farm

multiculturalism — a policy that embraces the idea of ethnic or cultural diversity; Canada is a multicultural society

natural increase — a rise in population because the birth rate is higher than the death rate

net migration — the difference between the number of people who emigrate and the number who immigrate each year

non-material wealth — those factors that improve our lives but are difficult to touch, describe, or measure, such as human rights and the freedom to worship as we wish

North American Free Trade Agreement (NAFTA) — a trading bloc consisting of Canada, Mexico, and the United States to allow tariff-free trade of goods and services

official plan — land use plan adopted by municipal governments to shape future directions for development within the municipality; land use maps are produced to illustrate the official plan; these maps show how property can be used (residential, commercial, industrial, and so on) and where different land uses will be allowed in the future

outsource — when one company hires an outside company or individual to help produce goods or services

per capita income — the average amount of money earned by each person in a country for one year

point system — a method used by governments to assess a potential immigrant's suitability using different measures such as family ties, language, and work skills

population characteristic — a factor that describes how a group of people is doing or changing in a given country; for example, birth rate, death rate, life expectancy, literacy rate, or infant mortality rate

population density — how many people live within a given area; usually measured by the average number of people for each square kilometre (km^2)

population distribution — the patterns of where people live

population pyramid — a special type of horizontal bar graph that shows the number of people in each age group and the balance between males and females in a country's population

preferred treatment — people who have family ties established in a country are given preference over immigrants who do not have family ties

primary industry — economic activities that extract natural resources from the environment and make them into semi-finished products

productivity — the efficiency with which *inputs* (for example, labour, technology, capital) are used to produce *outputs* (for example, vehicles); more efficient ways of doing things usually result in greater productivity

protectionism — actions a country takes to protect its local industries by limiting competition from abroad; actions include reducing foreign imports and imposing taxes, or tariffs, on imported goods

pull factor — a factor such as education opportunity, employment prospects, security, or good climate that attracts a person to another place

push factor — a factor such as drought, persecution, lack of freedom, or lack of employment that influences a person to move away

quality of life — the amount of satisfaction we have with our lives, taking into account both material and non-material wealth

quaternary industry — a category of economic activities that mostly provides services dealing with ideas rather than with material goods

quota — the maximum number of immigrants allowed to enter a country per year

racism — hostile discrimination against people based on their ethnicity

refugee — a person who is displaced or who flees her or his country for social, economic, political, or environmental reasons

refugee status — a level of recognition given to people who claim to be refugees on entering a country; after government officials hear their case, a decision is made whether to grant or not grant refugee status

replacement level — the fertility rate required for a population to replace itself; usually, a fertility rate of at least 2.1 is needed, taking into account infant mortality rates

Sahel — the region along the southern fringe of the Sahara Desert across Africa, where long-term drought and desertification have occurred

scattered — type of settlement pattern in which the population is spread over a large area with no grouping together

scatter graph — a type of graph that shows the relationship or interconnection between two population characteristics

secondary industry — economic activities that take semi-finished products from the primary industries and manufacture them into finished consumer goods

semi-finished product — a good produced by a primary industry; semi-finished products are not refined enough to be used by consumers; for example, a roll of steel produced by the steel industry needs to be manufactured into goods like pots and pans before consumers can use it

settlement pattern — how people arrange themselves as they live on the land, usually in either urban or rural regions

site — physical features in an area where a community is located

situation — the general position of a city in relation to human features such as transportation routes, other cities, and natural resources such as good farmland

sparse — referring to low population density, in which a relatively small number of people is spread over a large area of land; that is, there is a low ratio of people to land area

squatter settlement — a makeshift community, often on public lands in or around large cities, where people gather and live in poor conditions

Stone Age — an early time in human history when technology was not well advanced; tools were often made of stone or bones

structural adjustment — changes in employment patterns that occur as a country tries to change its economy to compete in a global market; often, unemployment and closing of businesses are results of structural adjustment

tariff — a tax charged on goods imported into a country; it makes imported goods more expensive than locally made products

tertiary industry — economic activities that provide services to consumers, such as auto repairs, bookkeeping, and dry cleaning

trading bloc — a group of nations that have agreed to treat the goods and services of fellow members in a special fashion, giving them preference over goods and services from non-member countries; a partnership among countries that makes exporting and importing goods and services cheaper, easier, and more efficient

transnational corporation — a large company that operates in many different countries; it operates across national boundaries and is sometimes beyond the control of any government; its annual sales can be more than the earnings of many developing countries

urbanization — the shift of the population from rural areas to cities, with resulting changes in people's lifestyle

urban sprawl — when urban areas spread out and grow into the surrounding rural areas

visible minority — "persons, other than Aboriginal peoples, who are non-Caucasian in race or non-white in colour," according to *Canada's Employment Equity Act*; persons belonging to visible minority groups include Chinese, South Asian, Black, Arab, West Asian, Southeast Asian, Filipino, Latin American, Japanese, and Korean, among others

xenophobia — fear of strangers; particularly, a mistrust of people who look and act differently

zoning bylaw — law passed by a community government to control the type and amount of development in an area; for example, zoning bylaws control what people can build and how big buildings can be on different properties

Index

Visual and Text Credits

This page constitutes an extension of the copyright page. We have made every effort to trace the ownership of all copyrighted material and to secure permission from copyright holders. In the event of any question arising as to the use of any material, we will be pleased to make the necessary corrections in future printings.

4.18 (left to right) Courtesy of Florida Atlantic University, College of Engineering and Computer Science; Michael Jacobs/ WireImage/Getty Images; Ethan Miller/Getty Images **4.20** (left to right) Comstock Images/Jupiter Images; JSTHR/Shutterstock **4.21** (clockwise) Harald Sund/Photographer's Choice/Getty Images; Andrew Geiger; Minden/Getty Images **4.22** Robert Nickelsberg/Getty Images **4.24** Data from Industry Canada, Canadian ICT Statistical Overview **4.25** Data from Statistics Canada, CANSIM, table (for fee) 228-0003 **4.26** Data from Statistics Canada, CANSIM, table (for fee) 228-0003 **4.27** (top) Lynne Milgram; (bottom) Lew French **4.28** Courtesy of National Aboriginal Achievement Foundation **4.30** Michael Zysman/Shutterstock **4.31** Courtesy of Soil to Sky/Photo by Angela Wilson **4.32** U.S. Census Bureau, International Data Base **4.33** (top) Jean Louis Bellurget/Stock Image/Jupiter Images; (bottom) Tony Bock/*Toronto Star*

Chapter 5: 5.1 © imagebroker/Alamy **5.4** Norman James/ Toronto Star Syndicate/CP Images **5.5** Steve White/CP Images **5.6** © Bill Brooks/Alamy **5.7** Kristiina Paul **5.9** Bob Blanchard/ Shutterstock **5.10** Andy Maluche/OnAsia/Jupiter Images **5.11** Roger Tully/Stone/Getty Images **5.12** www.CartoonStock.com **5.13** Trends in Urbanization, by Region, Population Reference Bureau. Used with permission. **5.14** Reza/Webistan/Reportage/ Getty Images **5.16** Chad Ehlers/Stone/Getty Images **5.17** John Boykin/Stock Connection/Jupiter Images **5.18** Ron Bull/*Toronto Star*/First Light **5.19** Richard Goldberg/Shutterstock **5.20** Rene Johnston/*Toronto Star* **5.21** © Jim West/Alamy **5.22** © Bob Johns/Expresspictures.Co.uk/Alamy **5.23** *Toronto Star*, June 9, 2008. Used with permission. **5.26** AP Photo/Damian Dovarganes

Unit 2 Opener: 1 Robert Llewellyn/Workbook Stock/ Jupiter Images **2** © McCord Museum, MP-0000.2082.2 **3** Jack Hollingsworth/Brand X Pictures/Jupiter Images **4** AP Photo/Dado Galdieri **5** Ward Perrin/CP PHOTO **6** BananaStock/Jupiter Images **7** Data from Statistics Canada, CANSIM, table (for fee) 228-0003 **8** (left to right) NASA; John De Bord/Shutterstock

Chapter 6: 6.1 Robert Llewellyn/Workbook Stock/Jupiter Images **6.2** Paul Chesley/Stone/Getty Images **6.4** © McCord Museum, MP-0000.2082.2 **6.5** © Peter Turnley/CORBIS **6.6** Leesa Price **6.7** Data from Statistics Canada **6.8** Data from Expenditures per household, Canada, 2006, Statistics Canada **6.9** CP PHOTO/Winnipeg Free Press/Ken Gigliotti **6.10, 6.11** Data from *The 2008 World Factbook*, CIA **6.13** Jack Hollingsworth/Brand X Pictures/Jupiter Images **6.15** THE CANADIAN PRESS/Tom Hanson **6.18** AP Photo/Andre Penner **6.19** GIANLUIGI GUERCIA/AFP/Getty Images **6.20** Carol Waldock **6.22** © SHOUT/Alamy **6.23** © john t. fowler/Alamy **Page 137 Be a Global Citizen: Made in Canada?** Based on information from *Globe and Mail*, July 6, 2007, and *Toronto Star*, July 16, 2008 **6.25** Data from *The 2008 World Factbook*, CIA **6.26** Gerald Bourke/WFP via Getty Images **6.27** REUTERS/ Jason Reed **6.28** Data from *The 2008 World Factbook*, CIA and UN Data

Chapter 7: 7.1 Paula Bronstein/Getty Images **7.2** Ward Perrin/ CP PHOTO **7.4, Fact File, 7.5** Data from *Human Development Indices: A statistical update 2008*, UNDP **7.8** From the *Human Development Report 2007*, United Nations Development Programme. Used with permission of Macmillan Publishers.

7.9 Knauer/Johnston/Workbook Stock/Jupiter Images **7.10, 7.11** Data from *Human Development Report 2007–2008*, UNDP **7.12** Ontario Black History Society **7.15** AP Photo/Kent Gilbert/CP Images **7.16** © 2008 Compare Infobase Limited **7.18** AP Photo/Dado Galdieri **7.19** From *Population Bulletin: World Population Highlights Key Findings From PRB's 2008 World Population Data Sheet*, September 2008, p. 3. Used with permission of Population Reference Bureau. **7.21, 7.22** Free the Children **7.24** Data from *The 2008 World Factbook*, CIA **7.25** © Images of Africa Photobank/Alamy **7.26** Andrea Booher/Stone/Getty Images **7.27** *Human Development Report 2007*, United Nations Development Programme. Used with permission of Macmillan Publishers.

Chapter 8: 8.1 Sallows Collection, Archival & Special Collections, University of Guelph Library **8.3** BananaStock/ Jupiter Images **8.4** BHP Billiton **8.6** John de Visser/Masterfile **8.7** Donovan Reese/Stone/Getty Images **8.9** Bruce Forster/ Riser/Getty Images **8.10** © Gene Chutka/iStockphoto **8.11** Mark Edward Atkinson/Blend Images/Getty Images **8.12** Olivia Barr/Photonica/Getty Images **8.13** (left to right) © Richard T. Nowitz/Corbis; © Robert Harding/Jupiter Images **8.14** Data from *Human Development Indices: A statistical update 2008*, UNDP and *The 2008 World Factbook*, CIA **8.15, 8.16** Data from *The 2008 World Factbook*, CIA **8.17** Celcom/Ministry of Environment and Nature Protection Yaounde Cameroon **8.18** Statistics Canada, CANSIM, table (for fee) 379-0027 and Catalogue no. 15-001-X. **8.19** Data from Statistics Canada, CANSIM, table (for fee) 379-0027 and Catalogue no. 15-001-X. **8.21** Lynne Milgram **8.22** Data from *People, Places and Themes*, Wendy Keeling, Mike Ridout, Alan Bilham-Boult, Second Edition, Heinemann, 2002; and *The 2008 World Factbook*, CIA. **8.23** Gaden Choling Mahayana Buddhist Meditation Centre **8.24** Internet World Stats **8.26** SONDEEP SHANKAR/ BLOOMBERG NEWS/Landov **8.27** Internet World Stats **8.28** *The 2008 World Factbook*, CIA

Chapter 9: 9.4 Data from Statistics Canada, CANSIM, table (for fee) 282-0008 and Catalogue no. 71F0004XCB. **9.5** Data from Statistics Canada, CANSIM, table (for fee) 282-0087 and Catalogue no. 71-001-XIE. **9.6, 9.7, 9.8, 9.9** Data from Statistics Canada, CANSIM, table (for fee) 228-0003. **9.10** September 19, 2007, *Toronto Star*. Used with permission. **9.11** Tracy Ferrero/Alamy **9.12** GIPhotoStock Z/Alamy **9.13** John De Bord/Shutterstock **9.14** NASA **9.15** CP PHOTO/Fred Chartrand **9.16** Data from *The 2008 World Factbook*, CIA, and 2005, IMF WEO Database **9.19** Marmaduke St. John/Alamy **9.20** *Cars on the Brain: Canada's Automotive Industry 2007*, Industry Canada. p. 3. Reproduced with permission of the Minister of Public Works and Government Services Canada, 2009 **9.21** Data from *Automotive Trade 2007*, Industry Canada **9.22** *New Motor Vehicle Sales: 2006 in Review*, Statistics Canada Catalogue no. 11-621-MIE - No. 054

Unit Opener 3: 2 © Dèsirée Martín/epa/Corbis **3** (top to bottom) Province Newspaper, Vancouver Public Library, Special Collection, 1397; Leonard Frank, Vancouver Public Library, Special Collection, 14917 **4** AP Photo/Teh Eng Koon **5** Originally published on the Migration Information Source (www.migrationinformation.org), a project of the Washington, DC-based Migration Policy Institute, an independent, non-partisan, nonprofit think tank dedicated to the study of movement of people worldwide. **6** © Bryan & Cherry Alexander Photography/Arcticphoto **7** CP PHOTO/*Toronto Star*/Rick Eglinton **8** Data from Statistics Canada, 2006 Census of Population. **9** Courtesy of Lord Elgin P.S.

Chapter 10: 10.1 (left) Jesse Allen, Earth Observatory/NASA; (right) Liu Yang/ChinaFotoPress/Getty Images **10.2** Canadian Pacific Railway Archives NS.13561.2 **10.6** Statistics Canada, 2006 Census of Population **10.8** © Dèsirée Martín/epa/Corbis **10.9** CP PHOTO/Andrew Vaughan **10.10** DIMITAR DILKOFF/AFP/Getty Images **10.12** THOMAS COEX/AFP/Getty Images **10.13** Data from UNESCO UIS Data, UNESCO Institute for Statistics **10.14** Norm Betts/Rex Features/CP Images **10.15** Saskatchewan Archives Board R-B6776-1 **10.16** *Application for Permanent Residence*, Immigration Canada, p. 10. Reproduced with the permission of the Minister of Public Works and Government Services Canada, 2009 **10.17** *Facts and Figures 2006, Immigration Overview: Permanent and Temporary Residents*, Citizenship and Immigration Canada. **10.18** CIDA 994-54-07 **10.20** World Vision Canada **10.21** Dmitri Kessel//Time Life Pictures/Getty Images **10.23** Library and Archives Canada/PA-034014 **10.24** © Àngel Castillo/MSF **10.25** AP Photo/Sarah El Deeb **10.26** Ontario Black History Society **10.27** CP PHOTO/Jonathan Hayward **10.28** (left to right) Leonard Frank, Vancouver Public Library, Special Collection, 14917; Province Newspaper, Vancouver Public Library, Special Collection, 1397 **10.29** World Bank Development Indicators, 2008. Used with permission. **10.32** Originally published on the Migration Information Source (www.migrationinformation.org), a project of the Washington, DC-based Migration Policy Institute, an independent, nonpartisan, nonprofit think tank dedicated to the study of movement of people worldwide. **10.34** Data from "Canada set to boost 'family' immigrants," Bruce Campion-Smith, *Toronto Star*, November 2, 2007

Chapter 11: 11.1 World Vision Canada **11.3** AP Photo/Contipress, Peter Leibing/CP Images **11.4** AP Photo/Thomas Kienzle/CP Images **11.5** Library and Archives Canada/PA-118185 **11.7** Robert Van Der Hilst/Stone/Getty Images **11.8** Paul Chiasson/CP Images **11.9** Dilip Mehta/CIDA, 468-01-15 **11.10** Michael S. Yamashita/National Geographic/Getty Images **11.12** AP Photo/Teh Eng Koon **11.13** AP Photo/Fernando Proietti/CP Images **11.15** Mario Tama/Getty Images **11.16** AP Photo **11.17** AP Photo/Michael Probst/CP Images **11.18** AP Photo/B.K.Bangash **11.19** Originally published on the Migration Information Source (www.migrationinformation.org), a project of the Washington, DC-based Migration Policy Institute, an independent, nonpartisan, nonprofit think tank dedicated to the study of movement of people worldwide. **11.20** CP PHOTO/Peterborough Examiner-Clifford Skarstedt **11.21** (left to right) National Archives of Canada/Rosemary Gilliat/C-007108/CP Images; AP Photo/Bullit Marquez **11.23** AP Photo/Lenny Ignelzi **11.24** CP PHOTO/Chuck Stoody **11.26** Christie Johnston/IHT/Redux **Page 259** The Associated Press, February 19, 2008. Used with permission.

Chapter 12: 12.1 (top to bottom) Ontario Archives; Olga Skalkina/Shutterstock **12.4** From *People and Places 7*, 1e, © 2006 Nelson Education Ltd. Reproduced by permission. www.cengage.com/permissions **12.5** R. Ian Lloyd/Masterfile **12.6** Ontario Archives I0012329 **12.9** (left to right) © Eddi Boehnke/zefa/Corbis; © Anthony Bannister; Gallo Images/CORBIS **12.10** Frances Anne Hopkins, "Canoes in a Fog, Lake Superior, 1869," 1869, oil on canvas, Glenbow Museum, Calgary, Canada, 55.8.1 **12.11** © Jeff Greenberg/Alamy **12.12** Donald Nausbaum/Stone/Getty Images **12.13** © Bryan & Cherry Alexander Photography/Arcticphoto **12.14** TV Ontario **12.15** Lynne Milgram **12.16** Richard Lautens/*Toronto Star* **12.17** Copyright © David Young-Wolff/PhotoEdit **12.18** The Canadian Press/Frank Gunn **12.19** AP Photo/Tibor Illyes/CP Images **12.20** (top to bottom) AP Photo/Aranberri; AP Photo/Javier Bauluz **12.21** CP PHOTO/*Toronto Star*/Rick Eglinton **12.22** Matt Trommer/Shutterstock **12.24** VisionsofAmerica/Joe Sohm/The Image Bank/Getty Images **12.25** AP Photo/David Cheskin/CP Images **12.28** © Andrew Holbrooke/Corbis

Chapter 13: 13.1 (left to right) William James Topley/Library and Archives Canada/PA-010264; Jason Hosking/Stone/Getty Images **13.3** ColorBlind Images/Iconica/Getty Images **13.5** Statistics Canada, Census of Population and *The 2008 World Factbook*, CIA **13.6** Data from Migration Policy Institute **13.7** CP PHOTO/Tim Krochak **13.8** From Canada's Ethnocultural Mosaic, 2006 Census, Statistics Canada, Catalogue no.: 97-562-XWE2006001 **13.9** Peter Mintz/First Light **13.10** Data from "Globalization from Below: The Ranking of Global Immigrant Cities," Lisa Benton-Short, Marie D. Price, and Samantha Friedman, *International Journal of Urban and Regional Research*, Volume 29, Issue 4, 2005 **13.11** Data from Canada's Ethnocultural Mosaic, 2006 Census, Statistics Canada, Catalogue no. 97-562-X, p.6 **13.12** Dick Hemingway **13.13** CP Images **13.14** Clement Allard/CP Images **13.15** Lynne Milgram **13.16** (left to right) CP PHOTO/The *Record*, Kitchener-Robert Wilson; Andre Pichette, The *Gazette* (Montreal); Courtesy of Sunfest/Alfredo Caxaj **13.17** *Toronto Sun*/Paul Henry/CP Images **13.18** Data from *Facts and Figures 2007–Immigration Overview: Permanent and Temporary Residents*, Citizenship and Immigration Canada **13.19** The Strategic Counsel, *Globe and Mail*, CTV **13.20** THE CANADIAN PRESS/Adrian Wyld **Page 302** (Canadian flag) Matt Trommer/Shutterstock **13.22** THE CANADIAN PRESS/Larry MacDougal **13.23** Data from Statistics Canada, 2006 Census of Population. **13.24** CP PHOTO/Michelle MacAfee **13.25** Phill Snel/CP Photo **13.27, 13.28** Courtesy of Lord Elgin P.S. **13.29** Isaac Erb & Son/Bibliothèque et Archives Canada/C-045083